# AUSTRALIAN POLICIES AND ATTITUDES TOWARD CHINA

# AUSTRALIAN POLICIES AND ATTITUDES TOWARD CHINA

BY HENRY S. ALBINSKI

PRINCETON, NEW JERSEY
PRINCETON UNIVERSITY PRESS
1965

L. C. Card: 66-10548
Printed in the United States of America by
Vail-Ballou Press, Inc., Binghamton, New York

*To Barbara*

# PREFACE

THE RISE and influence of Communist China have produced a profound impact on Australia, a Western nation situated on the rim of Asia. One purpose of this book is to indicate the nature and strength of Australia's interpretation of China as a power in her own right and as an influence on the course of Asian developments of special concern to Australia. A second purpose is to trace and appraise the various policy lines which Australia has devised to defend her interests in the face of the Chinese presence. These policies have had many facets—military, diplomatic, commercial, and others. Australia has tried to synchronize them as far as possible, but invariably has found that, as a middle power with limited resources and leverage, she has had to seek and maintain friends and allies. Much of the discussion in the book therefore revolves around relations with those whom Australia feels she must attract. The most prominent ally has become the United States, and the dilemmas which this necessary yet unequal relationship has created have constantly intruded into Australia's handling of Chinese problems.

But politics and personalities have invariably left their cast on Australia's China policy. Some of this has occurred within the ranks of the men and parties charged with making appraisals and policies. Some of it has come from the movements and pressure groups within the country which have developed an interest in China and Australia's relations with her. Much of it has been a reflection of the party battle in Australia, and in turn of the conflicts which have pulled at the parties from within. The book therefore also devotes itself to the imprint left by the Chinese problem on politics, and the manner in which politics have affected the tone of debate and policy direction on China. While the book is concerned with Australia and China, it is hoped that its treatment will provide some appreciation of Australian foreign policy and politics in the round, and especially of how they impinge on one another.

Research for this book was made possible through a Visiting Fellowship in International Relations at the Australian National University, Canberra, during 1963–64, and a Rockefeller travel grant. The materials consulted for this study came from many sources, including political parties, interest organizations, and private collections and individuals in Australia. A list of relevant bibliography is reproduced at the end of the book.

The preparation of the book has been greatly assisted by the factual and interpretative comment supplied by over one hundred individuals whom the author interviewed. Among the Australians interviewed were officials of various Government departments, diplomats, members of various political parties, representatives of interest groups, business figures, academicians, and journalists. Representatives of several foreign missions in Australia were interviewed, and the author also benefited from certain discussions conducted in New Zealand.

Some of those interviewed had no objection to being identified and openly quoted. Most asked not to have their remarks directly attributed to them, but did not mind being included in a list of acknowledgments. A few desired to have their names left out of the book entirely. The author finally decided not to include a list of those willing to be acknowledged. This was done with much regret, since the author is deeply indebted to the many persons who gave generously of their time, hospitality, and above all candid observations. In certain instances, however, the perceptive reader could probably logically connect the nature of privately obtained material reproduced in the text with certain listed informants. It was therefore thought best to preserve the anonymity of all save those who raised no objection to being named and quoted and who are mentioned at several points in the text.

At all events, cross-checking on interview statements of both fact and opinion was carried out as often as possible. In the text of the book privately obtained information has sometimes been qualified by a comment about the reliability of the source or sources. For the screening, sifting, and presentation of this and other material, the author naturally assumes responsibility.

Several individuals gave much-appreciated and critical reading to various portions of the manuscript, namely, Professor J. D. B. Miller, Dr. George Modelski, Dr. Peter Boyce and Sir Alan Watt of the Australian National University, Dr. Coral Bell of the University of Sydney, Mr. Josef Wilczynski of the Royal Military College, Duntroon, and Dr. Richard Rosecrance of the University of California at Los Angeles. Thanks are also due to Mr. John Bennett for research assistance in United Nations sources, and to Miss Beverley Male and Mrs. Sally Ohlsen.

Portions of this book have appeared elsewhere. Chapter I was published in the August 1964 issue of the *Australian Journal of Politics and History* under the title of "Australia and the China Problem Under the Labor Government." Chapters II and III appeared as a monograph published by the Department of International Relations, Australian National University, as *Australia and the China Problem During the Korean War Period.*

*University Park, Pennsylvania* HENRY S. ALBINSKI
*February 1965*

# CONTENTS

# GLOSSARY

| | |
|---|---|
| ABC | Australian Broadcasting Commission |
| ACFTU | All-China Federation of Trade Unions |
| ACS | Australia-China Society |
| ACTU | Australia Council of Trade Unions |
| AFCA | Australia-Free China Association |
| AIIA | Australian Institute of International Affairs |
| ALP | Australian Labor Party |
| ANZAM | Australian, New Zealand, and British Defense Planning Arrangement for the Southwest Pacific and Malayan Area |
| ANZUS | Australia, New Zealand, and United States Security Treaty |
| APACL | Asian People's Anti-Communist League |
| CHINCOM | China Committee, Coordinating Committee of the Consultative Group (Strategic Materials) |
| COCOM | Coordinating Committee of the Consultative Group (Strategic Materials) |
| CPA | Communist Party of Australia |
| CPR | Chinese People's Republic |
| DLP | Democratic Labor Party |
| EPIC | Export Payments Insurance Corporation |
| ICFTU | International Confederation of Free Trade Unions |
| ILO | International Labor Organization |
| KMT | Kuomintang (Nationalist) Party |
| LCP | Liberal-Country Parties |
| MHR | Member of the House of Representatives |
| NCC | National Civic Council |

| | |
|---|---|
| PKI | Communist Party of Indonesia |
| RSL | Returned Servicemen's League |
| SEATO | South-East Asia Treaty Organization |
| UNRRA | United Nations Relief and Rehabilitation Administration |

# AUSTRALIAN POLICIES AND ATTITUDES TOWARD CHINA

# I

# THE CHINA PROBLEM UNDER THE LABOR GOVERNMENT

ON DECEMBER 10, 1949, after eight years in office, Prime Minister J. B. Chifley's Australian Labor Party Government was defeated at the polls and replaced by a Liberal-Country Party coalition. Labor's departure from office occurred at a time when the situation in Asia was only beginning to assume its familiar postwar contours of nationalist agitation, European disengagement, Chinese interposition, and sporadic military crises. The advent of the Menzies Government was, however, carried out against a background of developing public attitudes and official policies. On the subject of China, Australians were already wondering how the competing claimants for the control of China should be regarded, what foreign and defense policies would best suit Australia's interests, and so on. The questions then being raised continue to be pertinent. The answers then being offered were perhaps more tentative than at present, but in many ways the line of continuity is impressive.

Full Australian consciousness of the import of a "Chinese question" was understandably slow in manifesting itself. In part this resulted from the general condition of Australia's international involvement. Until the second war Australia had barely any interest in foreign affairs, diplomatic relations, or diplomatic initiatives. The war destroyed the old complacency, but it took a while for even the more alert sectors of the community to sort and reason out the various facets and implications of the postwar Asian setting. In part, too, it stemmed from continuing preoccupation among nearly all shades of political opinion with devising restraints against renewed Japanese ambitions. Finally, Australian thinking on China in particular lagged behind for special reasons. Chinese consular representation existed in principal Australian cities even before the first war, but there was no Australian representation in China until the appointment of a trade commissioner in 1935 and a minister in 1941. The Sino-Japanese war produced some sympathy for the Chinese people, but was mainly reacted to in terms of Japanese intentions. Historically, conflict with Chinese in the gold fields and concern with China's role as part of the "yellow peril" which might sweep from the north had attracted Australia's attention, but there was small appreciation of China's importance in a mid-twentieth century world. Writing in 1943, even after Australia had been jarred into a fresh awareness of the impact of Asian events, P. D. Phillips gave a depressing but largely accurate picture of the typical Australian's image of the Chinese: "Resident Chinese are confined to very few occupations—most of them market gardeners and laundrymen. In consequence the Australian tends to think of a rather mild, industrious, and easygoing "cabbage grower" when without critical attention he permits his mind to summon the stereotype provoked by the title 'China.' " Furthermore, although the Australian business community had been devoting some thought to Sino-Australian trade, "The distinctive mark of Australia's attitude, not substantially modified by war experience to date, is an apathy that has neither feeling nor deliberate aloofness but merely the insular preoccupation of a people mostly interested in themselves and in those like them." [1]

[1] P. D. Phillips, "War Trends in Australian Opinions," in Australian Institute of International Affairs, *Australia and the Pacific*

By about 1946–47, however, Australian perception of China as a huge, strife-torn, and ominously significant country was sharpening. It seems that Australians began to form opinions about the character and merits of the competitors in the Chinese civil war before they started to sense the full dimensions of how the victory of one or the other would fit into the face of a changing Asia—aside from tending to agree that a "strong, united, and fully democratic" China would serve as a stabilizing factor in Asian affairs and would be of "prime importance" in security terms.[2] Since Australian judgments about the ability of either the Nationalists or the Communists to satisfy the above conditions came to affect judgments about the role and position of China in Asia, as well as about appropriate reactions in Australian policy, an analysis along these lines must be attempted.

## AUSTRALIAN REACTIONS TO THE NATIONALISTS

AUSTRALIAN reactions to the Nationalists deserve first attention. The Nationalists were, after all, the incumbent authority; furthermore, several explicit and critical points of Nationalist Chinese-Australian relations in the late 'forties developed in a way which unmistakably conditioned both popular and party thinking, and have, at least in broad outline, continued to do so.

Probably the most highly publicized—and most disappointing—Australian contact with the Chinese Nationalists was over Australian aid through UNRRA. When implementing legislation was introduced in Parliament in 1944, bipartisan support was forthcoming, and many shared External Affairs Minister H. V. Evatt's feeling that this aid was both an expression of obligation toward the allied nations and a humane act which would appeal to the

(Princeton: Princeton Univ. Press for the Institute of Pacific Relations and the AIIA, 1944), pp. 67–68.

[2] *Sydney Morning Herald,* January 7, 1946.

higher instincts of all Australians.[3] In time, Australia became the fourth largest donor of UNRRA assistance. Evatt himself was the leading spirit in the creation of the Australian Council for UNRRA, which he chaired. In March 1946 Australia was admitted to the Central Committee of UNRRA.

The Australian UNRRA effort was directed at China, first and foremost. Some £6,563,000,[4] or fully two-thirds of Australia's basic UNRRA commitment, went to China. There was also a large bulk goods allowance, mostly wool, which raised Australia's total UNRRA contribution to £24,000,000, but even after that addition China remained the largest single recipient of Australian UNRRA aid, receiving such items as small craft, locomotives, iceplants, and agricultural machinery—some of which were in short supply in Australia.[5] In 1945 a voluntary, UNRRA-sponsored clothing drive netted almost £5,000,000 of goods for China, at a time when rationing was in force in Australia.[6] By early 1947, Australians were the third largest national group serving UNRRA in China, following the U.S. and Britain. Even after UNRRA was disbanded, generous post-UNRRA relief was supplied to China.[7]

All of this suggests commitment, expense, and sacrifice by the Australian Government and the community toward the relief and rehabilitation of China. But with what re-

[3] *Commonwealth Parliamentary Debates,* House of Representatives, Vol. 179, September 7, 1944, p. 590.

[4] £1 Australian = $2.24. All citations hereafter are in Australian pounds unless otherwise indicated.

[5] See *CPD,* HR, Vol. 192, June 5 and 6, 1947, pp. 3695–3698; N. O. P. Pyke, "Australia's UNRRA Contribution," *Australian Outlook,* Vol. 3 (March 1949), pp. 79–80; Wilfred Prest, "Economic Problems," in Gordon Greenwood and Norman D. Harper, eds., *Australia in World Affairs 1950–55* (Melbourne: F. W. Cheshire for the AIIA, 1957) pp. 141–142.

[6] George Woodbridge, ed., *UNRRA* (New York: Columbia Univ. Press, 1950), Vol. I, p. 141.

[7] Nicholas McKenna, *CPD,* Senate, Vol. 200, November 24, 1948, p. 3352.

sult? The whole tone of both official and informal reports received in Australia during the years from 1946 to 1948 was that UNRRA aid in China was being squandered by inefficient and even corrupt Nationalist officials—mainly through the Chinese National Relief and Rehabilitation Administration, an agency designated to negotiate with UNRRA and to administer operations in the field, created by and directly responsible to the Executive Yuan of the Chinese Government. In 1946 the Australian press carried notices that dozens of ships laden with UNRRA supplies were lying idle in Chinese ports.[8] The following year, nearly all Australians on UNRRA's Shanghai staff were reported to have joined in addressing a cable to UNRRA's Central Committee in Washington, urging cessation of relief shipments to China because the Nationalists were preventing distribution in Communist-held areas.[9] Then, in 1948, Labor MP Leslie Haylen brought back more disquieting reports to Evatt and his colleagues. Some years later Haylen wrote, "Clothes donated by Australian workers, bearing Australian trademarks, were hawked along the [Shanghai] Bund or sold openly in the shops," two modern Australian trawlers "finished up some Chinese creek, after all the machinery had been looted," and he told of seeing Australian refrigeration machinery piled up on docks, scheduled for black market sale.[10] Just to make Australia's negative impressions of her China aid complete, an Australian UNRRA official in China, H. R. Heath, charged with embezzling UNRRA property, was reported to have been detained for months without trial, and locked in chains under intolerable sanitary conditions. Chinese authorities were unmoved by protests from other UNRRA officials, who believed that Heath had been made a scapegoat to shield implicated Chinese officials.[11]

[8] *SMH,* August 12, 1946. [9] *Ibid.,* August 20, 1947.

[10] Leslie Haylen, *Chinese Journey* (Sydney, London, Melbourne, and Wellington: Angus and Robertson, 1959), pp. 63–64.

[11] *SMH,* April 28, 1947.

The Australian Government was privately furious but publicly circumspect over the fate of its Chinese UNRRA program. At one point, reports of open market flour sales in Shanghai led the Government "to threaten peremptorily to discontinue the supply of wheat flour to UNRRA for China unless assurances were received that such stocks would in fact be delivered to famine sufferers." [12] But while Labor was still in office it kept its temper in check mainly because, the author has been told, it did not wish to reflect on and jeopardize the UNRRA program at large.[13] Once in opposition, Chifley said bluntly that his Government had known of the waste for some time and that this was striking evidence of the "utterly corrupt" Nationalist regime of the period.[14]

The second black mark Australia pinned on the Nationalists concerned Australia's Manus Island. Manus, some 150 miles south of the Equator, had been developed during the war by the U.S. Navy as a great staging base at a cost of about £50,000,000. When subsequent negotiations between Washington and Canberra failed to produce a satisfactory arrangement for their continuing utilization of the island, the Americans withdrew. The U.S. then sold the rights to all remaining movable property to the Chinese Government, which was given a set time within which to remove it. Australia purchased all nonmovables at a nominal price, and was entitled to all movables the Chinese might fail to carry off.

Then the Chinese set to work. According to one, essentially correct account, "Before they left, late in 1948, they wrecked as much equipment as they conveniently could, to prevent it from falling intact into Australian hands. They

[12] J. Franklin Ray, Jr., "UNRRA in China" (New York: IPR, 1947), Secretariat Paper No. 6, IPR Conference 1947, p. 53.

[13] For official reactions at this time, see Prime Minister Chifley, *CPD,* HR, Vol. 198, September 9, 1948, p. 334, and Vol. 201, March 2, 1949, p. 838.

[14] *CPD* HR, Vol. 206, March 23, 1950, p. 1174.

gashed open tins of paint and drums of oil with axes. They smashed toilet bowls and washbasins with crowbars. They drove trucks into the jungle. They cut steel arms off mobile cranes."[15] This description of malicious destruction was accepted in a number of Australian quarters, not the least of which was the Liberal Party. A 1949 Liberal Party campaign booklet, while criticizing Labor for failing to reach agreement with America over Manus, spelled out in some detail how the Chinese had contributed toward reducing the island to a junk pile.[16] What made the situation especially galling to Australia was that the Chinese had been enabled to buy the American equipment under a special UNRRA grant of £12,000,000.

The Chinese on Manus had yet one more indignity to bestow on Australia. While the Chinese were on the premises there were several unhappy encounters with the Australian Administration, especially over the treatment of natives. On one occasion four Chinese, suspecting a theft, seized an available native, tied his hands behind his back, hung him upsidedown, and left him there. The District Officer sentenced each Chinese to three months' imprisonment. The episode might ordinarily have remained unpublicized, but litigation continued and the High Court of Australia ultimately confirmed the District Officer's decision.[17] To many Australians, the combined allegations of an UNRRA officer being kept in chains and a Manus native being tortured hardly enhanced the Nationalists' reputation.

The final encounter between Nationalist China and

[15] "Manus Equipment Scandal is Still Unexplained," *SMH,* February, 5, 1951. Also see Leslie Brodie, "Neglect and the Jungle are Ruining Manus Installations," *ibid.,* June 2, 1949, and *Sydney Sunday-Herald,* April 3, 1949.

[16] Liberal Party of Australia, Federal Secretariat, "The Case Against Socialist Labour," Background Notes for Candidates, Speakers and Canvassers (Sydney: 1949), p. 127.

[17] George Dickinson, "Manus: Land of Beginning Again," *Walkabout,* Vol. 18 (October 1, 1952), p. 31.

Australia involved Chinese charges against Australia, not the reverse. By mid-1949 the UNRRA and Manus Island imbroglios were fading but still clear in memory. In July of that year the Chinese delegate on the UN Trusteeship Council opened fire on what he alleged to be flagrant racial discrimination in Australia's immigration policy and treatment of the natives in New Guinea. During a two-day debate in the Council on Australian administration of New Guinea, the Philippine delegate also mentioned the subject, but the Chinese attack was the more sustained and direct.[18] In October, before the Fourth (Trusteeship) Committee of the General Assembly, China again moved to the offensive, this time adding criticism of Australian treatment of Chinese workers on Nauru Island;[19] ultimately, China was instrumental in passage of a General Assembly resolution of reproval.

The merit of the Chinese accusations falls outside the concern of the present study.[20] What is important is the Australian reaction to the *idea* of a Chinese challenge to Australian administration and racial policies in New Guinea. One should first remember historic concern over fostering a security cushion in New Guinea, and especially a New Guinea free of unrestricted non-European migrants. William Morris Hughes fought for this objective at Versailles, and certainly in the late 'forties the Labor Government was convinced that the security interests of Australia dictated no outside tampering with the restrictive migration policy.[21] Nor should it be forgotten that

[18] Liu Shih-shun, UN Trusteeship Council, *Official Records,* 5th Session, 14th Meeting, July 6, 1949, pp. 178–179.

[19] UN General Assembly, *Official Records,* 4th Session, Fourth Committee (Trusteeship), 90th Meeting, October 3, 1949, pp. 8–9.

[20] For the substantive Australian Defense, see J. D. L. Hood, *ibid.,* 92nd meeting, October 5, 1949, p. 22, and H. V. Evatt, *CPD,* HR, Vol. 204, October 5, 1949, pp. 901–902.

[21] H. V. Evatt, *CPD,* HR, Vol. 190, March 25, 1947, pp. 1135–1136; Evatt's "Foreword" in Robert J. Gilmore and Denis Warner,

this was the period of Arthur Calwell's tenure as Minister for Immigration. Australia's own exclusionist policies were being inflexibly administered by a man who claimed that "No matter how violent the criticism, no matter how fierce and unrelenting the attacks upon me personally may be, I am determined that the flag of White Australia will not be lowered." [22] The Minister for External Territories, under whose jurisdiction New Guinea, Nauru (and Manus) fell, was then E. J. Ward. Blunt and often dogmatic, Ward's anti-Chinese Nationalist record until his death in 1963 was unflagging. It was in his time, in 1945, that something of a "new deal" for the New Guinea natives was introduced, after many years of neglect. The Government was proud of its improvement program in New Guinea, which it now saw under captious challenge by Nationalist China.[23]

What the Chinese had done, in other words, was to join battle with certain sacred cows of Australian policy and to irritate some important ministers. Against the backdrop of UNRRA aid and Manus Island, it seemed hypocritical to Australians of many political shades that the Nationalists, now in full flight in China, should have had the audacity to adopt the role of preacher and reformer. It may have struck some UN members as an admirable posture to assume, but it left Australians not only unimpressed but resentful. Early in October, an Opposition MP inveighed at what the Chinese were doing and complained about the periodic questioning of Australia's New Guinea administration by "Chinese, Mexicans and the representatives of

---

eds., *Near North* (Sydney and London: Angus and Robertson, 1948), p. vi.

[22] Remarks cited in *SMH,* March 24, 1949.

[23] Regarding Labor's New Guinea program, see J. D. Legge, *Australian Colonial Policy* (Sydney, London, Melbourne, and Wellington: Angus and Robertson for the AIIA, 1956) pp. 188–224.

other foreign countries,"[24]—a severe insult to China, or at least to its Nationalist remnants. For several years the Opposition had made sneering remarks about Evatt's misplaced exertions—aimed, it was asserted, at currying the favor of faraway, internationally impotent, and politically ludicrous countries, illustrations almost invariably being drawn from Latin America. Hence, the pairing of China and Mexico—it could have been Peru or Panama—was a way of insulting the Nationalists.

Irritations arising out of the UNRRA, Manus, and New Guinea situations tended to affect not just the Labor Government, but the country generally. It is difficult to demonstrate the precise cause and effect relationship: did these incidents tear down the Australian image of the Nationalists, or did an already besmirched opinion of KMT (Nationalist) rule and behavior simply serve to exaggerate their meaning? There is probably an element of truth in both directions, and they worked to reinforce one another. At all events, it is unquestionably true that in the three years 1947 to 1949, the Nationalists had few admirers and a host of critics in Australia. A close inspection of the Federal Parliamentary debates during this time fails to reveal a single instance of any Member, either Government or Opposition, actually praising and justifying the political, economic, or military conduct of the Nationalist authorities. In August of 1946, only a few months after arriving at his post as Minister to China, Sir Douglas Copland wrote to Canberra describing the Nationalists as inept and incapable of pulling the country together, and expressed his opinion that they would inevitably be displaced by a Communist regime. Early in 1948, shortly after his return from China, Copland addressed a public meeting at which members of the Chinese consular staff in Australia were present. He said that China's greatest need was the development of a political opposition in place of

[24] Hubert Anthony, *CPD,* HR, Vol. 204, October 5, 1949, p. 951.

the warring Nationalist and Communist factions, and no one seemed to think that his remarks were either exceptional or out of place.[25] Late in 1948 the Australian Embassy in Nanking received an interesting offer. The Nationalist Government had recently undertaken massive currency reform, with the death penalty applicable to violators. However, the Vice-Minister for Finance notified the Embassy that he could supply preferred accommodations for the Australian mission in exchange for rental payments in U.S. dollars, to be made payable to his private account in a New York bank. In this climate, not surprisingly, the press rarely made apologies for the Nationalists, and editorials on any aspect of the China situation often included some derogatory comment about the inability of the KMT to win the confidence of the Chinese people, to reorganize the administrative network, to abandon a losing military strategy, to shake off ultraconservative elements within its own ranks, and so on. When the U.S. State Department published its White Paper on China in August 1949, the previous Australian criticisms seemed vindicated. In the words of the Melbourne *Age,* the White Paper was a "pathetic revelation of ill-based hopes and a severe indictment of colossal waste, inefficiency, fraud, and feckless incompetence associated with his [Chiang's] regime." [26]

From the Government back benches in Parliament came an occasional jibe against the Nationalists. Senator Donald Grant, a venerable radical of first war IWW vintage, talked about the corrupt, nepotistic Chiang regime which no more reflected "the needs of the 400,000,000 Chinese peasants than does the man in the moon," [27] while the equally irascible Max Falstein beginning in 1947

[25] *SMH,* May 13, 1948.

[26] Melbourne *Age,* August 8, 1949. Other representative editorials: Hobart *Mercury,* November 25, 1947; *SMH,* November 2, 1948; Melbourne *Herald,* January 5, 1949.

[27] *CPD,* Senate, Vol. 196, April 9, 1948, p. 786.

alleged that the Nationalists were unfit to enjoy a permanent seat on the UN Security Council because the ruling families of China pulled wires, bargained, and sought gold from America "or any other country to which they might sell their vote on the Security Council."[28] But such expressions were occasional and emanated from the ALP's unreconstructed left wing. What of the Government itself? Aside from its annoyance over such episodes as UNRRA, Manus, and New Guinea, was it generally badly disposed toward the Nationalists? When Falstein made his indelicate suggestion in the House, the Chinese chargé in Canberra called on Chifley and inquired if this was also the view of the Australian Government. The Prime Minister was reported to have fielded the query by replying that he had not previously heard or read Falstein's speech, but that in any event the views of a private Member should not be confused with the thinking of the Government.[29] More than a year later, under heavy questioning in the House, he allowed himself the observation that, while the administration of China had not been such as to inspire great confidence, it was not his province to criticize the management of other countries.[30] But Chifley in these years was Prime Minister, playing the role of unruffled statesman quite aptly. We need instead to go to his biographer, Professor L. F. Crisp, who quotes from a personal letter written by Chifley in 1948: "I never did have much faith in the possibility of that [KMT] administration surviving. I always had a strong suspicion that they were more interested in establishing the Chiang Kai-Shek dynasty than in the welfare of China."[31]

[28] *CPD,* HR, Vol. 193, September 25, 1947, pp. 225–226.

[29] *SMH,* September 27, 1947.

[30] *CPD,* HR, Vol. 200, December 2, 1948, p. 3891. For a similarly guarded comment by Evatt see *CPD,* HR, Vol. 192, June 5 and 6, 1947, p. 3690.

[31] L. F. Crisp, *Ben Chifley* (London: Longmans, 1960), p. 294.

## AUSTRALIAN REACTIONS TO THE COMMUNISTS

IF AUSTRALIANS had, before 1950, become generally unsympathetic toward the Nationalists, it does not follow that the Chinese Communists were the darlings of Australia. There were some cautious hopes that Mao Communists were different in kind from Stalin Communists, that they might be willing to compromise on honorable terms with their Nationalist adversaries, that even if in full control of China they would turn inward toward reconstruction rather than outward for conquest.[32] These sentiments were, of course, by no means limited to Australia. But Australian opinion in general had special reason to take notice of the increasing string of Communist successes and the increasingly cocky and, indeed, belligerent Communist voices. Australia had only recently survived a war in which her metropolitan territory had been barely scratched, but her nerves had been shaken as the Japanese pushed down through South-East Asia and stopped short of Australia only in New Guinea. Now South-East Asia was undergoing a ferment which could be welcome only to China, or Russia working through China, or to both: the Chinese rebellion in Malaya, the Viet Minh in Indo-China, the Huks in the Philippines, a Communist coup recently thwarted in Indonesia, etc. All of this was, by Australian geographic reckoning, taking place on Australia's doorstep. By late 1948, for a variety of reasons, including the rising red star in China, opinion surveys in ten countries —the U.S., Britain, and Italy as well as Australia— indicated that Australians had the highest expectation that

[32] For instance, Hobart *Mercury,* June 18, 1947; *SMH,* November 10, 1948; Melbourne *Argus,* January 6, 1949. The setting is reviewed in Werner Levi, *Australia's Outlook on Asia* (Sydney, London, Melbourne, and Wellington: Angus and Robertson, 1958), pp. 150–151.

another world war would occur within ten years.[33] Quite understandably, appeals were being lodged to strengthen Australia's defenses, to search for improved contacts with allies, to construct a suitable alliance system in the region, and so on.[34] Perceptively, the Melbourne *Herald* concluded that the triumph of militant Communism in China required that Australia and other Western nations set themselves the task of mounting an economic and technical assistance scheme to bolster the resistance of the vulnerable countries of free Asia [35]—which later came to pass in the form of the Colombo Plan. Typical of subsequent Australian thinking on China, there was wide support for assorted preventive and defensive measures, but almost total silence in 1948 and early 1949 respecting Western military intervention to "save" China; later the silence continued on the subject of building a reconquest springboard on Formosa. Perhaps the Chinese Nationalists would have had it otherwise. When Frank Clune, an Australian writer, visited China late in 1948, he was told by high Nationalist officials that Nationalist China's struggle was Australia's struggle and that by fighting Communists the Nationalists were helping to defend Australia, but that unfortunately Australia failed to appreciate the implications of a Communist conquest of China.[36] Australians were then and still are widely agreed on the difference between deterrence and provocation.

The Labor Government's own assessment of the dangers posed by Communism in China was not substantially different in kind from the above characterization. In 1947

[33] *Australian Gallup Polls,* nos. 548–558, October–November 1948.

[34] For instance, Perth *West Australian,* November 24, 1948; Adelaide *Advertiser* April 25, 1949; Brisbane *Courier-Mail,* April 27, 1949.

[35] Melbourne *Herald,* April 23 and 26, August 6, 1949.

[36] Frank Clune, *Ashes of Hiroshima* (Sydney and London: Angus and Robertson, 1950), p. 278.

and 1948, to be sure, statements offered voluntarily by the Government on the situation in China were few and far between, and Opposition contributions on the subject were equally conspicuous by their absence. Part of the explanation certainly lies in the fact that Australians generally were slow to appreciate the full implications of the Chinese civil war. The Government also wished to observe and to remain uncommitted at a time when the situation was still extremely fluid. Another and rather unflattering interpretation came from the redoubtable Billy Hughes, who accused Evatt of being so overawed by the United Nations and its capabilities that he had completely lost sight of the trouble which the victories of Communism in China spelled for Australia.[37] This criticism of Labor, and of Evatt especially, was neither new nor entirely misplaced. From the time of the first UN Conference in San Francisco, Evatt had almost reflexively thought of the UN first when an international problem required attention. Regarding China, Evatt ran true to form. On February 9, 1949 he presented a formal statement on international affairs to the House, including many topics but omitting developments in China. When an interjector asked him for his thinking on China, he simply said that there had been a long and tragic war there, with much suffering. Then he added, "In my opinion, it would be strictly proper for the United Nations to endeavour to mediate there for the purpose of saving lives of countless of innocent people." [38] Within the week reports from New York indicated that Evatt, who at the time was President of the General Assembly, was considering the presentation of a proposal for UN mediation in China. Secretary General Lie had been noncommittal, but raised no objections.[39] Aus-

[37] W. M. Hughes, "U.N.O., Dr. Evatt and World Peace" (Sydney: 1949), *passim*.

[38] *CPD,* HR, Vol. 201, February 9, 1949, p. 88.

[39] Melbourne *Argus,* February 14, 1949.

tralian representatives at Lake Success had not been informed; the Australian Ambassador in China had been neither consulted nor informed. But Herbert Evatt's solo flight into UN diplomacy never really left the ground, for as soon as the Chinese Communist authorities got wind of what was being planned they branded the as yet unborn offer as "ridiculous" and an interference in China's domestic affairs.[40] Little was gained or lost in this episode, but it is probably enlightening as to what Evatt did, and how he did it, when he did decide that China deserved his diplomatic attention.

Nevertheless, it is necessary to indicate that regardless of why Labor had been uncommunicative in the past, in late 1948 and early 1949 a fairly coherent evaluation of the China problem began to emerge, and policies quite apart from the UN began to be formulated. At the source of Labor's reconsidered view of China lay its appreciation of Asian nationalism. For several years Labor had stood committed to furthering the orderly translation of nationalist demands into independent nation states in the South and South-East Asian region. Some of this was an extension of Labor's ideological commitment on behalf of "underprivileged" peoples against their more privileged masters, but, in Professor Greenwood's neat phrase, "realism was married to sympathy."[41] Moreover, Australia could never contract out of her Asian environment, and it was only common sense to live among neighbors who were content rather than disaffected.

As the Communist absorption of China came closer to being an accomplished fact, Australian Labor apparently

[40] *New York Times,* February, 14, 1949.

[41] Gordon Greenwood, "The Commonwealth," in Greenwood and Harper, *op.cit.,* p. 76. Also see in this connection Levi, *op. cit.,* pp. 71–72, and P. H. Partridge, "Developments Since 1939 Affecting Australia's Role Within the Commonwealth and in International Affairs," in Norman D. Harper, ed., *Problems of Contemporary Australia* (New York: IPR, 1949), pp. 41–43.

saw things in a new light. At the end of 1948, Chifley clearly stated that "the Communists go to every fire to pour oil on the flames. They have concentrated on the movement known as the Communist movement in China. Their influence is being exercised over a wide area of an important country. That contributes a grave danger to peace in Asia." [42] By mid-1949, Evatt was warning that all countries in South-East Asia had organized Communist movements whose objectives were the same as those of Communism everywhere; the majority of genuine nationalists in the area were not Communists, resented identification with Communism, and were "embarrassed by Communist activities that are carried out in the guise of progress towards freedom and independence." China seemed to hold an interest in sponsoring the disruptive, dangerous, Communist-oriented nationalism in South-East Asia, but no reason should be given China for suspecting that future accommodation with the West was impossible since that might lead her "to adopt an extreme course and sever all . . . traditional contacts with the democracies." Much was to be gained, according to Evatt, by establishing working relations with whatever regime was in *de facto* control of China.[43] In sum, Labor's evaluation was that Chinese Communism was dangerous, especially its potential power to upset the fragile balance of emerging nations in Asia, but that China was not so rigid in her aims and methods as to preclude a *détente*. The focus must now shift to Labor's efforts to design suitable policies which would blend deterrence with cooperation.

## SECURITY PLANNING

ALTHOUGH prominent alliances such as ANZUS and SEATO were joined by Australia under Liberal Governments, Labor maintained a fairly sustained interest in

[42] *CPD,* HR, Vol. 201, December 2, 1948, p. 3891.
[43] *CPD,* HR Vol. 203, June 21, 1949, pp. 1221–1222.

promoting collective security arrangements in the Asian-Pacific area almost from the end of the war. Although the various plans and negotiations connected with this interest fall beyond the scope of this study, a few relevant aspects need to be mentioned. First, it should be made plain that between 1946 and 1948, the Chifley Government desired a regional alliance for reasons quite divorced from the Chinese problem. Japan's recent adventures were vivid, and they inspired thinking about a protective shield in case of renewed trouble from Japan. Second, given the rapidly changing and volatile nature of the new Asia, it was believed wholesome to bring affected and interested parties together in a common and cooperative defense effort. Labor's thinking at this time was not uniform either as to how firm and explicit the security features of a pact might be or as to membership,[44] and no agreements were transacted.

By late 1948 and early 1949, however, roughly the time when the Government's perception of the danger of a Communist China began to sharpen, Labor energetically resumed the initiative in building a collective defense system in the region. If possible, Australia wished to attach not only New Zealand and Britain to such an alliance, but Asian states and the U.S. as well, with the clear connotation that Canberra sought a mutual security pact and not simply a glorified cultural association. Labor was also forced to admit that the UN was not proving itself able to supply the necessary internationally sponsored security to protect Asia in time of trouble; in addition, the new NATO system demonstrated that regional groupings were consonant with and complementary to the provisions of the

[44] On pact proposals in this period, see Richard N. Rosecrance, *Australian Diplomacy and Japan 1945–1951* (Melbourne: Melbourne Univ. Press for the ANU, 1962), pp. 128–147; Henry S. Albinski, *Australia's Search for Regional Security in South-East Asia,* Ph.D. thesis, Univ. of Minnesota, 1959, pp. 212–222.

UN Charter.[45] Indeed, as Evatt told a New York audience in April of 1949, NATO's creation reminded him that "We must beware lest over-concentration on Europe obscures the crucial importance of the immense changes going on in China and South-East Asia." [46] Events in China, the Government had decided, were now another stimulus governing the need for a security pact.

But Labor's efforts were again almost wholly unrewarding. The notion of a security alliance was broached at Commonwealth Prime Ministers' Conferences, at the ministerial level in Washington, through regular diplomatic channels, and at the service level. By midyear it was apparent that the Asian members of the Commonwealth and the Americans too, each for their own reasons, were most reluctant to participate in an Eastern security system. But in July and August support arrived from other quarters. The heads of state of the Philippines, South Korea, and Nationalist China held meetings among themselves and from Baguio broadcast their desire to found a Pacific security alliance in which Australia, New Zealand, and eventually America would be included. President Quirino of the Philippines even made a personal pilgrimage to Washington to explain the project.

What was Australia to do? Was this scheme a nucleus, something she might help to cultivate in the hope of ultimately drawing in the U.S. and the Asian Commonwealth states? Shortly after the Baguio proposals appeared, Canberra was reported as being "not interested" in them, but anxious to continue its own promotion of a Pacific

[45] Defense Minister J. J. Dedman, *CPD,* HR, Vol. 202, March 15, 1949, p. 1402; Evatt, *ibid.,* February 17, 1949, p. 479; Chifley's statement of March 19, 1949, in *Current Notes on International Affairs,* Vol. 20 (March 1949), p. 410; Chifley's broadcast of May 15, 1949, in *CNIA,* Vol. 20, (May 1949), p. 645.

[46] Address of April 12, 1949, American-Australian Association, New York, in *SMH,* April 14, 1949.

defense pact among Commonwealth members and other parties.[47] When Parliament met in September, Chifley confirmed his Government's lack of interest in the project.[48] America and the Asian Commonwealth members were not themselves, to be sure, interested, but Australia's own reaction was heavily conditioned by the auspices of the scheme. What the Government could not say publicly, the press said for it. The sponsors of the pact hardly inspired confidence as the hard core of an alliance; anti-Communism was not in itself enough to solve the many complex problems in the area and, argued the Perth *West Australian,* Chiang's own preoccupation with the scheme was "obviously to build up outside support for the Nationalist Government in the Asian and Pacific area with the dual purpose of recovering some credit lost by the Kuomintang and restoring in the West a measure of confidence." [49] The *Sydney Morning Herald* sarcastically characterized the offer as having "more the effect of a tin whistle than a trumpet." [50] At a time when the Government, the Opposition in Parliament, and the press were conscious of a danger in China and sought a protective alliance, a call from Nationalist China drew no encouraging cheers from any quarter. The Nationalist image was badly tarnished and Australia had no craving for heroic efforts on behalf of a tottering regime; she saw no resemblance between the proffered scheme and a genuinely satisfying Pacific alliance. All that Labor was able to secure from its 1949 search for an alliance was a military planning arrangement among Australia, New Zealand, and Britain in the South-West Pacific—Malayan area; it came to be known as ANZAM.[51]

[47] *Sydney Sunday Herald,* July 17, 1949.

[48] *CPD,* HR, Vol. 204, September 21, 1949, p. 388.

[49] Perth *West Australian,* July 14, 1949. Also see Hobart *Mercury,* July 14, 1949.

[50] *SMH,* August 10, 1949.

[51] On ANZAM, see Sir Alan Watt, "Australian Defence Policy

If the Labor Government's behavior on a security alliance tended to coincide with the views of the country at large, its reception respecting the defense of Hong Kong was a somewhat different story. By May of 1949 Communist armies were making huge strides forward, and it was an open question whether they would push straight on to capture Hong Kong. Britain sent reinforcements, and debate arose in Australia over possible Australian assistance. On the one hand, there were public demands that the Labor Government should offer material help to Britain, not only to improve the military situation in Hong Kong, but to demonstrate to Asia a genuine interest on the part of the West in stopping Communism. Australia, in particular, had to prove her active interest in the area.[52] An opinion poll confirmed this feeling among the public: 52 per cent favored the dispatch of forces to the defense of Hong Kong in the event of Chinese attack.[53] In early June, British Far Eastern commanders held discussions in Hong Kong regarding the defense of the Colony plus related questions; Australia sent no representatives and earned some sharp rebukes at home.[54]

Labor's reply to these developments consisted of two parts. In the first instance, the Government denied indifference toward Hong Kong. It had been kept fully informed of the Hong Kong talks and was thoroughly apprised of Britain's confidential intentions. It was, furthermore, meeting whatever defense requests the British Government was making—in this instance, keeping a transport ship in readiness—and maintained that the

---

1951–1963" (Canberra: Dept. of International Relations, ANU, 1964), pp. 53–55, and Royal Institute of Internationl Affairs, *Collective Defense in South-East Asia* (London and New York: RIIA, 1956), p. 20.

[52] Especially Melbourne *Herald,* May 9 and August 19, 1949.

[53] *AGP,* nos. 600–606, June–July 1949.

[54] *SMH,* June 7, 1949; Percy Spender, *CPD,* HR, Vol. 202, June 9, 1949, p. 772.

British Cabinet knew that Australia would assist in every way possible if need arose. Second, Labor felt that Hong Kong was primarily a British responsibility, and furthermore its own intelligence suggested that an attack from China on the Colony or indeed on South-East Asia was not imminent.[55] These publicly stated explanations were not untrue, but they require qualification. The Australian Department of Defense had submitted to its Minister a report which described Hong Kong as indefensible. Cabinet accepted this argument and this view was transmitted to the British; this undoubtedly limited both British appeals to Australia and Australia's contribution.

Although the Australian Labor Government was not asked to make any contribution save to keep a vessel in readiness, the New Zealand Labor Government, on British request, sent a flight of three Dakota aircraft "to assist and afford relief to the United Kingdom Air Force in Hong Kong," and arrangements were made to order three RNZN frigates to Hong Kong should they be required.[56] Since London knew of Canberra's reluctance to assist and kept its requests minimal, Australia never refused a British request for aid; it should not be overlooked, however, that at this time Australia was contributing elsewhere in the area. There were Australian occupation troops in Japan, and the commander of Commonwealth forces there was an Australian general officer. Australia was also supplying arms and ammunition to the British counterinsurgency effort in Malaya. Finally, Australian warships took their turn in the periodic voyages up the Yangtze River to provision and otherwise relieve Nanking. It probably was coincidental that in April of 1949 it was a British ship, HMS *Amethyst,* rather than

[55] Chifley, *ibid.,* and statement of May 10, 1949, cited in *SMH,* May 11, 1949; press report in *ibid.* of April 28, 1949.

[56] Prime Minister Peter Fraser, *New Zealand Parliamentary Debates,* HR, Vol. 286, August 18, 1949, p. 1381.

an Australian frigate or destroyer that was struck by Communist shells and spent tortured weeks under the nose of Red Chinese artillery. In retrospect, the conclusion is inescapable that the Chifley Government was right and its critics overexcited, since Hong Kong has yet to be attacked by the Chinese Communists. Labor at that time, it should not be forgotten, was thinking not purely in terms of forceful containment of Chinese Communism, but also of a *démarche* making coexistence possible, and on this hangs the tale of diplomatic recognition.

### REACTIONS TO THE CHINESE RECOGNITION QUESTION

EVIDENCE from several quarters makes it abundantly plain that the Labor Government believed in the desirability of recognizing the new Chinese regime. To begin with, Australian official (i.e., nonpolitical) quarters overwhelmingly gave advice toward this end. When the Communists occupied Nanking in April, nearly all diplomatic missions, including the Australian, decided to remain, although one Australian was detached and sent to Canton to act as liaison with the new Nationalist capital there. Both the Embassy and the Government agreed that the Nationalist cause was hopeless and no useful purpose would be served in chasing the Nationalists from one refuge to another.[57] In Nanking itself the Australian mission not only escaped any physical molestation, but was able to consult with its Commonwealth and other associates and to send and receive messages in cipher through the British Embassy's transmitter. Not long after Nanking fell, there were informal approaches by Communist authorities to Australian Ambassador F. Keith (later Sir Keith) Officer, which were reciprocated by the Ambassador. About the middle of the year, the Embassy was formally requested to transmit a Communist wish for diplomatic recognition.

[57] In public sources, see Chifley, *CPD*, HR, Vol. 203, June 22, 1949, p. 1299.

Canberra gave no reply, presumably because the Communist move was premature, no central government having as yet been formed.

In the meantime, the Australian Embassy was preparing for the very strong contingency of Australia's recognition of a Communist government. Plans were set in motion to acquire a location for an Australian embassy in Peking, the Ambassador himself taking a hand in the investigation of prospective sites. In October, shortly after the Communist Central People's Government had been announced, the Embassy was withdrawn from Nanking. The Ambassador returned to Australia, but some Embassy members established themselves in Hong Kong, with the clear inference that both the Embassy and the Government were leaving them there as a kind of forward post from which a *cadre* group could quickly be moved to Peking when recognition was granted. Indeed, after the Hong Kong group appeared, they maintained their interest in the topic of embassy quarters in Peking; when Professor C. P. Fitzgerald was passing through Hong Kong late in October on his way to dispose of some personal affairs in China, he was explicitly asked to look after the matter while in Peking. Although the search for premises in Peking seems to have been inspired by the Embassy rather than Canberra, the stationing of the "advance guard" in Hong Kong was an official decision pointing toward the prospect of recognition.

Early in November, the Department of External Affairs called a meeting in Canberra to discuss China and related Asian subjects. In attendance were Keith Officer, several other Australian diplomats and officials, plus British and New Zealand representatives. The official communiqué following two days of discussion gave no hint as to conclusions reached,[58] while Evatt's own summary was largely a rehash of his own earlier public pronouncements

[58] For the official account, see *SMH,* November 11, 1949.

on China.[59] From the then Secretary of External Affairs, Dr. John W. Burton, however, has come a fuller printed version—namely, that the Canberra conference participants *unanimously* recommended that Australia should follow the impending British recognition of China.[60] From another source the present author has been led to understand that the views of the participants were in fact known in advance, including the position of Ambassador Officer. Indeed, about this time, former Ambassador Copland was occasionally being consulted by External Affairs, and his advice was unswervingly in favor of recognition.

Regarding Burton himself, the highest official in the External Affairs Department at the time, there is no problem in ascertaining his posture on China. Burton then and steadily afterward held to the view that Australian recognition of China was desirable if not imperative for her own self-interest. Even while serving as Secretary he published a short article under the ill-disguised initials "J.H.W.B." in which he vigorously championed recognition and warned that delay could only help isolate the Communist regime and "serve to crystallize the beliefs of Peking in Australia's hostility toward it." [61] What made Burton's position rather special was his intimate relationship with Evatt, whom he had previously served as private secretary, and from which position he had been moved to Secretary of External Affairs at a remarkably early age. Furthermore, Burton was well liked and admired (though by no means uncritically) by the Prime Minister. It would be unfounded to allege that in this period Aus-

[59] *Ibid.,* November 12, 1949.

[60] John W. Burton, *The Alternative* (Sydney: Morgans Publications, 1954), p. 90.

[61] J.H.W.B., "Australia and Communist China," *Anglican Review,* No. 8 (November 1949), pp. 18–21. Also, under same initials, see his "Australia and the Asiatic Area," *Anglican Review,* No. 7 (August 1949), pp. 8–12.

tralian foreign policy was somehow the creature of John Burton, but his place in the Department should not be regarded strictly in accordance with his title.

There was also a powerful conviction on the political level that recognition would be valuable. In May 1949, the U.S. State Department contacted eight friendly governments, including Australia, with the purpose of first stressing the disadvantages of leaving an impression with the Communists that their search for recognition would be uncritically received, and second that it was desirable to adopt a concerted Western policy respecting any eventual recognition moves.[62] Consultations were indeed very close, both between Australia and her Commonwealth partners and America. Chifley himself observed discretion, as the occasion demanded, and time and again fell back on assuring questioners that the subject was under careful review as confidential exchanges with friendly powers continued.[63]

On June 21, Evatt made some remarks in the House that reflected the Government's predilections—consultations and exchanges of ideas aside. He denied the assumption that a Communist regime in China would slavishly follow the Moscow line, and thought that if the West gave the Communists grounds for believing that no cooperation or friendship could ever be expected or forthcoming, this could well tempt the new China to snap all ties with the democracies. Much was to be earned from regaining relations with whatever authorities controlled China. Every area of contact, every "breathing point," political or commercial, between China and the West could only serve to improve the international climate [64]; this interpretation thoroughly coincided with Burton's.

[62] *NYT,* May 26, 1949; "U.S. Policy Toward China, 1949–50," statement by Philip C. Jessup, reproduced in *Department of State Bulletin,* Vol. 25 (October 15, 1951), p. 604.

[63] *CPD,* HR, Vol. 202, May 26, 1949, p. 205, and *ibid.,* June 8, 1949, p. 648.

[64] Evatt, *ibid.,* June 21, 1949, pp. 1222–1223.

Perhaps a slight digression is in order at this juncture about Evatt's allusion to commerce, especially in light of the continuous Australian controversy in recent years about the usefulness of Chinese recognition as a stimulant for further Sino-Australian trade. In 1949 relatively little public attention was drawn to the possible connection between the two subjects. Neither Copland nor Officer, both of whom strongly advocated recognition, seem to have argued from a commercial premise. In the press and in Parliament the references are too negligible to report. Evatt did, however, make the above comment, and then again in early 1950, once his Party had passed into opposition, he stated that recognition would be "an enormous advantage from the trading point of view." [65]

The answer to this outward indifference toward the commercial aspects of the matter is probably easily explicable—trade promotion was regarded as highly important and it was simply assumed among the exponents of recognition that the two naturally marched together, with small need to labor the point. In the 1930's Australia was in certain years a prominent exporter of wheat and flour to China, and by the close of the decade began to make some significant wool deliveries as well. In the early postwar period, trade revived; in 1946–47 goods valued at over £6,000,000 were exported to China, and diversification began with shipments of metals, machinery, and chemicals.[66] The unsettled conditions of the civil war greatly handicapped this promising trade, Australian exports declining to £1,438,000 in 1948–49 and to £502,000 in 1949–50. In previous years, Chinese commentators themselves had kept the prospect of a vast Chinese market

[65] *CPD,* HR, Vol. 206, March 16, 1950, p. 919.

[66] Jack Shepherd, *Australia's Interests and Policies in the Far East* (New York: IPR, 1939), pp. 26–27, 67–69, 171–175; M. W. Oakley, "Australia's Trade with Asia," ANZAAS paper, section P, Canberra, January 1954, p. 15; W. Y. Tsao, *Two Pacific Democracies, China and Australia* (Melbourne: F. W. Cheshire, 1941), pp. 89–99; *CPD,* HR 4, September 7, 1954, pp. 1022–1025.

alive.[67] Late in 1948, the Chinese Vice-Minister for Industry and Commerce told Frank Clune that the products of the two countries were complementary and that a bright and profitable era in trade relations was bound to appear.[68] The problem in the late 1940's was that China had been torn asunder, and her normal trade relationships had suffered accordingly. The corrective, as offered by two Australian writers in mid-war, seemed self-evident: trade prospects could be expected to flourish, but only in the event of "a prolonged period of peace accompanied by a strong Chinese government with a sense of social reform and responsibility." [69] In many minds the eviction of the bungling Nationalists and the arrival of a Communist regime in China might well accomplish these conditions, and it stood to reason that diplomatic ties between Australia and the new China would be the obvious *entré* to commercial intercourse.

In any case, the Labor Government was convinced that recognition would be a judicious move. When the Central People's Government was proclaimed, "official circles" in Canberra were reported to believe that recognition by Britain would be followed swiftly by comparable Australian action.[70] A few days later a U.S. State Department press officer remarked that consultations among interested governments were proceeding, but the *New York Times* placed Australia and India in the same category as Britain and described them as being "somewhat more willing to recognize the Chinese Communists than the

[67] William J. L. Liu, "Chinese-Australian Trading Relationship" (Sydney: 1932) p. 14; Pao Chun-Jien, "Economic Co-operation—the Way to Peace," in Pao Chun-Jien, ed., *A Century of Sino-Australian Relations* (Sydney: 1938), pp. 34–39; K. D. Hung, "Opportunity for Australian Commerce in China," in *ibid.*, pp. 53–58; Tsao, *op. cit.*, pp. 89–99.

[68] Clune, *op. cit.*, p. 277.

[69] S. M. Wadham and K. H. Northcote, "Australian Markets Particularly for Primary Products," in AIIA, *op. cit.*, pp. 151–152.

[70] *SMH*, October 1, 1949.

United States," a view which persisted in informed American newspaper circles.[71] In point of fact, American Congressional hearings later disclosed that Washington had almost throughout the lengthy negotiations of 1949 identified Australia and Evatt in particular with a wish to recognize at the earliest possible moment.[72] In March of 1951, speaking as Leader of the Opposition, Chifley told the House that in 1949, "There could be no question about the mind of my Government with respect to the recognition of that [Chinese Communist] government." [73]

And yet, given Labor's unquestioned interest in recognition, in October and November of 1949 Dr. Evatt behaved in a curious manner on this issue. On October 25 Evatt produced a public statement on Chinese recognition. "Definite and convincing" answers would have to be given to three conditions if, as Secretary Acheson had indicated before, the democratic countries were to extend recognition: the new Chinese Government was in fact in control over the area it claimed; it was prepared to and capable of discharging its international obligations; it was supported by the free will of the majority of its subjects. Furthermore, recognition could not be granted, nor Peking's admission to the UN considered, in the absence of "firm and specific assurances that the territorial integrity of neighbouring countries, notably Hong Kong, will be respected." To cap it off, the Minister claimed that Australia, Britain, and the U.S. were all in accord on these principles, and had arranged to harmonize action when and if recognition arrived.[74]

[71] *NYT,* October 4, 1949; also see *ibid.,* October 23, 1949, and *Washington Post,* November 9, 1949.

[72] Walton Butterworth, remarks of October 6, 1949, cited in U.S. Senate, Committee on the Judiciary, *Hearings on the Institute of Pacific Relations,* 82nd Congress, 1st Session, 1951. Part 5, Appendix, p. 1566.

[73] *CPD,* HR, Vol. 212, March 7, 1951, p. 85.

[74] *CNIA,* Vol. 20 (October 1949), pp. 1084–1085.

To be sure, Evatt's three guidelines were nearly identical with the principles enunciated less than two weeks earlier by Acheson on behalf of the American Government.[75] The British Foreign Office had no comment on Evatt's statement, but was understandably reported to be incensed. Evatt had no right to speak for all three Governments, either as to the recognition principles to be followed or the proposed concerted action, especially since by then Britain was unequivocally leaning toward recognition and the U.S. was leaning in the opposite direction. Hence, common action was almost impossible even at that stage, and to speak of it could only embarrass the parties concerned. Furthermore, the British Government and various traders and officials in the East were appalled at possible Chinese reactions to the Hong Kong guarantee ingredient in Evatt's remarks. Britain wished to salvage her investments in China and to preserve Hong Kong, but scarcely believed that the new Chinese Government would be willing to rush forward with formal assurances of polite behavior. Evatt's intervention in the problem, wrote *The Times,* "merely obfuscates the main issue, which is the desirability of establishing as early as possible normal relations with what is the effective Government of the Chinese people, so that questions arising between the two countries can be dealt with through the normal official channels." [76] By coincidence, also on October 25, Canadian External Affairs Minister Lester Pearson had produced his own Government's China position. There was no flourish about squaring the circle of concerted action, no talk of demanding guarantees for Hong Kong's safety, and even no moralizing about the West's censorious eye keeping watch on the new China's strict adhesion to inter-

[75] *NYT,* October 13, 1949.

[76] *The Times* (London), October 27, 1949. Also see *Christian Science Monitor,* October 26, 1949; Melbourne *Herald,* October 28, 1949.

national obligations. Canada would need to find the new China independent of external control, exercising effective authority over the territory it claimed, and claiming territory reasonably well defined. In the meantime, close touch was being maintained with like-minded Governments on all aspects of the China question.[77] The comparison between the statements made by Evatt and Pearson hardly benefited the former.

About two weeks after Evatt's unhelpful strictures came the Canberra meetings of Australian officials and British and New Zealand representatives. In itself, a serious conference, pooling the thinking of career diplomats and public servants, could only be regarded as a constructive exercise. This conference certainly did no harm and may have shed some fresh light on the China problem, but probably not much. As was earlier suggested, the participants were agreed in advance on the propriety of recognition, and their views were mutually known. Then too, Ambassador Officer had been comprehensively briefed on the British discussions just concluded in Singapore, and could easily have delivered a résumé in Canberra without the trappings of a large conference; Britain's Esler (later Sir Esler) Denning, who had come to Australia from the Singapore discussions, could also have done this. But these were minor objections; what stood out was that when the talks ended, in complete agreement that Australia should recognize China, Evatt said that insofar as his Government was concerned on Chinese recognition, his remarks of October 25 still held, although he backtracked a bit by hoping for Commonwealth coordination, making no mention of the U.S.[78]

On this and subsequent occasions before the elections of early December, Evatt was reported to wish that the

[77] *Canadian Parliamentary Debates,* House of Commons, 2nd Session, 1949, Vol. 2, October 25, 1949, p. 1109.

[78] *SMH,* November 12, 1949.

various Commonwealth Governments defer recognition until they could talk things over at a Commonwealth Foreign Ministers' Conference in Colombo at the opening of 1950.[79] By the close of November, Evatt and his Department, for the record, had climbed to the very edge of conservatism on the China question. It was *officially* stated in Canberra that Australia would "strenuously oppose" any move by the Chinese Communists to gain representation on the UN Security Council (Australia was *not* then a member of the Council) until Peking had been formally recognized by all [*sic!*] members of the Commonwealth,[80] which would have meant Canada, New Zealand, and South Africa as well as Britain and the Asian members.

## LABOR'S CHINESE RECOGNITION BEHAVIOR APPRAISED

THE APPARENT contradiction between the Government's convictions and its public expressions on Chinese recognition was, at bottom, a reflection of the Australian domestic scene. Broadly, but not in every detail, it was a reaction of caution in the face of a general election in which the theme of Communism was worked and reworked by the Liberal and Country opposition parties. By late 1949 it was plain that Communist influence in a number of Australian trade unions was considerable. One result was a series of dramatic and publicly inconvenient industrial stoppages, involving Communist led unions and culminating in the great coal strike of mid-1949. There also were revelations of Communist ballot-rigging in union elections, plus, as the late Professor Leicester Webb suggested, a widespread tendency for the public to hold Communists responsible for nearly all the country's eco-

[79] *The Times* (London), November 14, 1949; *NYT,* November 17, 1949; *SMH,* November 23, 1949.

[80] *Ibid.*

nomic ills.[81] As the coal strike was about to be broken, an opinion survey inquired about the most important problem with which the Federal Government would have to cope in the next few months: 25 per cent replied "coal," 22 per cent "Communists," and 17 per cent "industrial unrest"—all issues which tended to link together and to carry the common denominator of "Communism." [82] Early in 1948 the Opposition moved censure against the Government for imputed laxity in dealing with internal Communism. A year later Liberal Leader R. G. (later Sir Robert) Menzies had been converted to the cause of outlawing the Communist Party, a position adopted several years earlier by the partner Country Party. By this time fully 70 per cent of the electorate supported such a ban.[83] In other words, even before the 1949 campaign had opened in early November, there were unmistakable signs of what the national mood was and of the line of attack the Opposition parties would select.

Reviewing the campaign speeches and propaganda literature of the Opposition in this election is a rather unedifying exercise. Time and again the ALP was accused of coddling Communists, of pursuing socialist programs (e.g., the abortive attempt to nationalize banks) which blurred into Communist programs, and of living in a cuckoo-land respecting the commotions which international Communism was stirring up. If the Menzies-Fadden electoral criticism were to be believed, one could imagine the uncompleted statue of George V facing Parliament House being wrecked and replaced by a monument to some Communist saint in case the Chifley Government

[81] Leicester Webb, *Communism and Democracy in Australia* (Melbourne: F. W. Cheshire for the ANU, 1954), p. 11. See a general treatment of the problem on pp. 10–15.

[82] *AGP,* nos. 607–618, July-August 1949.

[83] *Ibid.,* nos. 569–578, February-March 1949.

was reelected. One Country Party political advertisement pictured Stalin and Chifley, both smoking their pipes:

Two Pipes with but a Single Smoke.
Whether it's called Socialisation or "Joe"-Cialisation.
It's the same thing in the long run.
All Communists Begin as Socialists.
The Rest Follows.[84]

A Country Party political booklet contained "evidence" of Communist barbarity: the annexation of Manchuria, the nationalization of industries in Burma, industrial unrest in Japan, and "strikes in Australian coal mines and widespread unemployment and suffering of women and children throughout Australia, because of lack of power." What a frightful prospect the country faced if the Australian Constitution were replaced by the ALP platform: "Is the Australian coat-of-arms to be our symbol under free enterprise, or is the kangaroo to be bludgeoned to death by the hammer, and the emu hacked to pieces by the sickle?" [85] Shortly after having fought and lost the election of December 10, Chifley wrote to a friend, "the constant barrage over the radio and in the press, whereby the Opposition succeeded in linking Communism with Socialism and Socialism with the Labour Party, and so creating a fear complex in the minds of a percentage of the middle class vote, was the outstanding reason for the Government's defeat." [86]

Foreign policy was not, to be sure, a prominent feature of the 1949 campaign. Indeed, peacetime Australian elections have not been decided by external affairs, as Arthur

[84] As it appeared in *SMH,* November 15, 1949.

[85] Australian Country Party, "The Red Twins. Communism. Socialism" (Sydney: 1949), p. 16. Also see the Country Party's "You Won't Vote Labour When you've Read *This* Story!" (Sydney: 1949), *passim.*

[86] Cited in Crisp, *op. cit.,* p. 374.

Calwell has recently testified,[87] and the 1963 election, despite its relatively strong foreign and defense policy emphasis, was probably no exception. In 1949, nevertheless, while the Opposition talked only in broad terms about closer Commonwealth ties, cooperation with America, and the ominous threat of international Communism, it managed to paint an undifferentiated picture of Communism within Australia and without, and at every opportunity indicted Labor for its mistaken if not subversive behavior.[88]

It is in this context that the Government decided to postpone its desired recognition of the Chinese Communist Government, although it is proper to note and exclude from our analysis certain outwardly plausible considerations. First, the Australian press, starting considerably before the electoral campaign got under way, could certainly not be described as hostile to Australian recognition. There was no enthusiasm for a Communist regime in China, but widespread acceptance of the need to deal with such a regime as best one could, diplomatically and otherwise.[89] It was very much the exception rather than the rule to read apocalyptic comments like those of the Sydney *Bulletin,* which predicted that recognition would help install Peking in the UN and from this position it would direct pressure against Australian control of New Guinea. Communism would then be taught in New Guinea schools, the "White Australia" policy would crumble in New Guinea, and eventually metropolitan Australia's re-

[87] Arthur A. Calwell, *Labor's Role in Modern Society* (Melbourne: Lansdowne Press, 1963), p. 160.

[88] For example, see Spender's speeches of November 3 and 28, in *SMH,* November 4 and 29, 1949; Joint Liberal-Country Party policy speech and supplement, in *ibid.,* November 11 and 12, 1949.

[89] Brisbane *Courier-Mail,* April 27, 1949; Hobart *Mercury,* October 4, 1949; Launceston *Examiner,* October 4, 1949; Sydney *Daily Telegraph,* October 5, 1949; *SMH,* October 6, 1949.

strictive migration policy would vanish.[90] Although the press did incline toward the wisdom of recognition, it usually qualified its recommendations by cautioning against precipitate action and counseled a synchronized Commonwealth-American approach—this qualification was recommended by Australia's most important and influential newspapers.[91] Only in this limited sense would the Government's behavior on Chinese recognition seem politically explicable.

Second, the author is convinced that the Government was not affected by an *established* Liberal-Country Party view which, to Professor Werner Levi, was simply that "The Opposition was against recognition." [92] Levi footnotes this assertion, otherwise unembellished, with reference to a remark by P. C. (later Sir Percy) Spender on October 5 in the House. In this comment, which was very brief, Spender alleged that the Communists had come to power and were governing by force, and were being abetted by Russia. At most, his feelings against recognition could only be derived by inference.[93] There is considerable internal evidence that Spender himself was more or less thinking aloud on this occasion and his views were still very much in a formative state. Additionally, not only was there no official or even semiofficial Opposition view on Chinese recognition at this time, but after Spender's statement on October 5 the Opposition failed to make any reference to Chinese recognition as such, either before or during the campaign.

Third, it has been suggested to the author that at this time, late in 1949, swift recognition of China would have opened an ugly public within the ALP itself. It is true that the Victorian Executive was already in the hands of

[90] *Bulletin* (Sydney), October 12, 1949.

[91] Melbourne *Age,* October 19 and November 30, 1949; Melbourne *Herald,* October 13, 1949; *SMH,* October 3, 1949.

[92] Levi, *op. cit.,* p. 153.

[93] *CPD,* HR, Vol. 204, October 5, 1949, p. 1964.

militantly anti-Communist elements identified with the industrial groups, and in the losing year of 1949 Victorian Labor was able to nominate and elect figures such as W. M. Bourke, S. M. Keon and J. M. Mullens—men involved in the 1954–55 ALP split who later entered the Democratic Labor Party. Nonetheless, careful questioning of Keon, Francis McManus, then a Victorian Executive member, and of B. A. Santamaria, currently the president of the fiercely anti-Communist National Civic Council, plus an examination of party records resulted in the following consensus: The concern at the time was with internal Communism, particularly in the trade unions. Foreign affairs hardly concerned the Victorian ALP people of that period, and the specific question of Chinese recognition almost not at at all. There was no Victorian pressure on the Chifley Government to avoid recognition, and no serious rift in the Party would have been precipitated by early recognition, although it would not have been welcomed by some within the ALP in Victoria. Although the Melbourne Archdiocesan organ the *Advocate* was then an unflagging opponent of recognition,[94] the *News Weekly*, already a recognized spokesman for the uncompromising anti-Communism industrial groups, wrote in November, "There is some justification for the recognition of the Chinese Red Government, because the Nationalists have quite obviously ceased to govern." The timing of recognition was important, and certain guarantees might need to be sought from Peking, but recognition must in time be offered to safeguard the Western stake, including missionaries and investments.[95] An interview with a prominent left-wing Labor Parliamentarian, whose distaste for the groupists and DLP is incontrovertible, confirmed the fact that the Victorian right was not an issue in Chinese recognition.

[94] *Advocate* (Melbourne), October 20 and 27, December 8, 1949.

[95] *News Weekly* (Melbourne), November 16, 1949.

If adverse press comment, an established Opposition resistance to recognition, and the threat of an internal ALP explosion were not compelling reasons for the Government to tread an inordinately cautious path in October–November, what then was the explanation? In March of 1951, when he indicated that his Government had been inclined to extend recognition, Chifley added that the step had not been taken because he "considered the subject to be of such importance that with a general election pending it should be decided by the incoming government,"[96] and this appears to have been his approach when he raised the question of postponement of recognition before Cabinet in 1949. There are two ways to interpret this. Chifley may have been invoking the English constitutional doctrine of mandate wherein (with an election immediately available to test opinion) an outgoing Government feels restrained from binding its successor to important policies. This is not the place to debate the validity of the doctrine, although it might be mentioned that a general election was staged in Britain less than two months after the Attlee Government recognized Peking on January 6, 1950. In any event, whether the pure constitutional question was meaningful to Chifley, his remark can also be interpreted in a looser political sense—an attempt to escape taking a step which might backfire among the electorate.

One substantiation for this reading is found in an alleged understanding reached by the Australian Labor Government and the New Zealand Labor Government under Fraser. It has been stated by a number of highly respected writers, including Chifley's biographer, that the two Governments, presumably at the prime-ministerial level, decided to shelve recognition until after elections had been completed in both countries: November 30 in New Zealand, December 10 in Australia. Part of the

[96] *CPD,* HR, Vol. 212, March 7, 1951, p. 85.

reason is seen to be a wish to coordinate action, but far more significant is the explanation that both Governments were afraid that their political opponents would exploit hasty recognition as an issue in the campaign, especially in Australia where the Communist issue was so lively. The literature on the subject is not definite as to when the agreement was concluded or which Government initiated it.[97] The present author has tried without success to pin down the details, but even Walter Nash, a senior member of the Fraser Government and himself later Prime Minister of New Zealand, could not clarify the episode. In general, however, the story is certainly true. Evatt at one time told Professor Fitzgerald of the arrangement, and two former Labor Ministers verified the story in general terms for the author.

The second piece of testimony confirming this thesis was, of course, the nature of Evatt's public treatment of Chinese recognition: his statement of October 25, his persistence in sticking to a rigid line in the face of the Canberra conference recommendations, etc., would appear to have been purely politically inspired. Burton says as much in his book,[98] certain information given in confidence to the author supports this view, and as a finale perhaps something should be said about the men in charge of Australian foreign policy at the time. It was Chifley,

[97] Crisp, *op. cit.*, p. 294; C. P. Fitzgerald, "Australia and Asia," in Greenwood and Harper, *op. cit.*, p. 206; Norman Harper, "Australia and the United States," in Gordon Greenwood and Norman Harper, eds., *Australia in World Affairs 1956–60* (Melbourne, Canberra, and Sydney: F. W. Cheshire for the AIIA, 1963), p. 214; E. J. Tapp, "New Zealand: The Seventh State of Australia?" *Australian Quarterly*, Vol. 34 (December 1962), p. 77; Levi, *op. cit.*, p. 153.

[98] Burton, *op. cit.*, pp. 90–91. During and after the Canberra meetings there was some press opinion that the Government's posture was essentially based on political calculations. See *SMH*, November 10, 1949, and *Sydney Sunday Herald*, November 13, 1949.

who, undeniably, sanctioned the delay in recognition on political grounds. But it was Evatt who executed the decision, and the almost irrational force with which he publicly resisted recognition in the closing weeks of the Labor Government was probably as much a reflection of the man as of the policy. It should not be forgotten that in the period from 1952 to mid-1954, while he was Leader of the Opposition, Evatt again assumed an extremely conservative posture on foreign policy and especially on China. In those years he felt it expedient to swing close to the right wing of his Party and to avoid alienation of the industrial groups, a necessary attitude, he thought, if Labor were to win the 1954 election and if he were to succeed to the prime-ministership. After the 1954 election had been lost, he broke with the right and by early 1955 was embracing the left-oriented Hobart program, which included recognition and the seating of Peking at the UN. In late 1949, probably sensing that he might shortly be in competition for his Party's leadership and ultimately for the highest political office, he thought it prudent to follow a respectable conservative course. As has been suggested to the author, Evatt as a person favored recognition, but as a politician opposed it.

Finally, there was Burton himself. Although not a politician, his views were well known and indeed respected by Chifley and Evatt, though in the case of Chinese recognition disregarded. Burton was upset not only by Evatt's cast-iron treatment of nonrecognition, but by the fact of nonrecognition *per se.* Some years later, delivering a Chifley Memorial Lecture, he bitterly said that Labor's refusal to recognize China late in 1949 "was a miserable decision" and that "Something vital to the Labor Movement was lost when principle was so uselessly ignored." [99]

[99] John W. Burton, "The Nature and Significance of Labor," Chifley Memorial Lecture, Melbourne, September 11, 1958 (Melbourne: 1958), p. 11.

There is, however, something rather unreal in Burton's accusation. When Labor was beaten at the polls on December 10, no nation outside the Communist bloc had as yet recognized Peking, while Britain herself, a principal advocate of recognition, did not make her formal move until the following January, *after* India, Pakistan, and Burma had done so. Technically speaking, Australia could have recognized any time she pleased. Practically speaking, except in the unlikely event that a man of Burton's unswerving, politically insensitive temperament had been Prime Minister, no Australian Government—Labor or Liberal—could sensibly have been expected to break the ice and become the first non-Communist Government to recognize. Negotiations within the Commonwealth and with Washington had not been entirely exhausted by December 10, and precipitate Australian action would only have embarrassed British efforts to persuade America to recognize.

Domestically, recognition by Labor in October or November might have given the Opposition one more issue in its strong anti-Communism campaign, although this is not at all certain: the Liberals had every expectation of winning the election, and would not have cared to tie their own hands in advance while the subject of Chinese recognition was still so fluid. The principal accusation would probably have been that Labor was not only indifferent to American wishes, but indeed was "anti-British" in not waiting for a safe lead from Whitehall; this would have been a predictable reaction from R. G. Menzies, a King's Man *par excellence*. Labor had long been under fire both for "anti-American" and "anti-Imperial" conduct, Evatt had consistently been abused for being a sort of diplomatic peacock, erratic and inclined to strut about in fruitless if not dangerous directions, and an early and isolated Australian recognition would therefore have offered a perfect target. In this sense, Labor's choice to delay recognition until after the election, and presumably until recognition could be taken in conjunction with Britain and as many other Commonwealth countries as possible, was hardly surprising and cannot be considered a true surrender of principle as alleged by John Burton.

If, following the above line of analysis, in October and November there were reasonable and apparent reasons for Australian Labor not to recognize China before the election, then any understanding reached with New Zealand at about this time would have been superfluous. The logic of the situation points instead to an understanding made somewhat sooner—perhaps midyear—when the variables were far less defined: a new Chinese government might be created considerably before October 1; Britain might recognize rather quickly before the New Zealand and Australian elections; China might keep on rolling into Hong Kong or South-East Asia. At midyear, in other words, it was not unreasonable to forecast that by October or November, Chinese recognition might become a real instead of a rather academic alternative for Australia to consider. Yet, if she recognized the new Chinese Government before December 10, her action might be followed either by violent Chinese misbehavior or well-advertised American pique or both, thus giving the Opposition parties an issue concerning the naïveté of the ALP in foolishly snatching the Chinese bait.

What was unnecessary was the contrived, almost "professional anti-Chinese Communism" displayed by Evatt in October and November. The country at large held no brief for the Nationalists, there was no powerful and mobilized resistance to the principle of entering into relations with Communist China at an appropriate time, and Labor would probably have forfeited few if any votes on December 10 had it, or more particularly Herbert Evatt, chosen to emulate the more reasonable, undramatic, but cautious Canadian example. If the Evatt stiffness had a residual effect it was surely unintentional: conditioning the country against recognition and easing the Liberal Government's decision to delay the step. After Korea, delay was, in practical terms, converted into denial.

# II

# AUSTRALIA AND CHINA DURING THE KOREAN WAR PERIOD: 1

FOLLOWING ITS electoral victory in early December of 1949 the new Menzies Liberal-Country Party Government was forced almost immediately to find its bearings on evaluating the new China and devising a suitable policy posture. Then, according to one account, when the North Koreans crossed the 38th parallel and the Chinese subsequently intervened in the war, "Australia . . . found her policy towards China frozen at a time when it was still in formation." [1] For a period of some three years Asian international relations were inescapably colored by perceptions of China and her behavior in and around the Korean perimeter. Australia too became affected, both in her external policy and at the level of domestic debate and political life. Once the war was over, its imprint lingered on, later affecting aspects of the China problem in Australia. Chapters II and III analyze Australian reactions to Communist China in a decisive stage of their development. The contention that Australia's China policy was "frozen" by the advent of war in Korea cannot be dismissed lightly—it implies fluidity before the initial Korean events and rigidity afterward. To test the truth or falsity of this assertion is in fact to write the story of the China problem during the Korean War period.

[1] C. P. Fitzgerald, "China, Korea and Indo-China," in Gordon Greenwood, ed., *Australian Policies Toward Asia* (Melbourne: Australian Institute of International Affairs, 1954), part *VI*, p. 5.

# THE KOREAN WAR PERIOD: 1

## PRELIMINARY APPRAISALS OF THE NEW CHINA

THE NEW Chinese regime had been in existence slightly over two months when the Liberal Party took over in December 1949. Only Communist bloc countries had extended diplomatic recognition, while intensive discussions continued among other Governments as the search for a possible common approach to China was pressed. Within the week, however, the Attlee Labor Government decided that it could not postpone its decision much longer; other Commonwealth countries and the United States were notified that the formal announcement of British recognition would appear early in January. By the opening days of January, India, Pakistan, and Burma had recognized Peking, and on January 6 Britain and Ceylon were added to the list. British spokesmen subsequently explained that although China had been on the agenda of the Commonwealth Foreign Ministers' Conference which opened in Colombo on January 9, it had been clear for some time that because of varying attitudes on the part of members of the Commonwealth, even a full discussion at Colombo could not have produced a joint move toward recognition.[2]

In what way did this British explanation apply to Australia? Can it rightly be said that by the time that Spender, the new External Affairs Minister, arrived at Colombo his Government had already charted a position on China, one explicitly opposed to Chinese recognition? For the moment, two aspects of the picture can be isolated. First, it must be remembered that prior to winning the 1949 election the then Liberal-Country Party Opposition gave no real hint about how it proposed to approach

[2] Kenneth Younger, *United Kingdom Parliamentary Debates,* House of Commons, Vol. 472, March 13, 1950, col. 26 (written answers). Also see Younger, Vol. 475, May 24, 1950, col. 2187, and Ernest Bevin, col. 2083.

the recognition question, despite its natural regret that Communism had assumed power in China.

Second, during the month's interval between the election and the meeting in Colombo, there was scarcely an opportunity for the Government to shape a policy on China. Cabinet met only once, and then for ceremonial and organizational purposes. The Christmas holidays intervened. Spender left Australia on January 3, before Britain had made her recognition public, and when Menzies replied "no comment" to a question about his Government's reaction to London's move, it was undoubtedly more a gesture expressing uncertainty than a deliberate concealment of a fixed Australian position.[3] At Colombo both Spender and F. Doidge, New Zealand Minister for External Affairs, criticized other Commonwealth states for having extended recognition before full Commonwealth consultation could be undertaken at the conference, though they "made it clear they understood the reasons which had prompted the other nations to grant recognition."[4] At least part of the reason that this criticism came from Spender and Doidge rather than their Canadian or South African colleagues, was that both men represented newly formed Governments which had recently replaced their opponents. While both Australia and New Zealand had received advice from Britian and other Commonwealth Governments, there had been slight opportunity for them to think through their own positions and to offer suggestions in return. Hence Australia was unprepared to move in step with Britain on recognition before the Colombo conference because she herself had lacked time to crystallize a policy—any policy—on the subject.

None of this should be construed to mean that the principal Australian figures of the time, especially Menzies and Spender, were not already disposed to pick and choose and weigh various ingredients in the China com-

[3] *SMH*, January 7, 1950. [4] *Ibid.*, January 11, 1950.

plex, and to build toward an eventual decision. Among the ingredients to which the Australian Government paid attention was the fact of British recognition. From the beginning of concentrated thinking on how to handle a Communist government in China, the British had been inclined to favor early recognition and spent the closing months of 1949 trying to persuade other Governments to adopt a similar view; they continued into the first half of 1950 to nudge others into supporting both recognition and UN seating for Peking.[5] Furthermore, in late 1949 and early 1950 the attitude of the British Government was not a party-political matter. Diplomatic officers, commercial interests, the press, and the Conservative Opposition agreed with the Government and favored rapid recognition by Britain and her friends. It was no less an anti-Communist than Winston Churchill who, respecting China, had declared in November that "one had to recognise lots of things and people in this world of sin and woe that one does not like. The reason for having diplomatic relations is not to confer a compliment, but to secure a convenience."[6] This British solidarity must have impressed the new Australian Government. It was a Government which had a traditional affection for the senior member of the Commonwealth, believed in Commonwealth unity to the extent that could be achieved, and perhaps above all had at its head that staunch Anglophile, R. G. Menzies. As the pressure from London was brought to bear in December and early 1950, the Australian Government was not insensitive.

[5] Bevin, *UKPD,* HC, Vol. 475, May 24, 1950, cols. 2084–2085; Younger, col. 2188; J. P. Jain, "Chinese Reaction to British Recognition of the People's Republic of China," *International Studies,* Vol. 4 (July 1962), pp. 41–42.

[6] *UKPD,* HC, Vol. 469, November 17, 1949, col. 2225. See summaries of British agreement on recognition in Evan Luard, *Britain and China* (London: Chatto and Windus, 1962), pp. 77–80, and in Leon D. Epstein, *Britain. Uneasy Ally* (Chicago: Univ. of Chicago Press, 1954), pp. 209–212.

Yet there was more to Australia's reception of Britain's prompting than a sentimental wish to follow the leader. Britain was promoting recognition for particular reasons,[7] and some of these had special meaning for Australia. For one, there was the British economic stake in China, which stood at some quarter-billion pounds sterling. The author understands that Menzies was impressed by Britain's argument that recognition by Commonwealth Governments would help protect not only this investment but economically valuable Hong Kong as well. It is likely that Menzies was then, as at most times, concerned about the erosion of British power and influence in the Far East. From this he derived the conclusion that concrete steps by Britain and her associates to establish working relations with China would operate toward preserving the economic arm of Britain's presence in the area, and could in turn enhance the British role in both politics and security.

A second explanation of Britain's recognition policy was the need to maintain direct Western liaison with China so that Peking would not regard the West as an intractable opponent and, indeed, might be dissuaded from emulating Soviet behavior. There is no doubt that the Australian Government pondered this point with considerable care. On February 20, a few days after the Sino-Soviet treaty of friendship and mutual assistance had been signed, Spender expressed pessimism concerning the hope that China would become nationalist rather than Communist, or that the treaty would "mean anything else but close cooperation of foreign policy." [8] Nevertheless, on reflec-

[7] For explanations of why Britain favored early recognition, see Bevin, *UKPD,* HC, Vol. 475, May 24, 1950, col. 2082, and Younger, cols. 2186–2187; Kenneth Younger, "An Analysis of British and U.S. Policies in the Far East," *Eastern World,* Vol. 7 (March 1953), p. 10; Clement R. Attlee, "Britain and America: Common Aims, Different Opinions," *Foreign Affairs,* Vol. 32 (January 1954), p. 198; Sir Alexander Grantham, "What Britain Has Gained Through Recognising Red China," *Vital Speeches,* Vol. 21 (December 1, 1954), p. 876.

[8] Cited in *SMH,* February 21, 1950.

tion, in his Cabinet-approved statement to the House a few weeks later, he apparently had not surrendered all hope of accommodation, and in fact saw the possibility of some useful working relations with China:

> It is not for us to question the kind of government the Chinese people choose to live under. If they are satisfied with the Communist Government, that is their affair . . . we do not accept the inevitability of a clash between the democratic and Communist way of life; there is no logical reason why democracy and communism, as distinct from Communist imperialism, should not be able to live together in the world. We would very much dislike seeing the traditional contacts severed between China and the Western World. We should like to think that the Chinese Communists would look for the sympathetic help of the Western democracies in the work of uniting and rehabilitating their country.[9]

What seems clear in the period of the Liberal Government's first half-year in office is that it accepted literally the British explanation that recognition could pave the way toward moderating Chinese behavior very quickly. By the end of January, not only Britain but the Netherlands, Switzerland, and the Scandinavian countries had accorded recognition to Peking. Australia surveyed Chinese behavior and, simply put, endeavored to find some semblance of the positive effects that non-Communist recognition, and particularly British recognition, might be producing. In general she was very much disappointed by what she saw, particularly by Peking's inhospitable reception of Britain. The UN Security Council between January 10 and 12, 1950 considered a Soviet resolution to eject the Nationalists and substitute the Chinese People's Republic as the legitimate representative of China. The move failed; unlike the U.S.A., France, and four other delegations,

[9] *CPD,* HR, Vol. 206, March 9, 1950, p. 626.

which voted against, Britain joined Norway in abstaining, on the grounds that "at this moment, not many Governments have recognized the new Government in China, and, therefore, it might be premature and precipitate on the part of this organ of the United Nations to take, or attempt to take, a definite decision in the near future." [10] The Chinese failed to appreciate the finesse of the argument and reacted contemptuously. Similarly, they could not countenance the retention of a British consul at Tamsui, in Formosa, although he was technically accredited to the provincial governor rather than to the Republic of China. Finally, they showed impatience over legal proceedings in Hong Kong respecting the disposition of aircraft whose ownership they claimed. As weeks and then months wore on, these instances of British "duplicity" were emphasized and the British negotiating representative in Peking was unable to establish formal diplomatic connections.[11] By May of 1950, Anthony Eden was saying that "the truth is, and I think the Foreign Secretary would admit it, that recognition has in fact brought out no advantage at all today." [12]

The Australian Government was also struck by the callous Chinese treatment of foreign persons and properties within China. For months, American consuls and other officials had been subjected to continuing snubs, beatings, and jailings. In mid-January the Peking Government seized former military compounds belonging to the U.S., French, and Dutch Governments, and applied this same tactic to Britain three months later. This, from the

[10] Sir Alexander Cadogan, UN Security Council, *Official Records,* 459th Meeting, January 10, 1950, p. 6. Also see his remarks in 460th Meeting, January 12, 1950, p. 17.

[11] For discussions of these Sino-British problems, see Luard, *op. cit.,* pp. 83–87; Jain, *op. cit.,* pp. 29–43; Michael Lindsay, *China and the Cold War* (Melbourne: Melbourne Univ. Press, 1955), pp. 10–11; G. F. Hudson, "British Relations with China," *Current History,* Vol. 33 (December 1957), pp. 329–330.

[12] *UKPD,* HC, Vol. 475, May 24, 1950, col. 2071.

American standpoint, was the last straw; all remaining American consulates were closed and personnel withdrawn. This Chinese action had been taken only two days after the membership debate in the Security Council, and the State Department remarked that if the Communists were serious about seeking a seat in the UN, they would need to accept the obligations encumbent on UN membership.[13] Indeed, as was later revealed, the United States then undertook some active diplomacy of its own; missions abroad were instructed to explain that in light of recent developments it was America's belief that "recognition of the Communists or any change in the existing position regarding diplomatic relations with the Nationalist Government would be premature." [14]

The reaction in Australia was again to assess Chinese conduct unfavorably. Throughout most of January, Spender had been out of the country. When the Colombo talks ended, he visited several Asian nations, and did not reappear in Australia until the end of the month. The fact of his absence—and therefore of no direct report to Cabinet, including his advice on recognition—in itself precluded any change in policy. Retrospectively, therefore, the *Canberra Times*' opinion of January 7 that pre-Colombo recognition by Britain had spoiled the probability that Australia would have awarded recognition "if given the opportunity of joining in a simultaneous announcement" [15] seems unfounded. By the time Spender returned, there had been considerable Chinese misconduct in the intervening two weeks since the end of the Colombo meetings. Had Spender not felt the need, as a newly initiated External Affairs Minister of a new Government, to tour Asia rather than flying home immediately after Colombo,

[13] *NYT*, January 15, 1950.

[14] Philip C. Jessup, "U.S. Policy Toward China, 1949–50," *Department of State Bulletin*, Vol. 25 (October 15, 1951), p. 606.

[15] *Canberra Times*, January 7, 1950.

had Cabinet already been able to build up a working assessment of the Chinese problem, it is conceivable that Australia might have recognized about mid-January. But that was not the actual situation.

Earlier in the month there had been general editorial agreement that, irrespective of its timing, Britain's decision to recognize carried merit; the Nationalists on Formosa had no future, the West would need to live and deal with the new China, and an Australian offer of recognition should follow speedily.[16] Even Sir Frederic Eggleston, Australia's first Minister to China and a man who was not disposed to regard the Nationalists as fully responsible for the triumph of Communism in the country,[17] stepped forward and publicly exhorted the Australian Government to fall into line with Britain.[18] By the close of January, however, when Spender reappeared in Australia and volunteered that his Government would not "for the time being" recognize China, the Sydney *Daily Telegraph* began to reflect a changing mood; it praised Spender's caution, reminded its readers of rising Chinese disagreeableness, her undisguised cordiality toward Russia, and the snubbing of Western Governments that had accorded recognition, and concluded that "we needn't be in a hurry to join their ranks." [19]

At least two writers have attributed the failure of the old Dominions to recognize the Peking regime in January to China's mistreatment of consular officials and the requisitioning of the property of various Governments

[16] For instance, Melbourne *Sun,* January 7, 1950; Melbourne *Argus,* January 9, 1950; Adelaide *Advertiser,* January 9, 1950; Hobart *Mercury,* January 9, 1950; Melbourne *Herald,* January 12, 1950. For a less favorable view, see *SMH,* January 7, 1950.

[17] F. W. Eggleston, *Reflections on Australian Foreign Policy* (Melbourne: F. W. Cheshire for the AIIA, 1957), esp. chapter on "America and Two Chinese Revolutions," pp. 32–86.

[18] *SMH,* January 9, 1950.

[19] Sydney *Daily Telegraph,* January 29, 1950.

contrary to previous treaty rights.[20] As far as Australia was concerned this certainly was a contributing influence, and Spender's comment on his return undoubtedly took Chinese behavior into account.

However, when he returned from Asia he had already adopted a different and more significant set of notions relative to China: concern for the safety of South-East Asia. Even without the benefit of his travels, Spender, and the Liberal Government generally, would have reached the conclusion that a stable Asia secure from revolutionary disturbances was indispensable to Australia's own protection. The Government's thinking amounted to this: The center of political gravity was perceptibly shifting from Europe toward Asia. Colonial regimes were increasingly withdrawing their control. Nationalism was wide-spread. New national states were emerging. Communism, at least temporarily checked in Europe, was concentrating its efforts on this unstable part of the world. Most countries in South-East Asia had active Communist movements and, in certain cases, particularly Malaya, Indo-China, and the Philippines, armed uprisings were in progress. The Communists had accomplished their conquest of China, and were now exerting their influence toward neighboring countries, with local movements taking heart from the events in China. Even if China did not resort to force in South-East Asia, she held a handy instrument in the overseas Chinese populations, whom she was already trying to manipulate for her purposes. At all events, China had given quick and enthusiastic recognition to the Viet Minh in Indo-China—a sensitive danger point—whose collapse would outflank and threaten Malaya, similar to the pattern of World War II. The

[20] O. Edmund Clubb, "Chinese Communist Strategy in Foreign Relations," *Annals of the American Academy of Political and Social Science,* Vol. 277 (September 1951), p. 164; Allen S. Whiting, *China Crosses the Yalu* (New York: Macmillan, 1960), p. 26.

greater the successes of Communism, the smaller the capacity for resistance of remaining non-Communist South-East Asian territories would be. Australia was on the doorstep of these rapid and alarming developments, and could not afford to be indifferent toward them.[21]

### CHINA AND AUSTRALIAN SECURITY: CONSIDERATIONS IN THE FIRST HALF OF 1950

AUSTRALIA was not, indeed, indifferent, and her actions reflected the prevailing anxiety in Canberra. The Colombo discussions had ranged over wide ground. Their main accomplishment had been the arrangement of the Colombo Plan, providing for technical and economic assistance to Commonwealth Asian members; Spender had personally played a notable role in seeing that this plan was adopted. But differences prevented agreement on concrete security measures.[22] By the end of May, however, after considerable negotiation with Britain, Australia met requests for transport aircraft and crews to participate in the antiterrorist effort in Malaya, and for servicing facilities on Australian soil for RAF planes stationed in the Far East,[23] supplementing the arms and munitions shipments that the preceding Labor Government had undertaken. At the diplomatic level, Spender announced Australia's recognition of the three Indo-Chinese states early in February. Spender admitted that these states carried the limitations of continuing French management of their

[21] See especially Spender's statements of February 8, 1950, in *CNIA,* Vol. 21 (February 1950), pp. 133–134, and March 9, 1950, in *CPD,* HR, Vol. 206, esp. pp. 623–627.

[22] See comments in Colin Bingham, "The Colombo Failure," *SMH,* January 15, 1950, and Gordon Greenwood, "Australian Attitudes Towards Pacific Problems," *Pacific Affairs,* Vol. 23 (June 1950), p. 161.

[23] R. G. Menzies, *CPD,* HR, Vol. 208, May 30, 1950, p. 3351, and May 31, 1950, p. 3464; Alan Barcan, "Australia and Malaya," *Eastern World,* Vol. 9 (September 1955), pp. 19–20; Albinski, *op. cit.,* pp. 246–248.

defense and external affairs, but their prompt recognition by Australia and other powers "should encourage moderate nationalist leaders in Indo-China who did not wish their country to become a satellite of Moscow or Peking." [24] This step by Australia, and the explanation attached, carried special significance. It recognized the importance of insulating nationalist development from Communist influence—perhaps specifically Chinese influence. It assumed that the act of diplomatic recognition could serve to bolster morale and status in an affected country. It also helped the Government formulate its opinions on the recognition of China herself. If an act of diplomatic recognition was politically helpful to friendly Governments, especially Governments which were trying to maneuver themselves out of the range of Chinese Communist penetration, then withholding recognition from the guilty party, China, would seem to be a logical inference. By early March Spender was justifying nonrecognition of China largely on these grounds.[25] On June 8, in his last public statement on the subject prior to the outbreak in Korea, he said that his Government would continue to watch developments in China closely, "in order to ascertain to what degree the new regime in Peking intends to live up to international obligations in both its internal treatment of foreigners and its external non-interference in the affairs of neighboring states." The Government had "no present intention" of recognizing Peking.[26]

But there was another, related, and perhaps equally compelling international consideration which deterred Australia from extending recognition, although its proof is largely inferential. This was the search for a Pacific security alliance which could deter or defeat aggression in the area. The fear of Japan as a potential troublemaker

[24] Statement of February 8, 1950, in *CNIA, op. cit.,* p. 134.
[25] *CPD,* HR, Vol. 206, March 9, 1950, p. 626.
[26] *Ibid.,* Vol. 208, June 8, 1950, p. 4012.

certainly persisted and should not be underrated, but the Chinese Communist presence lent urgency. Ideally, the Liberals would have desired membership in such a pact to include Australia, New Zealand, Britain, perhaps other Commonwealth nations, and certainly and irreducibly the U.S.—similar to the regional alliance scheme which Labor had unsuccessfully promoted in 1949. To begin with, then, the reactivation of a search for an alliance by the Liberals depended somewhat on the appraisal placed on Chinese intentions. American participation was vital, and Spender admitted on June 8 that if no other avenue were open, Australia alone, without Britain and other Commonwealth members, would join the U.S. in a bilateral defense pact.[27] The U.S. held back, still disinclined to move into an alliance until interested states in the region gave clear evidence of banding together among themselves first, but prior to the Korean War, Australia labored conscientiously toward her alliance objective.

In these circumstances, it would have been most imprudent for Australia to recognize China, especially after January, for beyond that time there was a general hiatus in the extension of recognition by other countries. It has already been shown that after the Chinese property expropriations in mid-January, the United States redoubled its efforts to discourage recognition among its friends. It was about that time too that Spender was returning from Asia, somewhat disturbed about the lack of tangible security decisions at Colombo and considerably disturbed by what he had seen and heard of Chinese deportment and intentions. By the time a Cabinet decision was taken in February to withhold recognition of China, at least for the foreseeable future, there was also a decision to press ahead for an alliance. Spender hardly made a statement

[27] *Ibid.*, p. 4006. On the Government's pact search at this time, also see Spender's address of February 20, 1950, in *SMH*, February 21, 1950; Rosecrance, *op. cit.*, pp. 181–183; Albinski, *op. cit.*, pp. 248–254; *Round Table*, no. 159 (June 1950), pp. 280–281.

between February and June, in or out of the House, in which he failed to underline the fundamental need for co-operation with America. Since by February the prospects for U.S. recognition of Peking were becoming increasingly remote, despite Washington's aversion to protecting Formosa or to praising the Nationalists, the conjunction of Australia's two policy decisions was natural. Even the publicly available record supports the conclusion that America was pleased with Australia's general diplomatic posture. In a speech at San Francisco on March 15, Secretary Acheson explicitly mentioned and lauded Spender's Parliamentary statement of March 9, especially the guidelines of international behavior which Spender had set down. He remarked that it was "encouraging to see growing agreement about the nature of the problem in Asia." [28]

## THE IMPACT OF POLITICS AND PUBLIC OPINION IN THE FIRST HALF OF 1950

THE ARGUMENT presented so far has almost entirely bypassed the internal situation in Australia. It is tenable that had there been no political complications which dictated caution on Chinese recognition, the Government would not have recognized anyway. The point is that the Liberal Government *did* acknowledge a domestic complication and added it to its catalogue of reasons for denying recognition. The 1949 electoral campaign had been bitterly fought, and the then Opposition parties had hammered incessantly on the theme of Communism, associating the Labor Government with Communist policies and Communist connections. Then, almost before it had completed congratulating itself on its victory of December 10, the new Government was thrown into the China problem. Since it enjoyed a comfortable majority in the House, it could ordinarily have expected to survive for the duration

[28] *Department of State Bulletin,* Vol. 22 (March 27, 1950), pp. 471–472.

of the three-year Parliamentary term. Although it had waged a powerful anti-Communist electoral campaign, any public confusion which might have sprung from prompt recognition of a Communist China would probably have dissipated itself by late 1952.

The potential political embarrassment lay elsewhere. In the 1949 campaign, the Menzies-Fadden parties had pledged themselves to outlaw the Australian Communist Party, and from the early moments of coming to office laid appropriate plans, the implementing legislation being introduced in Parliament in April of 1950. This factor counted in a special way. Even if the bill could clear its legislative hurdles, there was bound to be sharp and extended public debate over its propriety, fired perhaps by the Labor Opposition. Furthermore, there was always the prospect that contentious legislation of this sort would be challenged in court on constitutional grounds. Finally, and conclusively, the 1949 election, while creating a Liberal-Country Party majority in the House, had failed to wrest control of the Senate from Labor, which retained an eight seat margin there. Facing a hostile Senate, the Government could not confidently expect to carry all its projected legislation, the ban on the Communist Party included, through both houses of Parliament. If the Labor Senate became too obdurate, there was recourse under Article 57 of the Constitution to a double dissolution and fresh elections for both chambers. Although the Government felt reasonably certain that it could capture the Senate in such an eventuality, the fact remained that an electoral campaign might have to be organized in considerably less than three years. The Communist dissolution proposal might not yet have been removed from the public scene and even if it had, the coincidence of hurried Chinese recognition could have been politically damaging to the Government.

What evidence exists that this type of reasoning affected the Government's China policy? While attending the

Colombo meetings, Spender was reported to have had an encounter with Nehru, who was advertising the virtues of his already accomplished step of Chinese recognition. According to press versions, Spender retorted that Australia would not evince any desperate hurry to recognize Peking; she had a Communist problem of her own which had to be tackled before the Government could assume responsibility for telling Communist China that she had earned Australia's official recognition.[29] If reported accurately, Spender's riposte may have been a spontaneous flash of annoyance against a man who at the same conference was unwilling to pledge support for any coordinated Commonwealth defense planning. However, there is probably some hint in this comment that Spender was already aware of a delicate political situation at home; on the same day, *The Times* of London wrote that "the Australian Government is especially cautious in approaching the question of recognition, for it fought the election in a strongly anti-Communist campaign and is considering outlawing the Communist Party of Australia." [30]

At home in Australia, as suggested previously, the early enthusiasm for recognition had subsided by February 1. From January on, the Melbourne and Sydney Archdiocesan organs, the *Advocate* and the *Catholic Weekly,* plus the *News Weekly,* the voice of the right-oriented, heavily Catholic industrial groups, maintained a steady if not always journalistically responsible drumfire against Australian recognition or any weakening on China generally.[31] Catholic missionaries were under severe duress in China, and Vatican sources were warning countries which had not yet recognized China that 90 per cent of the

[29] *SMH,* January 11, 1950.

[30] *The Times* (London), January 11, 1950.

[31] For instance, *Advocate* (Melbourne), January 19, 1950, and D. G. M. Jackson's articles of January 26, March 30, and June 22, 1950; *Catholic Weekly* (Sydney), January 19 and 26, March 16, 1950; *News Weekly,* January 18 and 25, 1950.

Chinese people were opposed to the Communist regime.[32] The author has been given to understand that the Australian Government parties believed that a portion of their 1949 victory had resulted from a chipping away of some traditionally ALP Catholic votes. If this was so, fierce Catholic opposition to recognition, paired with the prospect of another election soon, could have influenced the Government's thinking. It is also perhaps not without interest to notice the reactions of the Labor Opposition, which in principle had favored recognition prior to vacating office. In March of 1950, after the new Parliament had opened, both Chifley and Evatt, Leader and Deputy Leader, respectively, spoke on behalf of *eventual* recognition; Chifley, however, admitted that he could "understand that there were many reasons" for the Government's decision not to proceed with recognition at the moment,[33] while Evatt felt some *quid pro quo* might be extracted from the Chinese in exchange for recognition.[34] In other words, even Opposition spokesmen were somewhat timorous, perhaps themselves reflecting the uncertainties of the political climate.

Finally, the author must report his own findings which he obtained through interviews. It seems reasonably plain that in the first few months following the election there was a measure of antirecognition advice rendered to the Government by some of its own right-wing Parliamentary supporters, and that the most persuasive argument dealt with the political hazards which recognition could entail. Because Parliament did not convene until February 22, the access that these men had to the Prime Minister and/or his ministerial colleagues was necessarily limited, but some contacts were made. Although the author was not told precisely which factors, including the relative

[32] *South China Morning Post* (Hong Kong), January 8, 1950.
[33] *CPD,* HR, Vol. 206, March 23, 1950, p. 1174.
[34] *Ibid.,* March 16, 1950, pp. 918–919.

importance assigned to them, of all those converging simultaneously in the early part of 1950, he is convinced from his own sources of information, in this instance unimpeachable, that the Government did consider domestic politics when fashioning its decision on Chinese recognition.

## THE GOVERNMENT'S PRE-KOREAN INTENTIONS EVALUATED

IT WAS proposed at the onset of this chapter to test the contention that the Korean War caught Australia's China policy in a state of formation. More specifically, two Australian academicians and a former Secretary of the Department of External Affairs have written that prior to the Korean War, the Liberals were waiting for an opportune moment to recognize Peking, with some sort of phased approach having been evolved in advance. Professors C. P. Fitzgerald [35] and Norman D. Harper [36] have agreed that the Liberal plan consisted of two parts: to sever diplomatic relations with the Nationalists on Formosa, and subsequently to recognize Peking. Burton, who was External Affairs Secretary in the last years of the Labor Government and continued in that position until early June of 1950, wrote several years later that "six months after being in office, the Liberal Minister (Mr. Spender) asked his advisers for suggestions as to how recognition could be accorded in politically tactful stages, and was prepared to accord de facto recognition of the Communist Government as a first step, though not to support immediate recognition by the United Nations." [37] Since the author has had contact with all three gentlemen, it seems ap-

[35] C. P. Fitzgerald, "Australia, Japan and Formosa," *Spectator,* no. 6455 (March 14, 1952), p. 318; Fitzgerald, "Australia and Asia," p. 206.

[36] Norman Harper, "Australia and the United States," in *Australia in World Affairs 1956–1960,* p. 214.

[37] Burton, *The Alternative,* p. 91.

propriate to attempt a direct evaluation of their assertions.

Professor Fitzgerald has offered a specific item of evidence in support of his position. It will be remembered that in October of 1949 the Australian diplomatic mission in Nanking was withdrawn. The Ambassador and others returned to Australia, but a small group, together with Embassy records, was installed at Hong Kong, undoubtedly with the view of being used as a *cadre* to move into China once Australia recognized Peking. When Fitzgerald passed through Hong Kong in late October on his way to China, he was explicitly asked by Australian officials to examine possible embassy premises in Peking. Later in Peking, Fitzgerald received a letter dated January 5 from an Australian officer in Hong Kong, requesting that the search for embassy quarters be continued, and expressing an opinion that Australia would recognize China very shortly. In the months that followed, Australia did not, of course, recognize Peking, but neither was a diplomatic mission installed on Formosa in spite of the fact that Australia continued to recognize the Republic of China and there was a Chinese Ambassador in Canberra. The Hong Kong group was not pulled out until after the Korean War had broken out. Professor Harper was also aware of the continuing presence of the Australians in Hong Kong throughout the first half of 1950, and thought that this helped to strengthen his own conclusion.

The author has concluded that the search for embassy quarters in Peking was instigated about mid-1949 by the Embassy in Nanking, and that subsequent moves in this direction were inspired by the officials in Hong Kong rather than by those in Canberra. It was probably a combination of the Embassy staff's expectation that Peking would shortly be recognized and simply precautionary planning since adequate accommodations were scarce in Peking. In this sense, even though Professor Fitzgerald was being urged to press his inquiries almost a month *after* the Liberals had entered office, the Government at home probably had no knowledge of what was being done. Certainly Spender himself, who was preoccupied in late December and early January with the large issues he expected to discuss at Colombo, could scarcely have had opportunity to address himself to something of this nature, and Burton has no recollection of any instructions being transmitted through his Department. In any case, the opinion expressed in the letter written Fitzgerald concerning impending Australian recognition was definitely a private one and in no way registered Government thinking—whatever it may have been at the time.

Australia's failure to send a mission to Formosa in the first half of 1950 could certainly be interpreted as the initial step in a calculated operation, the opening phase of ultimate recognition of the Peking regime. What should not be overlooked, however, is that in early 1950 there was widespread feeling, shared in Washington, that it was only a matter of time before the Communists would overrun Formosa. Plainly, America made no moves to guarantee the safety of Formosa against any attack from the mainland. Fitted into present context, this could well have meant that Australia, regardless of whether she favored recognition for Peking or Taipei, may have felt it pointless and even potentially wasteful to establish a diplomatic complex in a place which might shortly be overrun. Second, probably not too much should be made of the presence of the Hong Kong contingent. The "contingent" was, the author suspects, no more than two men throughout most of this period. Retaining them there entailed no great expense, and they could serve as intelligence personnel, appraising Chinese developments and assisting the Australian External Affairs liaison officer appointed to Hong Kong in January of 1950.

Professor Harper told the author that his own conclusion about a phased Australian recognition policy was based on the memory of conversations he had with certain knowledgeable persons, presumably in the Department of External Affairs. Due to the confidential nature of these talks, he could not reveal his sources. Sir Douglas Copland also intimated that he had picked up the same current of thought in Canberra, although his recollections seemed less vivid than Harper's. The accuracy of what Harper and Copland were told would naturally need to be matched with the people to whom they spoke and the sort of reasoning which had impelled these informants to reach such a deduction. In this regard it might be useful to comment on Burton's own evaluation, since almost up to the opening of hostilities in Korea he was the principal official figure in the Department, and it would be reasonable to expect that if any official knew of the Government's intentions it would be he.

This is said with full knowledge of the immediately relevant background, which requires exposition. In June of 1949 Burton was furiously attacked on the floor of the House by such leading Opposition members as Menzies, John McEwen, and Harold Holt. Burton had recently but unsuccessfully sought ALP preselection for the newly organized Parliamentary seat for the Australian Capital Territory, and the Opposition, particularly Menzies, felt this to be a breach of the spirit of an impartial and apolitical public service. In the circumstances, Menzies claimed, he could not for a moment tolerate such a man serving under him as the head of a major department.[38] Furthermore, under the Labor Government and consistently after it had been turned out of office, Burton was an enthusiastic advocate of Australian recognition of China.

Although these considerations would appear to disqualify Burton for any *entré* to his Minister later in the Liberal period, this apparently did not follow. Though

[38] See especially Menzies, *CPD*, HR, Vol. 202, June 8, 1949, p. 670.

Spender was in the House during his colleagues' attack on Burton, he remained in his seat. Later, until Burton's departure from his post as Secretary, there is every reason to believe that Burton and Spender coexisted happily and even had mutual respect for one another. Although Burton's replacement in early June seemed to have resulted, by mutual consent, from the divergent political philosophies held by him and the Government he was serving, he was not eased out over a quarrel on China policy or any other substantive matter. The author has heard some remarks about Burton being pushed aside in early 1950 and his energies being steered into harmless channels such as working up the Colombo Plan organizational conference in May. There may be some truth in this, but not enough to disqualify Burton from having been privy to what was brewing in Australian foreign affairs. Again, therefore, it should be emphasized that Burton *probably* knew as much about his Government's foreign policy intentions in the first half of 1950 as did his own subordinates in the Department. The "people" to whom Harper and Copland spoke, were they other than Burton himself, were unlikely to know more than he.

Burton's principal contribution of evidence in support of his conclusion that the Liberals were planning to recognize Peking was, it is recalled, that six months after assuming office (and presumably before Burton stepped down and went on extended leave), Spender had called for papers and advice on how to approach the recognition process. Burton's correspondence with the author was confidential, but the letter which he wrote, while sustaining the principle of the above contention, creates some confusion as to the timing and singleness of purpose which Burton attributes to his Minister's behavior. Parenthetically, it might be said that Burton's account of the China problem in Australia after the war had broken out in Korea, and admittedly dealing with a period when he was no longer strategically placed, is very uneven, factually and otherwise. In any event, the request for advice on recognizing China is not *per se* sufficient proof that Spender was reaching toward recognition in the immediate future. Any sensible foreign minister, in circumstances similar to the pre-Korean period, would certainly have apprised himself of the limits and possibilities of switching policy gears when and if conditions abroad (and within Australia as well) recommended a change. If Professor Harper and Sir Douglas were advised largely on the basis of someone's interpretation of Spender's call for memoranda, this by itself is inadequate to warrant the conclusion that Australia's China policy was cut short as it was reaching toward recognition.

Indeed, if anything, Spender's own temperament would suggest a different conclusion. For most of the time he was External Affairs Minister, including the pre-Korean era, Spender was extremely sensitive about China's international performance. But his sensitivity moved beyond a straightforward appraisal of how such performance was damaging the outside world, or whether given types of Australian policy would serve to inhibit or foster misconduct by China. There was also a strain of moral disapprobation which tinted his reactions. Chinese behavior was not only *dangerous,* but in fact *normatively reprehensible,* as he saw it. For instance, early in 1951 Copland publicly reproved the Liberal Government for having failed to recognize China.[39] In reply, Spender said that there were "strong international and moral grounds which make it difficult to grant recognition."[40] The inclusion of "moral grounds" was not just diplomatic rhetoric. With Spender it was genuine, and the author's own conversation with Sir Percy about China left the unmistakable impression of a man who permitted, and perhaps encouraged, his own perception of what was good and what was evil to condi-

[39] *SMH,* January 29, 1951. [40] *Ibid.,* January 30, 1951.

tion his China policy. With this in mind, it would be difficult to imagine Spender counseling the recognition of China until such time as Peking had set aside its bellicose words and actions for some suitable probationary period —which in June of 1950 was not in sight.

In sum, Australia's China policy before Korea claimed mixed parentage: the accidental conjunction of the 1949 election and the rather lengthy and unavoidable period of unpreparedness on the part of of the new Government to reach a decision on recognition; the advent of a distasteful Chinese behavior pattern immediately following Colombo, before Spender could even report to his Government; the Government's appreciation of disturbing events in Asia, for which China was held in part responsible; the pressing need to engage American support for an alliance; the potentially awkward domestic political situation which the Government inherited; and, to a degree, the personality of the External Affairs Minister himself. The Liberal Government did not step into office bound and determined to follow an uncompromising anti-Chinese Communist attitude at every turn with, in Professor Manning Clark's words, "no inhibitions or agonies of mind on the [Chinese] Communist issue." [41] The evidence does not sustain that conclusion. Moreover the conclusion that Korea somehow "froze" Australia's China policy, displacing a previous essentially fluid approach, is equally troublesome to justify.

## THE KOREAN WAR: IMPACT AND REACTION

IT STILL remains to be argued whether the Korean War period itself created a special "frozen" state of mind and behavior, allowing small room for initiative and maneuver. Among the questions that require some thought would be Australia's definition of the threat posed by the Korean

[41] Manning Clark, *A Short History of Australia* (New York: New American Library, Mentor Books, 1963), p. 236.

conflict and subsequent Chinese intervention there, and the corollary definition of why aggression in Korea called for resistance. A second question would inquire into Australian perceptions of how and why exacerbation of the Korean War would be contrary to Australian interests. A third would deal with the catalytic function of Korea as a factor in the strengthening of security arrangements in the event of future trouble in the Far East. Finally, some measurement must be made of Australia's wish or ability to allow leeway for accommodation with China—Korea and security planning aside. If these questions can successfully be related and answered, the Korean period can usefully be regarded as a pattern-setter for later developments in Australia's policies and attitudes toward China.

When war broke out in Korea, the Government's interpretation was, at bottom, that "every Australian . . . [should] regard Korea as his business, and not as some remote frontier incident." [42] The invasion of South Korea was seen not as a narrowly limited object of Communist intentions, but as part of a calculated strategy to encourage Communist movements in South-East Asia and to demoralize the will of native populations to resist, or it was seen even more directly as a springboard for direct action elsewhere. The fact that it was only North Koreans who first stepped across the 38th parallel did not matter; it was part and parcel of a plot hatched by the international Communist movement, and the Chinese were certainly and prominently featured in Communism's grand design for Asia. Spender's almost instant evaluation of the invasion was, for instance, that Formosa would probably be the next target of Communism [43] (meaning the Chinese

[42] Menzies, broadcast of August 28, 1950, in *CNIA,* Vol. 21 (August 1950), p. 590. A valuable source of Korean era documents and statements, emphasizing the Australian position, is Dept. of External Affairs, *Select Documents on International Affairs. Korea* (Canberra: Government Printer, 1950–1954), 3 parts.

[43] Statement of June 25, 1950, in *SMH,* June 26, 1950.

Communists), while Menzies visualized a North Korean victory translating itself into accentuated Chinese-inspired and often Chinese-led revolutionary turmoil in South-East Asia.[44] Rightly or wrongly, the Government sensed some Chinese connivance in the North Korean move, plus real danger that the next Communist move in the region might be by China herself, a frame of mind toward which the Liberals had been conditioning themselves since entering office. Once the Chinese had entered the fighting and then proceeded to drag out the war until the second half of 1953, a dark image of China became even more sturdily implanted. Although a revived Japanese militarism concerned nearly all Australians in the early 'fifties, there was a hard core of truth in a remark made in an interview in 1954 by R. G. (later Lord) Casey, who had succeeded Spender as External Affairs Minister early in 1951. Casey had mentioned that Japan was not then, in 1954, a menace, but that Communism was. Asked if even in 1951 Australia had had her eye on Communist China, his reply was "Oh, yes. You've got to live in Australia and be an Australian to have a proper realization of the enormous change that's come over the continent of Asia by reason of China having gone Communist." [45]

The presence of China in Korea and the death and imprisonment of Australian servicemen at Chinese hands there, plus the ascription to China of mischief-making in Tibet and Indo-China or elsewhere, were not the only bones that the Australian Government had to pick with Peking during the Korean period. Two items only will be noted, but they underscore the position well.

On December 15, 1950 a chartered Catalina flying boat, on its way from Pakistan, was forced down near

[44] Broadcast of September 22, 1950, in *CNIA,* Vol. 21 (September 1950), p. 664.

[45] R. G. Casey, "New Plan to Defend Southeast Asia," interview in *U.S. News and World Report* (July 16, 1954), p. 56.

China but in Portuguese Macao waters. A Chinese gunboat moved in, and three Australian airmen, all civilians, were taken into custody. For almost two years nothing was heard of the three Australians. Working through the British chargé in Peking, on at least five occasions Australia inquired about the men, but the Chinese authorities gave no explanation of the arrests and no information about their welfare or whereabouts. No access to them was allowed to British officials or legal advisers, nor was communication permitted with persons outside.[46] Suddenly, in August of 1952, the Australians were set loose in Hong Kong, suffering from considerable physical privation. Only three days before their release they had been brought to trial for smuggling opium from Burma. Once out of China, they explained that they had been threatened with further long years of imprisonment unless they agreed to confess to the smuggling charges. This they did in order to gain their freedom although the Catalina had been empty when apprehended.[47] All this was happening about the time when Wilfred Burchett, an Australian Communist and a favorite of the Chinese, published a book in Melbourne which repeated the Peking version of the episode in defense of China's honor.[48]

It was during the Korean War too that China began a forceful campaign of praise for local Australian Communists and the "toiling masses" of Australia, as well as gleeful denunciations of the Menzies Government. At a time when the Chinese were already in Korea and Australia was caught up in the Government's effort to outlaw the

[46] See Casey's statements of May 22, 1951, in *CNIA*, Vol. 22 (May 1951), p. 288, and April 21, 1952, in *ibid.*, Vol. 23 (April 1952), p. 194; Anthony Eden, *UKPD*, HC, Vol. 499, April 21, 1952, cols. 51–52; *The Times* (London), September 11, 1951; *Sydney Sunday Herald*, March 30, 1952.

[47] See accounts in *SMH*, August 14 and September 22, 1952; *Sydney Sunday Herald*, August 17, 1952.

[48] Wilfred G. Burchett, *China's Feet Unbound* (Melbourne: World Unity Publications, 1952), pp. 14–15.

Communist Party, congratulations were cabled from Peking when General Secretary L. Sharkey of the Australian Communist Party was released from prison. On another occasion, when Victorian railway workers struck, they were reassured that "all railway workers of China are closely following your struggles." [49] At another stage, Chinese newspapers applauded the Australian Communist Party's fight for peace, brotherhood, and the defeat of the Communist ban measure, and approvingly featured their Australian brethren's call of "Forward to victory over warmongers! Remove Menzies from office!" [50] It is not surprising that under these circumstances—captives being held incommunicado and accolades for Australian Communists—the Chinese were hardly endearing themselves to the Australian public, to say nothing of the Menzies Government, though the Liberals might well have quietly appreciated any political windfall that Chinese-Australian Communist amity might yield.

This point deserves amplification. In March 1951, Menzies did in fact secure a Parliamentary double dissolution, although it was over a Government banking measure and not on any obstruction by the ALP Senate to anti-Communist legislation. In the preceding months the Government had steered its Communist Party ban through both houses, after much anguish of both conscience and politics within the Labor Party. However, the measure was successfully contested on constitutional grounds before the High Court, Evatt acting as chief counsel for the plaintiff, the Communist Party. The Government now desired not only a chance to win the Senate from Labor, but also an opportunity to stage a constitutional amendment referendum which would nullify the High Court's judgment. The Government parties entered the campaign

[49] New China News Agency releases, December 12 and November 8, 1950.

[50] *Shanghai News,* March 20, 1951.

with fond memories of how handsomely an anti-Communist orientation had paid off in 1949, and saw no reason to change course. The timing was considered propitious also, since Labor was internally divided on such exploitable issues as Communist dissolution, National Service, and union ballots.

In his opening policy speech of April 3, the Prime Minister dedicated his Government to "make war on Communism" at all levels,[51] and subsequently let few opportunities slip by without insinuating Labor's half-heartedness on the subject. The Government's electoral campaign made little reference to foreign affairs or to China in particular but, when made, the references were carefully designed to attract votes, especially among Communism-conscious Catholics. It was at about this time that a pamphlet on "The Future of Australia" appeared and was widely circulated. The cover illustration depicted a globe—Communist countries shaded black, Australia magnified, and a great black arrow emanating from the direction of China into Australia's heart. A portion of the pamphlet was concerned with Asian Communism's threat to the remainder of the region, including Australia: Chinese Communism was as ruthless as Stalin's brand, "both founded upon the same evil principles, and these principles must issue in the same evil policies." [52] What made the pamphlet especially interesting was that it was "published with the Authority of the Archbishops and Bishops of the Catholic Church in Australia." The Government parties were certainly aware of the Church's vehement anti-Chinese Communist position, and it therefore made sense in more than one way for Menzies to declare that "The plain truth is that there is the gravest danger of war. Labour leaders must take the Australian

[51] Cited in *SMH,* April 14, 1951.

[52] "The Future of Australia" (Carnegie, Victoria: Renown Press, 1951), Social Justice Statement of 1951, p. 7.

people for fools if they think that they have not read the lessons of Korea, and the threatening intervention of Communist China. . . ."[53] The Government was in fact returned, with a slightly reduced majority in the House but now in control of the Senate. Broadly, conviction and political advantage coincided.

For the Government, however, a realization of the dangers posed by Korea and the Chinese involvement there was only a beginning. Failure to check aggression in Korea would only whet Communism's appetite and discredit promises of subsequent free-world counterstrokes against Communist imperialism. Australia could not expect to combat aggression at her own time and her chosen place; united and determined efforts were urgently required, even on a distant Korean battleground.[54] Prodded by the Korean emergency, the Government proceeded along various parallel lines. Speaking to the UN General Assembly in October of 1952, Casey reminded his listeners that Australians had been among the first to enter action in Korea, as indeed they had: air and naval units were dispatched almost immediately after the Security Council issued its appeal for support, within weeks ground troops had been pledged, and by 1952 two Australian infantry battalions were engaged as part of the Commonwealth Division. Although the war had sunk into a stalemate, Casey could promise that, as in past world wars, Australia would "see this situation in Korea through to the end,"[55] which she did.

Additionally, concerned over Chinese-abetted commo-

[53] Address of April 24, 1951, in *SMH,* April 25, 1951. Also see Menzies' final electoral speech, April 27, 1951, in *ibid.,* April 28, 1951.

[54] For instance, Menzies' broadcast of September 20, 1950, in *CNIA,* Vol. 21 (September 1950), p. 660; Spender, *CPD,* HR, Vol. 212, March 14, 1951, p. 482; Casey, *ibid.,* Vol. 213, June 21, 1951, p. 274.

[55] UN General Assembly, *Official Records,* Seventh Session, 384th Plenary Meeting, October 20, 1952, p. 106.

tions in South-East Asia, Australia undertook further assistance. Shortly after the North Koreans crossed the 38th parallel, a squadron of RAAF heavy bombers joined the transport aircraft already committed to Malayan service. A few weeks later a team made up of Australian military personnel arrived in Malaya to conduct a firsthand study of Communist guerrilla tactics and to make available to British authorities the jungle warfare experiences of the team's members; and a similar mission left for Malaya and Indo-China late in 1952. In March of the following year, a high French official visited Canberra on *Australia's* invitation, from which followed the provision of Australian arms and materials for the French effort in Indo-China as well as the initiation of plans to supply Colombo Plan assistance to the Associated States.[56] At home in Australia, late in 1950, machinery was set in motion to raise the defense budget, improve military production and modernization, reestablish the women's services, and adopt "National Service," under which Australian youth would be conscripted into the Citizen Military Forces (without liability for overseas service) or into the RAN or RAAF if consent was given for service beyond the limits of Australia.[57]

## THE ANZUS TREATY

THE AUSTRALIAN GOVERNMENT was, nevertheless, convinced that measures of this type were far from adequate to meet the country's security requirements. Not only were these measures in themselves mere token measures but, far more significantly, they in no way engaged the active

[56] See especially the Letourneau-Casey joint communiqué of March 11, 1953, in *CNIA,* Vol. 24 (March 1953), pp. 165–166.

[57] For particulars, see Fadden, *CPD,* HR, Vol. 209, October 12, 1950, p. 767, and Harold Holt, *ibid.,* Vol. 210, November 21, 1950, pp. 2724–2730.

and formal support of the U.S. What was desirable, if not indispensable, was the reactivation of the search for an alliance, which culminated in the ANZUS Treaty of mid-1951 between Australia, New Zealand, and the U.S. There can be no doubt that nearly all sectors of Australian opinion regarded American wishes for a lenient Japanese peace treaty as a crucial reason to forge a countervailing defensive alliance with the U.S. Moreover, the Korean conflict, including Chinese intervention and the West's obvious lack of preparedness to counter such Communist strokes, added materially to the desire for such an alliance. At minimum, in Casey's own words of mid-1951, "It is difficult to say which is the greater potential threat—that of a revived Japanese militarism, alone or in association with other aggressive forces, or of a Japan taken over by an aggressive power and incorporated into the Communist empire. But clearly, Australian security requires that we should endeavour to avoid both these dangers." [58] He wrote later, with the advantage of hindsight and perhaps some rationalization, that "well before the ANZUS Treaty was drafted, the spokesmen of the Australian Government identified the immediate menace in the Pacific not as Japan but as Communist imperialism." [59] If anything, protection against Japan and against Communism, and especially Communist China, were inextricably connected. The security of Japan herself from Communist political blandishment, subversion, or even direct military action, "revealed by the persistent Communist intervention in Korea," lent credence to the argument that there would be danger to Japan and ultimately to Australia if Japan were

[58] *Ibid.*, Vol. 213, June 21, 1951, p. 279.

[59] R. G. Casey, *Friends and Neighbours* (Melbourne: F. W. Cheshire, 1954), p. 73. Also see the comments in Norman Harper, "Australia and Regional Pacts 1950–57," *Australian Outlook*, Vol. 12 (March 1958), p. 8, and in Rosecrance, *op. cit.*, pp. 244–245.

wholly exposed and became disgruntled through lack of management of her own affairs.[60]

At all events, Australian diplomacy in 1950–1951 was aimed at winning American support for an alliance through which Australia could gain close consultation, planning, and a promise of assistance in case of danger. Even her behavior in Korea, before and after Chinese intervention, seemed to imply at least in part a desire to impress Washington and therefore to attract its support. When the swiftly taken decision to dispatch ground forces to Korea was announced, there was insight in the *Sydney Morning Herald's* comment that the move would "lay up for this country a store of good will in America, all the more desirable because in any extension of the Korean conflict the Commonwealth must once again lean heavily on the aid of her great Pacific ally. The value of Austral-American cooperation in the field will be by no means limited to the Korean campaign." [61] Although related aspects of Australia's China policy will be raised later in this study, it is sufficient for the present to note that on many occasions while pact negotiations were in delicate balance prominent Australians did point out the tie between uninterrupted Australian defense contributions in Korea and elsewhere and the formulation of a broader alliance system. These explanations were freely given, both to American officials and to the Australian public.[62]

The negotiations leading to the conclusion of the ANZUS Treaty fall beyond the reach of this study.[63] What needs to be noted, however, for the moment is that

[60] *CPD,* HR, Vol. 213, June 21, 1951, p. 276.

[61] *SMH,* July 27, 1950.

[62] For instance, Spender's account of his consultations in the U.S. in late 1950, *CPD,* HR, Vol. 211, November 28, 1950, pp. 3168–3169; Menzies, before Australian state premiers, Canberra, March 2, 1951, in *SMH,* March 3, 1951.

[63] The most extensive treatment is found in Rosecrance, *op. cit.,* pp. 188–225.

through the terms of the ANZUS Treaty, Australia gained—in addition to regular service as well as ministerial liaison with the United States and New Zealand —the pledge that "each Party recognizes that an armed attack in the Pacific area on any of the Parties would be dangerous to its own peace and safety and declares that it would act to meet the common danger in accordance with its constitutional process." [64] This obligation was superficially softer than NATO's but was correctly interpreted by Casey [65] and subsequent commentators [66] as being equally strong in intent. Yet in another sense the treaty created a mixed sense of disappointment and promise for the Liberal Government. Negotiations had caused difficulty over which nations would be included in the pact, and in the last resort only the Australia-New Zealand-United States core became a manageable combination. Australia had been eager to include Britain, but U.S. objections overrode that possibility. Strategic thinking in Washington opposed the assumption of obligations toward continental Asian territories, such as Malaya and Hong Kong, and Britain's inclusion would have violated this intention. Anglo-American differences over China have been mentioned as a possible cause of American disinclination to admit the British, but the allegation has never been proved and in any event could only have been a subsidiary factor.[67] Indeed, not only had Britain been excluded from

[64] Article IV. For full text, see *CNIA,* Vol. 22 (September 1951), pp. 499–500.

[65] See *CPD,* HR, Vol. 216, February 21, 1951, p. 218; statement of April 29, 1952, in *CNIA,* Vol. 23 (April 1952), p. 196.

[66] Leicester C. Webb, "Australia and SEATO," in George Modelski, ed., *SEATO: Six Studies* (Melbourne, Canberra, and Sydney: F. W. Cheshire for the ANU, 1962), pp. 52–55; Watt, *op. cit.,* pp. 10–13; John Foster Dulles, "Security in the Pacific," *Foreign Affairs,* Vol. 30 (January 1952), p. 181.

[67] The point is raised—and relegated to secondary position at best—in the fullest available treatment of British exclusion, Dean E. McHenry and Richard N. Rosecrance, "The 'Exclusion' of the United Kingdom from the ANZUS Pact," *International Organiza-*

ANZUS, but so had other European powers with Asian interests, as well as Asian states themselves. ANZUS protected Australia's own integrity, but not the safety of South and South-East Asian territories, whose immunization from Chinese Communist intrusions was vital to Australia's ultimate well being. The Government's disappointment over the limited geographic scope of ANZUS, however, was felt to be remediable, for ANZUS could serve as a first and important step forward, perhaps a nucleus around which a more comprehensive pact could be developed, despite the broad-ranging assessments of Chinese activity undertaken at early ANZUS meetings.[68] The position was well summarized by the Adelaide *Advertiser* in 1952: the U.S. had erected a series of treaties through ANZUS and with Japan and the Philippines, but "these three systems of mutual defence are, as it were, off-shore alliances; they have no foundation in the countries which China overshadows," and this "makes it clear that we are still only at the beginning of a general and effective design of collective security in the Pacific. The true significance of the [ANZUS Foreign Ministers'] Honolulu Conference is that it marked the beginning." [69]

## PROSECUTING THE KOREAN WAR

THE PRECEDING discussion has traced the Liberal Government's appraisal of the Chinese danger during the Korean

---

*tion,* Vol. 12 (Summer 1958), p. 325. Discussion with one of the authors corroborated the low rank assigned to this factor. Also see the discussion in J. R. Poynter, "Britain and ANZUS," *Australia's Neighbours,* 3rd series, no. 27 (January 1953), esp. p. 2.

[68] Casey, *op. cit.,* p. 85.

[69] Adelaide *Advertiser,* August 11, 1952. For some early official pronouncements, see Casey, *CPD,* HR, Vol. 213, July 13, 1951, p. 1709, and his statement of August 6, 1951, in *SMH,* August 7, 1951; Spender's statements of July 12, 1951, in *CNIA,* Vol. 22 (July 1951), p. 400, and of October 4, 1951, in *SMH,* October 6, 1951.

War and has indicated the principal lines of security reaction and preparation. But the story is nowhere near complete, especially if the question of whether Korea actually "froze" Australian policy is to be tested reasonably, and perhaps the best place to begin, concentrating on prominent highlights, is by examining the manner and force with which Australia believed that the war in Korea should be prosecuted.

It has already been shown why the Menzies Government felt that continuing resistance in Korea was in Australia's own self-interest. But the tactical questions of pursuing and punishing the Chinese enemy in his own home territory were separate matters altogether. The crossing of the 38th parallel after the successful Inchon landings had taken Australia by surprise as it had most other Governments, since it was done against a background of promises that no crossing would occur without a collective UN sanction. Afterward, especially after the Chinese presence was an established and massively disconcerting fact, Spender tried to show that the Chinese counterthrust had been calculated, deplorable, and unjustified.[70] Nevertheless, from the earliest stages of the Chinese intrusion, Australia fought shy either of preaching or condoning radical measures to blast the Chinese out of the war. In mid-1951 Casey summarized the position succinctly:

> It is not our objective to threaten Communist China or legitimate Chinese interests, nor is it our objective to extend the conflict beyond Korea. I agree with a recent statement by Mr. Lester Pearson, the Canadian Minister for External Affairs, that proposals for the blockade of the Chinese mainland or for the bombing of Manchuria, about which there has recently been some discussion, must be judged in the light of the possibility of so ex-

[70] *CPD*, HR, Vol. 212, March 14, 1951, pp. 480–481.

> tending the war. If war is to be extended beyond Korea, the responsibility for doing so should not rest with us.[71]

Government spokesmen were reluctant to embellish these principles with comment on how, when, and through whom Australia was working to limit the war and avoid overextension, although the author has encountered unimpeachable internal evidence that every available diplomatic and service channel was used, especially *vis-à-vis* the United States. However, in at least two related situations, the activities and subsequent dismissal of General MacArthur and the Eisenhower proposal to deneutralize the Nationalists—the "unleashing" of Chiang—there is interesting corroboration.

On January 31, 1951, as the UN was passing its resolution condemning China as an aggressor, Spender remarked that "it would be a good thing if military leaders were to confine their observations to factual military communiqués," [72] with obvious reference to the man who had been urging the employment of Nationalist troops in Korea and the bombing of targets across the Yalu River. Starting in late November of 1950 and onward, the Australian press had been heavily inclined to support the Government's policy in Korea, agreeing that while resistance to aggression should not be lowered, the risk of a third world war could hardly be gambled on by an exposed and ill-prepared Australia.[73] But as 1951 moved on, MacArthur's behavior failed to improve and, in fact, worsened. Even in the eyes of an Australian press, which years before had hailed MacArthur as a redeemer, a

[71] *Ibid.,* Vol. 213, June 21, 1951, pp. 275–276. For previous cautious expressions, see Spender, *ibid.,* Vol. 211, November 28, 1950, p. 3173; Menzies, *ibid.,* December 8, 1950, p. 4079, and Vol. 212, March 7, 1951, p. 75.

[72] Cited in *SMH,* February 1, 1951.

[73] For instance, Melbourne *Herald,* November 29 and December 16, 1950; Melbourne *Sun* and Adelaide *Advertiser,* November 30, 1950; Launceston *Examiner,* December 4, 1950.

man who had kept the Japanese away from the country's shores, his continuing demands for radical solutions in China, peremptory and boastful offers of negotiation, and unauthorized statements of all kinds were most unwelcome.[74] The *Sydney Morning Herald,* in particular, felt that MacArthur's impromptu proposals had brought an additional complication to Australia: they were serving to drive a wedge between British and American opinion, accentuate China-policy differences between the two countries, weaken the Western security partnership, and ultimately to dent the unity of purpose indispensable to Australia's survival on the circumference of a Chinese-confronted region.[75]

But the Government's own replies to the MacArthur controversy could not simply be taken on the basis of endorsements in the daily press. The 1951 Australian electoral campaign began exactly at the moment that debate over MacArthur was reaching its climax and the Government parties were committed to waging another Communist-overtone campaign on every front. Furthermore, important Catholic opinion had hardened on China. Those sectors of Catholic opinion represented by the *News Weekly* were unsparing in their attacks on China and on any "appeasers" of China. To the *News Weekly,* Acheson, the U. S. State Department (infiltrated by such "evil geniuses" as Owen Lattimore), and even Truman were apostles of shame—people who were utterly blind to the profound wisdom of "Solomon" MacArthur. This paper had elected MacArthur "Man of the Year" for 1951 and referred to Chiang Kai-shek as the "George Washington of the Chinese resistance." Not only should Nationalist forces be put to work in Korea, but they should be

[74] Brisbane *Courier-Mail* and Hobart *Mercury,* March 27, 1951; Melbourne *Argus,* March 27 and April 12, 1951; Melbourne *Age,* April 9 and 12, 1951; Adelaide *Advertiser,* April 9 and 13, 1951; Melbourne *Sun,* April 12, 1951.

[75] *SMH,* April 12 and 17, 1951.

backed by American air and naval power in an invasion of the mainland. Communist China should be knocked out of the war by every means available; "eliminate Red China and all the grass fires started by the Communists in Malaya, Indo-China, Burma and elsewhere will go out for lack of fuel." [76] Yet even *News Weekly,* or other extreme Catholic opinion, might be discounted if the public at large were unconvinced. But was it? In March the results of two Australian Gallup Polls were published and compared. The question had been whether military targets in China should be bombed. In December of 1950, 36 per cent had said "yes," 47 per cent "no," and 17 per cent were "undecided." In February 1951 nearly on the eve of the election, 49 per cent were in favor and only 34 per cent opposed.[77]

The Government therefore faced something of a dilemma in the MacArthur debate, and in the final judgment acquitted itself well. Just prior to MacArthur's dismissal, on April 10, Menzies and Spender made relevant statements. The Prime Minister spoke of the need to persevere in Korea, but added that Australia was "determined to limit the area of conflict. Nobody has even thought that the Korean campaign is something which gives rise to an attack upon China or Chinese territory. Nobody has contemplated it." [78] Spender, on his part, went so far as to explain that his Government had frequently applied diplomatic action to counter any proposals to spread the area of conflict beyond Korea, both officially and unofficially.[79] Two days later Spender refused to comment on MacArthur's removal, but forcefully

[76] *News Weekly,* May 23, 1951. Other representative comments: December 12, 13 and 20, 1950; January 17, February 7, April 18, and May 2, 1951. MacArthur's "election" was announced in the issue of January 2, 1952. Also see the remarks of the *Advocate,* esp. December 14, 1950.

[77] *AGP,* nos. 744–755, February–March 1951.

[78] Cited in *SMH,* April 11, 1951.

[79] Cited in *ibid.*

reiterated his remarks of April 10.[80] The Government had been discreet, but its position was unmistakable, and the author's own information completely confirms the printed record. Furthermore, to the Government's relief, there were no unwanted repercussions. On April 18 President Truman formally announced support for a tripartite treaty with Australia and New Zealand, and ten days later the Government won control of both houses of Parliament.

The next Korean-connected crisis which elicited Australian attention was President Eisenhower's announcement early in 1953 respecting the deneutralization of Formosa. The Chinese, said Eisenhower, had entered Korea and then rejected reasonable gestures for a cease-fire. But Truman's mid-1950 neutralization of Formosa had come to "serve as a defensive arm of Communist China," for it only permitted the Chinese to kill UN soldiers with greater impunity. Consequently, Eisenhower was removing the Seventh Fleet as a shield for Communist China, though without implying any aggressive design on America's part.[81] At the original point of Truman's order, the news had been received in Australia with a mixture of puzzlement and concern in some press circles, on grounds of intervention being staged in the Chinese civil war and possible Chinese provocation to enter the Korean fighting.[82] The Government, the author has learned, was at the time quite pleased, thinking that a neutralization policy would serve to halt still another Communist move and possibly avoid a chain reaction; Spender, it will be recalled, commented on Korea with the prediction that the Chinese might quickly jump on Formosa.[83] But by two and one-half years later some important changes had

[80] Statement of April 12, 1951, in *ibid.*, April 13, 1951.

[81] *NYT,* February 3, 1953.

[82] For instance, Melbourne *Age,* August 8 and 31, 1950; Melbourne *Argus,* August 8 and 17, 1950.

[83] For a supporting position, see *SMH,* August 10, 1950.

appeared, and in Australia's eyes they mattered a great deal.

There was, in the first instance, much the same complaint that had arisen over MacArthur's plans. A new American administration, pushed by its own extreme Republican Party faction, was courting deep trouble. The "trouble" was certainly not assessed as seriously as earlier projects to bomb China, but any military advantages which Eisenhower's order might yield "would surely be far outweighed by the political disadvantages of identifying the democratic cause in Asian eyes with support of the Nationalist regime. That would be grist for Peking's propaganda mills." [84] Again, as in the 1950–51 debate, the disquieting specter of an Anglo-American falling out, with adverse results for Australia, was prominent in the discussions, and now the awful prospect was added of the interminable Korean War being prolonged rather than shortened.[85]

A different complication was raised by the ANZUS Treaty, which had been ratified between the MacArthur and the deneutralization controversies. At the time of ANZUS's birth, scattered criticism had appeared about contingencies in which Australia might be dragged unwittingly into an American-inspired adventure in or around Formosa, where by then Washington had a heavy military stake. Article V of the treaty, it had been pointed out, defined an "armed attack" as including "the metropolitan territory of any of the Parties or on the island territories under its jurisdiction in the Pacific or on its armed forces, public vessels or aircraft in the Pacific." In other words, under ANZUS Australia might feel obliged to embroil herself in a conflict precipitated by some American misadven-

[84] *Ibid.*, February 3, 1953.

[85] For example, Hobart *Mercury*, February 3, 1953; Melbourne *Age*, February 4, 1953; *SMH*, February 5, 1953; Adelaide *Advertiser*, February 6, 1953.

ture in the Formosan area, even if in the beginning the spark had simply been the downing of a stray American aircraft.[86] Hence, Eisenhower's "unleashing" order, opening the possibility of Australian entanglement through the ANZUS connection, inspired Australian fears all the more.

Official reactions in Commonwealth capitals varied. The British and Canadian responses to Eisenhower's order were quick and critical.[87] The New Zealand response was delayed and circumspect.[88] The Australian reaction, however, was quick yet relatively unworried. Casey and Menzies described the action as one undertaken by the U.S. and governing only its own property, the Seventh Fleet. Menzies added that if an extension of hostilities were to result, Australia would naturally have "material interests," but neither man either praised or criticized what had been done; it was more dissociation than complaint.[89] Piecing together press comments, Casey's later evaluation, and the author's own findings, a picture emerges from the puzzle.[90] The Australian Cabinet had prompt and unequivocally reassuring information that Eisenhower's announcement was not, in effect, meant to do, or would result in doing, what its words may have implied. America was not going to launch Chiang hell-bent

[86] W. Macmahon Ball, "The Pacific Defense Pact," *Nation* (November 29, 1952), pp. 488–489; ALP critics Kim Beazley, *CPD*, HR, Vol. 216, February 28, 1952, p. 609, and E. J. Ward, *ibid.*, March 4, 1952, p. 756.

[87] Eden, *UKPD*, HC, Vol. 510, February 3, 1953, cols. 1672–1673; Pearson, *Canadian Parliamentary Debates*, HC, Session 1952–53, Vol. 2, February 5, 1953, pp. 1638–1640.

[88] Prime Minister S. G. Holland, statement of February 9, 1953, in *External Affairs Review* (NZ), Vol. 3 (February 1953), p. 2.

[89] Casey's statement of February 3, 1953, in *SMH*, February 4, 1953, and Menzies' statement of February 4, 1953, in *ibid.*, February 5, 1953.

[90] See especially *ibid.*; *Sydney Sunday Herald*, February 8, 1953; Melbourne *Argus*, February 9, 1953; Casey, *CPD*, HR, Vol. 221, February 24, 1953, pp. 163–164.

against the mainland, and would herself resist any expansion of the Korean War. With this mind, there was even an element in the Cabinet which received the news with pleasure, considering the Eisenhower action as a kind of study in maximum benefit (diversion of Communist troops) and minimum risk.

There is no foundation for any imputation that Australia slavishly followed the American line, or supported a powerful and risky stroke against China, or in any way sympathized with Chiang's own dreams for reconquest. The Government turned no emotional cartwheels in the manner of the *News Weekly,* which hailed the unleashing order as "the most heartening piece of news on the international front that the world has heard for some long time." [91] But when the "unleashing" of Chiang came to little and a widely rumored U.S. blockade of China failed to materialize, Casey and his colleagues had reason to congratulate themselves. ANZUS, rather than bringing embroilment for Australia, may well have promoted a climate of confidence so strong that the frank expression of one party was fully accepted by another.

The Government's unwillingness to tolerate Chinese troublemaking, even at the expense of open publicity on Australian-American differences, can be derived from a dispute which was brought before the UN almost before the Chiang unleashing plan was no longer a cause for discussion in chanceries and editorial columns. In April of 1953 a Burmese complaint was lodged against the continuing presence of irregular Chinese Nationalist troops, some of whom had drifted from China because of the civil war, others of whom had been recruited locally. At all events, the Nationalist authorities in Formosa were supplying arms to these troops, who were engaged much more in fighting Burmese than Chinese Communist soldiers. What stands out for present purposes was the attitude

[91] *News Weekly,* February 11, 1953.

assumed by the Australian UN delegation, led at the time by the Ambassador to Washington, Percy Spender. Although the Western powers generally showed sympathy for Burma, Australia went farther than most in scolding Formosa. Not only was it necessary to provide for suitable evacuation or internment of the troops, but they must be denied arms and other supplies; if an arms embargo could not with success be imposed by individual countries, the UN must take a hand.[92] Later, in September, Spender showed impatience with the slow pace at which the irregulars were being evacuated, and he plainly did not believe Nationalist professions of no more arms being smuggled from Formosa.[93] Australia was active both in debate and in the drafting of committee resolutions on the Burma-China issue. Time and again Australia openly scolded the Nationalists, urged meaningful measures against the arms shipments, and hardly hesitated to differentiate herself from the more conciliatory tone of the American delegation. The Australian Government, with substantial press support,[94] found the Nationalists' behavior embarrassing to the West and above all damaging to a strategically pivotal, non-Communist, South-East Asian country. South-East Asia had suffered enough from Communist Chinese molestation without having to be drained by Nationalist Chinese adventures. In Professor Geoffrey Sawer's words, "the episode serves as illustration of the willingness of the Spender-Casey regime to follow an independent line even when a major United States policy is involved." [95] This same episode also detracts from the thesis that Korea froze Australia's China policy.

[92] UN General Assembly, *Official Records,* Seventh Session, First Committee, 609th Meeting, April 21, 1953, pp. 673–674.

[93] *Ibid.,* 656th Meeting, November 4, 1953, pp. 163–164.

[94] See Hobart *Mercury* and Adelaide *Advertiser,* March 27, 1953; *SMH,* March 28, 1953.

[95] Geoffrey Sawer, "The United Nations," in *Australia in World Affairs 1950–1955,* p. 123.

# III

# AUSTRALIA AND CHINA DURING THE KOREAN WAR: 2

THE EFFORTS of the UN early in 1951 to come to grips with the Chinese presence in Korea were at the center of Australia's attempt at evolving a suitable China policy. By the beginning of January, UN forces had been pushed back over the 38th parallel, Seoul had been lost, and the Chinese had rebuffed the efforts of the UN's cease-fire committee to discuss terms. Some hard choices lay ahead.

## BRANDING CHINA AN AGGRESSOR

WITHIN the UN, successful efforts were launched to postpone further debate to provide more time for the cease-fire group, thereby allowing the scheduled Commonwealth Prime Ministers' Conference in London to discuss and formulate new moves. Despite their separate evaluations of and policies toward China, all the Prime Ministers subscribed to a formula through which they hoped accommodation could be reached in Korea. The plan was quickly brought to the UN's Political Committee and translated into a recommendation that the cease-fire group transmit the plan to Peking. The terms of the plan called for an immediate cease-fire and for all non-Korean forces to be withdrawn in stages; as soon as a cease-fire was in effect, the General Assembly would constitute an appropriate body, consisting of the United States, Britain, Russia, and the Chinese People's Republic, for purposes of discussing a general Far Eastern settlement—including questions arising over Formosa and Chinese representation in the UN.[1]

The Chinese reply was arrogant in language and made a set of unacceptable counterproposals. As debate resumed in the Political Committee, representations made by the British chargé in Peking produced a revised and somewhat more reasonable set of Chinese terms. A 48-hour adjournment was called by the Committee to study the new Chinese offer, after which an American resolution providing for the branding of China as an aggressor and arranging for sanctions if necessary was discussed. The Political Committee adopted the resolution on January 30, together with a Lebanese amendment, and on February 1 the Assembly took formal action. In addition to labeling China an aggressor, the final form of the resolution, *inter alia,* provided for the creation of an Additional Measures Committee, to be drawn from the Collective Measures Committee, and which would consider further measures, "to be employed to meet this aggression and to report thereon to the General Assembly, it being understood that the Committee is authorized to defer its report if the Good Offices Committee . . . reports satisfactory progress in its efforts." [2]

Australian diplomacy was put to a most severe test during the month of January. Large decisions, freighted with consequences, needed to be made. They involved not only judgments about requisite means by which to counter the Chinese in Korea, but also touched on the dangers of exacerbating the conflict, on relations with the United States, and on the unity of Australia's principal friends and allies. All these decisions ultimately concerned the

[1] Document A/C. 1/645. UN General Assembly, Fifth Session, *Annexes,* Agenda item 76. See discussions of the Prime Ministers' Conference in *The Times* (London), January 12, 1951, and *Sydney Sunday Herald,* January 14, 1951.

[2] UN General Assembly, Fifth Session, *Supplement* no. 20A, *Resolutions,* 498 (*V*), p. 1.

Chinese problem, and their handling by the Government therefore allows an excellent glimpse of how, under the pressure of Korea, Australia pursued her China policy.

Australia's endorsement of the Commonwealth Prime Ministers' formula in itself supplies a strong clue. The formula clearly reached beyond an offer that fighting be stopped. It also held out to the Chinese the prospect of their personal participation, on a footing with other great powers, in discussing, and presumably altering, the *status quo* position of Formosa and the Chinese UN seat, with possible gains to Peking along one or both lines. Indeed, as Menzies later admitted, the Prime Ministers agreed *as a group* on their willingness "to engage in direct personal negotiations not only with Marshal Stalin but also with Mao Tse-tung." [3] This certainly would have entailed a revision of standing Australian policy, but was regarded as a necessary price to pay in order to bring the Chinese to the conference table and out of the war. Despite wide argument in the press over the value or even morality of such a price,[4] Australia's UN delegate K. C. O. Shann defended the need for seeking accommodation; resisting aggression should not be confused with refusing peace, he argued in effect.[5] America, however, accepted the recommendations unenthusiastically. When the Chinese rejection was made known, the U.S. assumed an unmistakably hard tone, suggesting that further approaches were pointless and that

[3] *CPD,* HR, Vol. 212, March 7, 1951, p. 75.

[4] Among strong supporters of a moderate Australian position were the Melbourne *Argus,* January 9 and 13, 1951, Launceston *Examiner,* January 11, 1951, and Melbourne *Age,* January 12, 1951. The *SMH,* January 11, 1951, claimed that "the London conference advocates buying off Chinese aggression," while the *News Weekly,* January 17, 1951, accused Nehru and Attlee of being the "two prime appeasers of the year" for having induced their colleagues to accept the formula.

[5] UN General Assembly, *Summary Records of Meetings,* Fifth Session, First Committee, 422nd Meeting, January 11, 1951, Vol. 2, p. 484.

aggression would have to be recognized for what it was and dealt with appropriately. Speaking directly after Warren Austin, Shann again preached restraint; he expressed the hope that not every link of communication with the Chinese had yet been snapped, since the UN could not entertain sanctions against a major power without contemplating a general war.[6]

But the game could not be played this way indefinitely. On January 19, the U.S. House of Representatives passed a resolution demanding that China be branded an aggressor. The next day the U.S. delegation complied by offering such a resolution in the Political Committee. On January 22, against American opposition, India moved the 48-hour adjournment, largely on the basis that fresh contacts were being effected with the Chinese. The vote illustrated the split in opinion within the UN: 27 in favor of adjournment, 23 opposed, and 6 abstentions (including Australia—she made no comment on the motion).

The British saw reason for optimism in the new Chinese reply carried out of Peking by their chargé, and on January 23 Prime Minister Attlee told the Commons that the time to consider further measures against China *had not* yet arrived [7]—the same day that the U.S. Senate followed the example of the House and insisted on an aggression resolution. What was Australia to do? It was simple enough to criticize her delegation for its abstention on the adjournment motion and to preach that "the Australian Government should be courageous enough to make firm decisions and let the world know what it stands for." [8] A

[6] *Ibid.,* 426th Meeting, January 18, 1951, p. 504. For Austin's remarks, see pp. 501–503. It had been reported that the U.S. had voted for the original London recommendations fully expecting to draw a Communist rejection and therefore better placing itself to gather support for its own aggression resolution. See *SMH,* January 18, 1951.

[7] *UKPD,* HC, Vol. 483, January 23, 1951, cols. 39–42.

[8] Melbourne *Age,* January 24, 1951.

more pertinent question was *which way* Australia should move. Varying opinion in Australia continued waging private wars in favor of one course or another, but even when divided, a sense of the underlying problem began to be recognized. The American resolution, argued one paper, threatened to split the Western world and to render the UN impotent for future purposes; in the interest of unity, the aggression resolution must be opposed.[9] The real danger lay in the disunity on Far Eastern policy which was developing within the Western alliance, claimed another paper, but it was British intransigence which was responsible, weakening the Anglo-American front, encouraging the Sino-Soviet bloc, and in the long run playing into the hands of American neo-isolationists; in the interests of unity, the agression resolution must be supported.[10]

The Australian vote was cast for the latter course. Australia saw her friends at odds at precisely the point when menacing Communism required full allied cooperation and solidarity. Australia had sought delay and compromise, but successively unsatisfactory Chinese replies had now been received. The American position had passed the stage of deliberation and was demanding action. If anyone could be expected to budge, the British were far more likely to do so. At all events, America was not only indispensable to maintaining the military effort in Korea, but her support was being avidly sought in connection with a Pacific alliance. John Foster Dulles, Truman's emissary, was scheduled to arrive in Canberra in February for talks on a Japanese peace treaty and an alliance, and Australia could barely have afforded to make a last-ditch and undoubtedly futile stand on the aggression resolution with the crucial Dulles conversations so close at hand. Finally, Australia was well aware of, and concerned

[9] Launceston *Examiner,* January 24, 1951.
[10] Perth *West Australian,* January 26, 1951.

about, the war-hawk and isolationist factions in Washington, and it was reasonable for her to suppose that the longer the resolution remained unpassed, or the more defectors there were from its cause, the larger would be the opening through which these factions could drive—to Australia's detriment. Australia's choice to draw into line with America was, therefore, *not* unreasonable, not an ignominious striking of her colors, although in the circumstances the insinuation in the rhetorical question put by the Melbourne *Age* was: "Is our new policy one of saying 'Yes' to whatever emanates from Washington?" [11]

When the resolution was carried, another and meaningful question was put: "The Chinese Communist Government has been condemned for aggression. But how now is a cease-fire in Korea to be negotiated with a declared aggressor?" [12] No one could answer with confidence, but both in the UN, after having accepted the American resolution, and in subsequent and positively stated words, Australia made it plain that she did not regard negotiations with the Chinese as closed, nor the application of sanctions as something to be undertaken lightly. In particular, the Government was at pains to indicate that any sanctions proposed by the Additional Measures Committee would require General Assembly approval (i.e., receive full and open ventilation), that all Governments reserved the right to interpret and act upon such recommendations as they saw fit, and that at all stages the subject of sanctions should be handled with extreme caution. In no way should peaceful negotiations with the Chinese be impaired.[13]

[11] Melbourne *Age,* January 30, 1951.

[12] Brisbane *Courier-Mail,* February 1, 1951.

[13] Shann, UN General Assembly, *Summary Records of Meetings,* Fifth Session, First Committee, 430th Meeting, January 24, 1951, Vol. 2, pp. 540–541; Spender, *CPD,* HR, Vol. 212, March 14, 1951, p. 481.

## ECONOMIC SANCTIONS AND TRADE

VERY quickly, with respect to trade with China, a concrete situation arose in which Australia needed to weigh priorities. As the result of the successful aggression resolution, an Additional Measures Committee of 12 members (including Australia) was set up by the General Assembly. From this parent committee a subcommittee of five, again including Australia, was organized and charged with sifting out the most appropriate approach by which sanctions against China, when and if needed, could be undertaken by the UN. The subcommittee's suggestion of economic measures was adopted by the parent group and, in May 1951, it and later the Political Committee discussed the appropriateness and character of such sanctions, given the failure of UN cease-fire approaches in Peking.[14] On May 18, the Assembly formally ratified the Political Committee's action, recommending that all member states embargo for shipment to China war supplies and various categories of strategic materials. Members were requested to cooperate with one another in fulfilling this objective, and reaffirmation was given to the search for a settlement of the Korean War.[15] Australia's approach to Chinese trade—before, during and after the sanctions resolution was under discussion—presents still another test of how the Korean War might have affected the freezing and immobilization of her China policy.

The sanctions resolution did not, for any practical purpose, require any amendment of Australia's established practice in the matter. Shortly after South Korea was invaded, Australia blocked the shipment of strategic items to North Korea. When the Chinese intervened in force,

[14] See Document A/1799. UN General Assembly, Fifth Session, *Annexes*, Report of the Additional Measures Committee, May 14, 1951, pp. 20–21.

[15] UN General Assembly, Fifth Session, *Supplement* no. 20A, *Resolutions*, 500 (V), p. 2.

comparable action was taken against them and apparently was strengthened following the passage of the aggression resolution.[16] From all appearances some care was taken in policing this policy. In January, the Government prohibited the departure of two old RAN corvettes which had been purchased by a Hong Kong concern and were scheduled to be towed out of Sydney. Canberra apparently suspected that the ships would be sold to China, either intact or as valuable scrap metal.[17]

But when the sanctions proposal reached the Additional Measures Committee early in May, Australian reactions were positively hostile. At the opening meeting of May 3, the U.S. delegate outlined a China embargo plan not materially different from the one adopted two weeks later with Australia's support. At the May 3 meeting, however, little enthusiasm was generated for the American plan. Britain's Sir Gladwyn Jebb forcefully argued that such a resolution would have no more effect than did the previous condemnation of China, and would merely heighten Peking's intransigence and diminish chances for a peaceful settlement. According to the fullest available account in the *New York Times,* "similar criticisms came from Keith C. O. Shann, Australian representative, who was reported to have expressed even stronger opposition than Sir Gladwyn."[18] The *New York Times* reported that opposition to the U.S. proposals had virtually vanished by the time of the next Committee meeting on May 7. Jebb assumed a far softer line, while Shann, the Peck's Bad Boy of four days earlier, spoke not at all.[19] A week later, by 11 votes to none, Egypt abstaining, the Committee

[16] See Ballard, UN General Assembly, *Summary Records of Meetings,* Fifth Session, First Committee, 444th Meeting, May 17, 1951, Vol. 2, p. 635; Casey, statement of May 14, 1951, in *SMH,* May 15, 1951, and in *CPD,* HR, Vol. 213, June 21, 1951, pp. 274–275.

[17] *SMH,* January 6 and 25, 1951.

[18] *NYT,* May 4, 1951.

[19] *Ibid.,* May 8, 1951.

approved a slightly revised version of the American plan. By the time the Political Committee received the proposal, Australia was all smiles, and had even been instrumental in *adding* a category of strategic materials missing from the original American catalogue.

Fortunately, the background story can in large part be reconstructed from public and other sources. The first and fundamental point is that Australia agreed with Jebb and the British, gravely doubting the usefulness or effectiveness of such a resolution. Most countries, including Australia, had already imposed a strategic ban on China, and the resolution would not materially enhance the position. More significant, perhaps, was the fear—publicly expressed by Shann himself in the opening weeks of January—that China must not be antagonized to the point of refusing to negotiate. The February 1 resolution had brought a tirade from Peking and, if anything, the Chinese stiffened in the face of subsequent attempts to bargain with them. Australia's feelings were so strong that, as has been seen, she outdid all others at the initial meeting of the Additional Measures Committee.

What, then, persuaded Australia to modify her behavior so radically? In the background was Britain's own handling of strategic goods to China. Like Australia, Britain had voluntarily imposed a tight strategic embargo against China when the Chinese stepped into the war. But some strategically valuable materials, particularly rubber from Malaya, slipped into China through Hong Kong or by other means even after the aggression resolution had passed. In Britain, political damage was being inflicted on the Attlee Government's management of the problem. But from America came a chorus of protests about British duplicity. Douglas MacArthur, back from Korea and celebrated everywhere he stood, testified about British laxity in Chinese strategic trade the very same day that Gladwyn Jebb was opposing the American sanctions scheme. A large and ugly Anglo-American argument was being blown up until, on May 7, the day of the second meeting of the Additional Measures Committee, the President of the British Board of Trade advised the Commons that loopholes were being closed and the Government would *support* the American resolution.[20] Britain, for reasons of politics and amity with America, capitulated.

The British capitulation had, of course, been preceded by intensive discussions with the U.S., and the Australians were also widely exposed to these attempts to turn their thinking. On May 7, Shann had been silent in Committee. The British cave-in certainly failed to help his cause, but at the moment he was probably without instructions from Canberra. By the time of the next meeting, May 14, some events of note had transpired. On May 10, the U.S. Senate voted to cut off all economic aid to nations which exported war materials to any Communist country, indicating the inflamed mood of opinion in America, which even the Administration could not wholly subdue or control. On the following day the Australian Cabinet met and the whole affair, including the impact of MacArthur's allegations, was scrutinized. Even at this stage the matter seems to have been placed in temporary suspension, because urgent cables were dispatched to London and Washington seeking more advice. But the Australian Government finally did decide to side with what was now the Anglo-American position. Its judgment, it is reasonable to venture, may also have been influenced by reports that Australian goods, perhaps of a strategic category, were finding their way into China after sale to Hong Kong. Aus-

[20] Sir Hartley Shawcross, *UKPD,* HC, Vol. 487, May 7, 1951, cols. 1589ff., 2174ff. A valuable account of these Anglo-American differences is available in F. C. Jones, "China and Japan," in Peter Calvocoressi, ed., *Survey of International Affairs 1951* (London: Oxford Univ. Press for the RIIA, 1954), pp. 357–364. Also see J. P. F. Dixon, "U.N. Embargo on China," *Australia's Neighbours,* 3rd series, no. 11 (July 1, 1951), pp. 2–4.

tralia wanted no repetition of the vituperation leveled in America against the British. A day after Cabinet met, it was reported that Customs Department officials had been given further orders to keep strict watch over the matter.[21]

Australia also came to believe that, if a sanctions resolutions was unavoidable, it was desirable to avoid having a less overwhelming demonstration for it than had been given to the aggression resolution, probably on grounds that the Chinese might think UN resistance was weakening and could somehow be exploited—though in the final meeting of the Additional Measures Committee, Shann allowed himself the parting observation that his Government was still "not entirely convinced as to the wisdom of pressing ahead at this juncture." [22] But if unity—especially unbroken and close contacts with America—happened to be vital, then certainly the forthcoming ANZUS Treaty could not be discounted. The agreement had already been laid in principle, but a bitterly anti-Chinese Communist United States Senate, charged with ratifying all treaties by two-thirds majority was, or should have been, a factor firmly held in mind. In May 1951, unlike the previous January, there was no national debate taking place in Australia. Comment, when given, reflected acquiescence and even pleasure in the Government's decision to fall into ranks.[23]

But what goods *were* useful to China? Late in 1953 the Director of Foreign Operations explained in his report to Congress that the U.S. had imposed and was maintaining a *total* embargo on trade with China, not because every kind of merchandise was directly helpful on the battlefield, but rather because an aggressor nation like China "ought

[21] *Sydney Sunday Herald,* May 13, 1951.
[22] *NYT,* May 15, 1951.
[23] For instance, Melbourne *Age,* Perth *West Australian* and *SMH,* all of May 15, 1951; Melbourne *Sun,* May 21, 1951.

to be subjected to the maximum possible economic pressure, and that we ought not to supply its economy with any articles whatever, even civilian-type articles." Furthermore, denial of all trade would retard China's bid to build a war-potential base for her primitive industry. "A policy of total embargo to Communist China has been the consistent position of the United States. *And the Government suggested that other free nations take the same position*." [24] At no time, however, did Australia, together with other countries, accept this American invitation to stop all commercial intercourse with China. The Japanese situation was exceptional: first came a total embargo, undertaken at SCAP direction in December of 1950. After independence, Japan was at least temporarily "persuaded" to maintain an especially high strategic list and to hold her China trade in ordinary goods within limits.[25]

Australian trade with China in the Korean period was trivial due chiefly to China's concentration on Soviet-bloc commerce and her lack of foreign exchange. In the financial year 1951–52, Australian exports to China had shrunk in value to £282,000, then moved up to £680,000 in 1952–53, but were still considerably below the 1946–47 figure of over £6,067,000. Yet apparently what little trade there was was not going to be sacrificed. In mid-1951 New Zealand announced that she was barring the sale of wool to China as her own sign of observing the recent UN resolution.[26] Australia, whose sales to China at that time were almost entirely in the form of wool, paid

[24] Harold E. Stassen, "Enforcing Strategic Trade Controls," *Department of State Bulletin*, Vol. 29 (October 26, 1953), p. 571. Emphasis added.

[25] Dulles, testimony, *Japanese Peace Treaty and other Treaties Relating to Security in the Pacific*. Senate Committee on Foreign Relations, 82nd Congress, Second Session, January 22, 1952, pp. 49–50; Leng Shao-chuan, *Japan and Communist China* (Kyoto: Doshisha Univ. Press, 1958), p. 45.

[26] F. W. Doidge, statement of June 1, 1951, in *EAR* (NZ), Vol. 1 (July 1951), p. 2.

no heed to her neighbor's example. Australia maintained close liaison with CHINCOM, the special China Committee founded in September 1952 as an offshoot of the Paris-based COCOM (Coordinating Committee of the Consultative Group), which since 1949 had been coordinating the West's trade with the Soviet bloc. In conformity with CHINCOM's directives, she joined others in applying a tighter strategic list to China than to the remainder of the Communist world. She maintained export license controls on all goods shipped to China (as did Britain), allowing for Governmental intervention when and if needed. She even heard an occasional plea from her own people for a wider China trade, be it with commercial or political motive in mind.[27] In the last resort, Australia's China trade policy during Korea was of course adjusted to the exigencies of the times. But it was not a policy of unmitigated restriction and surely, judging by her sentiments on the sanctions resolution, not divorced from her very real apprehensions about allowing practice to become a dangerous international principle.

### PROBLEMS OF DIPLOMATIC CONTACT

As regards diplomatic recognition and the seating of China in the UN, the Korean period brought no changes in Australian policy. Relations were not established with Peking and, whenever Australia had a voting option in the UN, she cast it against replacing Nationalists with Communists. But this aspect of the Government's behavior also requires elaboration, including noting the manner in which it may have shown signs of independence.

Actually, the pressures of choice were more compelling for the Menzies Government until roughly mid-1951 than

[27] For example, William Morrow (ALP), *CPD*, S, Vol. 219, October 1, 1952, p. 2392, and Vol. 221, February 19, 1953, p. 88; Burton's statement of June 17, 1952, in Sydney *Daily Telegraph*, June 18, 1952.

during the balance of the Korean War, affording a convenient break for reanalyses. Once the Chinese had moved into Korea, there was strenuous debate about resisting agression, avoiding entanglement in a king-sized Asian war, and the rest. But in many quarters the debate was seen as incomplete, perhaps even unreal, unless it squarely faced the fact that a large, powerful, and suspicious China could not be expected to come to terms in Korea, or to refrain from misguided behavior elsewhere, unless formal channels of communication were opened with her. It was held that when states withheld recognition separately, or collectively denied a UN seat to China, they were stumbling into two unpardonable errors: assuming that outcast treatment would not further alienate China, and assuming also that keeping her away from orthodox diplomatic tables would not hinder a settlement. The Peking Government was, for good or evil, *the* government of China, and the Nationalists on Formosa very decidedly were not. The conclusion: China should be admitted to the UN as quickly as possible, and Australia should not only support her seating but also extend diplomatic recognition. Words to this effect were not just the rantings of fellow-travelers or crackpots. The Melbourne press unanimously leaned in this direction,[28] while a number of Protestant church groups, including the Australian Council of the World Council of Churches, placed themselves on record in support of these conclusions.[29]

Within the ALP Opposition the leaning was similar but somewhat more involved. Chifley, still the Leader, was perhaps the most straightforward in expressing distaste for

[28] Among examples of Melbourne press opinion: *Age,* December 5, 1950, and January 8, 1951; *Herald,* December 5 and 11, 1950, and January 9 and 11, 1951; *Argus,* November 14 and December 11, 1950; *Sun,* November 27, 1950.

[29] Sydney *Daily Telegraph,* February 16, 1951. For a follow-up decision by the Methodist conference, see Melbourne *Age,* March 8, 1951.

Western nonrecognition and failure to seat China in the UN.[30] Evatt, for public consumption, agreed with Chifley but was careful to attach qualifications about timing.[31] At the Party's Federal conference early in March of 1951, the presidential address included a call for Australia to proceed without hesitation "in following the British Commonwealth of Nations lead in recognising China." [32] But the Party was sufficiently cautious to avoid dogmatic pronouncements. It already contained a number of bitterly anti-Communist Parliamentarians. For the moment, these men raised no serious complaint about the inclinations of the leadership, but the leadership could not, in turn, disregard the growing influence of conservative, predominantly Catholic elements in the Party, especially among the Victorian industrial groups. Above all, Labor was uneasy about an early election and, when the double dissolution arrived in March, discretion overcame it. As the Government parties unpacked their Communist tar brushes, ALP thinking on recognition and the seating of China at the UN suddenly became impossible to detect.

The Government's refusal to carry out the changes of policy asked by its critics is not difficult to gauge. There were, of course, the electoral considerations involving the Communist issue, which have already been discussed. Suffice it to add at this juncture that just as the campaign was about to open, an opinion survey indicated that the public favored Australian recognition of the Nationalists rather than Peking by more than two-to-one.[33] In addition Spender's own moral perspective on the Chinese

[30] *CPD,* HR, Vol. 209, September 27, 1950, pp. 24–25; Vol. 210, October 24, 1950, p. 1268; Vol. 212, March 7, 1951, p. 85.

[31] *Ibid.,* Vol. 209, September 27, 1950, pp. 52–53, and Vol. 211, November 28, 1950, p. 3182.

[32] J. Ferguson, in ALP, *Official Report of Proceedings of the 19th Commonwealth Triennial Conference,* at Canberra, March 1951, p. 5.

[33] *AGP,* nos. 744–755, February–March 1951.

question, though not a dominant ingredient in dissuading the Government from recognizing and/or supporting a UN seat for Peking, cannot be entirely discounted. In September of 1950, before the Chinese intervened in Korea, their admission to the UN was raised by India. In debate on this issue, Spender went even farther than the American delegation in stressing that Chinese behavior continued to be unmindful of the higher principles of international morality and that this fact among others disqualified Peking from entering an organization sworn to uphold the peaceful resolution of disputes.[34] Late in January, it will be recalled, Spender spoke of strong international and *moral* considerations which complicated a grant of Australian recognition.[35] The following March, he told Parliament that simple *de facto* control of and public obedience within a country did not entitle a Government to recognition.

> Such a test may have been sufficient in the days of the early part of the century, but in the modern world, which has already endured communism and fascism, there are deeper issues of moral character which we disregard at our peril; for were this test of *de facto* control to be the only test, then the control exercised by an aggressor nation, whether that of North Korea, had it been successful in overrunning the whole of the Korean peninsula, or any other aggressor elsewhere, could often easily satisfy it.[36]

Then again, from Australia's special vantage point, there was the compelling need to forge a defensive alliance with America, and Australian recognition of Peking or a breach with the U.S. over seating the Chinese in the UN

[34] Especially UN General Assembly, *Official Records,* Fifth Session, 277th Plenary Meeting, September 19, 1950, pp. 11–12.
[35] Statement of January 29, 1951, in *SMH,* January 30, 1951.
[36] *CPD,* HR, Vol. 212, March 12, 1951, p. 479.

carried forward any time late in 1950 or in 1951, could have harmed Australia's cherished goal. Her commitment to resisting Communist aggression could have been doubted in Washington. Her ability to negotiate the most favorable terms both for ANZUS and for a Japanese peace treaty might have suffered. The Senate's ratification of ANZUS could then have brought forth allegations of an unfriendly and inconsistent Australian policy toward China. Indeed, Australia's support for Peking, diplomatically or at the UN, would have run counter to her other, already mentioned efforts to lay up a store of goodwill in America. It is in this context that one must stop to test Dr. Burton's and Professor Fitzgerald's contention that Australia acquiesced in a Dulles-proffered *quid pro quo* at Canberra in February 1951: Australia could have an ANZUS pact only if she promised not to recognize Communist China.[37]

The first point to take into account is that neither purveyor of this contention was privy to any such demand. Fitzgerald told the author that someone had told him of the deal, but he could not recall who it was. At the time of Dulles' visit to Canberra, Burton could hardly have had direct access to such conversations since after stepping down as Secretary of External Affairs he had gone on extended leave of absence, and when Dulles was in Australia, Burton had returned to active service as High Commissioner in Colombo—never exactly a nerve center of Australian foreign policy.

The second and related point is that the author firmly understands from persons who *were* privy to the Canberra talks that no such proposition was ever dangled before Australia. But the final and perhaps conclusive evidence has nothing to do with "who said what to whom" about the Canberra conversations. Because of the many reasons

[37] Burton, *The Alternative,* p. 91; Fitzgerald, "Australia and Asia," p. 207.

already given, the Australian Government would have been irrational in the extreme had it been giving intimations of reversing its China policy on the eve of the crucial talks with Dulles. One cannot underline too heavily the fact that the domestic political situation, Spender's own temperament, and above everything else the top-flight priority assigned to meshing Australian security with America had for months been leading in an opposite direction. Similarly, only an exceptionally myopic and naïve American diplomatic mission in Canberra could have concluded that Australia was about to break ranks over China, and that Dulles should therefore be advised to resort to arm-twisting and lay down his alleged ultimatum. Since in all likelihood the Government was not irrational nor were the American diplomats myopic, little if any substance remains in the Burton-Fitzgerald imputation. Even the Canadian Government, which had both in word and action taken a more moderate line on China than Australia, and which had no election to wage or ANZUS to negotiate, was prepared to say in February of 1951 that Chinese intervention in Korea had made it "inconceivable that countries which had hitherto withheld recognition could at that time decide to change their policies." [38]

Moreover the above position is not undermined by Australia's attempts to avoid a servile and handcuffed posture on China. At the January 1951 Prime Ministers' Conference, Australia had subscribed to a formula which, if accepted by China, would at least by inference have included serious consideration of placing Peking in the UN as well as involving prior or subsequent diplomatic recognition by various governments, including the Australian. This displayed some flexibility in Australia's thinking, but within controlled limits. It should be recalled that this

[38] Pearson, *Canadian Parliamentary Debates,* HC, Session 1951, Vol. 1, February 2, 1951, p. 55.

formula was not the result of independent Australian initiative, and in fact had received the blessing of the UN. It was, also, part of a broad plan to halt the Korean fighting and to normalize Chinese behavior in the East. In the absence of constructive Chinese reactions, the formula became inoperative.

But it is probably not without significance that Australia, without any diplomatic links with the Chinese People's Republic, maintained her consulate-general in Shanghai until August of 1951, long after all American official personnel had been withdrawn. Furthermore Spender himself, despite his practical and moral objections to recognition and UN seating for Peking, never tired of qualifying his public statements: Australia did not discriminate against China because of the Communist system there; if only China would "simmer down," her "leper-status" could be removed—"We all desire to have the great Chinese people as partners in the constructive work of the United Nations" [39]—diplomatic recognition had never been excluded as a possibility and was in fact under frequent review by the Government; the ultimate decision depended on China's conduct.[40]

Once the 1951 election had been fought and won, the crisis period reached and surmounted, and ANZUS signed and ratified, the Government's practical alternatives were at once narrower and wider. They were narrower because, starting in the second half of 1951, the United Nations initiated what was to become the annual ritual of shelving the question of Chinese representation. Since even the British Labor Government came round to agreeing that the question should be postponed in view of China's "persistence in behaviour which is inconsistent with the

[39] UN General Assembly, *Official Records,* Fifth Session, 280th Plenary Meeting, September 21, 1950, p. 45.

[40] Statements of January 29 and 31, in *SMH,* January 30 and February 1, 1951.

purposes and principles of the Charter,"[41] Australia would have found herself unproductively and unnecessarily isolated had she voted opposite. Moreover, the British experience with recognition seemed discouraging. Britain's chargé in Peking was still technically a "negotiating representative," while not a single Chinese diplomat of any title or capacity had been posted to London. When the British chargé made representations to Chinese authorities about the detained Australian airmen and other Westerners being held without trial, the Chinese reaction was one of indifference. By 1952 British commercial enterprises in China were facing impossible obstacles to normal operations: they could neither carry on their business in the country, nor withdraw their interests.[42] Under these circumstances it is no wonder that Britain's unrewarded patience with China was hardly regarded as a favorable omen for Australian recognition,[43] though the British themselves had never been inordinately sanguine about recognition and were not actually suffering disenchantment with the results.

What the Menzies Government could, however, have done, but chose not to do, was to dispatch a diplomatic mission to Formosa. Australia's failure to house a mission there before Truman's neutralization order, and perhaps for a time afterward, could be explained by the widely held assumption that the Nationalist refuge would in due time be overrun by the Communists. As time passed, however, America's interest and military investment in Formosa were extended, and the earlier contingency became increasingly remote. In these years of the early 'fifties it was true that Australia was attempting to build an ambitious diplomatic network abroad in the face of severe

[41] Herbert Morrison, *UKPD*, HC, Vol. 489, June 27, 1951, col. 137.

[42] See Eden, *ibid.*, Vol. 501, May 20, 1952, cols. 265–267.

[43] For instance, *SMH*, June 11, 1951, and Peter Russo in Melbourne *Argus*, July 24, 1952.

shortages of trained personnel, and Formosa might therefore need to wait her turn. But this could not have been the entire answer; at a time when the U.S. was elevating its Minister in Taipei to rank of Ambassador, in large measure as a gesture of its support for the Nationalists, Australia placed no one there at all.

The Nationalists have never enjoyed a particularly good press in Australia, and their missteps have usually been followed with uncommon interest. Before Korea, the Australian public was treated to elaborate accounts of Australian ship captains whose British vessels had been shot at, boarded, and detained by the Nationalists, and whose crews had been beaten, imprisoned, and subjected to assorted indignities.[44] In May of 1951, Kan Naikuang, the Chinese Ambassador to Australia, resigned; this in itself was not an exceptional event except that he proved himself a K.M.T. critic and settled in Australia. Later that year public complaints were voiced by the Chinese consulate-general in Sydney against ransom notes being sent to members of the Australian Chinese community from Hong Kong by Chinese Communist agents. Communist agents *in Australia* were alleged to be watching local Chinese, determining who could pay for the safekeeping of relatives in China, and passing the information on to Hong Kong. The consulate-general repeatedly asked the Australian Government to intervene by imposing controls over the transfer of private funds to Hong Kong.[45] There is some, though not conclusive, reason to believe that the Australian Government was annoyed by this open display of Nationalist indignation: first, because much of the ransom racket was shown to be managed by opportunistic extortionists rather than Communist agents in

[44] "Sydney Man Says Seizure of His Ship was Just Plain Piracy," *SMH*, May 5, 1950. Also see *ibid.*, May 31, 1950.

[45] *Ibid.*, November 25, 1951, and *Sydney Sunday Herald*, December 2. 1951.

Hong Kong, and second because of the undiplomatic manner in which the Nationalists called "wolf," perhaps more to scare Australia about Chinese Communists than anything else.

To be sure, Dr. Chen Tai-chu, Kan's successor at Canberra, worked diligently to sketch an improved image of his country. He began a weekly Embassy newsletter, later known as the *China News,* and toured Australia whenever and wherever interested people would invite him.[46] By mid-1953, the Chinese had found for themselves a powerful sympathizer. W. G. Goddard, a former Australian radio commentator and External Affairs employee, had by then begun his career as an archenemy of Chinese Communism and apologist of the Nationalists. He had already written, for instance, that "Formosa is rapidly becoming a lighthouse of democracy in the Eastern Seas," and that "Australia dare not betray this torchbearer of democracy in East Asia."[47] For his outstanding work, Goddard was decorated by Dr. Chen on behalf of Chiang Kai-shek,[48] and in the months that followed the Embassy news bulletin became a vehicle for nearly everything that Goddard said and wrote.

Still, however, the Australian Government failed to send anyone to Formosa, in part no doubt because it cared little for the regime there, and perhaps in part because it wished to keep its diplomatic channels uncluttered just in case the Korean War should end and a *rapprochement* with Peking become possible. In any event, it was plain that the Nationalist Government did not disguise its displeasure with Australia's snub. From 1951 until Dr. Chen Chi-mai was appointed Ambassador in September of

[46] Among available mimeographed speeches are "China, Past, Present and Future," at Wagga, July 22, 1952, 5pp., and "China in World Politics," at Temora, March 6, 1953, 4pp.

[47] W. G. Goddard, "Behind the Bamboo Curtain," *Australia and East Asia* (October 1952), pp. 14 and 16.

[48] *China News* (Canberra), June 4, 1953.

1959, there was an *Embassy* in Canberra but no *Ambassador*. Chen Tai-chu, who served as head of mission for most of this period, was variously identified in the Australian diplomatic lists as "Minister Plenipotentiary" and "Minister," *Chargé d'Affaires ad interim*. This was no accident or coincidence; the Nationalists clearly resented being denied even token Australian representation in Taipei.

## LABOR PARTY POLITICS

BE THAT as it may, the approach of peace in Korea in mid-1953 gave rise to fresh speculation about any about-turn in Australia's China policy. The British Government was reemphasizing that the UN was not an anti-Communist alliance and, that after a Korean peace conference, the issue of Chinese representation should be reexamined.[49] In Canada, Lester Pearson was saying that "the time is coming when we have to recognize facts realistically. One of these facts is that the Chinese Reds represent 500,000,000 people."[50] In Australia even the more reserved papers, such as the *Sydney Morning Herald,* were reviving talk of a broad-ranging Eastern settlement which necessarily and inevitably would include Australian diplomatic recognition of China and a vote for Peking's entry into the UN.[51] In the face of all this prediction and advice, the Government refused to play an open hand. Early in June, the China problem was broached at the London Commonwealth Prime Ministers' Conference. Press reports about Australia's inclinations were contradictory.[52] Afterward,

[49] R. A. Butler, *UKPD,* HC, Vol. 518, July 30, 1953, cols. 1557–1558.

[50] Statement of May 25, 1953, in Montreal *Gazette,* May 26, 1953.

[51] For example, *SMH,* April 2, July 23 and 27, 1953; Melbourne *Herald,* April 2 and June 9, 1953; *Canberra Times,* April 4, 1953; Melbourne *Argus,* June 9, 1953.

[52] Sydney *Daily Telegraph,* June 10, 1953: Despite pressure from most other Commonwealth Governments for a general Common-

however, as the armistice was being signed, Casey was scrupulously careful to deny any aggressive intent on the part of Australia against China; the war just fought had not been directed at the form of government under which the Chinese functioned; and Australia would "watch very carefully what takes place in the next month or so in the political conference and elsewhere for evidence of Communist China's desire to live at peace with the rest of the world." [53]

In other words, as the Korean problem was coming to an end, among those groping for new policies and a *modus vivendi* with China were the British Conservative Government, the Canadian Liberal Government, a Liberal Australian Government, and even normally conservative sectors of the Australian press. The missing piece was the ALP. By comparison with its earlier and then its post-party-split image respecting Chinese policy, Australian Labor between 1952 and late 1954 presented a curious sight indeed, and one which demands rather detailed attention. Evatt had succeeded to the leadership on Chifley's death in mid-1951, and Arthur Calwell was elected his deputy. Perhaps some notice of what these and other Labor men were saying at this time would be a helpful beginning to the account.

In January of 1953, Evatt told an audience in Perth that it would be quite inappropriate for Australia to recognize China while Australian and Chinese troops were fighting one another in Korea.[54] Several days *after* the

wealth recognition of China and support for a UN seat, "Australia and New Zealand still don't like the idea." Melbourne *Herald*, June 12, 1953: "The Australian Government's view is that after an armistice, Communist China's Government must be recognised as the de facto effective government of Continental China, just as the Soviet Government is already recognized."

[53] Statement of July 26, 1953, in *CNIA*, Vol. 24 (July 1953), p. 403.

[54] Statement of January 19, 1953, in *Canberra Times*, January 20, 1953.

armistice had been signed, he said in a radio broadcast that it would be wrong and unjust to admit China to the UN "while other applicants for membership are in position in the queue." [55] In mid-July, addressing the Federal ALP Executive in Melbourne, Calwell insisted that at the recent London conference Churchill had demanded that Australia recognize China, and that the Menzies Government was about to give in to this demand even though any benefits would accrue to the British and not the Australians.[56] In September, ALP Parliamentarian Kim Beazley told the House that America's China policy was more realistic than Britain's. By maintaining recognition of Nationalist China, the U.S. was providing a rallying point for all dissident elements in China, and this was marvelously desirable.[57] The following month, Beazley was guest speaker at a Melbourne public meeting which condemned any Government move to recognize China.[58] Again, in September, ALP Parliamentarian S. M. Keon took the floor of the House to rip into any Government gesture to abandon Nationalist China, since Formosa's survival was indispensable to the entire Pacific defense line which America was manning.[59] In October, C. W. Anderson, the General Secretary of the ALP branch in New South Wales, announced that the state Executive had gone on record as opposing Chinese recognition; recognition would be "an acceptance of [an] usurping authority which is bitterly hostile to democratic Australia and to our American allies." And yet, added Anderson, the Australian Government had committed itself to the fatal blunder of recognition, an action which would wipe out

[55] Broadcast of July 31, 1953, in *SMH,* August 1, 1953.
[56] Statement of July 14, 1953, in Sydney *Daily Mirror,* July 15, 1953.
[57] *CPD,* HR 1, September 15, 1953, pp. 202–203.
[58] *SMH,* October 20, 1953.
[59] *CPD,* HR 1, September 24, 1953, pp. 643–644.

the precious ANZUS pact.[60] During the 1952–1954 period, not a single ALP Parliamentarian visited the Chinese mainland, though in July 1952 the Deputy Leader of the Opposition in the Senate, John Armstrong, went to Formosa, walked the red carpet, took dinner with the Chiangs, and returned with a favorable report on the island's progress.[61]

Clearly, something strange had happened to Australian Labor. On foreign policy, and China in particular, it was more conservative than the "conservative" Government parties. Beazley's attitude can be explained; an intellectual moralist, he has consistently maintained an anti-Communist independence. Keon too can be understood; a bright, militantly anti-Communist Victorian Catholic, he later broke with the ALP leadership and became an Anti-Communist and then Democratic Labor Party spokesman and candidate. But Evatt and Calwell were different. In reading their statements in this period the impression is more of men scoring debating points than of men making serious contributions to a serious subject. Furthermore, these were the men who after the great ALP schism of 1954–55 became Leader and Deputy Leader of a party pledged to a far different China policy, and Evatt in particular in 1950–51, despite his circumspection, had leaned toward a moderate China course.

But after 1951 it was different. By the end of 1951 Evatt had not only successfully defended the Communist Party before the High Court, but had earned considerable personal notoriety in leading the campaign against the Government's anti-Communist constitutional referendum. After 1951 Evatt was Leader, not Deputy Leader of the Party, and hence a contender for the Prime-Ministership,

[60] Announcement and statement of October 19, 1953, in *SMH*, October 20, 1953.

[61] See interview remarks in Brisbane *Courier-Mail*, July 30, 1952.

an office which he coveted. To gain that office he needed to bring Labor out of opposition and into power. To gain power, he reckoned, would require the active support of the Catholic, industrial group elements in Victoria which dominated the ALP machine in that state. By mid-1952, right-wing elements had seized control of the ALP Executive in New South Wales. In other words, conservatives were in charge in the two most populous and politically potent states. But Evatt's behavior on the Communist issue had been vastly unpopular among the conservatives, and in April of 1951 the *News Weekly* had written that "to date, the disastrous Evatt influence in Labor's foreign policy, which would recognise Chinese Communism, and which by its indecisive Korean policy would, in effect, abandon the United Nations, has not gained the support of the Australian electorate." [62]

What Evatt set out to do was to gain the support of the Australian electorate by gaining the support of the right within his own Party, and he was able to carry his Parliamentary colleagues with him. In April of 1952, the *News Weekly* headlined Evatt's speech and broadcast before the Victorian Labor Party's Easter conference. In his remarks Evatt had praised the anti-Communist stand of the Victorian Executive, complimented the good work of the industrial groups, and maintained that Party differences on the recent anti-Communist referendum had been differences over the means of best combating Communism rather than on ends.[63] In time, the Federal ALP's ban on the *News Weekly* was raised. Labor's China policy, for one, became a combination of rightists speaking out of conviction, leftists speaking not at all, and center men, such as the Leader and Deputy Leader, flicking jabs at the Government in the hope that (1) their jabs would be noticed and applauded by the right wing, and (2) some

[62] *News Weekly,* April 25, 1951.
[63] Address of April 13, 1952, in *ibid.,* April 16, 1952.

of them would land on the Government's chin and perhaps draw some electoral blood. On one occasion in Perth, Evatt was confiding to a small circle of friends that of course Australia's China policy needed a realistic overhaul. There would need to be recognition, a vote for Peking in the UN, etc. Then a stranger approached the group. Discovering that the newcomer was a newsman, Evatt reversed gears and began to preach against the very proposition he had just laid down. The story, so typical of Evatt's tactics at the time, comes from a person who sat through the entire episode. As the 1954 election approached, Evatt stoked the right wing stoves with all his might. He was the very model of the modern anti-Communist militant. He sought out B. A. Santamaria, even hounded him, in search of support, advice, and a fraternal *bon mot*. He called on Dr. Daniel Mannix, Archbishop of Melbourne and a great political as well as religious force in Australian life. He offered a cabinet seat to Stan Keon, one of the hardest anti-China men in the Party (and is alleged to have promised the same portfolio to two other men). To Evatt, these were the very nuts and bolts of political necessity.

The comings and goings of Dr. H. V. Evatt did not go unnoticed, and his fawning approach to the Party's right was assailed by no less a figure than John Burton.[64] The unsuccessful electoral bid of May 1954 and the subsequent eruption within the ALP are not immediately relevant to this stage of the Party's behavior. It should be noted, however, that subsequent ALP writing admitted that 1952–54 was an abnormal phase in the Party's development. Once the Party had split and a left-oriented foreign policy emerged at the Hobart Federal conference

[64] Statement of August 2, 1953, in *SMH,* August 3, 1953. Also see J. A. McLaren's letter to, *ibid.*, October 23, 1953; Alan Barcan, "Australian Labour Party and China," *Eastern World,* Vol. 8 (May 1954), pp. 15–16.

of March 1955, *Labor,* the Victorian ALP organ now divested of group domination, praised the new look by showing it was not a new look at all, but a return to the tried and true days of Ben Chifley, who had urged the recognition of China in 1950 and 1951. The article was revealingly entitled "The Chifley Policy Still Lives." [65] In another issue of *Labor* appearing at about this time, ALP Parliamentarian Clyde Cameron reminded readers that in 1954 *News Weekly* had backed Evatt, "but, of course, Dr. Evatt was then supporting their policy of non-recognition of China; of opposition to issuing passports to Australian citizens believed to be communists; and ALP interference in the internal affairs of trade unions." [66] At all events, Labor's political requirements in 1952–54 made small contribution to a sober national appraisal of Chinese recognition and UN seating policy. There was no doubt, wrote the *Sydney Morning Herald* in September of 1953, that Australia's attitude to post-Korea China required review, and that "the Labour Party will have to produce better arguments than Dr. Evatt has so far done to justify a reversal of the attitude [previously] taken up by Mr. Chifley and endorsed by Dr. Evatt." [67]

## PASSPORT POLICY

THE FINAL aspect of the China problem in Australia during the Korean period—the right of Australians to visit China—pulls together many of the strands evident in previous discussion, especially insofar as dilemmas of choice were thrown upon the Government and political opportunity opened to the Opposition. From the beginning of the Korean War, even before the Chinese intervention, the Liberal Government tried to act the role of juggler,

[65] *Labor* (Melbourne), May 1956.
[66] *Ibid.*, February 1956.
[67] *SMH*, September 11, 1953.

balancing its passport policy between the extremes of restriction and permissiveness. A young Australian Communist was invited by the Chinese youth movement to participate in Chinese National Day celebrations. At about the same time the wife of Ernest Thornton, the former General Secretary of the Federated Ironworkers Association who for some period had been serving in Peking on the Australasian Liaison Bureau of the World Federation of Trade Unions, expressed a wish to join her husband in China. No move was made to interfere with Mrs. Thornton, but the Government refused a passport to the young man. Harold Holt, then Minister for Immigration, explained that on the advice of the Security Service he had denied the passport without hesitation; the trip would have abetted "the international conspiratorial network of which the Australian Communist Party is a part"; he subsequently added that, in future, passports for Australian Communists wishing to travel abroad would be withheld only if security precautions required it.[68]

Several weeks later, the Government decided that some consistent yet pliable guidelines were needed to govern future situations. Australian passports would not be issued to persons, Communist or otherwise, desiring to visit any Communist countries unless special and convincing reasons were given. If an applicant had a legitimate reason and was not a security risk, endorsement of a passport would receive consideration. The policy would be operative for a one-year period and then reexamined.[69] Interestingly, previous Labor and Liberal Governments alike had refused passports for political reasons: at the special

[68] Statements of July 21 and 23, 1950, in *ibid.*, July 22 and 24, 1950.

[69] Holt, statement of August 31, 1950, in *ibid.*, September 1, 1950; and *CPD*, HR, Vol. 209, October 3, 1950, p. 207.

request of the Indian Government, Australian passports had not been valid for travel there by Communists.[70] Now, on broader grounds, the Australian Government was trying to rationalize its own approach to passports.

By the end of November 1951, the Government had reviewed its policy and found it wanting. The earlier method of excluding undesirable persons from visits to Communist countries had shown itself subject to circumvention, while serious delay and inconvenience had been experienced by those who had legitimate reasons for travel into Communist areas. Under the new approach, although a declaration concerning the object of the journey was still required, valid passports would immediately be granted instead of requiring a wait while security checks were being conducted.[71] For practical purposes, of course, the new policy was tantamount to no restriction at all, be it to China or elsewhere, despite the continuation of the Korean War.

In May of 1952 it came to light that five Australians had been granted passports for travel to Peking to attend meetings preparatory to a full-scale peace conference scheduled for the same city later in the year. There were no Communists in the delegation, and in fact four were formal members of the ALP. Within the delegation were a Methodist clergyman, a social and temperance worker, an agricultural specialist, a businessman, and, most significantly, John Burton. Speaking for the group, Burton said he and his colleagues were convinced that the preparatory conference represented a genuine effort to break the Korean stalemate and to improve Chinese-Western relations generally: "As such, the opportunities presented by such a conference should not be missed. Equally, if the

[70] Holt, *ibid.,* Vol. 207, May 10, 1950, p. 2348, and May 11, 1950, p. 2480.

[71] Holt, *ibid.,* Vol. 215, November 29 and 30, 1951, pp. 3148–3149.

conference is a propaganda stunt, that should be exposed."[72] What followed was months of almost wild controversy. The Government and Opposition sniped at one another relentlessly. Government supporters openly fought their own ministers. Members were constantly rebuked and even expelled from the House. Political smears were the order of the day. The Government moved backward and forward. It contradicted itself. It contributed to one of the most bizarre episodes in recent Australian history. It was a sorry performance almost all the way round.

The issue was joined by a volley of protests both from Government backbenchers[73] and the Labor Opposition, and in time nearly everyone was accusing everyone else of something shameful. The gravamen of Labor's charge against the Government was that it was allowing Australians to attend a bogus, Chinese Communist sponsored and directed conference at a time when China was perpetrating aggression in Korea and was killing Australians. Just how honest was the Government when it thumped its chest and proclaimed unflinching opposition to Communism? Could it not perceive that the Peking meetings were designed to immerse the gullible in an ocean of fabrications about who was really responsible for the distracted state of affairs in Asia? The Government probably had ample power under the constitution to withhold passports, the critics continued. If it had doubts, it should block the passports and then discover if judicial opinion sustained it. At all events, it should not seek cover behind a screen of legal inhibitions.[74] The Government's reply was that its own legal

[72] Statement of May 16, 1952, in *SMH,* May 17, 1952.

[73] For back-bench criticisms, see Hugh Roberton, *CPD,* HR, Vol. 217, May 6, 1952, p. 9; Hubert Anthony, May 20, 1952, pp. 517–518; W. C. Wentworth, p. 518; Alexander Downer, p. 465; Henry Gullett, pp. 508–509.

[74] For instance, Evatt, *ibid.,* pp. 510–513; Calwell, p. 516; Keon, June 3, 1952, pp. 1290–1292; Calwell, pp. 1295–1297; Beazley, June 4, 1952, pp. 1297–1298.

advice suggested that it lacked the constitutional authority to deny passports, save possibly under the defense power of the constitution, which it was loath to invoke. For Holt, Minister of Immigration, however, what seemed to matter was that his Government had "always adhered to the principle that we should never restrict the movement of our citizens in time of peace," and he made no apology for it. "I am glad to think that a Liberal government stands true to liberal principles on an issue of this kind." [75] The defense of legal incompetence to withhold passports hardly coincided with the same Minister's restrictive policy of 1950–51, but Holt did not care to show how and why what had been possible before was probably impossible now. Indeed, Holt's brave and liberal words stood in contrast to Casey's, which were largely concerned with identifying the Burton band as a "lunatic fringe" which had allowed itself to be duped by a cunning and conspiratorial Communist China—a point he elaborated on at some length.[76] Holt and Casey, two Liberal ministers, were barely speaking the same liberal language. Many Government supporters were subverting rather than supporting the Government, both in Parliament and in the party rooms.[77]

Perhaps the whole affair might have been dampened down had it not been for the adventures and observations of the Burton group. It all started with the unhappy publicity, complete with photographs, of the Peking-bound delegation boarding the same aircraft in Sydney which was being used to ferry Australian troops to Korea *via* Hong Kong. Once in China, the delegation broadcast over radio

[75] *Ibid.,* May 20, 1952, p. 513. Also see Holt, June 3, 1952, pp. 1292–1295; statement of May 17, 1952, in *Sydney Sunday Herald,* May 18, 1952.

[76] *CPD,* HR, Vol. 217, May 20, 1952, p. 465, and June 4, 1952, pp. 1366–1367.

[77] For a report of disaffection within the Government parties, see *SMH,* May 22, 1952.

Peking, giving a taste of things to come. One by one, the Australians told of the awakening which they were experiencing: religious freedom was flourishing in China and Christian churches were pulling their weight in programs of reform; the Americans had committed unspeakable acts of germ warfare in Korea; Burton promised that when the delegation returned home he would "present a basis on which friendly Australian-Chinese relations can be established, and perhaps a basis for wider understandings." [78]

When they did return home, the Australian delegates immediately set out to educate their countrymen on what were the facts of life. They insisted they had gone to Peking with a healthy skepticism, but were now convinced and impressed. The meetings had been conducted on the basis of open and forceful discussion, and the Australians were able to bring about amendments to objectionable features of certain resolutions. Fundamentally, what they wanted to convey was their impressions of China and of the proper solutions to international tensions. G. R. Van Eerde, the Methodist clergyman, extolled the peaceful and constructive efforts found everywhere in China. "Love of peace," he remarked, "as a theme in education, is an important reason why about 340 million people in China last year endorsed the appeal for a Five Power Peace Pact opposing the re-armament of Japan." In his unbiased Christian judgment, "after witnessing what is going on in China to-day, the thought came to me time and again that maybe this is how the Kingdom of God will come to earth, in an unexpected way and through unexpected channels, like the Babe at Bethlehem 2,000 years ago." [79]

Burton did not dwell on Godly Kingdoms or Babes in Bethlehem, but he did indict the West for being the real

[78] Cited in *ibid.,* June 12, 1952. Also see earlier reports of the delegation's reactions in *ibid.,* June 9, 1952.

[79] G. R. Van Eerde, in John W. Burton, *et al,* "We Talked Peace with Asia" (Sydney: 1952), p. 12.

mischiefmaker in Asia. For instance, asked Burton, why except for reasons of fostering feudalism and injustice "are [there] American troops in Burma and Formosa, and why does America have bases in Tokio, Korea, Formosa, Hong Kong and Burma—the whole semicircle around China?" [80] He never did explain what he meant by his Burmese and Hong Kong illustrations. What mattered was what China was like:

> I am not sure what is meant by a Communist country. If religious freedom, family life, freedom of expression and freedom of association are tests, then I do not believe that China is a Communist country. If the test is whether the revolution was directed against the owners of capital, again China is not Communist because the revolution was directed against only those workers and capitalists whose motive was their own gain, and who used corruption, exploitation including serfdom, and gangsterism as means to their ends.[81]

Australia could help redress the misconceptions and misguided policies animating her own people. Australia, Burton maintained, should support UN principles to the hilt, resist colonialism and feudalism, recognize China, trade with all countries without any embargo, and refuse to follow America slavishly.[82]

With the tidings that peace rather than war with China was achievable, the organization of a delegation to attend the full Peking conference in October was quickly placed in motion. Support arrived from a number of quarters, including Dr. J. J. Booth, Anglican Archbishop of Melbourne,[83] and Lord (Michael) Lindsay, a China specialist from the Australian National University.[84] The

[80] Burton, in *ibid.*, p. 6.

[81] Burton, in *Australia-China News,* Victorian Branch, Australia-China Society, August 1952.

[82] "We Talked Peace with Asia," pp. 7–8.

[83] *SMH,* June 16, 1952. [84] *Ibid.,* June 21, 1952.

Government now had to make a decision on the granting of passports—this time against the background of the earlier experience with political pressure being exerted by both opponents and party kinsmen, in the face of the kind of reports brought home by Burton and his friends, and in the context of its own assessment of what had been broached at the first Peking meeting and would come up for further discussion in October: germ warfare in Korea, a militaristic revival in Japan, and suppression of legitimate nationalist movements in Indo-China and Malaya.[85] Indeed, Burton's group were not the first Australians to visit China under the prevailing generous passport system which had caused embarrassment to the Government. By late 1952, a left-wing trade union delegation had paid a call,[86] a dozen or so Australian Communists had gone to China for extensive indoctrination,[87] and Wilfred Burchett was sending back reports as well as book and article manuscripts which outdid even the Burton mission in unvarnished praise for China and untempered criticism of Western policies.[88] Informal pressures by Government supporters on their own Ministers intensified. Within the newly established Parliamentary Joint Committee on Foreign Affairs (with which the ALP has never associated itself), a report on the forthcoming Peking conference was produced. The whole scheme was denounced as a piece of Communist stage management, and Australian partici-

[85] For a résumé of discussions and resolutions enacted at the conference, see *Important Documents of the Peace Conference of the Asian and Pacific Regions* (Peking: Conference Secretariat, 1952?).

[86] See Tom Wright, "Australians Visit People's China" (Sydney: Federal Council, Sheet Metal Working, Agricultural Implement and Stovemaking Industrial Union of Australia, 1952).

[87] See Herbert Passin, *China's Cultural Diplomacy* (New York: Praeger, 1962), p. 56, and Denis Warner, *Hurricane from China* (New York: Macmillan, 1961), p. 154.

[88] Burchett, *op. cit., passim,* and "News from China" (Banksia Park, Victoria: World Unity Publications, 1951), *passim.*

pation—by Communists or non-Communists—was ridiculed since it would be futile to attempt to advance the cause of reasonable relations with China.[89] All these facts and events had to be taken into account by the Government in assessing its future course.

But the Government bungled the job from the very beginning. Signs of its stumbling moves were evident as early as late June. Burton had been the first delegation member to reappear in Australia, and had done so without incident. However, when he later met his colleagues at Sydney airport, all their literature and notes were confiscated by customs officials, who told Burton this had been done "on direction." [90] A day later a Government spokesman denied that the Department of Trade and Customs had issued instructions to seize the papers,[91] and two days afterward they were returned without comment or apology.

Then on September 10, the Government announced its passport policy. Holt and Casey were shunted aside, and the Prime Minister himself made the explanation. In effect, he said that the forthcoming conference was rigged to further Communist aims in Asia, "designed as an instrument of war" rather than peace. Any association by Australians with the conference would be contrary to Australia's best interests, and passports would be denied. However, Menzies added, no general passport restriction was contemplated, and travel to Communist countries would in future be treated on an *ad hoc* basis.[92] Suddenly, it seems, the Government discovered it possessed the power to deny passports; this was a return to the 1950–51 position and a direct reversal of the position assumed and so briskly defended earlier in 1952. No attempt was made explain these gyrations. On political

[89] "First Report from the Joint Committee on Foreign Affairs Relating to the Peking Peace Conference," *Parliamentary Papers,* General, Sessions 1951–52–53, Vol. 2, pp. 487–494.

[90] *SMH,* June 23, 1952. [91] *Ibid.,* June 24, 1952.

[92] *CPD,* HR, Vol. 218, September 10, 1952, pp. 1186–1187.

grounds the Government had decided to shift course, though "the law" was made to look tenuous and highly adjustable—resembling a neurotic chameleon.

Still, the Government had no peace. One final act remained to be played. Some of the 30 original Australian delegates to China simply admitted defeat and did no more. A few Australians, carrying British passports, were not obstructed by the Government and went on to Peking. But 11 or 12 determined individuals decided to defy the Government, and to set out for China without benefit of passports. They faced two handicaps: major Australian air and shipping lines did not carry people without passports (although it was not an offense to leave Australia without a passport) and, on September 15 Menzies said it was the "general idea" to place every obstacle in the path of prospective Australian delegates.[93] What ensued was a ludicrous game of cops and robbers, badly acted on both sides.

The story can be pieced together from printed sources and from the author's interview with Dr. Clive Sandy of Melbourne, one of the determined dozen, who had no objection to being quoted and identified. The intrepid Australians left for Brisbane from Sydney and Melbourne, traveling under assumed names but in full view of shadowing Australian security agents. The plan was to take a flying boat to Townsville, where waterside workers were presumed to be holding a ship which would carry the party away. But the signals were crossed, since no ship was available to them. Some returned home dejected, others kept on, getting as far as Cairns on the northern Queensland coast in the hope of making some on-the-spot arrangements. "Through all this," ran one account, "Cabinet had taken on the aspect of an air operations room during the Battle of Britain, with the shadowing security men turning in regular reports on the whereabouts of the

[93] Cited in *SMH,* September 16, 1952.

Pekes."[94] The RAN had been instructed to watch for any small ships approaching or leaving the Australian coast. Civil aviation officials sent one message which read: "Offer no facilities for boarding other plane. Refuse launch transport."[95] According to Dr. Sandy, R. M. Ansett told him afterward that he had been asked by Government spokesmen not to permit his airline to fly any of the wandering Australians to Hayman Island, off the Queensland coast. There was suspicion that a Soviet submarine would be lying off shore, waiting to carry them to China. Happily for Sandy and his compatriots, the Government's pursuit did not include acceptance of the *News Weekly's* advice: Australia should have declared war on the Communists fighting in Korea long before, and "it would then not only have cast-iron authority to prevent anyone from attending a conference in the enemy's capital but, if necessary, the legal right to hang anyone who did."[96] At all events, no Australians who lacked passports reached China for the conference.

Although the Government had refused passports for the conference travelers and then went to rather amusing extremes to enforce its ban, its subsequent policy was an almost complete return to the earlier permissive days—even Communists were allowed to travel to peace congresses in and outside the Soviet bloc. They were even allowed to visit China, be it as general tourists or as participants at Chinese labor conferences and the like. The Government justified its position by asserting that the September-October 1952 situation had been special, in that Australians were then going to a Chinese conference explicitly concerned with undermining and villifying the West. But the old Harold Holt small "l" liberalism was very much in

[94] *News Weekly,* September 24, 1952.
[95] *SMH,* September 19, 1952.
[96] *News Weekly,* September 24, 1952.

evidence, for "the Commonwealth Government does not want to turn Australia into a prison house." [97] Australian traffic to China became fairly heavy, and Dr. Sandy managed to reach Peking later in 1952 without further Government interposition. Although China's Australian visitors wrote glowingly of what they saw and/or nastily of Western policies,[98] their freedom from harassment was complete.

Throughout this entire episode the Government had evinced a certain disingenuousness of argument respecting the legal position governing passports. It had at one time appeared to be speaking with two voices—Holt's and Casey's. Someone made a botch of the seizure of the preparatory conference delegates' papers. The dragnet methods and pursuit of Australians across the length of the country verged on a burlesque. But, broadly taken, the Government proved itself "liberal" as well as Liberal, even in the face of massive criticism inside and outside of its own supporting groups. Its policy on travel could not, in all justification, be regarded as just another stereotype of a rigged symptom of the Korean War and of the Chinese presence.

The controversial Dr. Burton also provides a transition to some explanation of Labor's conduct during the passport debate. Late in March of 1951 Burton suddenly and without instructions left the Australian High Commission

[97] Howard Beale, statement of October 4, 1952, in *Sydney Sunday Herald,* October 5, 1952. Also see Neil O'Sullivan, *CPD,* S, Vol. 219, October 7, 1952, p. 2502; Holt, HR, Vol. 220, October 16, 1952, p. 3273.

[98] See Elizabeth Vasilieff, *Peking-Moscow Letters* (Melbourne: Australasian Book Society, 1953); Allan D. Brand, "I Preached Peace in U.S.S.R. and China" (Sydney: NSW Peace Council, 1953). For an account of China written by a British passport-bearing Australian who attended the Peking conference, see Helen G. Palmer, "Australian Teacher in China" (Sydney: Teachers' Sponsoring Committee, 1953?).

in Ceylon. The moment he alighted in Australia he announced his intention of seeking ALP endorsement for a Parliamentary seat. In addition, while still a public servant and a High Commissioner, he quickly accused his own Government of having resorted to mass hysteria to justify coercive legislation: Menzies was an archenemy of all socialist countries, and had concocted an atmosphere of fear conducive to waging war against China, Japan, Russia, or some British Commonwealth country with a socialist Government.[99] Within a matter of days Burton won preselection to the New South Wales seat of Lowe and then resigned from the public service entirely, surrounded by a storm of controversy which his uninstructed return and his remarks had blown up.

Almost as soon as Labor had shown its alarm over the award of passports, Arthur Calwell selected Burton as a target and claimed that he should resign from the ALP if he intended to visit China, since "no man can serve two masters. No person can honestly belong to the Labour Party and attend what, after all, can only be a Communist-inspired—if not Communist controlled—conference to weaken the Western democracies in their struggle with the Communist world." [100] Calwell's challenge was, strictly speaking, consistent with established Party policy, which prohibited, on pain of expulsion, united front activity with Communists. As recently as March 1951, the triennial Federal conference had reaffirmed this principle and adopted an Executive resolution which denounced "so-called Peace Councils" and warned all members "against being involved with appeals or organisations which exploit the desire for peace" in Communism's interests,[101] and

[99] Statement of March 26, 1951, in *SMH,* March 27, 1951.

[100] Statement of May 17, 1952, in *Sydney Sunday Herald,* May 18, 1952. Burton later had his pre-selection for the Lowe seat withdrawn but, after a personal appearance before the NSW Executive, was not expelled from the Party.

[101] ALP, *Official Report of Proceedings,* p. 10.

during the balance of its unity era the ALP echoed these sentiments frequently.[102]

But Calwell may also have been trying to cushion the political punches which dissident Government supporters might have wished to throw in view of the fact that Burton had ALP connections and ties with Evatt, the ALP Leader. This, in fact, is precisely what they tried to do, and the debate over passports degenerated into the exchange of heated irrelevancies about whether Evatt, who had defended Communists before the High Court and at the constitutional referendum, had not in truth also spawned and nourished his protégé Burton, the leader of the madcap delegation to Peking.[103] Even more fundamentally, Labor's attempt to dissociate itself from Burton and to beat the Government with one of its own political sticks, i.e., softness on Communism, was probably a manifestation of the new conservatism which had settled over the party by then. Evatt was among the leaders when the ALP tried to embarrass the Government on the passport issue. In May of 1953, as a Senate election drew near, Labor Senator W. P. Ashley again launched a soft-on-Communism attack against the Government because of Australian trips to China, with Evatt and Calwell joining in support of their colleague.[104] No wonder that the *News Weekly,* a notable Australian enemy of Burtonism, Communism, and various and sundry other left-looking evils, should have taken pride in Evatt's "clearly and unequivocally" stated position on the passport issue,[105]

[102] For instance, see ALP, *Federal Executive Report to the 20th Federal Conference,* at Adelaide, January 1953, pp. 23–24; ALP, State of Victoria, *Central Executive Report, 1952–53,* p. 6; "Communist Peace Propaganda Condemned," *Labor,* December 1953.

[103] See the exchange between Henry Gullett and Evatt, *CPD,* HR, Vol. 217, May 20, 1952, pp. 508–510.

[104] See Statements and accounts in *SMH,* May 5, 6 and 7, 1953.

[105] *News Weekly,* September 17, 1952. Also see *ibid.,* May 28, 1952.

and indeed that Evatt and his Party should have felt comfort rather than remorse in being congratulated by this new and politically usefull ally. In retrospect, however, the canvas assumes a different shade. After the great ALP split, Burton published a pamphlet in which he defended various canons of democratic socialism and the foreign policy planks of the Hobart program. In his introduction to the work, H. V. Evatt endorsed its contents in full and wrote of Burton as follows:

> John Burton has already made contributions of value to the defence of basic freedoms in Australia. He resisted the onset of McCarthyism and helped to beat it back. Like many others, he underwent and surmounted the "ordeal by slander" which is the very essence of McCarthyism. He took a leading part in the cultivation of true friendship of Australia with the new nations of Asia, including India, China [sic], Indonesia and Ceylon.[106]

Time, and a party split, heals all things.

### THE IMPACT OF THE KOREAN WAR PERIOD ON AUSTRALIA'S CHINA POLICY: A SUMMATION

AUSTRALIA'S China policy was not, properly speaking, thrown into a deep freeze by the Korean War. For its first six months in office the Menzies Government searched about, trying to assess the impact of Chinese Communism and to evolve suitable policies. But the guidelines were already drawn when war came; the Korean years brought no real changes and earlier perspectives were still largely valid. This is not to say that Korea had no effect. Far from it. What the Korean War did was to stimulate, but not originate, Australian conviction that aggressive Chinese activity threatened Australian interests, and that powerful remedies were required. The quest for an alliance with

[106] John W. Burton, "The Light Grows Brighter" (Sydney: Morgans Publications, 1956?), p. 5.

America, for instance, reflected the position well. It had been sought before Korea, but the need for its achievement was heightened afterward; strong discomfort over China's intentions made an alliance imperative. The achievement of ANZUS was therefore very much a part, and a successful part, of Australia's China policy, and if Australian attitudes in 1951 on Chinese questions arising in the UN, or with respect to recognition, were in any way scaled to reach this goal, it was still considered a first priority goal.

Nonetheless, actions such as ultimate endorsement of the aggression and economic sanctions resolutions, or withholding criticism of the Eisenhower deneutralization order, were palpably not the reflex actions of a deaf and dumb Government which was waiting for instructions from Washington. Australia did work to moderate and restrain American behavior, and on more than one occasion simply followed a separate road. In refusing to place a mission on Formosa, sharply and openly rapping the Nationalists when she thought it necessary, continuing her nonstrategic trade with China, pursuing a lenient passport philosophy, and in other ways, Australia differentiated herself from America. The differentiation, however, was not for its own sake, just as the fact that Australian policies broadly coincided with American policy was not due simply to a wish to conform, but was based largely on independent judgments shared by many other Western Governments.

There were, to be sure, political considerations which conditioned public statements and, perhaps to a degree, official behavior. Despite Australia's historic lethargy, however, about sophisticated thinking on foreign affairs, the press did not hesitate to weigh, debate, and criticize the Government's China policy, perhaps exhibiting a superabundance of apoplectic reactions on the part of the right fringes. Unfortunately, for a large portion of the

Korean period, constructive criticism was not available from the Opposition benches, or at least from the ALP leadership. The manner in which the Korean War brought Communist China out of the shadows and into bold relief on the international scene frightened and rallied the Catholic right, and also persuaded the ALP that its political future would be uncertain unless it fell into the embrace of men who, among other things, would both carry and use a big stick against China. In this rather special way, the shape of Australian political life, and with it the debate on China policy, became stultified by the events in Korea.

# IV

# CHINA AND AUSTRALIAN SECURITY PROBLEMS: 1

THE PRECEDING discussion has tried to underscore the interplay of elements—strategic, diplomatic, commercial, and the rest—which before and during the Korean War combined to shape Australian thought and action on the China problem. With the background material in mind, it becomes practical to detach some of these elements and to deal with them as thematic components of recent developments. Strategic and military considerations deserve first attention, if for no other reason than China's presence has in one fashion or another come to entail debate over her power and intentions concerning her neighbors in the Asian-Pacific complex. In itself, the security aspect of the China problem appears to offer a reasonable division of analysis. The conjunction of the Indo-China crisis, the formation of SEATO, problems related to the Chinese Nationalist territories, and the decision to dispatch troops to Malaya provides a meaningful focus for the interrelationship of security questions bearing on China. Other security perspectives, together with proposals to modify, replace, or supplement the network of pacts and commitments, have in large measure been conditioned by these events. Invariably, the appropriate balancing of resistance and risks has dominated the argument.

## THE INDO-CHINA CRISIS OF 1954

THE CRISIS in Indo-China presented Australian diplomacy with a stern assignment. As has been seen, the Government had come to regard the insulation of South-East Asia from Communist intrusion as a paramount requirement of Australia's own welfare. The disturbances in Indo-China had long scraped against the Government's nerves, and had brought a voluntary Australian contribution to the French effort there. By the second half of 1953 the Korean War had ended, but the tempo of Communist activity was beating more and more dangerously in Indo-China, despite massive American aid. From Australia's standpoint, Indo-China, closer than Korea, bordering China, and adjoining other pivotal South-East Asian states, could not simply be allowed to drift into Communist hands and mark a wholesale admission that the West was equipped to protest but incapable of striking any hard bargains. The tactical problem, as in Korea, was to halt the advance of Communism without running the danger of inviting reprisals and consequences more serious than the original difficulty carried, and again the enigma was China.

At the Big Four foreign ministers' meetings in January–February of 1954, it was agreed to assemble a conference at Geneva to deal with a Korean settlement and the tensions in Indo-China. Here, at least, was an opportunity for the major Western powers to deal with the Russians, Chinese, and Viet Minh in the atmosphere of a conference hall rather than a battleground. In December, the Viet Minh had launched a major offensive; in March, before the Geneva conference was convened, they concentrated their attack on the isolated stronghold of Dienbienphu. French resources and patience were already stretched to the limit, and the military situation deteriorated steadily. On March 30, Casey said that the pressing menace of Communism's southward march was keeping him awake at night.[1] The basis of Australia's anxiety was shared by the U.S. As Secretary Dulles explained almost coinciden-

[1] Statement of March 30, 1954, in *SMH,* March 31, 1954.

tally with Casey's insomnia complaint, what was at stake in Indo-China was the freedom of the population itself, the raw materials and rice surplus of the region, the protection of strategic routes to other parts of Asia and the Pacific, and the dampening of Communism's appetite for further conquest. China was always there in the background. She trained and supplied the Viet Minh, provided military advisers, and generally fed inspiration to the rebels. Without the Chinese presence, the military scene in Indo-China would have far less severe overtones.[2] Whether France had committed mistakes in her Indo-Chinese colonial policy was now rather beside the point; what stood out was the present and threatening situation.

But Casey, Australia, and indeed most reasonable men by then were developing cause for restlessness for reasons beyond the nature of the Communist threat in Indo-China, or the inverse ratio between the West's bargaining strength at Geneva and French setbacks at the front. The U.S., and in particular Dulles, had begun to talk the language of intervention in Indo-China. On January 12, Dulles had submitted that "massive and instant retaliation" should be available as a tool in America's armory, and hinted at an extension of the Monroe Doctrine to Indo-China.[3] Almost immediately after making this statement, he told the Senate Foreign Relations Committee that if the Korean armistice were broken, the U.S. would no longer feel confined by Korean boundaries, would recognize no privileged sanctuary beyond the Yalu, and would strike at China without ceremony.[4] On February 8, Sir Anthony Eden has written, the British Ambassador "was told at the State Department that the United States Government were per-

[2] Statement of March 29, 1954, in *NYT,* March 30, 1954.

[3] Statement of January 12, 1954, in *Department of State Bulletin,* Vol. 31 (January 25, 1954), pp. 107–108.

[4] *Mutual Defense Treaty with Korea,* Hearings, Senate Committee on Foreign Relations, 83rd Congress, Second Session, January 13 and 14, 1954, p. 8.

turbed by the fact that the French were aiming not to win the war, but to get into a position from which they could negotiate."[5] In his March 29 speech, Dulles stressed the need for facing and meeting serious risks in Indo-China. As this record of pronouncements built up, American policy seemed ready and willing to join with friendly air and naval forces for a strike at rebel concentrations in Indo-China and at Chinese coastal cities.

Whither Australia? As far back as September 1953, the ANZUS council meeting had discussed Indo-China against the background of a prior Dulles trial balloon which stated that Chinese intervention there could not occur without consequences not limited to Indo-China. Casey's reaction was guarded but not unsympathetic: Dulles' comments were of "very considerable interest to Australia," and "must inevitably have the effect of discouraging international Communist exercises in that part of the world."[6] But by early April of 1954 Dulles seemed disinterested in a calmly negotiated settlement, was preaching intervention *without* the provocation of overt Chinese presence in Indo-China, and was searching for active support from some of America's foremost allies. Prior to Geneva, the U.S. position dictated that the U.S., Britain, France, Australia, New Zealand, Thailand, the Philippines, and three Associated States should issue a warning to China that she break off her aid to the Viet Minh, otherwise there would be naval and air reprisals. In particular, Washington was searching for a firm declaration of support from Britain and the ANZUS partners.[7]

The Australian Government's initial response to this prospect was again guarded, but reflected a disposition first to find out what precisely America had in mind and

[5] Sir Anthony Eden, *The Memoirs of the Rt. Hon. Sir Anthony Eden* (London: Cassell, 1960), Vol. 2, "Full Circle," p. 90.

[6] *CPD,* HR 2, November 27, 1953, pp. 663–664.

[7] Eden, *op. cit.,* pp. 92–93, 95; *SMH,* April 7, 1954.

secondly to avoid public commitment. America's interest in protecting the integrity of Indo-China was "welcome," but the Geneva conference should be given ample scope to grapple with the Indo-Chinese question. At all events, when such matters are at hand, "we all have present in our minds the threat to mankind from the atomic bomb." [8] The press was more direct and forthright. The *News Weekly* was of course delighted to rap the knuckles of "appeasing" Britain, whose Far Eastern interests were shrinking, and to urge using every available force, including the deployment of Chinese Nationalist ground troops, to clean up the festering condition of Indo-China.[9] But the overwhelming sentiment was on the side of saner counsels. American threats and slogans, combined with minimal consultation with affected parties such as Australia, were hardly helpful, and "If the utterances of Mr. Dulles are to be studied as an indication of the American approach to the Geneva Conference, they leave an uneasy feeling that the prospect of anything coming from the meeting of those invited to confer is daily being prejudiced." [10] Some of the thinking, again reflecting Australia's unenviable position, was quite imaginative. In May, for instance, once the Geneva meetings had gotten under way, announcement came of a proposed Attlee-led British Labor Party delegation visit to China. Certain papers found no fault in the principle that China ought to be visited, but deplored the timing. The Geneva conference had to succeed, to calm the immediate threat in Indo-China, to avert a general war-spreading intervention, and to pave the way toward a subsequent and broader settlement of

[8] Casey, *CPD,* HR 3, April 7, 1954, pp. 123–125; Philip McBride, statement of April 28, 1954, in *CNIA,* Vol. 25 (April 1954), p. 294.

[9] Especially *News Weekly,* May 5, 1954.

[10] *Canberra Times,* April 7, 1954. For other representative comments during the controversy, see Melbourne *Argus,* September 4, 1953, and Melbourne *Age,* May 14, 1954.

outstanding differences with China—all of which would serve Australia well. But the Americans were violently anti-Chinese, were already displeased with Britain's conciliatory approach at Geneva, and the Attlee trip might trigger a "let's go it alone" response in Washington. Therefore, went the reasoning, the Attlee group had blundered and should postpone its trip.[11]

What, in the last analysis, was Australia's official thinking on intervention proposals? Although Australia was not formally a participant at the Indo-Chinese discussions in Geneva, Casey spent some time there as well as in travel elsewhere on consultation; in his absence at Geneva a senior Australian External Affairs officer, Sir Alan Watt, was deputized to take his place. In the first half of 1954 Eden more than anyone else worked diligently and skillfully to avert intervention and steered Geneva to a respectable compromise settlement; the Australians exerted themselves in the same direction. Shortly before the Indo-Chinese conversations opened at Geneva, Eden has reported, Casey, Pearson of Canada, and Webb of New Zealand all agreed with the British view which sought to avoid any involvement in the war that could jeopardize the negotiations.[12] In June, Casey met with Chou En-lai at Geneva, explained America's impatience, and urged a cooperative Chinese spirit which could prevent the application of drastic measures by the West. Once the Geneva accords had been drawn up, Casey told Parliament that he had consistently been aware of the political nature of the problem in Indo-China, where the substantial effort had shown the shortcomings of a military response. A negotiated settlement had been the only realistic outlet. When interventionist talk was rife, "Our Australian view was that such intervention would be wrong for the following reasons:—It would not have the backing of the United Nations. It would put us in wrong

[11] *SMH,* and Hobart *Mercury,* May 28, 1954.
[12] Eden, *op. cit.,* pp. 113–114.

with world opinion, particularly in Asia. It would probably embroil us with Communist China. It would wreck the Geneva conference, and it was most unlikely to stop the fall of Dien Bien Phu. These were the views that I expressed on behalf of the Australian Government to Mr. Dulles, Mr. Eden, and other leaders at Geneva." [13]

The final Indo-Chinese settlement was not perfect, but among its strong points, with reference to China, as Casey continued to explain, was that Peking had formally pledged itself to respect the integrity of the Indo-Chinese states. The fighting had been stopped—thankfully, because "Wars do not stand still. They either expand or contract"—and some foundation may have been laid for a wider set of understandings in the East, including of course Chinese questions.[14] This was a far cry from the American proposals to build a free-power coalition to warn and then possibly intervene, from the over-all suspicion with which Washington viewed the conference, and from America's refusal, in the end, to sign and associate herself with an agreement which delivered half of Vietnam into Communist hands. It was, however, strikingly similar to the approach and conclusion reached by Britain, with whom Australia had been cooperating throughout.[15]

The reasons why Australia was far more publicly circumspect than Britain in adumbrating her position during the crisis exceed the simple proposition that she found no purpose in advertising differences within the Western camp. During most of April and May, Government

[13] *CPD,* HR 4, August 10, 1954, p. 97.

[14] *Ibid.,* pp. 99–101.

[15] See Eden, *UKPD,* HC, Vol. 529, June 23, 1954, cols. 435ff. See summaries of Anglo-American differences in Charles O. Lerche, Jr., "The United States, Great Britain, and SEATO: A Case Study in the Fait Accompli," *Journal of Politics,* Vol. 18 (August 1956), pp. 459–478; Miriam S. Farley, *United States Relations with Southeast Asia* (New York: IPR, 1955), pp. 11–18; Greenwood, "Australia, the Commonwealth and Pacific Security," pp. 12–14.

spokesmen reiterated the absence of Australian commitments to fight in or for Indo-China because it was improper to do so just prior to a general election.[16] This explanation seemed to encompass the best of all relevant worlds: it was a constitutionally respectable position; it largely avoided embarrassing criticisms from sensitive right-wing sectors; and it also, for those who were pleased to read the matter in this way, dissociated Australia from the interventionist schemes being bandied about at the time. Public opinion seemed widely uncertain about the whole enterprise. A May survey asked "If the French are driven out of Indo-China, do you think Australia will be greatly affected?" To this query, 37 per cent replied "greatly affected," 17 per cent "affected a little," 16 per cent "won't be affected," and 30 per cent had no opinion.[17] The Government's circumspection—and indeed the Opposition's as well—was typical of the entire electoral campaign which, on May 29, ended in the return of the Liberal-Country Party coalition. Neither Menzies nor Evatt even mentioned foreign policy problems in their respective policy speeches, and in fact the entire campaign was almost equally devoid of any guidance to the electorate. The press deplored this condition,[18] and a mixture of public indifference and unstimulating party dialogue testified to the political wisdom of a leave-well-enough-alone philosophy. Among L-CP supporters, only 2 per cent felt their own party's best argument in the election would bear on foreign policy, while a blank was recorded for ALP followers.[19]

Beyond electoral considerations lay another, and quite

[16] For example, Menzies' statement of April 28, 1954, in *SMH*, April 29, 1954, and Casey's statement of May 16, 1954, in *ibid.*, May 17, 1954.

[17] *AGP*, nos. 1006–1021, May–June 1954.

[18] Adelaide *News*, May 12 and 25, 1954; Melbourne *Age* and Melbourne *Argus*, May 14, 1954; *SMH*, May 30, 1954.

[19] *AGP*, nos. 999–1005, April 1954.

strongly respectable diplomatic reason. Casey met with Chou at Geneva after, not before, the election. When he did so the meeting was unpublicized—even the fact of the interview was played down. Indeed, to this very date, the character of the discussion has never been publicly disclosed, and the author learned of its outlines through private contact. It must be remembered that Australia, like America, had no official relations with China, the Americans were especially antagonistic toward the Chinese at the time, and were not making a large contribution to ironing out the maze of problems facing the Geneva conference. The Australian wish to avoid any public criticism or offense toward America flared up in the House on April 8, while talk of intervention was widespread in Washington. E. G. Whitlam, later the ALP's Deputy Leader, charged that Dulles' countenancing of European tutelage in Indo-China had driven many native people into Communist rebel ranks, and that Australia should not participate in any Indo-Chinese police action save under UN auspices. Casey, although he privately agreed that intervention was wrong, replied that "The world is very disturbed. Anything could happen at any time, and this is a time when we have to stick to our friends and to our convictions. The United States of America is on our side. . . . I leave the honorable member to the contemplation of my remarks." [20] The Australian Government operated behind the scenes to calm the Americans, to allow the Geneva meetings to make headway toward a reasonable settlement, and to contain both direct and indirect conflict with China. But a public demonstration of rocking the boat of Austral-American relations was also inimical to Australia's vested security interests. A broad South-East Asian alliance was needed to deter further Chinese ambitions, and the talents of Australian diplomacy were being employed not simply to carry off such a pact but also to time its creation with-

[20] *CPD,* HR 3, April 8, 1954, pp. 244–245.

out prejudice to negotiations at Geneva and insure the participation of desired Governments.

### THE BIRTH OF SEATO AND THE CHINA FACTOR

THE AUSTRALIAN role in the preparation of SEATO has been treated elsewhere by several authors.[21] What is intended here is to show the bearing of the China factor on the subject, and likewise to note the connection between Australia's efforts at minimizing the risks of major war with China over Indo-China while planning for future security against the same contestant. It is well to remind one's self that, while ANZUS had been regarded by Australia as a diplomatic victory, it was only a partial victory, since its scope and membership had excluded Asia entirely. The termination of fighting in Korea was almost immediately followed by aggravation in the Indo-Chinese situation in which Australia, like the U.S., saw a heavy and ominous Chinese hand. The Indo-Chinese crisis therefore spurred thinking on fresh collective arrangements through which Chinese activity in South and South-East Asia, as distinct from the Pacific coverage of ANZUS, could be thwarted. The Geneva settlement itself, while representing to Australia the best bargain which could be struck without involving the West in an escalated conflict with China, was seen by Canberra as strengthening the Chinese position. Half of Vietnam was now explicitly Communist, and China, a full participant at the Geneva conversations, had shown herself to be independent minded and self-satisfied with her role of diplomatic player. Now that China's attention had shifted from Korea to South-East Asia, prepared, coordinated defensive measures of a sort that had been absent when Korea and then Indo-China became inflamed were necessary. The Govern-

[21] Webb, "Australia and SEATO," pp. 59–74; Levi, *op. cit.*, pp. 99–110; Watt, *op. cit.*, pp. 28–43; Albinski, *op. cit.*, pp. 352–376; Fitzgerald, "Australia and Asia," pp. 225–231.

ment recognized that if Australia were subjected to direct attack America would lend assistance under ANZUS, "But the problem of defending our shores in such circumstances and of maintaining our vital communications with the Western world would be tremendous. It is thus essential to keep the potential aggressor as far as possible from Australia's own shores."[22] This was—and still is—the nub of Australia's doctrine of buffer-zone strategy.

An inescapable question in early 1954 was precisely *when* serious steps should be taken to start building such an alliance. Dulles' call for united action in early April was regarded as a double-edged sword. That portion of it which urged an allied ultimatum for China to break off in Indo-China was received with utmost suspicion. However, Dulles was also opening the way to a long-sought Australian wish, because he construed the common front in the immediate context to be the basis for a concurrent effort to organize for permanent collective defense in South-East Asia.[23] This was a change of heart for America, a new willingness to become actively engaged on the Asian continent, "the greatest contribution to Australia's national security since the signature of the ANZUS Pact," rejoiced the *Sydney Morning Herald*.[24] The difficulty inherent in Dulles' call for an alliance was in his wish to arrange it without any delay. To him, its early conclusion would be tangible proof of the non-Communist world's intention to defend the area, and might therefore have the rewarding effect of influencing favorably the Geneva discussions, as well as serving a long-range South-East Asian defense purpose.[25]

[22] John Spicer, *CPD*, S 4, November 9, 1954, p. 1250. Also see Casey, *CPD*, HR 4, August 10, 1954, p. 100, and HR 5, October 27, 1954, pp. 2382–2383; Menzies, statement of July 22, 1954, in *CNIA*, Vol. 25 (July 1954), p. 469.

[23] Eden, *op. cit.*, pp. 92–93, 95.

[24] *SMH*, April 8, 1954.

[25] See Dulles' statements of May 3, 5, and 10, 1954, in *ibid.*, May 4, 7, and 13, 1954, respectively.

In principle, the British and Australian views converged once again, as they had in resisting intervention. Both Governments were convinced of the desirability of an alliance, though the Australian conviction was more positive and urgent, but firmly believed that zealous motions to begin the work while Geneva was wrestling with the problems of Indo-China would surely antagonize the Communist side and ruin chances for a respectable settlement—hence leaving the Chinese shadow lying across Indo-China and reinforcing the pressures for intervention. Australia was steadfastly oriented in this direction through May and most of June. As the conference discussions on Indo-China were opening, and as America was pointedly pushing for pact building, Casey plainly said that no positive steps should be taken until the pattern at Geneva had become obvious, and he emphasized that any treaty which might eventually be negotiated would be defensive in nature.[26] Casey then successfully undertook to organize a meeting of British, French, and ANZUS service personnel in Washington, in part to assess the prevailing military situation in Indo-China (and thereby to press home the futility of intervention), but also as a delaying gambit, designed to forestall American pressure to move on with formal pact discussions. The last point is inferential, but should be read against the general tone of Australian opinion at the time, plus Casey's own meticulous phrasing that the liaison group meetings should not be interpreted as a sign of any breakdown in the Geneva deliberations, and that no participating Government was to be bound by the group's findings.[27]

Casey must have been aware that his posture could create unwanted difficulties with America. In mid-May, U.S.

[26] Statements of May 1 and 6, 1954, in *ibid.,* May 3 and 7, 1954, respectively.

[27] Statement of May 26, 1954, in *CNIA,* Vol. 25 (May 1954), p. 351. Also see his remarks in *CPD,* HR 4, August, 10, 1954, p. 101.

delegate Walter Bedell Smith was reported to have said in Geneva that his Government would convene meetings to form an alliance even in the face of British opposition,[28] and a few days later President Eisenhower, asked if British membership in a South-East Asian treaty was necessary, replied that it was Australia and New Zealand from among the Commonwealth who were most intimately involved in the region.[29] Three days later New Zealand's External Affairs Minister, Clifton Webb, questioned in Washington if he felt a pact were conceivable without Britain, replied in the negative. The result was a shower of American press criticism that he was impeding the creation of an alliance, and this disturbed him considerably.[30] Casey no doubt was also disturbed, since he entirely shared Webb's thinking on the indispensability of British membership. Within Australia press opinion was beginning to express some uneasiness over the widening rift between America on the one side and the concerned old Commonwealth nations on the other, going so far as to charge that "Mr. Casey's wishy-washy statements have evidently encouraged the view in Washington that Australia is not interested [in a South-East Asian security treaty]." [31] Nothing could have been farther from the Government's mind, but as late as mid-June Casey was still talking in terms of awaiting the outcome of Geneva before plunging in with an Australian commitment to work on details of a treaty.[32]

Late in June, following the Churchill-Eden visit to

[28] See *NYT,* May 13, 1954.

[29] Statement of May 19, 1954, in *ibid.,* May 20, 1954.

[30] See Webb's statement of May 21, 1954, in *EAR* (NZ), Vol. 4 (May 1954), pp. 16–17; also Melbourne *Age,* May 22 and 24, 1954; *SMH,* May 22, 1954; criticism of the American position in Greenwood, "Australia, the Commonwealth, and Pacific Security," pp. 9–10.

[31] *SMH,* June 12, 1954. Also see *ibid.,* May 19, 1954; Sydney *Daily Telegraph,* April 27, 1954; Hobart *Mercury,* May 18, 1954.

[32] Statement of June 13, 1954, in *SMH,* June 15, 1954.

Washington, Britain did in fact agree to open treaty talks while the Geneva meetings were still going on, and Australia joined these preparatory discussions. If, however, fear of disturbing the Geneva talks, and therefore of inviting continuing Chinese truculence, was a prominent factor in Australia's bid to avoid treaty planning as long as possible, it was not the only factor. The other factor was the controversy over which powers ought to be included in a security alliance within the region, and one way to begin the analysis is to consider the membership of Nationalist China. Professor Harper has suggested to the author that at some point in 1954 Australia resisted the inclusion of Nationalist China in a prospective alliance agreement. His source of information was personal and confidential. The material on this point is scarce indeed, but Eden has referred to conversations with Dulles in early and mid-April in which he warned that any attempt to include India would be countered by American insistence on including the Nationalists. Judging from Eden's account, Dulles, against Eden's wishes, summoned a meeting in Washington of ambassadors representing Governments with an immediate interest in a pact to settle the membership question once and for all. While the ultimate focus of the meeting was somewhat different than Dulles had originally intended, there well may have been some mention of the Nationalist membership issue.[33] At all events, two points stand out. Throughout the Indo-China crisis and the intra-allied thrusts and counter-thrusts respecting a regional treaty, Australia and Britain were in extremely intimate contact. Also, Australia was among the powers represented at the Dulles-convened ambassadors' conference in April. In this sense, it is unlikely that Australia was ignorant of at least the possibility that the Nationalists might be included—aside from any direct intimations which Washington may have given her. There certainly

[33] Eden, *op. cit.,* pp. 97–99.

was some suspicion in the Australian press that a Nationalist inclusion plan was being propounded.[34]

If Australia ever really believed that the Nationalists were being considered, there is little question that she would have resisted. There certainly would have been apprehension on strategic grounds in committing Australia to the defense of Nationalist territories, especially the sensitive area of the offshore islands. This point will be elaborated later, but for the moment one bit of argument by analogy can be offered. In 1956, some reports appeared that Nationalist observers had been invited to attend forthcoming SEATO exercises near Thailand. Replying in the House to the significance of this occurrence, Casey said that when he heard these reports he immedately wired the Australian Embassy in Bangkok for clarification. He was satisfied that the invitation had been extended by the Thai Government, which had every right to act in this way. It had definitely not been an invitation issued under SEATO auspices, "and I think one can say with safety that there is no political implication to be drawn from those facts." [35] What Casey appeared to be doing was to assure Parliament that no back-door scheme for admitting the Nationalists into SEATO was being hatched. Earlier, in the first half of 1954 there was another reason for a possible Australian objection to the inclusion of Nationalist China: to do nothing whatever to prejudice the inclusion of additionial Asian states, and in particular India, within the coming security system.

Ultimately, only three Asian states—Pakistan, Thailand and the Philippines—came to Manila and entered the SEATO pact. From Australia's standpoint, this was a misfortune. Except for the special situation governing the

[34] *SMH,* May 31, 1954. At a press conference on July 21, Eisenhower intimated that the inclusion of Formosa had not been fully excluded from American thinking. See *NYT,* July 22, 1954.

[35] *CPD,* HR 9, February 16, 1956, p. 54.

three Indo-Chinese protocol states, nonparticipating Asian countries remained outside SEATO's protective umbrella and probably could not count on successfully resisting Communist infiltration or aggression if forced to rely solely on their own resources. Since the safety and independence of all Asian states was pretty much indivisible, a truncated SEATO likewise suffered, and security efforts on the part of the SEATO signatories would lose effectiveness and credence to the extent that the protective cover was the contribution of Western states. China's menacing presence simply did not allow for the complacent self-delusion that she could successfully be curbed after the fact of any aggressive motions.[36] The Australian Government had not been content to express its regrets. During the crisis in Indo-China Casey had visited nearly every Asian capital and had tried to persuade those countries that an alliance was as much in their interest as the West's. Casey's plan had been to promote a double-pronged approach to the situation. (1) When an Indo-Chinese settlement was reached, there should be a wide international guarantee for it—a treaty emphasizing peaceful intent to which free Asian states, the Western powers, Russia, and China would all presumably subscribe. (2) Beyond that there should be an explicit security alliance which could block any future intrusions in Indo-China or elsewhere in the area. To this arrangment free Asian and Western governments alike would link themselves.[37]

The difficulties facing Casey and his Government were severe. India, and probably most other neutralist states, would have been pleased to accept the first part of the treaty, but had an aversion to a military alliance. In any

[36] See especially Casey, *CPD*, HR 4, August 10, 1954, pp. 100–103, and HR 5, October 27, 1954, p. 2384.

[37] Casey, *ibid.*, HR 4, August 10, 1954, pp. 98, 100; Casey, "New Plan to Defend Southeast Asia," pp. 50–51.

event, under no circumstances would the neutrals have participated in any system which included the Chinese Nationalists. As an indication of this, at their Ceylonese talks in late April and early May, they had reaffirmed their view that the CPR's inclusion in the UN would materially assist peace-keeping in Asia.[38] On its part, the U.S. built up opposition to entering into any guarantee in common with Communist powers and, as has been seen, lacked interest in constructing a military arrangement with neutralist nations. Australia's chore, shared by Britain, was to harmonize the positions. But Washington was pressing for quick action on a collective defense system, and indeed one bereft of neutrals. Thus Australia's campaign to persuade and cajole on the terms of a guarantee *cum* security alliance project, including resisting Nationalist participation, was only part of the problem. Above all, she had to resist America's insistence on the rapid summoning of a treaty conference. To have agreed would have spelled the destruction of the Australian plan and, in the perspective of Australian thinking, would have ruined chances for an Indo-Chinese settlement and made China more obstreperous at exactly the moment when the opportunity for vulnerable Asian states to associate themselves with a protective alliance had been forfeited.[39] The various threads all tied together, and Canberra desperately feared that they would be tied in Peking in the form of a hangman's knot.

In time, of course, despite the temporarily successful delaying tactics, Australia failed to realize her objective of a multilateral guarantee or of widespread Asian membership in SEATO. By mid-July Washington had accepted the Anglo-Australian wish to approach the Colombo

[38] See the Asian Prime Ministers' final communiqué of May 2, 1954, in *CNIA*, Vol. 25 (May 1954), pp. 361–362.

[39] See discussions in Levi, *op. cit.*, pp. 104–105, and Webb, "Australia and SEATO," pp. 62–63.

powers about membership, but basic differences remained and only Pakistan became a SEATO partner. Yet the pertinacity of the Australian Government had not been fully spent. The U.S. wished to orient the SEATO alliance explicitly and solely against Communist aggression. Australia worked to expunge any such language from the pact; the participating Asian states took exception to this anti-Communist line and probably would not have ratified SEATO on such terms. Also, Australia had not lost all hope that in time new Asian members might still join, and she saw the absurdity of stressing this particular angle in dealing with sensitive and suspicious neutrals who had just indicated their wish to normalize relations with Peking.[40] Eventually, no anti-Communist clause was inserted into SEATO, though the U.S did attach a special protocol which limited its own obligation in the SEATO area to Communist aggression.

Despite its limited Asian membership, SEATO was welcomed in Australia. ANZUS remained, and indeed continued to serve as the basis of tripartite discussion and planning. But through SEATO America had at last extended her commitments to the Asian mainland, and there were now eight powers which could coordinate planning, act against common dangers (much in the language of ANZUS) through their respective constitutional processes, assist nonmember states under the "designation" terms of the treaty and, importantly, would devise antisubversion and economy-strengthening projects which could handle indirect encroachment in the area.[41] Out of SEATO's character two significant points furthering analysis can be derived respecting Australia's China policy. Considered abreast of one another, they again strengthen the Austral-

[40] Casey, *CPD*, HR 5, November 4, 1954, p. 6. Also see Professor Webb's succinct summary in "Australia and SEATO," p. 66.

[41] For the text of SEATO, see *CNIA*, Vol. 25 (September 1954), pp. 671–674.

ian tendency to avert dangerous gambles with China while continuing to press for needed measures of deterrence and resistance.

It has already been suggested that if Australia was aware of any plans to include Nationalist China in SEATO, she would in all likelihood have resisted them. The issue of Nationalist China's signatory status in SEATO was at all events not long pressed by America, but the prospect of defining Nationalist territories, or at least Formosa and the Pescadores, as being within the compass of SEATO's protective arc did explicitly arise before and probably during the Manila conference. It is known, for instance, that in August the British Foreign Office was at pains to deny that Formosa could be construed to fall within the South-East Asian or Pacific boundaries of a treaty.[42] In the last resort, the coverage of the treaty was defined by Article VII as being "the general area of South East Asia, including also the entire territories of the Asian Parties, and the general area of the South West Pacific not including the Pacific area north of 21 degrees 30 minutes north latitude." The effect of this geographic delineation was that all Nationalist-controlled ground fell outside SEATO's purview, and formal protection of Formosa had to await the signing of the *bilateral* Sino-American treaty of December 1954.

In presenting SEATO to Parliament in October of 1954, Casey explained that while a Chinese invasion of Formosa would be regarded with the "greatest concern" by his Government, its exclusion from SEATO's perimeter had been "wise and prudent." [43] These were measured words, not further embellished, but they mirrored a genuine Australian anxiety. The entire area in the Straits of Formosa was diplomatically and militarily volatile. There was diplomatic concern because, with both Korea and

[42] *NYT,* August 17, 1954.
[43] *CPD,* HR 5, October 27, 1954, p. 2389.

Indo-China now at peace, many governments, including the Australian, hoped for a general and long-term relaxation of tensions in the East, with a possible eventual Western diplomatic détente with China—recognition, UN seating, some rearrangement on the status of the offshore islands, etc., being part of the adjustment. Formosa's enclosure under SEATO's wing would surely have annoyed China and generally complicated normalization of the position in the East. For Australia, it also surely stood to reason that SEATO protection for Chiang and his Government, so widely distrusted in Asia, would almost certainly have slammed the gate on the subsequent entry of India and other Colombo powers into the alliance.

Militarily, the situation also dictated caution, even if the protective cover had not extended to the offshore islands. For one, a crisis in the Nationalist area would undoubtedly have created wide differences of opinion among SEATO members on how, when, and in what manner to react. America, on her part, was a close friend of Nationalist China, and in many respects her guardian angel. Britain had diplomatic relations with Peking and had never shown any enthusiasm for Chiang. Pakistan also recognized Peking, not Taipei, and her own vital interests were considerably removed from the region occupied by the Nationalists. At all counts, it was reasonable to assume that SEATO would have been beset by powerful internal strains if crisis had come and the Nationalists were covered by SEATO, discrediting the alliance and rendering its operations more difficult in future emergencies within South-East Asia.

Late in July of 1954, as machinery was rolling to establish SEATO, Chinese Communist planes shot down a British commercial airliner off Hainan Island. American aircraft involved in rescue efforts were then jumped by Chinese fighters, two of which were shot down in the ensuing battle. China reacted with surprising contrition. A formal apology was extended to Britain and compensation was offered for the losses in life and property. The airliner, Peking explained, had been mistaken for Nationalist. In the U.S, a predictable storm of anti-Chinese sentiment was blown up, and Admiral Felix Stump ordered his Seventh Fleet pilots to be "fast on the trigger" with intruding Chinese aircraft.[44] Australian press reaction did not excuse the attack on the rescue aircraft, nor acquit the Communists of any designs on Nationalist territory. What it did do, however, was to expose the folly of allowing the conflict between Communist and Nationalist Chinese to simmer indefinitely until it began to boil, regardless of who might be overzealous and fast on the trigger. Whatever might be the final solution—neutralization of Formosa or whatnot—the incident made clear the extremely volatile situation in this area on the eve of the Asian security treaty.[45]

To the Australian Government, the incident must have carried a lesson as well. The Eisenhower deneutralization crisis of early 1953 had been passed without serious incident, but it was difficult to predict how soon, and with what far-reaching results, Washington might again tinker with an anti-Chinese scheme, or when the Nationalists on their own initiative might step up their raids against their opponents, or when Peking might make a major move. Australian commitment through SEATO would therefore have been embarrassing and/or dangerous.[46] Professor Harper again supplies some food for thought when he writes that Australia "vigorously" opposed Nationalist China's inclusion within SEATO's protective ambit.[47] This goes considerably beyond Casey's "wise and pru-

[44] See *SMH,* July 27 and 28, 1954.

[45] For instance, Melbourne *Age* and *SMH,* July 28, 1954.

[46] For some Parliamentary expressions of relief that Nationalist territories were excluded, see Patrick Kennelly (ALP), *CPD,* S 4, August 12, 1954, p. 176, and John McCallum (Liberal), *ibid.,* September 9, 1954, p. 257.

[47] Harper's chapters on "Australia and the United States," pp. 187 and 210 in the 1950–1955 and 1956–1960 volumes, respectively, of *Australia in World Affairs.*

dent" characterization of Nationalist exclusion, but the author is satisfied that Harper is right. In the first place, the above discussion, although largely inferential, seems to build a plausible case on behalf of Australian representations to omit the Nationalists. Secondly, while Harper told the author that his information came from people whose identity he could not divulge, the author has verified the point from his own competent sources. The author has no proper option save to state the matter in this way, leaving his sources anonymous. At all events, though working without publicity, Australia's definition of her interests and security requirements had dictated that the Nationalists be exempt from SEATO's terms of reference.

## FORMOSA AND THE OFFSHORE ISLANDS

THE FOREGOING argument leads directly into an evaluation of Australia's attitude on the complexities inherent in the offshore island crises, the first of which was generated before the ink had dried on the Manila accord. Australia had reason to be grateful that SEATO's appearance had not engaged her in any fresh obligations toward any of the Nationalist territories, and her expressed wish to omit them from the alliance's coverage helps considerably in explaining her thinking on the events which followed, both in 1954–55 and subsequently. Once again the broad pattern of Korea and Indo-China was thrust upon Australian decision-makers and commentators—the need to define basic strategic interests and resolve to persevere in working toward them, while cutting losses in places where interests were marginal and where an extension of conflict was seen to be more dangerous than rewarding. The applied problem was by now familiar: support for America where vital interests were concerned, and the imposition of unspectacular but firm diplomacy to curb excesses.

The Chinese have consistently claimed that all the Nationalist-held territories, Formosa and the Pescadores as well as the several offshore island groups, are Chinese property, should be transferred to China *post haste,* and that any external interference in this claim constitutes a blatant intervention in China's domestic affairs. Because China is simply trying to recover what is rightfully hers, according to Peking, she can resort to any methods she chooses to gain her objective, and no question of external aggression arises. Before, during, between, and after the crises in the Formosa Straits the Australian Government put its position on many of the problems quite plainly, though again some of the presentation was kept out of public view. Juridically, it has regarded the status of Formosa and the Pescadores to be undetermined, since the Japanese peace treaty failed to settle the matter. Because the position was undetermined, Australia assumed that these territories were definitely not an integral part of the Chinese People's Republic, contrary to Peking's claim. Any Chinese encroachment on them, therefore, constitutes external aggression rather than the completion of the Chinese civil war's unfinished details. This is not merely legal hair splitting, because Australia has consistently believed that where Chinese aggression is involved, it cannot be disregarded. Communist Chinese gains *per se* are to be resisted, since they only encourage further adventures, demoralize non-Communist peoples and Governments elsewhere, and discredit the entire anti-Communist defensive system in the region. Especially in the first crisis of 1954–55, since Communism had just secured a foothold in Indo-China through the Geneva settlement and a brand new anti-Communist alliance had arisen in the shape of SEATO, it was necesarry to prevent a successful Communist bid against Formosa. The explicit protective mantle which was thrown over Formosa and the Pescadores by the U.S. through its treaty with the Nationalists in December of 1954 only reinforced this conclusion. If America had reneged on this obligation she, as the most powerful deterrent force in Asia, plus her allies, *mutatis mutandis,* would have been critically compromised.

More particularly, there have been special reasons why Formosa should not be cast adrift. Formosa and Australia are almost identical in population, and Australia can hardly see as many people as she herself houses suddenly handed over to Communist domination, regardless of what may be thought of Chiang or Nationalist rule. But in essence there has always been a strategic value assigned to Formosa. As the Prime Minister summarized the picture, "The strategic position of Formosa is such that it is a portion of an island chain, the southern extremity of which is Australia, along which defeat and danger travelled [*via* Japan] only a few years ago, and which today represents a great barrier against a new Communist aggression in a great war." [48] The Government's evaluation of the importance of not allowing China to take over Formosa has been widely shared and welcomed among Australian commentators, regardless of differences over other aspects of the Nationalist problem.[49] It has frequently been echoed in Parliament, mostly by Government supporters but with at least the tacit backing of the Opposition.[50]

Beyond this area of near unanimity, however, Austral-

[48] Statement of March 25, 1955, in *CNIA,* Vol. 26 (March 1955), p. 203. For other official comments on the status and importance of Formosa, see Menzies, *CPD,* HR 6, April 20, 1955, p. 48; Governor-General's address to Parliament, *ibid.,* HR 2, November 10, 1953, p. 21; various statements by Casey, esp. December 31, 1954 (with special reference to the U.S.-Nationalist treaty), in *CNIA,* Vol. 25 (December 1954), p. 858; October 6, 1958, in *ibid.,* Vol. 29 (October 1958), p. 660; October 25, 1958, in *ibid.,* p. 669.

[49] For instance, *SMH,* January 26, 1955; Denis Warner in Melbourne *Herald,* February 18, 1955; *News Weekly,* February 9, 1955, September 10, 1958, and March 8, 1961; A. J. Rose, "Strategic Geography and the Northern Approaches," *Australian Outlook,* Vol. 13 (December 1959), p. 308.

[50] Representative comments: Bruce Wight, *CPD,* HR 4, August 17, 1954, p. 335; John Gorton, *CPD,* S 4, September 16, 1954, p. 375; Edmund Maher, *ibid.,* S 19, April 13, 1961, p. 495.

ian opinion on the problem of the Nationalist territories has had to grapple with such vexing questions as the assessment of the offshore islands, the validity of American, Nationalist, and Australian maneuvers, and the types of commitments which should or should not be laid down. Although there have been many variations on this theme, there has been a strong indication of a definite turning-away from policies that aggravate the already tense situation in the area, so that neither China nor the Nationalists and their friends and allies would contribute toward open warfare, the danger of enlarging the dispute into a general war, or the peaceful working out of the future disposition of the Nationalist territories. Officially and publicly, the Australian Government has made its own estimate of the offshore islands quite unmistakable. Time and again, when speaking of Formosa and the Pescadores as being distinct from China proper, it has studiously failed to include the offshore islands. When it has mentioned the islands, it has taken care to distinguish between them and Formosa, with the inescapable conclusion that juridically it regards them as *part of China* and, regardless of their legal attributes, has dismissed them as not "worth another great war" [51] and not in themselves constituting a "worthy casus belli." [52]

The direct, unavoidable next question has been what should be done so as to prevent the offshore islands from becoming an irritant and the possible precipitant of a general conflict. The press and other critics in Australia have pulled very few punches in this regard. They have never condoned the Communist shellings of the islands, nor indeed the dogmatic, threat-laden fashion in which China has demanded their return. In plain language, however, they have viewed the Nationalist position as stubborn and

[51] Menzies, statement of February 9, 1955, in *SMH,* February 10, 1955. Also see his statement of March 25, 1955, in *CNIA,* Vol. 26 (March 1955), p. 204.

[52] Casey, UN General Assembly, *Official Records,* Thirteenth Session, 759th Plenary Meeting, September 25, 1958, p. 157.

provocative, calculated to assure neither peace in the area nor friendship for the Nationalists, while American policy has been seen as vacillating, overweeningly acquiescent toward the Nationalists, and guilty of having lost precious opportunities. "It seems important for us Australians to remember that American power in the Pacific does not, in itself, give Australia security," Professor William Macmahon Ball has written. "Everything depends on how the power is used." [53]

In the first instance, there was and continues to be doubt in Australia as to what American intentions about protecting the offshore islands might be. The 1954 treaty with the Nationalists pledged U.S. support only to Formosa and the Pescadores, but provided in Article VI that assistance would be accorded "to such other territories as may be determined by mutual agreement." [54] The subsequent Congressional resolution, which authorized the President to employ American forces in compliance with the treaty, again made specific reference to Formosa and the Pescadores, but included the proviso that the authority was "to include the securing and protection of such related positions and territories of that area now in friendly hands and the taking of such other measures as he [the President] judges to be required or appropriate in assuring the defense of Formosa and the Pescadores." [55] The consistent American interpretation of these clauses has been that the one and only obligation is toward Formosa and the Pescadores, but that when and if the Chinese tried to force their way into the offshore islands, Washington would be free to defend them if it thought such an attack was a prelude to an invasion effort against the formally

[53] W. Macmahon Ball, "Observations on Britain's Attitude to Asia," *Australia's Neighbours,* 3rd Series, no. 60 (February 1956), p. 2.

[54] The treaty's text is reproduced in *CNIA,* Vol. 25 (December 1954), pp. 859–860.

[55] For text, see *ibid.,* Vol. 26 (January 1955), pp. 55–56.

protected territories.[56] There have been, of course, the attached disclaimers about resort to force as a means of seeking solutions, but what has disturbed Australian opinion has been that the U.S., in the last resort, has the choice of determining when and if an attack on the offshore islands is a threat to Formosa. Surely the Communists would not painstakingly announce in advance that any strike against the islands was a limited operation, with no aggressive designs against Formosa. During various phases of the crises, Washington seemed to be fluctuating on just how quickly it would react if the islands were under siege, and there has always been the nagging danger that the reaction would include nuclear weapons—"massive and instant retaliation"—in the phraseology of Dulles. In one shape or form, Australian reaction during the crises were summarized by the Sydney *Daily Telegraph's* comment that "If the game of brinkmanship has to be played (and it is deplorable that it should be played at all) it should at least be played for tangible stakes affecting the interests of the free nations of the world. It would be tragic for the whole human race if it were played for such peanuts as these rocky and worthless outcrops." [57]

But if Australia was disturbed by the ambiguities of American policy about assisting in the defense of the offshore islands, she was dismayed by the Nationalists' own truculence and ability to get away with thrusting America and ultimately the rest of the world into compromising postures. The evacuation of the Tachen Islands in February of 1955, it was believed, had been an instance of

[56] For instance, Eisenhower's message to Congress of January 24, 1955, in *NYT,* January 25, 1955, and letter to Senator Theodore Green, in *Department of State Bulletin,* Vol. 39 (October 20, 1958), p. 605; Dulles, statement of March 8, 1955, in *NYT,* March 9, 1955.

[57] Sydney *Daily Telegraph,* September 9, 1958. Also see, for example, Melbourne *Age,* February 18, 1955; *New South Wales Countryman* (Sydney), March 1955; *SMH,* September 8, 1958; Hobart *Mercury,* October 6, 1958.

successful disengagement, and a useful precedent for reducing the Nationalist garrisons on other islands and eventual total withdrawal to Formosa. But in the three years which separated the two major offshore island crises, there was no removal of Nationalist garrisons from the Quemoy or Matsu complexes. Dulles admitted in 1958 that his Government had felt it unwise for the Nationalists to make a major military investment on the islands. Nonetheless, "In view . . . of the very strong views of the Republic of China, we were acquiescent in that. We did not attempt to veto it . . . after having used persuasion."[58] In fact, by the high point of the 1958 crisis, although repeating the absence of a formal U.S. commitment to the offshore islands, Dulles seemed to dismiss the argument that the islands were indefensible; so was Berlin, he continued. On the islands, as in Berlin, both moral and material factors operated, "So the United States is assisting the Chinese Nationalists logistically in their gallant and inspiring defense of these off-shore positions."[59] Meanwhile, ranking Nationalist officials were saying openly that they had no intention whatsoever of renouncing the use of force to regain the mainland and would alone decide the circumstances of their actions, that they would not reduce their "self-defense" garrisons on the islands, and that any hesitancy by America to lend outright pledges to defend the islands must be the result of "Communist propaganda" to blind world opinion.[60]

Australian opinion, which in 1954–55 had hoped that a pause in the fighting might create a climate in which the Nationalist garrisons could be pulled out, the islands

[58] Statement of September 30, 1958, in *Department of State Bulletin,* Vol. 39 (October 20, 1958), p. 600.

[59] Statement of September 25, 1958, in *ibid.,* Vol. 39 (October 13, 1958), p. 465.

[60] See announced agreement between Chiang and Vice-President Cheng, and statement of Ambassador to U.S. Yeh, as reported in *NYT,* September 30 and October 28, 1958, respectively.

abandoned directly or by some *quid pro quo* negotiation, was appalled by what was happening. Between the two crises Chinese and American representatives had discussed common problems at Geneva and then Warsaw, but the U.S. had refused to bargain for any Nationalist-controlled territory, while the Chinese had refused to countenance any renunciation of force toward any of the territories while America's military presence and guarantees were maintained. With negotiations stalemated the U.S., the patron, was being dictated to by the client—the Nationalists. The tail was wagging the dog, and the dog did little but utter a few squeaks of protest. The continuing Nationalist presence on the islands was a provocation to China, a threat to the peace, regardless of who shot first. American professions of peaceful intent were therefore suspect, and Nationalist attempts to involve the world in the morass of a war with China despicable.[61] Anger in Australia with both nations was only compounded when other U.S. and Nationalist behavior clashed with Australian interests at about this same time. Late in September of 1958, the U.S. imposed restrictions on the import of Australian lead and zinc. The reaction was immediately hostile, and at least one paper felt that Eisenhower's action was "astounding" at a time when the U.S. was seeking the support of its friends on its China policy.[62] The "fire-eaters of Taipei," on their part, were scored for allowing arms to be shipped and flights made from their soil to assist the anti-Government, anti-Javanese rebel forces in Indonesia—a country whose stability and freedom from external intervention have been of central concern in Australia for a long time.[63]

[61] For instance, Melbourne *Herald,* August 29, 1958, and Denis Warner in *ibid.,* October 4, 1958; *SMH,* September 10 and 22, 1958; Melbourne *Age,* October 1, 1958.

[62] *SMH,* September 25, 1958.

[63] *Ibid.,* April 3, 1958, and Frederick Howard in Melbourne *Herald,* May 10, 1958.

All told, therefore, it is not surprising that Australian opinion preached not only calm and disengagement over the offshore islands, but importuned the Government at home to do all in its power to prevent ensnarement for Australia. In 1955 the offshore island question had been brought before the UN Security Council, but the Chinese refused an invitation to attend and no action resulted. In 1958, the subject was not formally raised at the UN at all. Consequently, the diplomacy of the offshore islands needed to be conducted by other than collective means. Heart could be taken from the example set by Australia's closest Commonwealth associates. Both the British [64] and Canadian [65] Governments consistently maintained that they held no obligations to assist in the defense of the islands, that the islands belonged to China, and that the future of a neutralized Formosa, disencumbered of the island outposts, should be settled as soon as practical. To be sure, neither Britain nor Canada were vulnerable Pacific countries, dependent on American support and tied to the U.S. through ANZUS. Yet New Zealand did fall into this category, and under both National and Labor Governments she publicly spoke of having "no intention of entering into any sort of commitment involving New Zealand in developments around Formosa," and otherwise spoke of China's ownership of the offshore islands and of a long-term solution of an independent Formosa.[66] It was

[64] For instance, Eden, *UKPD,* HC, Vol. 538, March 8, 1955, cols. 160–161, and Macmillan, Vol. 594, October 28, 1958, col. 36.

[65] Pearson, *Canadian Parliamentary Debates,* HC, Session 1955, Vol. 1, January 25, 1955, pp. 498–499; Vol. 3, March 24 and April 21, 1955, pp. 2341–2343 and 3061–3063, respectively; Pearson's report to the Parliamentary Standing Committee on External Affairs, in *External Affairs* (Canada), Vol. 8 (August 1956), p. 245.

[66] T. L. Macdonald, Minister for External Affairs, statement of January 27, 1955, in *EAR* (NZ), Vol. 5 (January–February 1955), pp. 8–10. Also see Macdonald, *NZPD,* Vol. 305, March 29, 1955, pp. 56–58; Prime Minister Holland, *ibid.,* March 24, 1955, pp.

New Zealand, in 1955, who assumed the initiative in carrying the offshore island dispute before the UN Security Council, and helped to persuade a reluctant America that Chinese representatives should be invited to the discussions.

The Australian press was almost unanimous in it expression of the hope that the U.S. could be steered into a more temperate position, and that Australia, together with her Commonwealth allies, could find an escape hatch leading out of the offshore island imbroglio, since "Australia did not join the United States in contracting a treaty of mutual defence with the Formosa Government." [67] All this was coupled with a now typical Australian pattern of playing the game unobtrusively. ANZUS obligations moved both ways, and if there were an overzealous Australian demonstration over the offshore islands, vital Australian interests might suffer in any new crisis that might arise. At all events, whatever America's mistakes and fumblings on the matter, open carping against her would tend to break up rather than cement the Western alliance and perhaps detract from America's bargaining stature with the Communists.[68]

This exposition of Australian public appraisal of the offshore island crises has been given at rather considerable length because the Government's own perceptions were not materially different. A hasty examination of bits and pieces of the Government's pronouncements on the offshore islands can leave a misleading impression. For instance, both in the 1955 and 1958 periods of stress, Menzies and Casey *praised* the U.S. for standing firm re-

---

14–16 and Vol. 309, August 7, 1956, p. 889; Prime Minister Nash, Vol. 318, September 11, 1958, p. 1721.

[67] Brisbane *Courier-Mail,* September 2, 1958. Also see Sydney *Sun,* September 11, 1958, and *Sydney Sun-Herald,* September 14, 1958.

[68] Melbourne *Age,* September 17, 1958; *SMH,* September 18, 1958; *Sydney Sun-Herald,* October 5, 1958.

specting these islands, since giving way under pressure to the Communists could have led to further applications of force and the demoralization of various peoples in the region.[69] Then again, in September of 1958, Casey and Menzies made seemingly contradictory statements: Casey said in Washington that the U.S. and Australian views on the offshore islands were "quite close"; [70] Menzies, in Canberra, said that Australia had "no specific policy" on the subject.[71] It would be a mistake, however, to read these statements literally, interpreting them as a policy of least resistance, of following the leader no matter where the leader happened to be stumbling. Under questioning in the House, Philip McBride, then the Acting Minister for External Affairs, explained that Casey's allusion to a closeness of views with America referred to the concern of both Governments that there should be no resort to force in any territorial dispute in the Formosa Straits.[72] This intepretation of Casey's words not only served to equate Australia with nearly every other Government's noble wish for nonviolence, but by its failure to associate Australia with specific American policies about the garrisoning and retention of the offshore islands turned the remark almost wholly around. Menzies himself undertook to explain his "no policy" observation. His critics were quoting him out of context, he insisted, for "no specific policy" had meant that he had *no comment* to make to a question on whether Australia favored the retention of the islands by the Nationalists. He then immediately proceeded to advise the House, at much length, that while

[69] Menzies, *CPD,* HR 6, April 20, 1955, p. 48; Casey, statement of October 25, 1958, in *CNIA,* Vol. 29 (October 1958), p. 669, and "Australia's Relations with the United States," article provided for UPI for world release, November 28, 1958, in *ibid.,* (November 1958), p. 766.

[70] Statement of September 9, 1958, in *SMH,* September 11, 1958.

[71] Statement of September 10, 1958, in *ibid.*

[72] *CPD,* HR 21, September 16, 1958, p. 1229.

there had been differences among friendly Governments on this point,and he had worked long and hard at explaining the Australian position in Washington and elsewhere, it was best not to provoke open debate on sensitive topics.[73] The inference again was that Australian and American policies had points of divergence, and that Australia, rather than being silent, had set herself the task of redirecting American policy.

And what of statements seemingly agreeing that the offshore islands should not be abandoned? What Menzies and Casey had said, with methodical phrasing, was that the islands should not in the very midst of the emergency be evacuated lock, stock, and barrel. One moves closer to the basis of the Government's attitude by studying Casey's remarks of January 25 and February 15, 1955, the specific dates being important insofar as they spanned the Cabinet meeting of January 28, which devoted its attention to the crisis. In the first statement, Casey's words were quite plain: "we are not committed in any way to assist the United States in any military action it might undertake on any of these islands." [74] In his comment a few weeks later, he came as close as discretion permitted regarding the advisability of a Nationalist withdrawal: "if it is decided that other off-shore islands close to the Chinese coast should be evacuated in the same way as the Tachen Islands are at present being evacuated, then it is clear that American aid in such evacuations is not only no threat to mainland China, but will reduce the danger which the Chinese Communists seem to fear of an invasion of the mainland from Formosa." [75] The author feels that his own responsible sources of information confirm Australia's moderate conduct on the offshore islands. During the respective emergencies, Australian diplomacy

[73] *Ibid.*, September 18, 1958, pp. 1376–1377.
[74] Cited in *SMH*, January 26, 1955.
[75] Cited in *CNIA*, Vol. 26 (February 1955), p. 128.

worked for the reduction of Nationalist garrisons, because the islands were not viewed as necessary to the defense of Formosa and because heavy garrisoning represented a tinder-box type of harassment against China. During the three-year lull between crises, Australian diplomacy, for the same reasons, worked for a complete disengagement at an internationally suitable moment. When the second crisis arrived, and nothing had been done, Australia told Washington of its displeasure in no uncertain terms.

If further evidence that a moderate Australian position prevailed is required, the affair of W. S. (later Sir Wilfrid) Kent-Hughes can be mentioned. Early in 1955, at the peak of the first offshore island crisis, Kent-Hughes, then Minister for the Interior in the Menzies Government, undertook a tour of Asian countries to inspect Australian war graves in the area. He decided, however, to include Formosa on his itinerary. Although he ostensibly went there for a week's holiday, he was treated royally—a 19-gun salute, a personal welcome by the Acting Foreign Minister, etc. Later in February, while in Tokyo, he remarked that criticism of America's Formosa policy, especially in the British press, was "playing straight into the hands of Red China," and that a Korean-style cease-fire in the Formosa Straits, i.e. with the offshore islands passing to the Communists, would be a "colossal blunder" if discussed apart from China's "predatory programme" in Tibet, Korea, and South-East Asia.[76] Officially, the Government denied it was annoyed; privately, it was disgusted with Kent-Hughes' antics. No Australian minister had been to Formosa since the Nationalists took refuge there. Although Kent-Hughes went there on holiday, he still wore the trappings of a minister, and was therefore regarded as a representative of his Government, witness the booming guns and style of reception. It was bad enough

[76] Statement of February 20, 1955, in *SMH,* February 21, 1955. Also see *ibid.,* December 30, 1954.

that he had gone to Formosa without authority; it was worse that at a time when Australia was delicately working out a moderate offshore island policy, Kent-Hughes should deliver a statement which contradicted his Government's program. On his next stop, in Korea, Kent-Hughes was handed a note just dispatched from Canberra, telling him to cease and desist from further comment. Less than a year later, after the December 1955 general election in Australia, Kent-Hughes was unceremoniously dumped from the ministry. There were several factors involved in this decision, including a personal one, but a powerful reason was Kent-Hughes' embarrassment to his Government on China policy. The story of Kent-Hughes' dismissal has long been popular gossip in and around Canberra—most of what is said is absolutely true.

Although Australia's position *vis-à-vis* the offshore islands is clear enough to decipher, her commitment to the defense of Formosa cannot be established so readily. Here and again, comment has been made that through her ANZUS membership, Australia was and is committed to help a militarily involved America *both* on the offshore islands *and* Formosa.[77] Strictly speaking, ANZUS makes no discrimination between the offshore islands and Formosa and the Pescadores; all fall within the frame of the "Pacific" area where an attack on the armed forces of a signatory would be deemed grounds for joint action. As noted earlier, however, ANZUS does not impose any *automatic* obligation on a member to move his forces to the support of an attacked partner. Casey's statement of January 25 spoke of no Australian commitments in the offshore islands. This should probably be read not just that Australia had no prior pledge to assist in their de-

[77] For instance, Evatt, statement of January 26, 1955, in *ibid.*, January 27, 1955; J. R. Poynter, "Treaty Commitments," *Australia's Neighbours,* Fourth Series, nos. 3–4 (March–April 1963), p. 2.

fense, but also that in case of future fighting, even with America involved, she would react as the situation required—and probably not act at all. In other words, respecting the offshore islands, the Government found it possible, despite the bond with ANZUS, to dissociate itself. If it felt *legally* comfortable in adopting this attitude concerning the offshore islands, there was no less reason for feeling competent to do the same as far as Formosa was concerned.

Whether it actually did so is speculative. Professor Harper, again on the basis of private information, has written that after the U.S.-Nationalist treaty was concluded, Australia in effect made a gloss on the ANZUS pact, as New Zealand did, dissociating herself from any obligations on Formosa.[78] She surely would have preferred not to become involved, if that were feasible. But she also quite unmistakably, as has been shown, believed that Formosa should not be awarded to the Communists. The superior strength of the American Seventh Fleet could easily handle any Communist drive across the Straits, and the assistance of Australian air and naval units would have been token and in no way decisive. Ground forces, unlike in Korea, would not have been required apart from Nationalist China's own sizeable establishment. It is doubtful if in that set of circumstances the U.S. would ask a friendly but minor power such as Australia to contribute materially—contrasted with diplomatically—to the defense of Formosa and the Pescadores. The question of Australian military assistance would therefore not arise, and perhaps this was understood by both America and Australia at the time and thereafter. This in itself could be defined as a "gloss" on ANZUS, but it would be of a different sort than Harper appears to have in mind, and would entail not a

[78] Harper, "Australia and the United States," pp. 187 and 210 in the 1950–1955 and 1956–1960 volumes, respectively, of *Australia in World Affairs.*

unilateral but a joint Austral-American understanding—which if true was surely also extended to New Zealand, the third ANZUS member, whose resources fall short even of Australia's. The escalation of a conflict over Formosa into a general war would, of course, pull in Australia as well as most non-ANZUS nations.[79]

The position in the offshore island area has not materially changed since the last full crisis of 1958. China continues to assert that all Nationalist territories are rightfully hers, while the offshore islands, though subjected to intermittent shelling, continue to absorb large numbers of Nationalist forces. The Nationalists launch their own raids from time to time, using the coastal islands as springboards and refusing to renounce their reconquest dream. So far as most Australian opinion is concerned, this is not at all a happy predicament. The offshore islands continue to be denounced as strategically worthless and a provocation to China. America's lack of spine in not compelling a disengagement on the islands while there is comparative calm in the region is deplored, as is her reluctance to gag bellicose Nationalist pronouncements and activities. Australia, after all, cannot opt out of living on the flank of an aroused China.[80] An illustration of Australian perturba-

[79] For some brief speculations on Australia's commitments, see Julius Stone, "Problems of Australian Foreign Policy, January–June 1955," *Australian Journal of Politics and History,* Vol. 1 (November 1955), pp. 14–16; J. G. Starke, "Security in the Pacific," in London Institute of World Affairs, *Year Book of World Affairs 1956* (London: Stevens and Sons for the LIWA, 1956), pp. 120–121; Alexander, *op. cit.,* p. 18; Melbourne *Age,* August 15, 1955.

[80] Denis Warner in Melbourne *Herald,* August 26 and 29, 1959, and *ibid.,* August 27, 1960; *Sydney Sun-Herald,* October 4, 1959, and May 29, 1960; *Nation* (Sydney), October 10, 1959; Launceston *Examiner,* December 19, 1959; Hobart *Mercury,* June 28, 1962; *SMH,* July 25, 1962; James Monaghan (ALP), *CPD,* HR 36, October 3, 1962, p. 1120. For a recent defense of the maintenance of the Nationalists on the offshore islands, see Australia-Free China Association, New South Wales Branch, "China—Free or Red?" (Sydney: 1963), p. 10.

tion with both the Nationalists and America appeared in September of 1962, when a Nationalist U-2 reconnaissance aircraft was brought down over the mainland. The aircraft's presence was in itself reviled as provocative. What irritated Australian commentators even more, however, was that in 1960 the forcing down of an American U-2 over the Soviet Union had created an incident of world-reaching proportions. Although Eisenhower had cancelled further intelligence flights over Russia, now, two years later, the American authorities either were indifferent to or perhaps even encouraged comparable sorties over China. How, it was asked, could there be a détente in the East, in the face of such heavy-handed behavior by America and her Nationalist friends? [81]

The response of the Australian Government is somewhat more difficult to delineate than was possible for the 1955–58 period. There is every reason to believe that, by conviction, Australia continues to feel uneasy about the offshore islands and Nationalist activity in much the same way that unofficial comment has brought criticism to bear. The best assessment the author has been able to make is that for a time after the 1958 crisis, Australia continued to urge a disengagement policy on the U.S., obviously without success; it has been reported, however, that after the Kennedy Administration came to office, as part of a general scheme to improve relations with China, a group of advisers hoped to persuade the President to compel a Nationalist withdrawal from the islands and permit their transfer to the mainland.[82] Be that as it may, it would appear that Australian representations have subsided in recent years; perhaps because the prospect of budging America in the near future has come to be regarded as futile, perhaps because Australia has found it expedient to

[81] See Sydney *Telegraph*, *SMH*, and Melbourne *Herald*, all of September 11, 1962.

[82] Max Frankel in *NYT*, December 17, 1963.

conserve her diplomatic ammunition for other disputes of concern to her—such as the Indonesian claims to Dutch New Guinea, or Indonesia's Malaysian confrontation policy. There has been a measure of service-level contact between Australia and the Nationalist Chinese. In April of 1963 the Commander in Chief of the Nationalist Navy, Admiral Ni Yue-si, visited Australia for five days. In addition to touring various naval and air installations, his time in Canberra was spent as guest of the Australian Chief of Naval Staff, and calls were paid on the Chairman of the Chiefs of Staff Committee and the Minister for the Navy. Upon arriving in Sydney, Admiral Ni expressed the hope that some Nationalist naval officers could be trained in Australia, and that the subject would be raised with Australian officials.[83] Although Australia formally welcomed this ranking Chinese Nationalist officer to her shores, she did not forget the many political connotations which attach to her thinking on Formosa and the offshore islands. Now, almost two years after Ni's visit, absolutely nothing had been done to accept Nationalist naval cadets into the country.

## THE MALAYAN TROOP COMMITMENT

IF AUSTRALIAN diplomatic activity respecting the Indo-Chinese and offshore island crises was evidence of her wish to contain the spread of fighting with China and to create an atmosphere conducive to working toward a long-term thaw in Asia, her decision to station troops in Malaya, like her eagerness to create SEATO, represented the reverse side of the coin—the wish to devise a concrete deterrent posture. On April 1, 1955, Prime Minister Menzies announced that his Government was committing naval and additional air units to Malaya, as well as a battalion of infantry with supporting arms. The Australian

[83] Statement of April 21, 1963, in *SMH,* April 22, 1963. Also see *China News* (Canberra), May 7, 1963.

presence in Malaya was in part designed to assist in the prosecution of the counterinsurgency effort there. Also, however, the Australians were to join British and New Zealand forces as part of a Commonwealth Strategic Reserve which could serve as protection for Malaya-Singapore in the event of outright conflict there, or as a staging area from which forces could be moved to other trouble spots in South-East Asia as circumstances might warrant. For the moment, it is necessary to note that the Government made it entirely plain that this exceptional commitment—the first instance when Australian troops had ever been dispatched overseas in time of peace—was a reaction to China. Chinese meddling in Korea, Indo-China, and the offshore islands had followed one another in swift and disconcerting succession, and there was no indication that Peking would suddenly become more subdued. Malaya herself was strategically poised. Her survival as a viable political and economic enterprise, as well as the integrity of her frontiers, required protection. More broadly, her defense was required in the light of Australia's professed strategic doctrine of buffer-zone security, which was defined as lying in South-East Asia between China and Australia.[84] In part, then, the Malayan decision was an outgrowth of the immediate background of difficulties in Indo-China and to a smaller extent the offshore islands. But it also bore a relationship to SEATO, which by April had come into operation, and the position requires some clarification.

Early in August of 1954, when SEATO was already in

[84] See *CNIA*, Vol. 26 (April 1955), pp. 278–280. For further elaboration, see Menzies, *CPD*, HR 6, April 20, 1955, p. 49, and Casey, April 27, 1955, pp. 206ff. For comments supporting the connection between the troop decision and Chinese intentions, see Robert Wordsworth, *CPD*, S 5, April 28, 1955, p. 111, and Alexander Downer, HR 6, May 5, 1955, p. 483; *SMH*, September 23, 1955; Perth *West Australian*, December 1, 1955; Adelaide *News*, April 25, 1956.

preparation but its details had yet to be settled, Menzies stated the principle that Australia was prepared to join other countries in the defense of South-East Asia, and that he was not excluding the possibility that a troop commitment would be carried out under SEATO's aegis.[85] But, as it has been correctly stated, "The dramatic Menzies bid, committing Australian troops in advance of the signature of the treaty . . . failed to pin down the United States to a firm military agreement at Manila." [86] It is not completely clear from the public record, commentaries, and the author's own investigations precisely what sort of stronger military planning or troop earmarking provisions Australia was interested in securing from SEATO, but it is obvious that the Manila terms fell short of her expectations.[87] When the SEATO powers met in February of 1955 to lay the organizational framework of the alliance, no advance was made on the earlier position. Dulles had already made it completely evident that it would be pointless for America and her allies to maintain standing forces at all danger zones in Asia. The chopping up and segregation of forces "would mean real strength nowhere and bankruptcy everywhere. Therefore, we [the U.S.] are relying in most of the world primarily upon the deterrent [and mobile] striking power as an effective defence." [88] Casey's public comments on the subject, both before and after the Bangkok conference, seemed comfortably fitted to the Dulles position. First he expressed the obvious when he observed that a combined SEATO force could not be expected to be formed and sent to police the treaty

[85] *CPD,* HR 4, August 5, 1954, p. 66, and statement of August 6, 1954, in *SMH,* August 7, 1954.

[86] Harper, "Australia and the United States," 1950–1955 volume, p. 184.

[87] *NYT,* September 3 and 6, 1954; *Sydney Sun-Herald,* October 3, 1954; Webb, "Australia and SEATO," p. 66.

[88] Statement of December 21, 1954, in *CNIA,* Vol. 25 (December 1954), p. 862. Also see his Bangkok press release of February 23, 1955, in *ibid.,* Vol. 26 (February 1955), p. 21.

area for "the conditions do not at present exist which would make [this] possible or acceptable to the majority of the signatories." [89] When Bangkok had concluded, he sounded like an echo from the Secretary of State's speech-writer's office—the extensive stretch of South-East Asian territory would be almost impossible to garrison since, wherever forces were stationed, "the other side could avoid them and get through somewhere else. Better to rely on mobile allied power which could be applied at any threatened point." [90]

Less than a month later Menzies announced the Australian troop commitment to Malaya, which in effect was a contradiction of Dulles' and Casey's appraisals of the folly of scattering allied forces in South-East Asia in bits and pieces. Furthermore, while SEATO at large had created no standing forces of its own, Menzies was most emphatic in defending his Government's contribution to Malayan defense as a contribution to a very important portion of the Manila treaty area, and an "integral part of the defensive effort within the structure of the Manila Treaty. They are not to be regarded as exclusive matters. They are not to be treated as some evidence that the defence of Malaya is important, but that the defence of a country like Thailand is not. But unless we achieve strength somewhere while we can, we may end up by having inadequate strength everywhere." [91] To resolve these inconsistencies makes it possible to appreciate better Australia's security thinking, and her attitude toward the Chinese problem especially.

The primary element to be kept firmly in mind is that Australia's original desire for a stronger SEATO and her eventual commitment in Malaya were prompted by her definition of Communist China's presence and intentions in the area, and the rest follows. Dulles' strategic evalua-

[89] Statement of February 7, 1955, in *ibid.*, p. 118.
[90] Broadcast of March 10, 1955, in *ibid.*, (March 1955), p. 197.
[91] *CPD*, HR 6, April 20, 1955, p. 51.

tion and opposition to a SEATO standing force was put down before Manila, then at Bangkok, and affirmed resolutely afterward. It would have been senseless for Australia to beat her head against this wall for two reasons. For one, without U.S. support SEATO could never undertake a decision of this magnitude. For another, constant Australian nagging, in addition to achieving nothing positive, could in fact, in the circumstances attending the times, have produced negative results. Late 1954 and early 1955 was the peak period of the first offshore island crisis, and Australia was devoting her talents to toning down America. It must be restressed that sensible analysis in Canberra would have suggested that Australia carried only so much weight and influence with Washington, and that in needing to be selective in her representations it was far more judicious to press on the offshore islands alone than on both the offshore islands *and* on the probably fruitless point of a stronger SEATO. It is probably in this light that Casey's acquiescent remarks should be interpreted. The conclusion is inferential, but the inference seems to fit and make sense in the context of earlier discussion.

In late 1954 and early 1955, before the Bangkok meetings, Australia, Britain, and New Zealand took various political and service-level opportunities to plan for a joint Strategic Reserve commitment in Malaya, hopefully with SEATO's benediction. Casey was reported to have sounded out Dulles at Bangkok on the degree to which the U.S. was prepared to give assurances of air and naval support if Australia assumed a major defensive responsibility in Malaya,[92] and Menzies undertook a similar task during his visit to Washington in March.[93] Australia managed to

[92] *SMH,* February 26, 1955.

[93] *Ibid.,* March 16–19, 1955, and Guy Harriott in *ibid.,* March 14, 1955. For comments on the earlier Australian-New Zealand-British conversations, see *ibid.,* November 16 and 18, 1954, and January 27, 1955.

receive American endorsement for her commitment as an action of cooperation implicit in SEATO, and SEATO itself approved it in the same way.[94] All this preparation, plus the search for American and SEATO backing, served a purpose. For Australia, South-East Asia was *the* area of unrest and potential Chinese encroachment, direct or indirect, which threatened Australian interests. Malaya was a key segment of this area, and one where Commonwealth forces could conveniently be located. The American definition of the futility of scattering forces may have suited the U.S., but not Australia, who was not nearly as powerful in mobile and retaliatory capacity as her great Pacific ally.

Still, the question remains why Australia felt she required explicit American endorsement for her commitment, and why she emphasized the SEATO connection with the Strategic Reserve. The answer seems to lie in two places. First, while neither SEATO as such nor the U.S. in particular joined the combined Australian-New Zealand-British forces, in Malaya or elsewhere, gaining an admission in Washington and at SEATO headquarters in Bangkok that Australia was proceeding wisely and in consonance with SEATO's purpose was an indirect, somewhat back-door maneuver to loosen the Dulles strategic concept. In future, at time and place unspecified, the Strategic Reserve might be able to move to a South-East Asian brush fire with greater confidence and expectation of assistance from its members' SEATO partners, especially the U.S. A second and related explanation can also be found. America had preached intervention in Indo-China and was now rather tolerant of the Nationalist position on the offshore islands. From time to time Dulles had spoken of massive retaliation against the Chinese enemy and had brandished his country's nuclear arsenal. It is reasonable to infer that, for Australia, to the extent

[94] See Menzies, *CPD*, HR 6, April 20, 1955, p. 50.

that the Strategic Reserve represented an array of forces which could deal with outbreaks on a limited and contained basis, and could possibly engage SEATO's *collective* diplomatic or military support for such a venture, to that degree the risk of a massive strike by the U.S. might be reduced. When unscrambled, therefore, Australia's Malayan commitment, and the manner in which she went about enlisting support for it, reflected both an attempt to deter and deal with Chinese intrusion *and* to reduce the contingencies in which such intrusions might unnecessarily be expanded to dangerous proportions.[95]

The Government's handling of the troop commitment did, to be sure, leave something to be desired. The exact nature and purpose of the troops was fully defined only in the course of time, not immediately. The decision was announced shortly before elections were to be conducted in politically volatile Singapore. The Labor Opposition in Parliament opposed the commitment in full stride. There were accusations that the troops might be a sinister cover for an expedition to defend the Nationalist offshore islands.[96] There were accusations that Australian troops in Malaya would encourage rather than subdue strife, since no true settlement with the terrorists could be reached save by negotiation and conciliation and in keeping with the high principles of the UN Charter.[97] There were accusations that Australian troops would only serve to prop up British colonialism, delay Malayan independence, and abet the subjugation which had long been im-

[95] For some general discussions of the Malayan commitment, see Albinski, *op. cit.*, pp. 433–446; Levi, *op. cit.*, pp. 190–194; Watt, *op. cit.*, pp. 49–52; Fitzgerald, "Australia and Asia," pp. 238–240.

[96] Henry Bruce, *CPD,* HR 6, April 28, 1955, pp. 285ff, and Norman Makin, May 4, 1955, p. 408.

[97] Evatt's statements of March 20, April 1, May 17, June 16, June 26, and November 9, 1955, in *SMH,* March 21, April 2, May 18, June 17, June 27, and November 10, 1955, respectively; Sidney O'Flaherty, *CPD,* S 5, April 27, 1955, p. 69.

posed on the country by "the interests of Chinese millionaire merchants, British exporters, and the wealthy owners of tin mines and rubber plantations." [98] There was criticism that the troops were provocative, for China or other Asian states might be tempted to allocate troops wherever they could throughout the region.[99] Lastly and fundamentally, there was the objection that the troop commitment made strategic nonsense: if China or some other major power such as Japan or Russia chose to strike in force, with Australia as an eventual target, the troops in Malaya would be outflanked and bypassed, left out on a limb, as it were, while a defenseless Australia waited for the enemy's unhindered arrival.[100]

### THE LABOR PARTY SPLIT AND THE HOBART CONFERENCE

THESE were strangely pungent words from a Labor Party which had only recently been so careful to cultivate a conservative image, to ingratiate itself with the right-wing elements whose support it coveted. The truth of the matter was that the Labor Party of early 1955 had become something other than the Labor Party of 1952, 1953, and early 1954. It was now an internally convulsed party, purging itself of much of its right-wing and stepping before the public with a fresh, very differently oriented foreign policy platform just approved at the most controversial Federal conference in its history.

No systematic attempt can be made in this work to review and unravel the events which split the ALP in 1954–55. In essence, however, what is clear is that as of the Federal election of May 1954 and onward, there was increasing alienation between Evatt and a number of right-

[98] Clyde Cameron, *ibid.*, HR 8, September 29, 1955, pp. 1129–1130; Justin O'Byrne, *ibid.*, S 5, May 11, 1955, p. 330.

[99] Evatt, *ibid.*, HR 6, April 27, 1955, p. 201.

[100] Evatt, *ibid.*, pp. 200–201, and Nicholas McKenna, Senate Leader of the Opposition, *ibid.*, S 5, April 27, 1955, p. 55.

oriented, mostly Catholic, elements in the ALP and within the trade unions. By October of 1954 Evatt was denouncing the grouper element, originally constituted to rid the unions of Communists, as an ambitious force which wished to invade the Labor Party and to dominate its work. The lay Catholic "Movement" (later translated into the National Civic Council), its organ the *News Weekly,* and its head, B. A. Santamaria, were identified as moving spirits in this subversion, and some Victorian Parliamentarians were also linked with the alleged conspiracy by Evatt. In reply, the accused denied any complicity in trying to infiltrate or capture the Party, and turned on Evatt for his dramatic and compromising intervention in the controversy surrounding the defection of one Petrov, Soviet third secretary in Canberra, and the subsequent royal commission investigation into espionage in Australia. For good measure, they charged Evatt with deliberately raising a sectarian, anti-Catholic bogey to deflect attention away from his own misbehavior and shortcomings as Leader.[101]

Toward the turn of 1954–55, the Party seemed ready to burst at the seams. In the Parliamentary Labor Party, within the trade unions, around Australia generally, protagonists of one side or another began to recruit supporters. Evatt's own leadership was challenged in the Federal Parliamentary caucus, and the challenge just barely missed its mark. The Victorian Executive, saturated with right-wing and grouper-oriented men, was dissolved by order of the Federal Executive, again by the narrowest margin, and replaced by a "loyal" Executive. The Federal ALP conference, held at Hobart in March of 1955, again highlighted the Party's divisions, 17 out of the 36 delegates walking out over the disputed seating of the Vic-

[101] For an able summary of the events of 1954–55, see Tom Truman, *Catholic Action and Politics* (Melbourne: Georgian House, 1959), pp. 1–17.

torian delegation, there being one group representing the "bogus" and one the "loyal" Executive from that state. In the last resort, the remaining delegates, a bare quorum, wrote platform planks which banished industrial groups and expounded a new direction in foreign policy. The ensuing developments sealed the split. A number of ALP men voluntarily resigned from the Party, others were expelled. The Party's Victorian delegation to Parliament sliced itself in two, 7 of the 14 breaking off and eventually moving into a new, Anti-Communist Labor Party, later the Democratic Labor Party. The persisting Labor split has been a first-order tragedy for countless individuals, for the Labor Party, and for Australian political life at large. Various aspects of the problem will be introduced and appraised in later contexts, but it is now necessary to return to the China problem aspects of the 1954–55 ALP disorders.

The truncated Hobart conference, *inter alia,* pronounced against the stationing of Australian troops in Malaya and in favor of rapid admission of Communist China into the UN, China's seating being coupled with the need to include a number of then-excluded states and explained simply in terms of the desirability of universal membership in that organization.[102] In May the Federal Executive of the Australian Council of Trade Unions, the largest collection of trade unions in Australia and the ALP's organizational and financial backbone, considered the Hobart decisions. Some delegates held reservations, but in the end only one member dissented, it being considered "advisable that there should be a common approach to international affairs by both the political and industrial wings of the [Labor] Movement."[103] In

[102] Australian Labor Party, *Official Report of Proceedings of the 21st Commonwealth Conference,* at Hobart, March 1955, pp. 52–53.

[103] Australian Council of Trade Unions, *Executive Report 1955,* p. 29.

September the Executive's recommendations were brought before the ACTU Congress in Melbourne. Emasculating amendments both on Malaya and China's UN seating were introduced by fledging DLP men representing the right-wing Clerks' union, but were defeated,[104] and the ACTU officially went on record as embracing the ALP's new foreign policy statement. Australian diplomatic recognition of China had not been explicitly mentioned in the Hobart platform—probably inadvertently, since the China-in-the-UN clause was widely assumed to imply the other, complementary policy step. In any case, at the ALP's next conference, held in Brisbane in 1957, the omission was corrected,[105] and for practical purposes Labor has been on record as advocating both recognition and UN seating of China since 1955.

While the 1954–55 tremors in the Party and the Hobart platform were not at bottom activated by a cleavage on foreign policy, such differences, especially over China, played some role in finally alienating one faction from the other. As has been noticed, the electoral campaign of May 1954 was a dreary performance on both sides, and the ALP gave no outward hint that it was departing from the conservative China policy it had been pursuing for over two years. By August of 1954, however, some months before the Hobart platform was written, Parliamentarians began to speak publicly on behalf of recognizing China and placing her in the UN.[106] The first reason for this appeared to be the rising alienation between the left and right wings of the Party, and the reluctance of those who favored a fresh approach to China to remain under wraps

[104] ACTU, *Congress Minutes 1955,* at Melbourne, September 1955, mimeo., p. 27. Also see report in *SMH,* September 10, 1955.

[105] ALP, *Official Report of Proceedings of the 22nd Commonwealth Conference,* at Brisbane, March 1957, pp. 94–95.

[106] For example, Donald Cameron, *CPD,* S 4, August 5, 1954, p. 49; E. G. Whitlam, HR 4, August 12, 1954, p. 275; and Clyde Cameron, August 24, 1954, p. 577.

indefinitely. More specifically, the Attlee-led British Labor Party delegation's visit to China imposed an additional strain on a Party already showing evidence of internal discomfort.

The delegation's trip was, strictly speaking, not Australia's concern, but in two ways it did involve her. In the first instance, the person chosen to accompany the delegation as its interpreter was Lord Lindsay, an Australian academician. Because he carried a British passport there was no official obstruction thrown in his way, but before he left for China, just as the Geneva conference had closed and SEATO was being mapped out, Lindsay expressed the view that any sensible Australian policy must be based on accurate rather than speculative accounts of China, implying that not only was the British delegation performing a useful service to Britain, but that Australia would need to reconsider her own policy.[107] The very fact of Lindsay's connection with the British delegation undoubtedly contributed to the agitation in right-wing Australian quarters about the trip in general. The Sydney *Daily Mirror* launched a scathing attack on Lindsay, writing that his "sorry adventure" was an "affront and most offensive to the great majority of the Australian people. . . . The suspicion exists that the Australian National University has been set up by the Australian taxpayer as a sort of home away from home for scholarly political dilettantes, and the Lord Lindsay affair will do little to dispel that suspicion." [108] S. M. Keon, who was later condemned by Evatt as one of the conspirators against the Party, described the Attlee mission as a "pilgrimage of shame to the masters of Red China." [109]

[107] Statement of July 30, 1954, in *SMH,* July 31, 1954. Also see *ibid.,* June 19, 1954.

[108] Sydney *Daily Mirror,* June 22, 1954. The paper already held a powerful animus against allegedly left-wing academicians. See its attack on Professor Fitzgerald's endorsement of Chinese recognition in its issue of May 11, 1954.

[109] Statement of July 4, 1954, in *SMH,* July 5, 1954.

But what really set the gears grinding was the Menzies Government's invitation to Attlee and his colleagues to visit Australia after their China tour. The *News Weekly* very nearly exploded over this "scandal." In June of 1954, as the result of contacts between Eden and Chou En-lai at Geneva, agreement had been reached between Britain and China to formalize diplomatic relations at long last, with accredited missions to be posted in Peking and London, and arrangements were also made to explore trade prospects between the two countries. While in China, the British Laborites met top Chinese officials, including Mao Tse-tung, who since the 1949 takeover had never previously granted an audience to Westerners. The British MP's organized a dinner party at the British Embassy, creating another precedent—Chinese officials had never before entered the compound. This concatenation of events alarmed the *News Weekly* because, it claimed, Attlee and his brainwashed crew would influence Australian policy on China. Indeed, the whole affair was a "masterstroke of political subtlety" by Menzies. The Government, according to the *News Weekly,* really wanted to recognize China and support a seat for her at the UN, but was afraid of the electoral damage which an ALP counterattack could inflict. Therefore, the Menzies Government was counting on the delegation's visit to Australia to jockey Australian Labor, the political kinsman of the British Labor Party, into a position favoring the same ends. If this were carried off, the Liberals could safely change their China policy, because Labor would have been politically neutralized.[110]

Early in September the British group arrived in Australia. On several occasions, including an address at a luncheon at which Parliamentarians of all parties were present, Attlee indicated that he did not feel China to be a threat to the West, and that her leaders, while mis-

[110] *News Weekly,* July 7, 14, and 21 and September 1 and 8, 1954.

guided, were genuine idealists who had cleaned up many of their country's perennial evils. Closer contacts with China would serve everyone well.[111] Two Australian Parliamentarians explicitly refused to attend the Attlee luncheon because of their disgust with Attlee's behavior in China and the ideas he was now disseminating. One was Jeff Bate, a New South Wales Liberal whose cardinal claim to prominence has been his consistently violent anti-Communism. The other was J. Mullens, Labor MHR from Victoria, another forthcoming Evatt target and defector to the Anti-Communist Labor Party. Keon attended under protest. Evatt's reaction to Mullens' and Keon's conduct was that they were entitled to their opinions, but as ALP Leader he praised Attlee fulsomely.[112] By then and subsequently, even before Hobart, Labor people were speaking up for recognition and a Chinese UN seat. After the Hobart conference, the *News Weekly* insisted that the Attlee trip had materially pushed the ALP into a definite "pro-China" stand which reflected itself in the new platform.[113]

Is there any validity in the *News Weekly's* allegations? The notion that the Menzies Government wanted to exploit the Attlee visit for purposes of reorienting its own China policy was transparent nonsense, as later discussion of the recognition question should demonstrate. Nevertheless, there is probably a segment, but only a segment, of truth in that part of the *News Weekly's* later allegation that Attlee's visit to Australia helped to influence ALP thinking on China. The author has heard several informed versions of who actually wrote the foreign policy planks which were adopted in the Hobart platform, and Evatt has been among those mentioned, but people of present ALP

[111] Statements of September 7 and 9, 1954, in *SMH*, September 8 and 10, 1954, respectively.

[112] *Ibid.*, September 10, 1954.

[113] *News Weekly*, May 4, 1955.

and DLP coloration who were involved in the events of 1954–1955 are uniformly agreed that Evatt fully endorsed these points. There is also not much doubt that as the 1952–1954 embrace with the right-wing wore on, it also wore thin, and more and more ALP personalities grew restless in observing a conservative China policy. Some of them broke their silence on Chinese recognition before Attlee's group came to Australia, but the combination of the closing down of the Indo-Chinese troubles, the marked improvement in Sino-British relations, and the soothing words of a respected British Labor Party colleague probably helped to nudge the ALP into informal and then official expression of a fresh China approach.

But there is also a case to be made out that the almost fanatical attack on Attlee and his beliefs by the right-wing may have been as influential as the substance of what Attlee did and said. The behavior of men such as Keon and Mullens and of the *News Weekly,* so blistering and derogatory to Attlee and any ALP association with him, may in fact have induced a counterreaction. The strain within the Party was already intense, and the charges respecting Attlee and China may have contributed to Evatt's final alienation from the right, his imputation of subversive conduct to it, and a final commitment to a shift in policy on external affairs. After the Hobart conference, Evatt said that the foreign policy items decided on there were an indication that "Labour has called the bluff of the small subversive clique within its ranks whose ideas on foreign policy are . . . inimical to Australia's chance of peaceful and independent survival in the Pacific." [114] It is an open question whether Evatt and others who came to accept the Hobart program would have tried to devise a comparable policy had there been no frictions in the Party, no impending split, no exit by the 17 delegates, most of whom would not have received a new platform

[114] Statement of March 20, 1955, in *SMH,* March 21, 1955.

with equanimity, whether they eventually wound up in the DLP or stayed in the parent party. The *News Weekly* had its own version of why, late in 1954, the Evatt group in the ALP was leaning toward an "appeasing" China policy: it was a cynical political tactic, "an attempt to place his [Evatt's] present fight on the basis of 'principle'; to create a divergence of opinion around a policy, irrespective of whether that policy was in the interests of Australia or not." [115] There was a double irony to the *News Weekly's* position. In the first place, it probably *assisted* in thrusting Evatt and his associates into a revised China policy. In the second place, once the ALP had officially clothed itself in a new China policy, it became an *advantage* for the Menzies Government to exploit the differences for political gain. It relished the appearance of an uncompromisingly anti-Chinese Communist DLP which pulled votes away from the Labor Party. In the last resort, the Government's own maneuverability on Chinese policy was therefore inhibited, not enlarged, as the *News Weekly* had otherwise predicted.

[115] *News Weekly,* October 27, 1954.

# V

# CHINA AND AUSTRALIAN SECURITY PROBLEMS: 2

"WE MUST accept, I believe, for the present that China constitutes the greatest threat to the security of the region in which we live. Indeed, there is no other major threat at this time." So spoke Sir Garfield Barwick, then Australia's External Affairs Minister, before the Australian Institute of Political Science in January of 1964.[1] The aim of the present chapter is to underscore Barwick's thesis by illustrating the pervasiveness of the Chinese factor in Australia's external relations, to show how the alliance system has been affected, and to point to the reappearance of this factor in the alternative security proposals which have recently been mooted in the country.

## AUSTRALIA, CHINA, AND WEST IRIAN

Perhaps Australia's outlook and policies *vis-à-vis* Indonesia offer the most striking example of how the China factor has increased its influence in Australian conceptions of security. In particular, the disputes over Dutch New Guinea (West Irian) and Malaysia tie into the picture. They are in themselves enormously complicated topics, but for present purposes the Chinese factor will be culled out of them. It is proper to recall that Indonesia holds a rather special relationship to Australia. She is Australia's

[1] Sir Garfield Barwick, "Australia's Foreign Relations," in John Wilkes, ed., *Australia's Defence and Foreign Policy* (Sydney, London, and Melbourne: Angus and Robertson for the AIPS, 1964), p. 22.

nearest neighbor, some 100 million strong, placed across the northern tier of Australia and constituting the geographic link with mainland South-East Asia. She has also undergone considerable domestic stress since gaining independence in 1949, and has often followed a foreign policy which has clashed with Australia's own defined interests. Naturally enough, Australian concern with Indonesia has been consistent and often agitated. For years Indonesia persisted in claiming for her own the Dutch-controlled western half of the island of New Guinea, whose status had not been settled by the original independence settlement, and it is this which sharpened Australian thinking on Indonesia considerably. Bilateral negotiations between Indonesia and the Dutch broke down, since each side declared its own right to sovereignty over the territory. Indonesian appeals to the UN between 1954 and 1957 failed to bring her satisfaction. Ultimately, her behavior became more strident, and in the early 'sixties actual sea and airborne operations against Dutch New Guinea began to be staged.[2]

Official and unofficial opinion in Australia found various legal, historical, administrative, and moral faults in the Indonesian claim, but at bottom the security element seemed paramount. There were voices, coming from assorted political and professional sectors, which increasingly denied the strategic preeminence of New Guinea, largely on grounds that intercontinental nuclear delivery systems had seriously reduced its buffer advantage to Australia and that, even without nuclear arms, a determined invader, should he seize Indonesia, could handily bypass

[2] For a general survey of Australian-Indonesian relations, see J. A. C. Mackie, "Australia and Indonesia, 1945–60," in Greenwood and Harper, *Australia in World Affairs 1956–1960,* pp. 272–326. For an account of Australia's behavior throughout most of the West Irian controversy, see Henry S. Albinski, "Australia and the Dutch New Guinea Dispute," *International Journal,* Vol. 16 (Autumn 1961), pp. 358–382.

New Guinea if he wished to enter Australia. Wild and undeveloped New Guinea did not, at any rate, offer an aggressor any comfortable facilities.[3]

Yet most of Australian opinion was wedded to the notion that even in a mid-twentieth century war, tangled as it might become in the exchange of missiles fired from hundreds if not thousands of miles away, it was prudent to deny to a potential aggressor all proximate bases and subversion sites. Some of this thinking was undoubtedly a residue from the days of World War II, when the Japanese established themselves on New Guinea and had no other land barrier between them and an open and largely undefended Australia. But with it was blended the feeling that a West New Guinea in friendly and responsible hands was a protective wall, both for the integrity of the eastern, Australian portion of the island and for metropolitan Australia as well. The conclusion reached by the great majority of Australians, with almost no distinctions on party lines, was that the island of New Guinea—all of it—was not yet obsolete as a protection for Australia, and the author understands that about 1959 this was the basis of an American military appraisal conveyed to Australia.[4]

[3] For some sample thinking, see Lt. General Sir Sydney Rowell, "Defence Problems Involved if Indonesia Takes Over," *SMH,* January 12, 1962; Edmund Maher (Country Party), *CPD,* S 14, February 25, 1959, p. 173, and Reginald Wright (Liberal), S 21, April 5, 1962, p. 831; Leslie Haylen (ALP), *CPD,* HR 31, April 27, 1961, p. 9.

[4] For a military appreciation, see the views of Generals K. W. Eather (Australia) and R. L. Eichelberger (U.S.), in *SMH,* February 20, 1959. For an academic appreciation, see John Andrews, "New Guinea and Australia's Defence and Foreign Policy," in Australian Institute of Political Science, *New Guinea and Australia* (Sydney, London, Melbourne, and Wellington: Angus and Robertson, 1958), esp. pp. 184–185. On the political side, see Menzies' statement in Washington of May 25, 1959, in *CNIA,* Vol. 30 (May 1959), pp. 269–270; Evatt, *CPD,* HR 22, February 24, 1959, p. 200, and Calwell, *ibid.,* p. 207; McKenna, S 14, February 25, 1959, pp. 169–170; George Cole (DLP Parliamentary Leader), *ibid.,* pp. 175–176.

In point of fact, what increasingly alarmed Australia about the abandonment of West New Guinea by the Dutch was not so much that a neutralist Indonesia would hold it, but that the Communists and especially Chinese Communists might become established there, as in the rest of Indonesia. Australia has taken grave—perhaps exaggerated—notice of the zig-zag course of Indonesian life. She has minutely debated the decline in economic viability, the revolts within the country, the suspension of normal political activity, the "Guided Democracy" experiment of President Sukarno, attempts on the President's life and, above all, the role of Communism there. She took notice of Communist Party (PKI) successes in the 1955 national elections and in the Javanese provincial elections of 1957. She noted the huge size of PKI membership in Indonesia and the high positions and respectability enjoyed by the Party as Sukarno performs his political trapeze act. The great Australian anxiety has been that Communism in Indonesia might either push the present non-Communist regime into reckless acts and/or overreliance on the Communist bloc, especially China, or that the Communists might some day achieve power themselves.[5]

Indonesia's actual relations with the Communist bloc, with emphasis on China, have not exactly been encouraging from Australia's standpoint. Tensions between Djakarta and Peking arising out of the status and treatment of the Chinese minority in Indonesia have been noted but the larger picture has been disquieting. There were reciprocal visits by high personages between Djakarta and Peking and Moscow. The Indonesians acquired large stocks of

[5] See Denis Warner in Melbourne *Herald,* October 8, 1955; Launceston *Examiner,* October 10, 1955; *News Weekly,* December 14, 1955; Adelaide *Advertiser,* March 6, 1956; Casey, *CPD,* HR 18, April 15, 1958, p. 871; Wilfrid Kent-Hughes, *ibid.,* HR 17, December 5, 1957, p. 2946; Denis Killen, *ibid.,* May 1, 1958, p. 1408; George Cole, "Joint DLP-QLP Policy Speech," at Melbourne, November 8, 1961, mimeo., p. 5.

modern military equipment from the Russians and in 1961 China, suffering economic dislocations of her own, granted credits. Chinese and Indonesian leaders exchanged pledges quite unsuited to Australia's interests—Djakarta was fully committed to promoting China's seating in the UN and the eventual regaining of Formosa, while China supported the Indonesian claim to Dutch New Guinea.[6] But Australians read these expressions as something more than amity recitations. As the West Irian dispute grew increasingly critical, Indonesian spokesmen intimated that the Communist powers stood prepared to back Djakarta by material as well as moral means.[7] In September of 1961, Kuo Mo-jo, the vice-chairman of the CPR, visited Indonesia. He remarked at the time that he favored Sukarno's proposal for a "Three A Group"—Asia, Africa, and Latin America as neutralist states—but that it would be even better if these three A's were expanded into four, so as to include Australia.[8] Australia understandably boggled at such Sino-Indonesian intimacy, which she saw as a drift by Djakarta into the arms of a China already well served by the large and active Communist element within the country.[9]

In addition to her disquiet over the strength of Indonesia's Communist movement and the convergent points of Indonesian and Chinese foreign policy, Australia held more specific apprehensions about what would come of all this. If Indonesia were to pass under Communist control,

[6] See Subandrio-Chen-yi joint communiqué in Peking, in *SMH*, October 12, 1959; Sukarno's statement in Peking, June 14, 1961, in *ibid.*, June 15, 1961.

[7] For example, Nasution, April 26, 1961, in *ibid.*, April 27, 1961; Indonesian Moscow-Peking mission delegate, June 24, 1961, in *Sydney Sun-Herald*, June 25, 1961; Sukarno, December 19, 1961, in *SMH*, December 20, 1961.

[8] See Melbourne *Age*, September 23, 1961.

[9] For typical reactions, see Adelaide *Advertiser*, December 16, 1957; Melbourne *Herald*, October 12, 1959; *SMH*, October 13, 1959.

with the Chinese being the principal beneficiaries, the strategic implications for Australia were forecast as disastrous. Malaya and Singapore, where Australian troops were stationed to safeguard South-East Asia and to supply defense in depth, would be outflanked and cut off, while SEATO itself would be compromised by the intrusion of a Communist government in such a crucial location.[10] B. A. Santamaria and the National Civic Council inflated the problem to even wider dimensions, warning that Communist and especially Chinese bases, including nuclear ones in time, would be put down in Indonesia and West New Guinea, ringing and neutralizing Australia according to Communism's laid-out plan for dominating the entire region.[11] The emphasis on the character of the danger flowing from the Communist prospects in Indonesia varied in Australia, to be sure, but without doubt a climate of real concern for Australia's safety was prevalent.

In theory, Australia would have preferred that the Dutch presence be maintained in West New Guinea for a suitable period and without any Indonesian duress, and that ultimately the Dutch and Australian portions of the island could undergo some parallel political evolution. But duress there was, and Indonesian flirtations with Communism were always at the surface of Australian reactions. What was to be done? Was it prudent to resist Indonesian claims to West Irian in the fullest and most uncompromising way? There was a sector of Australian opinion which concluded that strategic considerations *required* the territory to be transferred to Indonesia. The reasoning was that as the Indonesian campaign to retrieve Dutch New Guinea gained momentum, Djakarta was becoming increasingly dependent on Communist arms and diplomatic

[10] *Ibid.*, January 1, 1958; Denis Warner in Melbourne *Herald*, April 7, 1958; Perth *West Australian*, April 10, 1958.

[11] B. A. Santamaria, "Peace or War?" (Fitzroy, Victoria: NCC, 1958), pp. 6–8, and "New Guinea. The Price of Weakness," (Fitzroy, Victoria: Australian Catholic Publications, 1959), pp. 4–5; *News Weekly*, December 18, 1957.

support. Asian opinion of almost all persuasions, including SEATO members, supported Indonesia. At home, Sukarno's balancing act could be upset if he continued to threaten West Irian without actually taking over, since the PKI might then fill the political void left by his failure. Australia's first priorities lay in reducing Djakarta's ties with the Communist powers, in preserving SEATO and the goodwill and trust of Asian states both in and out of that organization, and in limiting the internal maneuverability of the PKI. Perhaps Indonesia feared China and Communism as much as Australia, but her hands were tied because of the deep involvement over West Irian. In sum, the territory might need be sacrificed in a higher cause: "New Guinea is strategically important to this country, but the friendship of Indonesia is a matter of life or death." [12]

What tipped the scales for Australia was the threat of war and lack of support for the Dutch by the U.S. in particular. There were words of caution in Australia that if Indonesia went to war over Dutch New Guinea she would so exhaust herself materially, and perhaps become so reliant on Communist assistance, that she would, willy-nilly, stumble into the arms of Communism.[13] But the fear of war itself was a nightmare. Indonesian spokesmen seemed to be saying that while they might need to rely on Communist support if war came, they did not welcome a war which could be disastrous to all concerned.[14] This was believable, for it raised the specter of a chain-reaction

[12] *Nation,* February 1, 1961. Also see *ibid.,* June 4, 1960; A. J. Rose in *ibid.,* January 31, 1959; Charles Meeking in Sydney *Sunday Mirror,* March 5, 1961; Peter Hastings in *Bulletin,* January 13, 1962; John McCallum (Liberal), *CPD,* S 14, February 18, 1959, pp. 74–75; and Charles Anderson (Country Party), *ibid.,* HR 22, February 19, 1959, p. 143.

[13] Kim Beazley, *ibid.,* HR 35, March 29, 1962, p. 1173, and Victor Vincent, *ibid.,* S 21, April 4, 1962, p. 805.

[14] Subandrio, statement in Canberra of February 11, 1959, in *SMH,* February 12, 1959; L. N. Palar, Ambassador to Canada, statement in Ottawa of January 9, 1962, in *ibid.,* January 10, 1962.

conflict—with the Chinese contributing "volunteers" to Indonesia, Australia, Britain, and America becoming involved, and a war of perhaps general proportions developing on Australia's doorstep. West New Guinea might be valuable but, like the Nationalist offshore islands, it was not worth a great war.[15] In any case, the Australian Government worked hard with London and Washington to dissuade Indonesia from taking over Dutch New Guinea, just as she tried to reason with Indonesia herself. But by late 1961 Canberra was beginning to realize that its "great and powerful friends" would not risk conflict, and that the territory would probably pass to Indonesian ownership. The author understands, for instance, that certain Australian journalists were privately called in by a minister, or ministers, and asked not to overdo the dispute before the public, since it was probably only a matter of time before the inevitable transfer would be effected. In any event, once the U.S. in particular had set its mind against over-antagonizing the Indonesians and subsequently promoted the Bunker plan, Australia could not demur. Even a new Australian enthusiasm for some form of international control over West New Guinea was now inapplicable.

What Australia counseled and was herself prepared to do at the crest of the crisis is illuminating. Arthur Calwell made some embarrassingly intemperate comments which by implication could be read as a call for Australia to resist Indonesian ambitions by arms if necessary,[16] but most Australians, including ALP supporters, could join in Menzies' sentiment that a war over Dutch New Guinea "would solve no problems, but would create animosities from which nobody except the Communist Powers would

[15] See Denis Warner in Melbourne *Herald,* July 11, 1961; Adelaide *News,* December 20, 1961; Ewen Mackinnon, *CPD,* HR 34, March 29, 1962, p. 1175; Reginald Wright, *ibid.,* S 21, April 5, 1962, p. 831; Malcolm Scott, *ibid.,* April 12, 1962, p. 980.

[16] Statement of February 9, 1962, in *SMH,* February 10, 1962; *CPD,* HR 34, March 29, 1962, pp. 1152ff.

profit. . . . No responsible Australian would wish to see any action affecting the safety of Australia on the issues of war and peace in this area except in concert with our great and powerful friends." [17] There actually were two separate notions in Menzies' comment. Australia and Holland could not have afforded to risk war with Indonesia. This was true first, because it would have isolated Australia as an enemy of Indonesia and ruined chances for future peaceful and cooperative living; second, because with only Australia and Holland to contend with, i.e. without the threat of American and/or British armed intervention, Indonesia might be inclined to request, and the Chinese to award, some form of external assistance. What is especially interesting—and the point is entirely authentic—is that Australia had asked the U.S. to warn Indonesia that if she persisted in applying force she would meet with physical resistance. Furthermore, Australia *was* prepared to join the U.S. in a shooting conflict with Indonesia if Washington's admonition were disregarded. It was Australia's belief that the Communist powers would not have intervened if the risk involved fighting with the U.S. Therefore, a policy of strength would have paid off without producing an East-West clash, and likewise without exposing Australia as an isolated white "colonialist" enemy of Indonesia. This is what Menzies meant when he said he could not countenance any action affecting issues of war and peace in the area "except in concert with our great and powerful friends."

[17] Statement of January 12, 1962, in *SMH,* January 13, 1962. Also see Menzies, *CPD,* HR 31, April 27, 1961, p. 1249, and statement of June 26, 1962, in *CNIA,* Vol. 33 (June 1962), p. 40; Barwick, *CPD,* HR 34, March 15, 1962, p. 903. A February 1962 opinion poll indicated that only 22% of the public would support Australian military intervention on the side of the Dutch. See *AGP,* nos. 1581–1591, February–March, 1962.

## SECURITY PROBLEMS: 2

### AUSTRALIA, CHINA, AND MALAYSIA

THE CLOSING of the West Irian dispute was almost immediately followed by another piece of unwanted Indonesian policy—her confrontation against Malaysia. The concept of Malaysia, or the fusion under a single national standard of Malaya, Singapore, and the North Borneo, Sarawak and Brunei territories, was first broached by Malayan Prime Minister Tunku Abdul Rahman in mid-1961. At bottom, its motivation was to join Singapore to Malaya. But the giant Chinese-origin population of Singapore required a counterweight, hence the Borneo areas were included in the scheme. The Tunku saw the project as an economic stabilizer for the member parts, but also appreciated very keenly the opportunity to neutralize potentially dangerous radical elements in Singapore. By late 1962 the British had given their blessing and preparations were put in motion to effect the merger. Although Brunei chose not to join the federation, the remaining territories were formally constituted as Malaysia on September 16 of 1963.

Australian opinion expressed well-nigh unanimous endorsement of the Malaysia concept, because the political stability and economic viability of the concerned area was a contribution to Australia's own security. It was stressed that discontented Chinese elements in Singapore, or the Chinese minorities in the Borneo areas, could wreck hopes for a vigorous and thoroughly non-Communist state whose location was a buffer for Australia's fear of encroachment by China. The Tunku's moderation and leadership talents, as well as those of Lee Kuan-yew in Singapore, were admired and regarded as promising signs that the Strategic Reserve could stay on to fulfill its functions without undue difficulties. It is significant that Arthur Calwell, the ALP's Leader since Evatt's retirement in early 1960, should have remarked that the "overriding" reason for Malaysia to survive was "the common threat from Communist China

—and that is a threat which Malaysia shares in common with Indonesia, the Philippines and Australia."[18]

The difficulty, of course, has rested in Indonesia's implacable opposition to Malaysia. Australia, like most other interested onlooking states, has found it hard to sympathize with Indonesia's explanation of her hostility toward the Federation. The PKI, which helped to set off the anti-Malaysian agitation in the first instance, has at least a clearly understandable argument—"that the activities and prospects of the strong Chinese Communist element in Singapore (and to a lesser degree in northern Borneo) will inevitably be curbed by the imposition of the authority of a central Government uncompromisingly hostile to Communism."[19] But the publicly expressed motivation of non-Communists such as Sukarno, Foreign Minister Subandrio, and Defense Minister General Nasution has been regarded as utterly misguided and/or specious. These men claim that the presence of Malaysia on Indonesia's borders is a menace to Indonesia herself. They say that Malaysia is fragile; her large Chinese component can in time take over Malaysia and also bring influential assistance to bear on Indonesia's own Chinese minority. Likewise, the Chinese factor in Malaysia could be an invitation for Communist China to become established around Indonesia in a way which would threaten the integrity of not just Indonesia but of the region at large. "How can Malaysia, with its 10 million population, put up a blockage against Communist Chinese influence?" Subandrio has asked rhetorically.[20] The Indonesian intention therefore

[18] *CPD,* HR, September 25, 1963, p. 1368. Also see, for instance, John McEwen, *ibid.,* p. 1372; Sydney *Daily Mirror,* November 30, 1961; Geoffrey Fairbairn in *Bulletin,* February 3, 1962; *Canberra Times,* January 23, 1963; Perth *West Australian,* February 5, 1963; *SMH,* July 22, 1963.

[19] Guy Harriott in *ibid.,* November 1, 1963.

[20] Speech of December 20, 1963, in *ibid.,* December 21, 1963. For a sample of interview opinions from Indonesian leaders, see

seems to lie in establishing Indonesian hegemony over the Borneo segments of the Federation, and excluding the British military presence from the area.

But Indonesia's objections to Malaysia have by no means been confined to polite diplomatic notes. She encouraged the Brunei rebellion of December 1962. When in mid-1963 Indonesia, the Philippines, and Malaysia agreed to form the Maphilindo confederation among themselves, the project was hailed in Australia not just as the closing of Indonesia's confrontation policy, but as a useful vehicle for containing the Chinese elements in the region, for providing a framework of cooperation against China, and for allowing Indonesia to return to her efforts of improving her internal situation.[21] But Indonesia disappointed the optimists. The Tunku promised to delay Malaysia's appearance until a UN opinion survey could be taken. When Malaysia finally was established, the Indonesians caviled at the UN findings, returned to undisguised confrontation, broke off commercial relations with and refused to recognize the new Malaysia, allowed mobs to demonstrate and to burn down and loot the British Embassy in Djakarta, intensified their assistance to dissident elements in northern Borneo, and introduced their own "volunteers" into the area, with loss of life on both sides. By the close of 1964, Indonesian infiltrators had been landed in Malaya proper.

In Australia's eyes, these actions are bewildering when set against the purpose that Malaysia was supposed to achieve. Instability rather than stability is being fostered, enmity rather than friendship between Malaysia and Indonesia promoted and, to top it off, the hand of China seems

---

Guy Harriot in *ibid.,* September 16, 1963; Robert Raymond, "How We Met President Soekarno," *Bulletin,* December 14, 1963; Subandrio interview of April 5, 1964, in *The Times* (London), April 6, 1964.

[21] Sydney *Sun,* June 11, 1963; Sydney *Daily Telegraph,* June 13, 1963; Hobart *Mercury,* June 20, 1963; *Canberra Times,* July 9, 1963; *SMH,* July 10, 1963.

to rest more rather than less heavily on Indonesia. The PKI itself has now committed itself to a pro-Peking line in the Sino-Soviet dispute, yet some recent changes in the Indonesian army, long a steadfast opponent of the PKI, suggest an even wider influence for the Communists than before.[22] Indeed, Malaysian Deputy Prime Minister Tun Abdul Razak has gone so far as to allege that PKI leader D. N. Aidit "pulled the strings which made Dr. Soekarno dance like a puppet. But Aidit's strings are pulled by his Communist masters in Peking." [23] Sino-Indonesian friendship has, on the surface, increased rather than decreased from the high level it achieved in the last phases of the West Irian controversy. In April of 1963 Liu Shao-chi paid a state visit to Indonesia. Once again the Indonesians affirmed their support for China's claim to Formosa. Again the Chinese offered their wholehearted support for an Indonesian objective; with West Irian out of the way, it was now Malaysia's turn to be denounced as a "neo-colonialist intrigue opposed by the peaceloving people of the world," [24] and in their final communiqué Liu and Sukarno expressed "full support" for the "Korean People's struggle for the reunification of Korea" and advanced sympathy for the fight of the "gallant Cuban people" to maintain their own development and independence.[25] When anti-Chinese riots broke out in Indonesia in May of 1963, Sukarno charged that they had been the handiwork of "counter-revolutionaries" who were trying to overthrow him "because of my policy of friendship with the Chinese People's Republic." [26]

Sino-Indonesian ties have become stronger and there-

[22] For a sharply drawn account of the situation from an Australian source, see Sir Wilfrid Kent-Hughes, "Appreciation of the S.E. Asian Situation. January-February, 1964," private paper, mimeo., p. 4.

[23] Statement of October 13, 1963, in *SMH,* October 15, 1963.

[24] *Nation* (Rangoon), April 20, 1963.

[25] Djakarta *Daily Mail,* April 22, 1963.

[26] Broadcast of May 19, 1963, in *SMH,* May 20, 1963. Also see his comments of the following day in *ibid.,* May 21, 1963.

fore more disturbing to Australia. In November of 1964 Subandrio warned that if Australia's recent defense buildup was designed to bully and subjugate Indonesia, Indonesia would have to reply to such a challenge. Menzies ought to realize the nature of Asia's development; he should "look at the Chinese People's Republic which today has the atom bomb. Asia's growth today constitutes a symbol and sign that imperialist and white domination over Asian nations is coming to an end." [27] In December Chen Yi was cordially received in Djakarta. In January of 1965 Subandrio obtained Chinese credits worth at least $50 million during his trip to Peking. On both occasions, more pledges to crush Malaysia were exchanged. Also in January, Indonesia withdrew from the United Nations giving as her reason the fact that Malaysia had been allowed a seat on the Security Council. Even the Soviets opposed this Indonesian move; the Chinese were almost alone in praising it.[28]

All of this has been received with the utmost consternation in Australia, coming as it has on the heels of the violent campaign to absorb West Irian and the subsequent repudiation of Indonesia's promise to allow genuine self-determination in the area.[29] Indonesians are seen as mercurial at the least and as probably the witting or unwitting promoters, not opponents, of Communist China's cause in the region. Chinese policy is to destroy Malaysia and Indonesian policy has the same objective, while Indonesia makes no effort to hide the encouragement which China is giving her. Since the success of Malaysia is regarded as considerably more significant to Australia's security interests than the preservation of West New Guinea in Dutch

[27] Statement of Nov. 12, 1964, cited in *Sydney Sun-Herald,* Nov. 22, 1964.

[28] See *NYT,* Jan. 4, 8, and 29, 1965.

[29] Note Sir Robert Menzies' own wry comment on the connection between Indonesia's West Irian policy and Malaysian confrontation. Statement of July 14, 1963, in *SMH,* July 15, 1963.

hands had been, the whole discussion in Australia has developed a crisis atmosphere, with more predictions about Indonesia sliding behind the bamboo curtain—a kind of Asian Cuba, perhaps in time including the establishment of Chinese military bases. China, however, would not be amenable to backing down as Khrushchev did in Cuba.[30]

The Australian Government's reactions to the Malaysian confrontation must be seen against the background of the West Irian dispute. When the dispute was over, Australia hoped that Indonesia would then turn her attention to domestic improvement, that she would no longer need to be wedded as intimately to the Communist powers, and that Austral-Indonesian relations would prosper. Australian spokesmen went out of their way not to offend Indonesia, but when a confrontation developed over the establishment of Malaysia, some hard choices lay ahead.

While trying to convince Djakarta that Malaysia was no threat and indeed an asset to Indonesia, Australia studiously avoided any untoward and captious criticism. The Maphilindo scheme was warmly received, in fact given "positive encouragement" by Australia, but Indonesia again turned on her fledging neighbor.[31] Finally, on September 25, 1963, after Malaysia had come into existence and as Indonesia was stepping up her confrontation by leaps and bounds, Menzies laid down a firm attitude.

[30] For sample comment, see *News Weekly,* October 23, 1963; *SMH,* August 29, 1963; *Canberra Times,* December 6, 1963; Melbourne *Sun,* March 11, 1964; Sir Wilfrid Kent-Hughes in *Bulletin,* November 10, 1962; Clyde Cameron (ALP), *CPD,* HR 36, October 3, 1962, p. 1126; Beazley (ALP), *ibid.,* HR, September 25, 1963, p. 1379; James Arnold (ALP), *ibid.,* S, September 26, 1963, p. 883; George Hannan (Liberal), *ibid.,* S, May 16, 1963, pp. 517–518; T. B. Millar, "China's Policy in Asia" (Sydney: AIPS, 1964), monograph no. 4, pp. 22–24.

[31] For commentary on Australia's diplomacy in the early stages of the Malaysian controversy, see Peter Boyce, "Canberra's Malaysia Policy," *Australian Outlook,* Vol. 17 (August 1963), pp. 149–162.

After consultation with Britain, Malaysia, and others concerned, Australia was making public her determination to resist armed invasion or subversive activity inspired against Malaysia from the outside, and that Australian military assistance would be available if needed; the terrorists being employed in Malaysia under Indonesian supervision were as much a threat to Malaysia's integrity, as much an act of war, as overt invasion.[32]

Gradually, Australia matched her promise with performance, first providing stores of ammunition and other supplies to Malaysian and British forces fighting in Borneo, opening training facilities in Australia for Malaysian personnel, and sending Australian instructors to Malaysian forces on secondment.[33] By April of 1964, decision was taken to station air and naval units in the area, and to dispatch an army engineer squadron.[34] Australia was pursuing a deliberatively phased response to the Malaysian troubles. She still hoped that the Indonesians would see reason and withdraw confrontation. Combat troops as such were not yet being posted. But Canberra's concern was sufficiently high, the stakes of protecting Malaysia and giving a boost to the British military involvement there so important, that a kid-gloves approach to Djakarta had been set aside. Indeed, it is understood on excellent authority that once Malaysia had been formally proclaimed, Australia pressed the U.S. very hard to use economic aid to Indonesia as leverage in the hope of bringing Sukarno to his senses. This was done with full appreciation of the possibility that unwanted ricochet effects would result, but the sanctions policy was urged nonetheless. Chinese Communism could not be allowed to have its way in disrupting the Malaysian experiment, and Australia was responding accordingly.

[32] *CPD,* HR, September 25, 1963, pp. 1338–1339.

[33] Paul Hasluck, Minister for Defense, *ibid.,* March 17, 1964, p. 523.

[34] Hasluck, *ibid.,* April 16, 1964, pp. 1192–1193.

But Sukarno was unimpressed. By the end of 1964, Australian land and naval units had come into contact with and inflicted casualties upon Indonesians infiltrating into Malaya. In February of 1965, after much soul-searching and weighing of consequences, Acting Prime Minister John McEwen announced that Australian combat elements would be moved to Malaysian Borneo.[35]

The Labor Party's reaction to Malaysia must be mentioned before the account can be closed. At its 1961 conference, by unanimous vote, the Party approved a resolution which, in effect, repeated the 1955 policy of withdrawing Australian forces from what was then Malaya.[36] At a special conference on foreign and defense affairs, held in Canberra in March of 1963, a resolution was adopted urging that Australian forces should not be committed overseas, with special reference to Malaya, without a "clear and public treaty which accords with the principles of this declaration, and which gives Australia an effective voice in the common decisions of the treaty powers." An emasculating amendment which in essence urged a return to the policy established in 1955 was lost on a deadlocked 18–18 vote. When the original motion was brought forward, it was also lost by 18–18.[37] Four months later, at the regularly scheduled ALP conference in Perth, a resolution styled on the defeated March motion was approved by *unanimous* vote of all 36 delegates, although Malaya-Malaysia was not specifically mentioned.[38] In sum, the Party had very rapidly converted itself to supporting a troop commitment in Malaysia, though with the proviso that any such commitment should

[35] Statement of February 3, 1965, cited in *SMH*, February 4, 1965.

[36] ALP, *Official Report of the Proceedings of the 24th Commonwealth Conference,* at Canberra, April 1961, pp. 35–36.

[37] ALP, *Official Report of the Proceedings of the Special Commonwealth Conference on Foreign Affairs and Defence,* at Canberra, March 1963, pp. 12–13.

[38] ALP, *Official Report of the Proceedings of the 25th Commonwealth Conference* at Perth, July-August 1963, pp. 23–24.

be formally spelled out. There is no question that Malaysia's forthcoming appearance was favorably regarded, and that Indonesia's confrontation was deplored. As has been shown, Calwell himself underscored the Chinese threat to the region. The Parliamentary leadership, and Calwell especially, worked strenuously both before and after the 1963 Canberra conference to swing the ALP into line with new external conditions. Indeed, the defeat of both the original and the amending motions at Canberra bore the result that Labor had not only failed to produce a fresh policy, but had repudiated the old as well, leaving itself with no official position whatsoever regarding Malaysian troops. The "clear and public treaty" clause of March and July made the final changeover more palatable to those who still harbored reservations about changing policy respecting troops overseas. Not all members of the ALP have yet fully reconciled themselves to it. But the Party did come out of its outdated shell, and there was no concealing the fact that many in the ALP expected to gain some political capital as a result. The Menzies Government had been returned to office in 1961 with a considerably smaller popular vote than Labor's, and held on with a bare two-seat majority in the House, reduced to one after the Speaker's election. Just a bit more effort, perhaps a refurbished policy here and there, and Labor could at last emerge from the political wilderness, or so it imagined.

In point of fact, the Government parties still found room for attacking Labor over Malaysia. The September 25 commitment had been undertaken through an exchange of letters between Australia and Malaysia, corresponding to an informal understanding of 1959 which had broadly indicated the Malayan Government's acceptance of Australian troops under the aegis of the Strategic Reserve. Britain's military presence, first in Malaya, then in Malaysia, had been brought under formal agreements. But

Malaysia was not interested in a formal, well-defined treaty with Australia which would clearly establish the duties and obligations of both signatories. The Australian Government was willing to accept a treaty if Malaysia were to offer one, but in its absence it asserted that no Australian interests were being sacrificed. Malaysia required protection, Canberra and Kuala Lumpur enjoyed excellent relations, and in any case formal commitments within the Commonwealth association were most exceptional.[39]

The ALP took a while sorting out its own position. During the two 1963 conferences, the applied question of whether a Labor Government would have to pull Australian troops out of Malaysia if no treaty could be negotiated simply failed to arise. In early September E. G. Whitlam, the ALP's Deputy Leader, told the House that unless a "clear and public treaty" were transacted, he would bring Australian troops home.[40] The Party continued to agitate for a treaty, claiming that the definition of obligations was both for Malaysia's and Australia's benefit and protection, and that in any event Australia had treaties with all sorts of countries with whom she was on the best of terms.[41] But as the 1963 elections drew near, Calwell chose to put a different interpretation on what an ALP Government would do. If Malaysia were attacked "tomorrow," a Labor Government would "of course" help to defend her. Labor would "exactly and immediately" render aid even without a treaty, "but that's in an emergency. On the long-

[39] See Menzies, *CPD,* HR, September 25, 1963, pp. 1338–1339; television interview of October 27, 1963, in *SMH,* October 28, 1963. For texts of the several Australian and British agreements with Malaya-Malaysia, see *CNIA,* Vol. 34 (September 1963), pp. 42–48. Also see the discussion in Watt, *op. cit.,* pp. 49–65.

[40] *CPD,* HR, September 10, 1963, p. 766.

[41] For example, Calwell's remarks in *ibid.,* September 25, 1963, esp. pp. 1368–1370; 1963 television policy speech of November 6, 1963, in "Labor's Policy" (Melbourne: 1963), p. 22; television interview of October 20, 1963, in *SMH,* October 21, 1963.

term view we of the Labour Party are not prepared to commit Australian troops to the defence of Malaysia without a clear, open treaty with some mutual obligations." [42] Calwell did not define an "emergency," nor did he state how long a Labor Government would wait for a treaty before electing to remove troops. In point of fact, the author's queries leave no doubt that a Labor Government's actual approach would have differed little if at all from that of the incumbent Government. An attempt—gesture might be a better word—would be made to obtain a treaty. If none could be had, the armed forces would stay, and would be utilized in much the same manner that they would be deployed by the Liberals. There is reason to believe that Whitlam is not to be exempt from this interpretation.

But the Government parties imputed bad faith to Labor. In the weeks preceding the 1963 elections, Labor's summons for a treaty was caricatured as a half-hearted and insincere advocacy of Malaysia, a denial that Malaysia's survival was vital to Australia, a symptom of the "ambiguous, uncertain, fluctuating and almost mumbling attitude of our opponents." [43] At the climax of the campaign, a Liberal Party political advertisement appeared in a national news magazine; it was headed "Look to Our Perilous North Before You Vote": Mao Tse-tung had declared that the world could only be remade with the aid of a rifle. Security inside Australia depended on security on the outside, and the Government's policies were directed toward that end. The electorate was enjoined to reject the "confused, dangerous, and frustrating policies of the Labor Party on the critical issue of Communist aggression." Among the featured Opposition faults was that "the

[42] *Ibid.*

[43] Menzies television policy speech of November 12, 1963, in "Federal Election, 1963" (Canberra: Federal Secretariat, Liberal Party of Australia, 1963), pp. 6–7. Also see his television interview of October 20, 1963, in *SMH,* October 21, 1963.

Labor Party strongly opposed the stationing of Australian forces in Malaya."[44] This was rather dirty pool, but it probably had its effect. The advertisement used the past-tense *opposed,* and spoke of *Malaya* rather than *Malaysia.* The statement was true, but undoubtedly was designed to be mixed up with the prevailing debate and the Government insinuations about Labor's call for a Malaysian treaty. It was to be but one of several Chinese-related themes on which Labor has found itself politically vulnerable despite evidence that in practice it would implement something remarkably proximate to the *status quo.*

## THE SECURITY SYSTEM: IMPUTATIONS OF SHORTCOMINGS

DIFFERENCES with Indonesia, and especially as they bear on the Chinese aspects of the Malaysian controversy, are also important to the alliance structure to which Australia subscribes. The ANZUS treaty continues to receive the endorsement of nearly everyone in the country, the Labor Party not excepted. One reason is that Indonesian antics and flirtations with China continue to disturb Australia, and the flat and unequivocal promises made by the U.S., in the context of ANZUS—that it would "fight to defend" Australia's portion of New Guinea against Indonesian or any other aggression—have been most reassuring.[45] The second reason is that there is no mistaking the applicability of ANZUS to the northern Borneo (Sarawak and Sabah) Malaysian territories, in case Australian armed forces are attacked, and Sukarno has known this for some time. By late 1963 he had been told by Australia the ANZUS could be invoked. U.S. Ambassador Howard Jones also brought the point to Sukarno's attention, but Australia concluded that he, as simply an ambassador,

[44] *Bulletin,* November 30, 1963.

[45] See the ANZUS Council communiqué of May 9, 1962, in *CNIA,* Vol. 33 (May 1962), pp. 6–7; Secretary Rusk's statement of May 8, 1962, in *SMH,* May 9, 1962; Averell Harriman's comments of June 4, 1963, in *ibid.,* June 5, 1963.

was not being taken seriously enough. Hence Barwick's comments in April of 1964 which publicly, and in consonance with American thinking, reaffirmed the position.[46] The precise circumstances in which an Australian engagement with Indonesians would bring assistance from the U.S., and the nature of that assistance, is of course problematical. But the fact that Australia feels confident of a sympathetic American reaction, on whatever terms, strengthens Canberra's determination to assist Malaysia materially and reinforces her faith in ANZUS. SEATO, however, is another matter. It is under criticism from quite divergent quarters, which in turn have been inclined to offer substitute plans.

Malaysia fits into the over-all picture of SEATO's criticisms. Malaya and then Malaysia expressed their opposition to entering SEATO, the Tunku having described it as "negative, ineffective, outmoded and under the stigma of Western domination." [47] Under the terms of the original Anglo-Malayan agreement, repeated in the 1963 agreement, the Strategic Reserve in Malaya could not be used outside of Malaya-Singapore or British territories in the Far East without prior agreement of the Malayan (Malaysian) Government,[48] and in fact Australian units were not allowed to move to Thailand during the Laotian crisis

[46] See Barwick's press conferences in Manila and Sydney, April 16 and 17, 1964, respectively, and his television interview of April 17, in Dept. of External Affairs, "Sir Garfield Barwick's Statements on Possible Applicability of ANZUS and Australian Forces in Malaysian Borneo," mimeo., pp. 1–2; Barwick, *CPD, HR*, April 21, 1964, p. 1234 and April 22, 1964, p. 1306; Sydney *Sun-Herald,* May 17, 1964.

[47] Cited in Gerald Caine, "Towards the Pacific Community" (Ballarat: Cripac Press, 1963), p. 13. Also see Vernon Bartlett, "Why Malaya Does Not Want to Join SEATO," *Straits Times* (Singapore), January 8, 1959. For a general review of Australian security in Malaya-Singapore, see Henry S. Albinski, "Australia's Defense Enigma," *Orbis,* Vol. 4 (Winter 1961), pp. 452–466.

[48] Article VIII, 1957 Agreement; Article VI, 1963 Agreement.

without first regrouping in Singapore. The Tunku remarked in November 1961 that Australia could withdraw her troops from Malaya anytime, if she wished—he did not mind if they "leave tomorrow or today." [49] During the Anglo-Malayan negotiations respecting the status of Singapore under Malaysia, considerable anxiety was voiced in Australia lest that base would also fall subject to the whim of a Malaysian Government.[50] As it turned out, while Singapore was not and can not be converted into a SEATO base, it can be employed for purposes extending to South-East Asia generally,[51] though of course there are always undefinable political considerations which could qualify its use in future—the distinction between employing Singapore in the defense of South-East Asia as against using its as a SEATO base for the same end being a fine one indeed.

To be sure, Malaysia's difficulties with Indonesia have made the Tunku's Government reliant in large measure on the support of Britain, Australia, and New Zealand. But despite this reliance, the ability of the Strategic Reserve to move to trouble spots beyond Malaysia is uncertain. During the Maphilindo meetings in 1963, the Tunku advised the Indonesians and Filipinos that British bases and the Strategic Reserve were necessary, and only "when we can live in peace and sleep safely in our beds" could they be dispensed with.[52] The Maphilindo agreement did, however, provide that foreign bases in the three nations (meaning in effect Malaysia and the Philippines) were

[49] Statement of November 30, 1961, in *SMH,* December 2, 1961.

[50] *Ibid.,* October 3, 1961; Adelaide *News,* October 4, 1961; Adelaide *Advertiser,* October 5, 1961; Perth *West Australian,* November 22, 1961.

[51] Article VI, 1963 Agreement. Also see Duncan Sandys, *UKPD,* HC, Vol. 650, November 28, 1961, col. 242; *SMH,* November 24, 1961.

[52] Statement to Parliament of August 13, 1963, in *ibid.,* August 15, 1963.

only temporary in nature and should not be used in any way to subvert the national independence of any of the signatories.[53] Put in another way, despite Malaysia's present involvement, it can be argued that the Government there does not hold a firm conviction that when the current troubles are cleared up the Strategic Reserve can remain indefinitely, or if it can, that it will be usable anywhere and anytime in South-East Asia, as circumstances dictate to Britain, Australia, and New Zealand. Australia, it should not be forgotten, regards the Strategic Reserve as a central contribution to the SEATO effort in the region. These difficulties have not gone unnoticed in Australia, and their mention has contributed to the general disparagement of SEATO's capabilities.[54]

Shortcomings have also been attributed to SEATO in other aspects of recent South and South-East Asian developments. The recurrent crises in Laos have been most frustrating to Australian opinion for various reasons. Conditions in Laos herself have been perennially confused and fragile as factions coalesce and part, fighting erupts sporadically, the whole of South-East Asia becomes increasingly exposed, and the Communist powers reap benefits. For present purposes it is sufficient to say that the Australian Government, appreciating the need to promote Laotian integrity against an internal or external Communist take-over, has consistently taken the view that a peaceful solution must be had, and that a neutral Laos is the only type of Laos able to avert tearing herself apart or inviting interference from neighboring North Vietnam or China. SEATO should keep a watchful eye, however, and in the last resort be prepared to take necessary steps, for "if, unhappily, collective Seato action is forced upon us,

[53] Article x. Text in *ibid.,* August 6, 1963.

[54] For instance, E. G. Whitlam, "Australian Foreign Policy 1963," Roy Milne Memorial Lecture, Armidale (Melbourne: AIIA, 1963), p. 8; S. J. Benson, *CPD,* HR, March 19, 1964, p. 693.

we will need to act together or find Seato weakened and destroyed." [55]

In the first half of 1962, the Laotian situation again deteriorated as the Pathet Lao assumed the initiative and Thailand's own safety was placed in question. In March, the American Government announced its intention of defending Thailand even if other SEATO members chose not to assist.[56] By the end of May, American, British, New Zealand, and Australian forces were installed in Thailand, Australia supplying a squadron of fighter aircraft. The immediate importance of these events was the circumstances in which Thailand received support. Barwick explained that all participating nations, who were also SEATO partners, had acted in pursuance of their treaty obligations. He said that such obligations could properly be discharged without the prior agreement of all parties to the treaty, since they were individual as well as mutual, although joint consultation was assumed at all junctures of such action.[57] Once the various national contingents had been established in Thailand, Barwick complimented SEATO on its ability to react swiftly and purposively in an emergency.[58]

Developments arising out of Viet Cong activity in Vietnam again stimulated concern and reaction in Australia.

[55] Menzies, *CPD,* HR 30, April 11, 1961, pp. 657–658. Also see Menzies, HR 29, December 6, 1960, pp. 3570–3571, and HR 31, April 27, 1961, p. 1251; Barwick, TV interview of September 13, 1959, in *SMH,* September 14, 1959; *CPD,* HR 24, September 17, 1959, p. 1125; HR 34, March 8, 1962, p. 610; "Australian Foreign Policy 1962," p. 12. For reviews of Australian reactions on Laos, see Harper, "Australia and the United States," *Australia in World Affairs 1956–1960,* pp. 198–205, and Webb, "Australia and SEATO," pp. 74–78.

[56] *SMH,* March 8, 1962.

[57] *CPD,* HR 35, May 1, 1962, p. 1801, and May 17, 1962, pp. 2451–2452; Statement of May 23, 1962, in *SMH,* May 24, 1962.

[58] Statement of June 25, 1962, in *ibid.,* June 26, 1962; SEATO Council address of April 8, 1963, in *CNIA,* Vol. 34 (April 1963), p. 17.

Various forms of strategically significant materials have been supplied by Australia to Vietnam under SEATO's aegis. In May 1962, at the time that the fighter squadron was dispatched to Thailand, 30 military advisers were pledged to assist in training the Vietnamese army, on grounds that a SEATO protocol state had made the request. By July 1964, the Australian commitment was increased by over 50 additional instructors and 6 transport aircraft,[59] and in early 1965 17 more instructors were committed. After the April 1964 SEATO Council meetings in Manila, the Government again was compelled to interpret the character of SEATO's obligations, this time under the shadow of a French search for neutralization of South-East Asia and French abstention on a SEATO resolution which placed the reestablishment of security ahead of any broad political settlement affecting Vietnam. In his own report on the Council meetings, Barwick made special efforts to praise SEATO's past performance and to defend its utility for the future. To be sure, there had been differences at Manila, but no member had entertained reservations about SEATO as such. French views on neutralization were mistaken, since under prevailing conditions North Vietnam and China wanted neutralization for South Vietnam, which would give them all the advantages. Countries such as Vietnam lacked sufficient defensive capacity of their own, stood in danger of being picked off one by one, and must therefore be protected by concerned friends and allies. This, he said, was what certain SEATO members had done in assisting the Vietnamese authorities. SEATO need not act unanimously; *some* members can legtimately act in keeping

[59] Defense Minister Townley, statement of May 24, 1962, in *ibid.,* Vol. 33 (May 1962), pp. 36–37; Barwick, *CPD,* HR 36, August 21, 1962, p. 581, and statement of January 25, 1963, in *CNIA,* Vol. 34 (January-February 1963), p. 62; Defense Minister S. D. Paltridge, statement of June 8, 1964, in *SMH,* June 9, 1964; Government statement of July 7, 1964, in *ibid.,* July 8, 1964.

with SEATO obligations—a desirable feature in that "it gives great flexibility and strength to Seato." [60]

A large number of critics have appeared in Australia who simply have not been satisfied with the Government's brave and sanguine evaluation of SEATO. The striking feature of the debate is not just that criticism has flowed from various and even opposite quarters, but that some of the alternative solutions offered have become imbedded in Australian politics and in particular have generated still another slant of dialogue where China is concerned. Some of this has sprung from allegations concerning the fragility of the alliance system as it regulates the Strategic Reserve and Malaysia, but most of it has resulted from the nature of SEATO activity, or inactivity, in Laos-Thailand and in Vietnam.

The first basis of criticism has been that SEATO is not equipped to cope with the kind of subversive and guerrilla activity that has come to characterize life in the old Indo-Chinese states. These states, debarred under the terms of the Geneva accords from entering military alliances, are the targets of undermining operations which, if successful, would open the way for Chinese, or at least Chinese-oriented, hegemony in the area. SEATO passes resolutions, it threatens to interpose itself from time to time, but the choices are unenviable. "If we elect to stand firm," wrote the Melbourne *Herald* during the 1961 Laotian crisis, "we may become involved in a war we cannot win. If we back down under pressure we will scuttle SEATO and perhaps find ourselves [Australia] denied the support of our strongest ally in the difficult years that certainly lie ahead." [61] When Australia and others sent armed units to

[60] *CPD,* HR, April 21, 1964, esp. pp. 1264–1267. Also see John Gorton, Senate, April 16, 1964, p. 704.

[61] Melbourne *Herald,* March 21, 1961. For related comments, see Melbourne *Age* and Brisbane *Courier-Mail,* March 21, 1961; *Canberra Times,* March 22, 1961; Hobart *Mercury,* March 25, 1961; Bruce Wight, *CPD,* HR 24, August 26, 1959, pp. 617–618.

Thailand, in discharge of "individual" rather than "mutual" SEATO obligations, SEATO was disparaged again. The formula under which the forces were sent was said to expose the organization as indeed a "paper tiger"—a collection of countries who meet to discuss common problems, stage a few defense exercises, provide some aid to affected regions, but who countenance running out on responsibilities by any member who chooses not to participate. Troops and aircraft in Thailand were fine, but to say they were the result of a sturdy and united SEATO front would be a mockery—events had shown that "there would be more teeth in an R.A.A.F. Sabre squadron—even as a token addition to United States forces along the Mekong —than there is in all the collective 'commitments' of SEATO." [62] The critics felt vindicated when, just as allied forces were being set down in Thailand, a study mission of the Foreign Affairs Committee of the U.S. House of Representatives published a report to the effect that SEATO's shortcomings prevented it from offering any meaningful security to the nations of South-East Asia.[63]

Events in Vietnam in early 1964 sharpened another criticism which had been raised against SEATO before, a criticism which to a number of observers is at the heart of the organization's inability to produce a united and credible front. This criticism, which points out the disparate interests and behavior of members of SEATO, has found its strongest spokesmen on the political right, though not exclusively. Fault has been found with nearly all SEATO

Also see Professor W. Macmahon Ball's general criticisms in "A Political Re-Examination of SEATO," *International Organization,* Vol. 12 (Winter 1958), pp. 17–25.

[62] Douglas Wilkie in Melbourne *Sun-Pictorial,* May 29, 1962. Also see Melbourne *Age,* March 16, 1962, and Sydney *Sun,* March 18, 1962.

[63] See U.S. House of Representatives, Committee on Foreign Affairs, *Report of the Special Study Mission to the Far East, South Asia, and the Middle East.* House Report no. 1946, 87th Congress, 2nd Session, esp. p. 38.

signatories save the ANZUS members. Pakistan seems intent on concentrating her attention elsewhere than in South-East Asia, and her antagonism toward India and flirtations with a China which has an invasion of India on her record has been resented. The Philippines have been a disappointment because of support lent to Indonesia's confrontation against Malaysia, a critical factor in Australia's defense calculations and where, of course, the Chinese element operates. Britain is seen as rapidly disengaging in Asia and therefore can not be counted upon to stiffen SEATO's posture in critical times. France is now viewed as perhaps worst of all. Whatever interests she retains in Asian affairs point to weakness and concession, for example, her neutralization proposals. To cap it off, three of SEATO's partners, Britain, Pakistan, and France, now recognize China, SEATO's principal antagonist, while French recognition has been interpreted as an almost deliberately malicious move *vis-à-vis* SEATO.[64]

## THE SECURITY SYSTEM: ALTERNATIVE PROPOSALS

THESE tendencies have been taken so seriously in recent years by the DLP, the National Civic Council, and certain individuals that a substitute policy has been evolved and in fact incorporated into the DLP's program. At the start and at a minimum, the DLP is now calling for the expulsion of France from SEATO.[65] More broadly, there is the scheme of a Pacific Confederation: the proposal opens with the unmistakable assertion that China poses a dreadful threat to all free nations in Asia and the Pacific, Aus-

[64] For instance, see B. A. Santamaria in *Bulletin,* February 16, 1963; Caine, *op. cit.,* pp. 13 and 53; Democratic Labor Party (Victoria), "Speakers' Notes-Part 2. 1961 Elections" (Melbourne: DLP Victorian State Secretariat, 1961), pp. 80–84, 86; *Bulletin,* April 20 and 27, 1963; Adelaide *News,* April 16, 1964; Sir Wilfrid Kent-Hughes, *CPD,* HR 34, March 6, 1962, p. 461.

[65] See Frank McManus, DLP Organizing Secretary, in *News Weekly,* February 6, 1964.

tralia included. The Chinese are seen as holding a diversity of instruments by which to establish their influence: subversion, political blackmail against those who trade with them, and, in the last resort, reliance on undisguised aggression. Kuo Mo-jo's 1961 comment in Djakarta about the neutralization of Australia is accepted at face value rather than as a bluff, and as part of a long-range program to expel American power from the region and to establish a series of helpless or perhaps even Chinese-vassal states. Yet SEATO, the widest anti-Chinese alliance in Asia, is divided and irresolute, and its very weaknesses are a constant and irresistible invitation to China to operate unmolested and to play upon the internal troubles of the organization.

The Pacific Confederation envisaged by the NCC-DLP calls for the construction of an alliance among Asian and Pacific states which share not only a geographic location, but also have a stake in resolutely opposing Chinese Communist expansion. As a nucleus, Australia, New Zealand, Japan, Thailand, the Philippines, South Vietnam, Malaysia, and Nationalist China would come together. India has recently been added to this list. They would interlace their military planning and build up their armed forces, and would be prepared to employ them in a way that SEATO has found impossible, mostly because of its European members. Foreign policies would be coordinated though not merged. "Neutralist" states such as Indonesia would not be welcome in the foreseeable future because of their equivocation on meeting the Chinese threat in a head-on, uncompromising fashion. In order to strengthen their own well-being, serve as an example to other Asian states, and interchange goods so extensively as to permit the suspension of all commerce with China, close and preferential economic ties would be developed, since the respective members are seen as being economically complementary to one another. Although no Asian-Pacific counterpart of the European Common Market is envisioned, nor indeed is political union, great strength is said to inhere within such a confederation, especially since links with the United States would be intimate at every level.[66]

Just how meaningful is the Pacific Confederation? The author has questioned some leading DLP and NCC figures rather closely on the possibility of achieving such an organization in the near future. There is agreement among them that, while China's threat grows ever more ominous and SEATO's sickness lingers, the chances for a Confederation are dim. Australia and New Zealand show no disposition to turn their backs on SEATO and to search for fresh solutions. Japan is both constitutionally and politically inhibited from joining an alliance to which she would need to make a substantial military contribution. Several of the countries suggested for membership now carry on a profitable trade with China that they would not care to jeopardize. The inclusion of Formosa would be an embarrassment to many. For instance, Malaysia recognizes neither "China" and has a delicate domestic Chinese problem; Australia and New Zealand have avoided placing diplomatic missions in Taipei; Japan recognizes Formosa but strives to cultivate good relations with both Chinas; India is still in no mood to enter into an anti-Chinese alliance despite the events of late 1962. The exponents of Confederation dismiss the argument that forceful criticism of SEATO, in the absence of prospects to construct a Pacific Confederation, only undermines whatever prestige SEATO retains, for they allege that SEATO has arrived at

[66] The fullest exposition is in Caine, *op. cit., passim.* Also see B. A. Santamaria, lecture in Melbourne of September 1, 1963, in Melbourne *Age,* September 2, 1963; his articles in *Bulletin,* February 16, 1963, "An Australian Defence Policy," *20th Century,* Vol. 17 (Summer 1962), pp. 136–155, and "A Pacific Confederation," *Quadrant,* Vol. 6, no. 1 (1962), pp. 25–35; "The Idea of a Pacific Confederation," in Institute of Social Order, *A Pacific Confederation?* (Melbourne: The Institute, 1963), pp. 7–20,

the stage of virtual worthlessness. The best they can offer is some vague hopes that quiet and patient diplomacy by Australia could at some future, unspecified date condition the other prospective members to weigh the alternatives and to opt for a Confederation in preference to the *status quo*. Their project raises a number of crucial yet unanswered questions, however: how could the Confederation contain either direct or indirect aggression against nonmember states such as Laos, where SEATO's failures have been held up as evidence that a new alliance system is urgently required? [67]

Is the Pacific Confederation therefore a piece of complicated nonsense so far as its promotion in Australia is concerned? From the DLP's standpoint, not entirely. Even if something approximating such a plan is never attained, it serves as a useful arguing point for the DLP. In the first place, the DLP uses the Confederation as a kind of audio-visual aid to educate the public to the horrors of Communist China and the danger that Australia faces. In the second place, the emphasis on military strength and cooperation with like-minded countries serves to remind everyone of the general need to be strong in arms and fighting forces and to resist China's threats and blandishments courageously. In the third place, the Confederation scheme, whatever its drawbacks, lends a special authority to the DLP cries about Communist dangers. The DLP has again and again been vilified as paranoically and professionally anti-Communist. Be that as it may, the Confederation lends a certain constructive and positive quality to its political attacks that blunts the charge of negativism. Fourth, the emphasis on Formosa as a member of the project serves a special purpose. Attention is called to the so-

[67] For criticisms, see P. J. Boyce, "Politico-Cultural Obstacles to a Pacific Confederation," Rene L. S. Starling, "A Pacific Confederation?—The Economic Possibilities," Herbert Feith, "Future Australian Foreign Policy," all in *ibid.*, pp. 29–41, 42–51, and 95–108, respectively; *SMH*, Sept. 3, 1963.

cioeconomic progress achieved in Nationalist China and to the considerable military machine which exists there. Since Australians are regarded by the DLP as either ignorant of or hostile toward Formosa, this free advertising is all to the good, perhaps helping to create a climate in which a diplomatic mission would be installed there, greater trade contacts secured, and tendencies to recognize Peking dampened. The final special advantage of the publicity given to one aspect of the Confederation, i.e. diversion of trade from China, can best be examined later in the context of Sino-Australian commercial relations.

Forceful attacks on SEATO have not been confined to the DLP however. The most vociferous single individual has unquestionably been W. G. Goddard, whose writings and lectures in Australia have gone considerably beyond praise for Formosa and condemnation of China. Goddard's theory is plain and stark. China is determined to absorb Australia in her march across Asia and the Pacific. She hopes to be seated in the UN in order to mobilize Afro-Asian sentiment on behalf of breaking down restricted Asian migration into Australian New Guinea. From there and from Indonesia, which Goddard predicts is scheduled for Chinese absorption, leverage would be exerted to open northern metropolitan Australia to Chinese migrants. These migrants would prepare the route for a Chinese invasion, and the Australian Government might have to retreat to Tasmania, holding out there much as the Chinese Nationalists hold Formosa, Hobart becoming the Australian Taipei. SEATO is no shield in Goddard's estimation. What is needed is not simply absolute military firmness against China, but a grand mobilization of spiritual resources throughout Asia and the Pacific. Christians, Muslims, Buddhists, and others must close ranks to instill spiritual energy into people threatened by China. Spiritual officers, publishing houses, all manner of devices and all operating under the aegis of the South-East Asia Spiritual Offensive, or SEASO, must be mobilized, and to whose formation Australia must offer leadership.[68]

The final source of criticism worth mentioning is the small group of articulate and unflinchingly anti-Communist Liberal Party back-benchers in Parliament. Although they tend to be individualists *par excellence,* what unites them is their hatred of Communism and their apprehensions about China. Like the DLP, they claim that the Government is insufficiently aware of the danger from China and of the traps and snares which the Chinese set. Like the DLP, they tend to write off SEATO as ineffectual, or at least of falling short of being a reliable deterrent against China. As to alternative programs, they are far less helpful than the DLP, if the concept of a Pacific Confederation may be called helpful. They are furious with French behavior but are vague about the propriety of instigating France's expulsion from SEATO. They think SEATO ought to be beefed up, but have no specific formula as to how and by whom this should be done. In general, while they sympathize with the broad idea of a Pacific Confederation, they are inclined to admit that it is impractical if not illusory. Among them would, however, be found figures who privately hint that in a situation such as the Vietnamese, the risks of bombing North Vietnam and perhaps even China need to be taken if Vietnam is to be salvaged.

The Menzies Government is aware of these assorted criticisms, though it does not accept them. Public affirmations of support for SEATO aside, the author is reasonably certain that the Government feels that the alliance is functioning acceptably, and definitely feels that no Pacific Confederation or SEASO can or should be attempted. For

[68] See especially his *The Story of Formosa* (Taipei: P.O. Box 337, 1960), and *The Story of Chang Lao* (Melbourne: Australian League of Rights, 1962).

example, the Government is not worried about the future of the Strategic Reserve or of Malaysian ties to the West. At bottom, it believes that when Malaysian spokesmen insist that Malaysian bases cannot automatically be employed for actions elsewhere in South-East Asia, they say so largely for purposes of domestic consumption. Similarly, the anti-foreign bases clause of the Maphilindo agreement is seen as an innocuous diplomatic gambit designed to please Indonesia but with no serious intention of being carried out in the foreseeable future. Private assurances that Malaysia will not restrict Commonwealth forces in times of real danger have apparently been conveyed to and accepted by Australia. The Government is not interested in Malaysian membership in SEATO, reasoning that any such move might unduly excite certain portions of the Chinese population, and that in any event the diverse nature of SEATO's existing membership could lower rather than enhance the available defense assistance now forthcoming from like-minded Britain, Australia, and New Zealand. Indeed, the Government feels that despite the varied national interests and behavior among SEATO's eight signatories, there is no advantage in rocking the diplomatic boat by, for instance, working to expel France. As long as France or any other partner does not throw impossible obstacles in the path of action such as was taken in Thailand, the ability of interested parties to block Communist expansion remains. Also, since it is now understood that SEATO obligations can be executed "individually" rather than "mutually," new flexibility is available, as Barwick claimed. The linchpin of SEATO has always been America, and as long as she does not disengage from Asia, SEATO need not be abused or dismantled.

Aside from disagreeing with the critics of SEATO, however, the Government has seldom if ever engaged in public debate with them. It is understandable that Goddard, as an individual, or his fantastic scheme for spiritual mobilization, should be ignored, but the general neglect of DLP and Government back-bench criticisms requires some explanation. Trying to debate the DLP on the merits of SEATO or the Pacific Confederation would accomplish nothing constructive and perhaps do some harm. The only electoral threat to the Liberal-Country Party coalition stems from the ALP. If the ALP is beaten, the Government is safe. The Government parties therefore train their fire on Labor, and to train it on the DLP would distract from the central objective. In addition, to reply to the DLP over SEATO or the Confederation might create a public impression that the Government is not really as anti-Communist as it avows to be, since the DLP is absolute in its anti-Communism, and in foreign policy is tenaciously anti-Chinese. Since the Government strives to hang a soft-on-Communism label on Labor as part of its political strategy, no reward would come of a dialogue with the DLP. Finally, the DLP performs a vital service to the Government even when it differs with it on such issues as the containment of China. The DLP's announced and recognized function is to alter ALP policy or, failing that, to keep Labor out of office. When the DLP scolds the Government on foreign policy, it simultaneously is being infinitely more severe with the ALP, which suits the Government nicely. Elections to the Australian House of Representatives are held in single-member districts but with preferential voting. If no candidate secures an absolute majority, the winner is not determined until the second and if necessary further preferences cast by voters who supported eliminated candidates have been redistributed. Because in the nature of things DLP voters are instructed by the DLP leadership to cast their second preferences for Liberal and not ALP candidates, and do so with high regularity, they prop up the Government. The DLP would forfeit its *raison d'être* if it allowed its supporters to give second preferences to the Labor Party, the Government knows this, and therefore can largely ignore DLP complaints directed at itself.

Criticisms emanating from Government back-benchers are usually disregarded as well, but for other reasons. Most of the men who criticize the Government for a soft line on China, or condemn SEATO, or something of the sort, are an isolated minority within the coalition parties. They have standing reputations as mavericks and most do not aspire to ministerial office. Probably the two most prominent are Sir Wilfrid Kent-Hughes and W. C. Wentworth, both of whom serve conservative and exceptionally safe Liberal constituencies. Kent-Hughes was a Rhodes scholar, an Olympic athlete, and served in two wars. Although dumped from the Government years ago, in part for his indiscretions on China policy, he later was an active chairman of the Parliamentary Joint Committee on Foreign Affairs and now publishes a private newsletter which stresses foreign relations. Wentworth is the descendant of one of Australia's most famous families and an Oxford M.A. During the war he staged a token simulated invasion of New South Wales just to prove Australia's vulnerability. He has had a long and deep personal feud with Menzies. Another back-bench critic, D. J. Killen, who has been studying law in his spare time, carries considerable personal appeal in a marginal Queensland electorate. Victorian Senator George Hannan, who was narrowly defeated in December of 1964, a successful Melbourne solicitor and national president of the Asian People's Anti-Communist League, was useful because he was one of the very few Catholics on the Government benches. Because these men are in certain ways special, because they represent a small minority, and because they vote with their party when the division bells ring, there is no need to punish or silence them, even when they use the floor of Parliament, or the innocuous Foreign Affairs Committee, or letters to the press to expound their views about SEATO's deficiencies or other matters. Moreover, in an essentially two-party system, a range of opinion within each is predictable.

## THE LABOR PARTY AND SEATO

THE ALP's approach to SEATO is a story in itself, and is pertinent not only to the controversy about security but to politics as well. In the aftermath of the great split, Australian Labor came to share the view of right-oriented critics that SEATO had lost its relevance, though its remedies to meet this situation were indeed different. The first major statement on SEATO was drawn up at the Party's Brisbane Conference in 1957, declaring that "This Conference is of the opinion that S.E.A.T.O. has failed to perform its basic [security] functions, that it is fast becoming an instrument for bolstering reactionary regimes as in Thailand, and that the Liberal-Country Party Coalition Government has contributed to S.E.A.T.O.'s ineffectiveness." [69] By the time of the 1961 conference, the Party had produced an alternative program, arguing that SEATO must be replanned on a cultural, educational, medical, and technical basis rather than on military lines, and should include "all the peoples of South East Asia." [70] Taken literally, this conception of SEATO was especially pleasing to the Party's left-wing. The position took no heed of any Chinese-inspired threat in the region. It denigrated SEATO's military functions to the vanishing point. It reduced the conditions under which Australians might be expected to fight away from home, consistent with the Malayan troops decision adopted at Hobart in 1955. It reprimanded "reactionary," unprogressive regimes and

[69] ALP, *22nd Commonwealth Conference,* p. 95.
[70] ALP, *24th Commonwealth Conference,* p. 35.

looked to penicillin and plows as effective in implanting resilient and democratic systems in the region.[71]

At the time that the special foreign and defense policy conference was held in Canberra in March of 1963, some recognition was given to the fact that Labor could be—and in fact was being—boiled in the Government's and the DLP's political oil for trying to scuttle SEATO completely and therefore to give in to China. Without repudiating its earlier characterization of SEATO, or its scheme for a social reorientation of the organization, the Party declared that Australia should not withdraw from SEATO while it was being reshaped.[72] Recent ALP comments on SEATO have not been especially helpful, although French recognition of China and neutralization proposals for South-East Asia have been used to point the incriminating finger at SEATO once again. One Labor Parliamentation has seen hope in France's neutralization plan: China's shadow is now lying over South-East Asia, and she has invaded both Tibet and India. SEATO had proved itself incapable of any contructive reactions, and in any event is upholding inefficient and corrupt governments. Perhaps de Gaulle's neutralization plan should be explored since U.S. policy, so faithfully imitated by Australia, is obviously fighting a losing battle. "While the neutralization of this area will mean nothing without Chinese good faith, it cannot even start towards being a fact without Chinese participation." [73] In Parliament, French behavior occasioned comments from the leadership itself. While denying that a Labor Government would withdraw

[71] See the comments of L. R. Johnson, *CPD,* HR 31, April 13, 1961, pp. 848–849, and Leslie Haylen, HR 33, October 5, 1961, p. 1730.

[72] ALP, *Special Commonwealth Conference,* p. 12. Also see the majority report of the Standing Committee on Foreign Affairs, pp. 21–22.

[73] Gordon Bryant, in *Fact* (Melbourne), March 5, 1964. Also see L. R. Johnson, *CPD,* HR, March 19, 1964, pp. 710–711.

from SEATO, Whitlam pointed to the absurdity of existing conditions: SEATO had been formed to contain China, but Pakistan was flirting with China, the Philippines had incriminated themselves over Malaysia, France had extended recognition to Peking and was preaching South-East Asian neutralization, etc.[74] Calwell, while leveling other indictments, derided SEATO for its unrepresentative character—for instance, Malaysia was not a member.[75]

The interested spectator may be excused if he is puzzled by just exactly what Labor wants and how it hopes to accomplish it. The clear implication of the ALP's position is that aside from ANZUS, which includes no Asian states, neither SEATO nor any other military alliance can perform a useful function in defending South-East Asia and containing China. Socioeconomic programs have been extolled so much that one is left with the impression that they can handle what arms cannot—for instance, block a Chinese invasion of India, rid Laos of the North Vietnamese and Chinese-sponsored Pathet Lao, or call a halt to Sukarno's confrontation of Malaysia. If it is to be admitted that there are immediate and pressing problems of subversion and military threat in the region, how could they be managed if years, or perhaps decades, were required to banish malaria, increase literacy, build recreational centers, and the like? There was point to Killen's cutting query whether recent Chinese behavior could be so interpreted that "entering into a discussion with Mao Tse-tung about the benefits of Shakespeare to the twentieth century would be of any advantage." [76]

Labor also cavils at SEATO because it props up undemocratic regimes in Thailand and Vietnam. But Labor also wants universality of South-East Asian membership

[74] *CPD,* HR, April 21, 1964, p. 1284.
[75] *Ibid.,* p. 1271.
[76] *Ibid.,* HR 37, October 25, 1962, p. 1973.

in its reconstructed SEATO, which certainly implies that Thailand and Vietnam would be included. How could a reconstructed SEATO drive undemocartic and unprogressive tendencies out of these countries? If Thailand and Vietnam are governed as heavy-handedly as Labor suggests, surely the ruling elites there would not allow political interference, and would assure themselves that socio-economic aid could not be converted into a political threat against them. And, for that matter, which would come first, universality of membership among South-East Asian countries or SEATO's reconstruction along "cultural" lines? While the organization retains its present orientation, Malaysia and Cambodia, to mention but two, would surely not enter. But a reconstruction of SEATO could not be carried forward without the present members' consent, and is Australia willing to risk spoiling whatever is left of SEATO unity and offending the U.S., while searching for a fresh orientation?

Questions of this sort must confound people who are trying to unscramble Labor's SEATO policy, and indirectly its attitude toward China. The Government parties and the DLP know this, and blast Labor whenever they can for muddle-headedness on the real threat that China poses in the region. The almost monumental irony of the whole business is that under a Labor Government there would probably be no change of any consequence, and nearly all the above questions and dilemmas would assume academic interest at most. The author's understanding is that, if in office, an ALP Government would strive to persuade its SEATO partners to place greater emphasis on the social and economic assistance features of SEATO *already* provided for in the treaty. However, Labor would *not eliminate,* only *supplement,* the defense discussions, planning, and exercises now a feature of the organization. The admission was obtained that since Labor already regards SEATO's military functions as minor and ineffective, there would be no compulsion to abolish what is there.[77] And yet, of course, the Menzies Government feels that what is there is both important and efficient. Hence, for practical purposes, both sides, for entirely separate reasons, are satisfied with the *status quo* as far as the military aspects of SEATO are concerned. It is legitimate to ask whether a Labor Government, i.e. a Calwell or Whitlam Government, would simply not be helpful when occasion arose to show some of the "paper tiger's" remaining teeth. This entails speculation about unknown circumstances, but it should be remembered that by now Labor is prepared to retain Australian troops in the Strategic Reserve, that it did not object to forces being committed to Malaysian Borneo, that it would not pull forces back if a treaty could not be negotiated with Malaysia, and that in principle it did not condemn the stationing of an air squadron in Thailand or instructors in Vietnam.

But what if, even in the above context, Labor could not convince other SEATO members to accelerate socioeconomic operations? The most likely answer is that nothing would happen. Australia, having diplomatically tried to steer a fresh course, would not withdraw from SEATO. Both Calwell and Whitlam realize the political disaster that would follow such a step, and both are sufficiently aware of American sensitivities and sufficiently committed to ANZUS, so that they would not consider taking such a spectacular step. Above all, Labor admits that the chances for a major increase in SEATO's nonmilitary activities are not promising. Even assuming Labor was wrong in its assumption, a "reconstructed" SEATO would still carry its military features. What chance then of attracting Cambodia, Laos, Indonesia, or Malaysia in order to universalize South-East Asian membership? The old Indo-Chinese states, in any event, are debarred from joining military al-

[77] See Nicholas McKenna, *CPD,* S, August 8, 1964, p. 64, and Reginald Bishop, *ibid.,* September 2, 1964, p. 351.

liances. Malaysia and Indonesia would hold the same objections to joining as they do now. The net result would probably be no change in membership, certainly not raising membership—the SEATO picture would hold the same focus which it now does, one favored by the Government. These are not the sorts of admissions that Labor wishes to make public, in part because of sentimental attachment to some of the precepts of the official program, in part because it feels it must differentiate itself from the Government, in part because the left-wing of the Party, be it in Parliament or in conference or otherwise, would not stand for it. In the meantime, the ALP squirms in opposition as it is sharply criticized and berated for what it could not or would not implement if in power.

### THE PROBLEMS AND POLITICS OF NUCLEAR DEFENSE

CONTROVERSY surrounding the United States naval communications center in Western Australia, and the ALP's proposal for a nuclear-free zone in the southern hemisphere, once again point up the pervasiveness of the Chinese factor in security matters and in Australian politics. In May of 1963, after considerable discussion between the two Governments, Australia and the U.S. signed an agreement providing for the construction by the Americans of a powerful transmitting station at the North West Cape, Exmouth Gulf. The station's basic purpose was to improve communication with American naval units in the Indian Ocean and the South-West Pacific, and particularly to signal submarines, polaris or otherwise. It was not designed as a storage area for nuclear weapons, or as a naval or air base of any sort. Australian sovereignty over the station's area is retained, and the facilities are available for Australian use. Although Austral-American consultations on the various uses of the station are provided for, Canberra has agreed without reservation to the terms of a memorandum from U.S. Ambassador William Battle, who indicated that "it was clearly understood that consultation connoted no more than consultation and was not intended to establish Australian control over use of station nor to imply any Government of Australia design to restrict at any time United States Government use of station for defence communications including, for example, communications for polaris submarines. It is also understood that it was not intended to give Australia control over or access to the contents of messages transmitted over the station." [78]

The signaling station at the North West Cape was another very sizeable stride along the road to defense cooperation between the two countries. In 1957 the Menzies Government began a systematic program of integrating its arms with American weapons.[79] Under an agreement in the same year, an atomic information exchange was announced, relating to defense planning, enemy nuclear capabilities, and civil defense information sharing.[80] By the time the North West Cape agreement was completed, the Americans had space and research tracking facilities at Woomera and Muchea, a high-altitude atmospheric sampling establishment at Mildura, a joint weather station at Alice Springs, air sampling operations at Laverton and Avalon, and other assorted facilities sponsored by U.S. military and scientific groups.[81] American U-2 aircraft have been employed, though Chinese accusations that they have flown over China for purposes of espionage have been hotly denied.[82]

At all events, the Government has viewed the Cape

[78] Memorandum of May 7, 1963, in *CNIA,* Vol. 34 (May 1963), p. 7. For text of the agreement, see *ibid.,* pp. 17–32.

[79] See Menzies, *CPD,* HR 14, April 4, 1957, p. 573.

[80] Statement of Howard Beale of July 13, 1957, in *CNIA,* Vol. 28 (July 1957), pp. 557–558.

[81] See William Spooner, *CPD,* S 22, December 4, 1962, pp. 1659–1660.

[82] Menzies, statement of July 6, 1960, in *SMH,* July 7, 1960, and David Fairbairn, Minister for Air, *CPD,* HR 36, October 16, 1962, pp. 1586–1587.

agreement as a logical extension of its intimate and productive cooperation with the U.S., while recognizing the prominent role the China "problem" played in its inauguration. Broadly taken, the Menzies Government, applauded both by the press and the DLP, has seen the North West Cape installation as a contribution to the deterrent and retaliatory capacity of the Western coalition, in which of course the U.S. figures most conspicuously. Chinese troublemaking has again been cited as a reason for keeping defenses strong and efficient. The presence of a great Chinese land army is seen as being offset by nuclear capabilities. The determination of China to develop nuclear capability, and her contemptuous sneer at the nuclear test-ban treaty of 1963 and refusal to join the Geneva disarmament discussions, have been interpreted as additional reasons to maintain high-pitch readiness.[83] Beyond this, however, is a definite motive to prove to the United States that Australia is indisputably an excellent ally—she is pulling her weight in the security system. The point of this is to heighten U.S. concern for Australia's own security interests in the region, a kind of insurance policy, with the signaling station serving as a premium which Australia might someday wish to cash in. Time and place and manner of "cashing in" are unspecified, but, as has been shown, Australia has a vested interest in the Malaysian-Indonesian-New Guinea complex, where a "Chinese factor" is seen to operate, and it is all to the good to implant the U.S. on Australian soil physically so as to make it more psychologically disposed to listen to and/or protect Australia in special situations. As the *Sydney Morning Herald* summarized it, the Cape station is "doubly welcome because its establishment amounts to an implicit admission by the United States that this country is

[83] See Barwick, *ibid.,* HR 38, May 9, 1963, pp. 1224ff.; William McMahon, *ibid.,* May 16, 1963, p. 1506; Perth *West Australian,* March 8, 1963; Melbourne *Herald,* April 30, 1963.

the secure southern baseline of its global strategy and because it physically engages the United States on this continent." [84] It is probably with these considerations in mind that Canberra accepted without protest the "consultation but no interference" statement made concerning the signaling station. According to the Prime Minister, the U.S. must always be kept at Australia's side; if the Americans could be told when and how to employ their polaris submarines, the Chinese would be more than pleased.[85]

In order to understand the ALP's reaction to the Cape installation and to gauge the surrounding political debate, the Government's position on the acquisition of nuclear weapons must first be explained. Menzies laid down the guiding principles in September of 1957. The first point he made was that the danger of global nuclear war was remote, but chances were that there would be recurring limited conflicts, especially in South-East Asia; for such conflicts conventionally armed Australian forces were sufficient. In any event, "nuclear play" in such outbreaks could only invite escalation—a comment no doubt inspired by memories of brinksmanship during the 1954 Indo-Chinese troubles. Second, he stressed the enormous drain of both money and resources involved in any attempt by small Australia to create her own nuclear arsenal. Finally, he warned against any tendency toward the proliferation of nuclear arms—again, perhaps, with the idea of not stimulating Chinese ambitions in that direction.[86] But that was 1957. By 1962, Australia held a new although not a diametrically opposed view. Early in 1962,

[84] *SMH,* May 10, 1963. Also see Sydney *Daily Telegraph,* March 8, 1963; *Canberra Times,* March 11, 1963; Adelaide *Advertiser* and Melbourne *Herald,* May 10, 1963; Sydney *Mirror,* May 12, 1963; George Cole, *CPD,* S 23, May 23, 1963, pp. 720–721; "The United States Radio Communications Station," *Facts* (Melbourne), National Civic Council (May–June 1963), pp. 1–2.

[85] *CPD,* HR 38, April 3, 1963, p. 344.

[86] *Ibid.,* HR 16, Sept. 19, 1957, pp. 795–798.

U Thant circulated a letter among various UN members asking their opinions on undertakings not to manufacture or acquire nuclear weapons. Barwick's reply was that Australia could not give such an understanding. At bottom, she needed the flexibility of deciding on the matter as security considerations demanded, and particularly had to take into account the emergence of "a military power of great dimension and some ambition," namely China. "This power is convinced of the inevitability of war and is consciously working for the elimination of the type of society of which Australia is a part . . . [and China] already has massive conventional forces, which it has used against the United Nations, and has nuclear weapons potentialities which may be close to fulfilment." [87]

Here and again some of the Government's own supporters in Parliament have urged the acquisition of such weapons from the U.S. or Britain, or at least the stationing of American-controlled nuclear delivery systems on Australian soil.[88] In June of 1963 the NSW convention of the Country Party defeated a motion urging establishment of U.S. strategic bases in Australia, but the motion lost by only a handful of votes. [89] The following month the DLP's Federal conference opted for U.S. nuclear bases in all areas affected by American NATO, SEATO, and ANZUS commitments,[90] and the Party's 1964 Senate campaign policy speech called for the development of Australia's

[87] Cited in *SMH,* April 6, 1962. Also see Barwick, "Australian Foreign Policy 1962," p. 20. See comments by Charles Meeking, "Long-Range Dilemma," *Eastern World,* Vol. 16 (June 1962), p. 19; Sydney *Daily Telegraph,* Adelaide *Advertiser,* and Hobart *Mercury,* April 6, 1962; Perth *West Australian,* April 7, 1962; Sydney *Sunday Mirror,* April 8, 1962.

[88] William Bostock, *CPD,* HR 15, May 7, 1957, pp. 1104–1106; W. C. Wentworth, *ibid.,* May 8, 1957, pp. 1155–1156; Robert Wordsworth, S 10, May 8, 1957, pp. 614–616; J. D. Killen, HR 28, October 11, 1960, p. 1872; George Branson, S, September 2, 1964, p. 351.

[89] See *SMH,* June 27, 1963.

[90] *Ibid.,* July 29, 1963.

own nuclear deterrent.[91] Since its 1962 national congress, the Returned Servicemen's League of Australia, an influential body of 250,000 members, has been on record favoring a comparable step.[92]

It is true that the Government has explicitly rejected a Chinese disarmament scheme designed to strip the West of its nuclear advantage in the face of the continued preservation of large conventional Chinese armies.[93] It appears that the U.S. has promised at least tactical nuclear weapons to Australia in case of emergency.[94] Although the Government has categorically denied any American plans to establish a nuclear base of any sort in Australia,[95] the 1962 exchange of letters with U Thant and the presence of the communications center can be inferred as meaning that nuclear arms for or in Australia are no longer precluded in principle.

But the Australian Government has not discarded its anxieties about nuclear proliferation. It readily and enthusiastically acceded to the nuclear test-ban treaty. It still believes that local rather than global war is more likely to occur. It still could not afford the investment connected with becoming a self-made member of the nuclear club. China's success with nuclear tests may, on balance, act as a deterrent to any Australian temptations to acquire nuclear capacity or station U.S. nuclear forces on Australian territory. A nuclear arsenal in Australia, as a response to China, could trigger exactly the kind of reactions in Asia

[91] George Cole, policy statement in Melbourne, Nov. 24, 1964, in *ibid.*, Nov. 25, 1964.

[92] Returned Sailors', Soldiers' and Airmen's League of Australia, 47th national congress, standing policy resolution no. 94. Material supplied by courtesy of A. G. W. Keys, National Secretary, RSL, Canberra.

[93] See Barwick, *ibid.*, HR, August 15, 1963, pp. 196–197; statement by D. O. Hay to the UN First Committee, October 23, 1963, in *CNIA*, Vol. 34 (October 1963), esp. pp. 48–49.

[94] *SMH*, January 18, 1960.

[95] Menzies, *CPD*, HR 37, November 7, 1962, p. 2116.

that Australia wishes to avoid. One could well be Asian exaggeration of present Chinese nuclear strength and a corresponding sense of panic. The other would be the urge of Asian states to climb on the nuclear bandwagon by one means or another. Hasluck's comment on the October 1964 Chinese nuclear test is instructive. He said that while the test was a depressing event, it was not unexpected. Much time would elapse before China would become a major nuclear power in any significant sense, and the successful test had not materially enhanced her relative power position. Hasluck then went on to discourage nuclear proliferation in Asia and promised continued Australian efforts toward the universal acceptance of the nuclear test-ban treaty, including China.[96] Consider Indonesia's boast in November 1964 that she would have an atomic bomb in the following year and that appropiate rocket delivery systems were already being tested.[97] While Australia reacted with incredulity to the Indonesian nuclear claim, it is probably of more than passing interest that Menzies said that "Indonesia, like Australia, is a signatory to the partial nuclear test ban treaty and is therefore, with us, involved in a state of affairs in which we will not have atomic testing ourselves and we do not want to see the spread of atomic weapons beyond those countries in which they now exist. I would hope that Indonesia would observe the terms of that ban just . . . [as] we do." [98] Nuclear weapons in Australia would surely not contribute toward these stated Government objectives.

It is in the light of all these elements that Labor's response can be measured, and indeed some of the Australian academic criticism as well. Labor has always possessed an idealistic quality which preaches that all possible measures must be taken to avert war or provocation of

[96] Statement reported in *Australian News Weekly Round Up* (New York), Oct. 21, 1964.
[97] *SMH*, Nov. 16, 1964.
[98] *CPD*, HR, Nov. 16, 1964, p. 2976.

war. It has also had a tradition of looking inward in matters of defence, some would call it isolationism, and has been suspicious of undue entanglement in the power-politics decisions of other nations. In addition Labor has contained a neutralist group whose members tend to assume a "plague on both your houses" view of the East-West conflict. Nevertheless, in spite of some of the tendencies described, it is also a Party that is not unmindful of the Chinese cloud over Asia, nor is it blind to electoral expediency. It is quite impossible to reconstruct the political interplay which occupied the ALP for most of 1962 and up to the time of the special conference at Canberra in March of 1963, when formal and binding decisions were taken on the North West Cape and nuclear affairs. A small book could probably be written on this alone, but a few lines will be sketched in here to serve as prelude to the Canberra conference policy decisions.

The Party became doubly troubled in early 1962 because the first announcement of a station at the North West Cape and the exchange of letters between U Thant and Barwick closely coincided, and the Government was very slow indeed in clarifying the exact purposes for which the Cape facility was intended. An abhorrence of nuclear warfare was a traditional preoccupation with the Party, and now the prospect of nuclear involvement for Australia seemed to be spreading. In 1962 and early 1963 the Parliamentary and organizational wings of the Party were caught up in heated controversy over whether to opt for a total ban on atomic arms for Australia or a qualified one, over the type of nuclear disengagement plan that was most desirable, and eventually over whether to sanction the Government's Cape proposal and, if so, on what terms.[99] Throughout the period the Parliamentary group, of which

[99] For some résumés, see Ian Turner, "Nuclear Bases in Australia?" in *The Questions for Labor–Foreign Policy and Defence,*

only 10 to 15 per cent is "neutralist," was, for reasons of conviction and electoral judgment, disposed toward a moderate line. Calwell and Whitlam, and especially the former, found themselves doing everything in their power to avert adoption of a policy that would be substantively and politically unrealistic.

The result was the convening of the special conference in March of 1963. Even then the outcome was uncertain. Most of the 36 delegates were trade unionists with small appreciation of what the facts of life were in Canberra or on the hustings. Only two of the six state delegations came instructed—the West Australian to vote against the North West Cape station, the South Australian to support it. Other delegates divided about evenly. Finally, in an atmosphere almost as supercharged as Hobart had been eight years earlier, after furious behind-the-scenes activity and impassioned appeals by Calwell and Whitlam, a binding statement was approved by the bare margin of 19–17. What was this decision, "this miserable compromise" as Menzies described it, "dangerous and frustrating" to Australia interests and arrived at not by Labor's Parliamentary leadership but by 36 unknown and politically irresponsible figures, the "36 faceless men" as they later were stigmatized? [100] The language of the decision was one thing. Public interpretations of it by the ALP added something else. Comments made to the author by leading figures in the Party introduce still different elements into the picture.

---

an *Outlook* publication (March 6, 1963), pp. 6–9; Report of the Federal ALP Secretary, F. E. Chamberlain, in ALP, *Special Commonwealth Conference,* pp. 5–7; R. G. Neale, "Problems of Australian Foreign Policy January-June 1963," *Australian Journal of Politics and History,* Vol. 9 (November 1963), esp. pp. 137–141. For a DLP interpretation, ascribing ALP policy to Communist influence, see G. Healey, "The Nuclear-Free Zone Campaign" (Carnegie, Victoria: Renown Press, 1963), *passim.*

[100] Statement of March 21, 1963, in *SMH,* March 22, 1963.

It is important to consider the highlights of the March 1963 statement against Labor's explanations and interpretations as well as Government and public reactions, and finally to consider the political impact within the framework of Australia's policies and attitudes toward China.

The Canberra conference statement opens with a denunciation of nuclear tests generally and urges the Australian Government to initiate a conference of the Antarctic treaty powers, China, South and South-East Asian nations, and all African and South American countries, "directed towards making the Southern Hemisphere a nuclear-free zone"; furthermore Australia should submit to the conference her own pledge "not to manufacture, acquire or receive atomic weapons." It goes on to say that a radio signal station, such as the North West Cape installation *would not* be inconsistent with Labor policy under certain conditions. One condition laid down was that the facility come under "joint control and operation" of the U.S. and Australia. Another stated that in no circumstance should Australia automatically become involved in war, and that if America were at war or was threatened with war by another power, "Australian territory and Australian facilities must not be used in any way that would involve Australia without the prior knowledge and consent of the Australian government." Finally, such a communications center must not become a base for the stockpiling of nuclear arms in peacetime. Australia, the statement continues, "will not be the first nation in the Pacific to stockpile nuclear arms in its territories in peace time." [101]

The first major public encounter was precipitated when the Government introduced the North West Cape agreement before Parliament. Labor decided not to oppose the measure—in itself a victory for the leadership—but to ask that it be renegotiated in a way that would allow for

[101] The relevant decisions are contained in ALP, *Special Commonwealth Conference,* pp. 36–37.

joint control and that safeguards be incorporated against automatic Australian involvement in a war arising out of the utilization of the station. There are variations within the ALP, and within the academic community on the theme of how Australia could be embarrassed diplomatically or dragged into war if she were unable to control "attack" signals from the station to submarines and nuclear-armed planes. One broad line of argument has been that the station would facilitate the issuing of orders to fire on China should the offshore islands dispute flare up again, or into North Vietnam or China if America became exasperated with the conflict in Vietnam.[102] Connected with this argument is the proposition that the center's presence as a sender of American operational signals could invite atomic retaliation against Australia, or the holding of Australia as a "nuclear hostage" unless she were prepared to capitulate in a war. At the moment this could only be done by the Russians, but the Chinese will also eventually own the nuclear capacity to behave in the same manner.[103]

The Government's reply to all this has been to say that in the first place the U.S. did not and will not consent to joint control over the messages carried from the North West Cape, and there is public record, aside from Ambassador Battle's memorandum, that this is in fact so.[104] But rather than patiently explaining that no nuclear attack

[102] Patrick Galvin, *CPD,* HR 38, May 16, 1963, pp. 1495–1496; E. J. Harrison, *ibid.,* May 16, 1963, p. 1540; L. R. Johnson, *ibid.,* May 21, 1963, p. 1566; George Gray, *ibid.,* May 21, 1963, p. 1578; Whitlam, "Australian Foreign Policy 1963," p. 7; A. L. Burns, "Overseas Bases and Alliances: The Australian-American Case," *Australia's Neighbours,* Fourth Series, nos. 3–4 (March-April 1963), p. 7.

[103] James Cairns, *CPD,* HR 38, May 21 and 22, 1963, p. 1637; Coral Bell, "Australia and the American Alliance," *The World Today,* Vol. 19 (July 1963), p. 310; Turner, *op. cit.,* pp. 10–11; Turner, in *Bulletin,* April 27, 1963, and in "The Base," *Dissent,* Vol. 3 (Winter 1963), pp. 9–10.

[104] See Averell Harriman's statement in Canberra of June 7, 1963, in *SMH,* June 8, 1963.

could be launched without Presidential consent, that such an attack is in practice almost wholly unthinkable save as a second strike, and that political and service consultations between the two countries might help to clear up American thinking for Australia and might indeed present Australia with an opportunity to dissuade Washington from hasty and dangerous policies in Asia which could evolve into a major war, the Government has largely picked at the ALP. Renegotiation cannot bring fresh terms, therefore Labor would only succeed in frightening the U.S. out of the Cape facility, the American alliance would be irreparably harmed, and the only victor would be the Communist powers, especially China. These insinuations were especially brought to bear during the 1963 electoral campaign, as part of the strategy to expose Labor's foreign policy weaknesses and alleged willingness to countenance Chinese ambitions.[105]

The Government's substantive reply was both right and wrong. It was right because a Labor Government would most likely fail in renegotiating the treaty. But it was wrong when it imputed crippling effects to Labor's *wish* to renegotiate. In point of fact, what emerged both from responsible Labor statements and the author's own queries, is first that Labor would definitely not repudiate the treaty even if it failed to renegotiate, and perhaps even more importantly that it really would not ask for anything dramatic in the first instance. Calwell has publicly affirmed that the ALP desires consultation at the political and not the military level, does not care to impose a veto over what the station can do, and did not wish access to American secrets, codes, or ciphers.[106] On his part, the Senate

[105] For example, Menzies' statement of November 17, 1963, in *ibid.*, November 18, 1963; Liberal Party advertisement in *Bulletin*, November 30, 1963; "Liberal Facts. Federal Election Campaign, 1963" (Canberra: Federal Secretariat, Liberal Party of Australia, 1963), item 12.

[106] Statement of June 7, 1963, in *SMH*, June 8, 1963; TV inter-

Leader of the Opposition has stated that his Party was realistic enough to realize that if an atomic attack were launched against Australia *or* the U.S., "there would be no time for consultation whilst a nuclear missile was in the air on the way." [107] A well-situated ALP source told the author that his Party, when in office, would approach "re-negotiation" not to alter the treaty terms, but to expunge the hard tones of Battle's memorandum which, it is charged, only obfuscated an agreement through which even Labor could establish a working, consultative arrangement with America. This is certainly not a view congenial to the left-wing of the Party, and is probably not in the spirit of the Canberra declaration. Oddly enough, if the Australian public understands "consultation" in the meaning of the March 1963 declaration, then Labor *in fact* holds a position almost identical to that of the Government, and *both* are slightly out of step with public sentiment. Opinion surveys have shown wide support for the Cape installation,[108] but also exceptionally strong feeling that no messages which could involve Australia in war should be transmitted without Australian consent (71 per cent to 21 per cent; 8 per cent "don't know"), and that joint control of the center *would* work (65 per cent to 25 per cent; 10, "don't know").[109]

With respect to the nuclear-free zone proposal, Labor's critics have had a veritable field day. The Government has claimed that it does not have a "closed mind" on nuclear-free zone schemes, but that four requirements must be satisfied for such a zone to be meaningful: unanimity, balance, verification, and the absense within such a zone of nuclear targets. So far as the Pacific is concerned, none of

view of October 20, 1963, in *ibid.*, October 21, 1963; Calwell, "Labor's Policy," p. 20.

[107] *CPD*, S 23, May 23, 1963, p. 713. Also see the comment by Don Dunstan, "The Base," *Dissent*, Vol. 3 (Winter 1963), pp. 6–7.

[108] *AGP*, nos. 1676–1687, May-June 1963.

[109] *Ibid.*, nos. 1688–1697, June-August 1963.

these requirements is at the moment satisfied.[110] More particularly, especially when attacking nuclear-free zone proposals in the Australian political setting, the Government has been scornful and mocking in its tone. A proposal on Labor's lines would be "suicidal" to Australia. It would push the U.S. out of the southern hemisphere, neutralize the benefits of the North West Cape, expose Australia, damage ANZUS and SEATO, and invite Communist penetration beneath the equator. The equator is an imaginary line, not a buffer that would prevent enemy submarines from firing across it into the southern hemisphere. The Chinese presence was especially distressing. China was committed to building nuclear weapons, yet she, the closest Communist power threatening Australia, was also the most irresponsible Communist power. She could not be trusted, and in any event policing such an agreement would be next to impossible. Yet even without nuclear capacity China would welcome such a zone, for the elimination of the nuclear deterrent of the U.S. from the region would grant China's giant land forces an enormous advantage and perhaps even invite encroachment into the southern hemisphere.[111]

The Government not only used Labor's nuclear-free

[110] See Barwick, *CPD,* HR, March 11, 1964, p. 486; D. O. Hay to the UN First Committee, November 19, 1963, in *CNIA,* Vol. 34 (November 1963), pp. 35–36.

[111] For sample Government reactions, see Menzies, *CPD,* HR 38, May 16, 1963, p. 1519, and May 22, 1963, p. 1704; addresses of November 2, 1962, and April 23 and November 19, 1963, in *SMH,* November 3, 1962, and April 24 and November 20, 1963, respectively; Menzies' Policy Speech, "Federal Election, 1963" (Canberra: Federal Secretariat, Liberal Party of Australia, 1963), pp. 7–8; Liberal Party of Australia, " 'Dangerous and Frustrating'—A.L.P. Decisions on Defence and Foreign Relations" (Canberra: Federal Secretariat, Liberal Party of Australia, 1963), esp. p. 9; John Gorton, *CPD,* S 22, October 17, 1962, p. 920; Barwick, "Australian Foreign Policy 1962," p. 21; "Liberal Facts," item 10; "Peace Through Security" (Canberra: Federal Secretariat, Liberal Party of Australia, 1963), pp. 3–4.

zone proposal as a whipping cane in ordinary Parliamentary circumstances and in the 1963 election but, as R.G. Neale has properly argued, it deliberately brought the Cape agreement before Parliament for ratification—which constitutionally it was not required to do—in part to exploit divisions within the ALP and to hammer at such Opposition "absurdities" as the nuclear-free zone.[112] Nor was the Government lacking in allies. The press was nearly unanimous in berating Labor on the issue,[113] while the DLP, especially as the election approached, could not find adjectives abusive enough to describe the position taken by Labor as it toiled to pin labels of fantasy and China-coddling on the ALP.[114] It is probably safe to say that to the extent that foreign and defense policy played a part in the 1963 elections to incriminate and discredit Labor, the nuclear-free zone was the single most damaging issue.

In a way, Labor has deserved some of the brickbats thrown at its nuclear-free zone proposal. There is considerable confusion within the Party as to what the plan implies. Although the Canberra statement called for a conference to de-nuclearize the entire southern hemisphere, the author has heard much talk of proceeding piecemeal, with stress on de-nuclearizing only the Asian-Pacific region as a start. Dr. James Cairns, who is on the Labor front bench, has publicly stated that, contrary to what was decided at Canberra, the major powers would not need to subscribe to such a scheme; it would be sufficient to gain approval from existing nonnuclear nations. Also, contrary to the Canberra declaration, he has sug-

[112] Neale, *op. cit.,* pp. 140–141.

[113] For example, Sydney *Sunday Telegraph,* November 4, 1962; Melbourne *Herald,* November 5, 1962; Brisbane *Courier-Mail,* November 6, 1962; Hobart *Mercury,* May 10, 1963; *SMH,* November 2 and 4, 1963.

[114] *News Weekly,* March 6 and 13, November 6, 1963; Healey, *op. cit.,* pp. 3–4; George Cole, "DLP Policy Speech," November 7, 1963, mimeo., p. 4.

gested that China's agreement to such a scheme would not be necessary.[115] Another Labor man admitted that policing de-nuclearization would be tremendously difficult, but that even the hortative effect of an unenforceable agreement of this kind among great powers might have some significance. Still another Labor figure, with a strong interest in foreign affairs, said that he had not given any thought to whether a nuclear-free zone and the North West Cape installation were compatible—but on the spur of the moment he thought not. The Canberra statement, under listed conditions, does make the two compatible.

But in the last analysis what emerges is that the effect of Labor's nuclear-free zone program is more like that of a pop-gun than an explosion on the Australian defense scene. Labor's leadership has set its sights so low as to assert simply that Australia should take the initiative in convening the appropriate multination conference. The main purpose would be to avoid atomic proliferation in the Asian-Pacific region,[116] rather than the barring of great power presence and activity there, though the latter is not regarded as undesirable if it could be achieved with suitable guarantees. Labor figures are almost at one in agreeing that there are serious practical difficulties in reaching *any* sort of agreement. Whitlam's Roy Milne lecture of July 1963 is very instructive as to the minor key in which the nuclear-free zone is in fact played. In the course of his remarks he stressed that

> The core of our proposal is that a conference should be called to consider the establishment of a nuclear-free zone. Only if the conference could agree to a watertight arrangement would Australia agree not to manufacture, acquire or receive nuclear weapons. To obtain such a

[115] *CPD,* HR, March 19, 1964, p. 723. Also see Alan Reid's comment in *Bulletin,* March 28, 1964.

[116] Calwell, statement of June 11, 1963, in *SMH,* June 12, 1963; "Labor's Policy," p. 21.

> watertight arrangement would require the support of all the nuclear powers. If the United States or any other nuclear power found the proposal unacceptable, clearly the conference would be abortive and nothing would be achieved. But neither would anything be lost. The emphasis is on calling a conference, on taking a diplomatic initiative. The Australian Labor Party is not pledged to renounce nuclear weapons in advance of the conference or following the conference if it proves unsuccessful. Defense measures cannot be defined till disarmament agreements are achieved. . . . No country in the southern hemisphere has nuclear weapons at this stage. Accordingly Australia's defence is not immediately prejudiced by a proposal to ban them. If, however, our neighbors were to acquire them, then probably Australia would have to match them.[117]

Whitlam's public view largely coincides with what the author himself has been able to learn. It is in substance very close to the Government's own position. For instance, while U.S. officials have not spoken favorably of a Pacific nuclear-free zone under the present circumstances,[118] the ALP leadership admits that without great power support the whole scheme collapses. In view of China's nuclear test and her ambition to acquire operational nuclear capability, plans for a nuclear-free zone are apt to become even more untenable. It is instructive that Calwell's response to the Chinese nuclear explosion was a call for invigorated disarmament negotiations, but not for

[117] "Australian Foreign Policy 1963," pp. 16–17.

[118] See Barwick, *CPD,* HR, August 15, 1963, p. 198; Sydney *Daily Telegraph,* October 31, 1963; U.S. Admiral John H. Sides, statement of April 29, 1963, in *SMH,* April 30, 1963; ANZUS Council communiqué of June 6, 1963, in *CNIA,* Vol. 34 (June 1963), pp. 6–7. Also see the discussion in A. L. Burns, "A Regional Problem: The American Signalling Station in Western Australia," *Disarmament and Arms Control,* Vol. 2, no. 1 (1964), pp. 28–29.

the convening of a conference to construct a nuclear-free zone.[119] A month and a half later, during the Senate electoral campaign, Calwell averred that while the ALP still wanted a nuclear-free zone, if but a single nation (presumably including all nuclear powers) did not want it Australia could not accept it.[120] Whitlam leaves room for nuclear weapons in Australia, and so does the Government. The only difference is that the ALP, through the Canberra platform, recommends that Australia not be the *first* nation in the region to acquire such weapons, while the Government has made no similar pledge. Since in practice there is no immediate prospect that the Government will buy nuclear arms, or that U.S. controlled arms will be invited, operationally Labor and the Government are far more alike than different. Yet the charges against the ALP continue to fly, and the Government portrays its policy as the only one capable of saving Australia from Chinese adventures. While Labor has only itself to blame for much of the confusion and inconsistency which affects its nuclear-free zone attitude, debate on the issue, as on other key questions of Australia's security requirements opposite China, carries an uncomfortably unreal ring.

[119] Calwell's statement of Oct. 18, 1964, supplied by courtesy of Ian Hamilton, Director, Australian News and Information Bureau, New York.

[120] Television statement in Brisbane, Nov. 29, 1964, in *SMH*, Nov. 30, 1964.

# VI

# THE CHINA TRADE: INCENTIVE AND PERFORMANCE

AUSTRALIA'S TRADE with China supplies excellent insight into how economic, political, and diplomatic ingredients of the China problem interrelate. Because it is a subject of great variety and has figured so prominently in Australia's attitude and behavior toward China, it deserves special and extensive treatment.

## AUSTRALIA'S OVERSEAS TRADE POSITION

ALTHOUGH the discussion here will highlight political implications, it is appropriate to outline some of the economic considerations which impelled serious thinking about trading with China. Australia is a prosperous society, and becoming more so. She wishes to maintain an annual growth rate of 2 to 2.5 per cent *per capita* and a Gross National Product increase of over 4 per cent, and to keep the unemployment level no higher than an enviable 1 to 2 per cent. To do so she must continue to attract investment from abroad, and to sell and earn overseas at an accelerated pace to pay for her large volume of imports.[1] The Australian emphasis on exports is obvious. Although a country of but eleven million people, Australia ranks twelfth in size as a world trader. She exports about 16 per cent of her GNP annually, compared with only 4 per cent

[1] See especially comments by Sir John Crawford, former Secretary, Dept. of Trade, in "The Jolt of the Common Market," *Saturday Review,* January 12, 1963, p. 31, and address in Adelaide of September 4, 1963, in Melbourne *Age,* September 5, 1963.

of GNP exported by the world's largest trader, the U.S.[2] A lowering of the volume of her exports, or the price they earn, or serious imbalances in trade, are therefore all deleterious to Australia's economic well-being.

At the heart of Australia's export market are primary products—wool, grains, fruits, minerals, and the like, whose share of the country's overseas earnings lies between 80 and 90 per cent. Yet for many years the prices earned on such products have been deteriorating. Between 1953 and 1963, the terms of Australia's trade declined from an index of 100 to 68, largely because of falling primary products prices. Between 1948–49 and 1960–61, despite a 50 per cent increase in volume of rural output, net farm income declined almost a third.[3] Rapid population growth, hire purchase (credit) buying, and inventory stocking have led to a high pitch of consumption and development spending, which in turn has required heavy imports. But the weakness of primary goods prices overseas has created drains on foreign exchange. Counting both actual imports and exports and invisibles, Australia accumulated foreign exchange debits of £152,000,000, £184,000,000, £222,000,000, and £368,000,000 in the financial years between 1957–58 and 1960–61, a condition which prompted the tightening of import licensing and brought the celebrated "credit squeeze" of 1960 and 1961.

But the weakness of export prices has not by any means been Australia's only complaint about her foreign trade. She has been inordinately sensitive about being shut out of traditional and profitable markets, usually placing gloomy interpretations on any signs of shrinking opportunities.

[2] See *Yearbook of National Accounts Statistics 1963* (New York: United Nations, 1964), pp. 6, 285; John McEwen, Minister for Trade, in *SMH,* July 15, 1963.

[3] "Costs and Returns in Primary Industry," *Bank of New South Wales Review,* no. 48 (March 1962), pp. 3–7; McEwen, statement of April 30, 1963, in *SMH,* May 2, 1963.

The share of Australian exports now finding their way into traditional markets has been declining, both absolutely and proportionately, and the trade balance has suffered accordingly. To take the most extreme case, exports to Britain, long Australia's best customer, dropped from £359,000,000 in 1952–53 to £209,000,000 in 1962–63. In 1962–63 Australia had an import-export deficit of £107,000,000 with Britain and £105,000,000 with North America, while her favorable balance with the EEC countries declined from £88,000,000 to £55,000,000 between 1961–62 and 1962–63. These are only examples, but they underscore the trend sufficiently.[4] Indeed, in part because of these secular tendencies, Australian trepidation about fresh blockages to a reasonable trading relationship with traditional markets became especially acute in the late 'fifties and early 'sixties.

Take the United States. In 1960, John McEwen, Minister for Trade (now Trade and Industry), Deputy Prime Minister, and the Leader of the Country Party, told a meeting of the Australian-American Association that no great trading nation had obstructed Australia's battle for overseas trade in the previous eight years more than America.[5] Australia has been irritated by American trading policies in many ways. In 1958 the United States slashed the quota on Australian lead and zinc imports, a "savage" decision which damaged a significant dollar-earning source. America is the only major wool buyer which main-

[4] See especially Angus Paltridge, "Australia's Trade with the United Kingdom and Western Europe," *Australian Accountant*, Vol. 32 (November 1962), pp. 575–582; Sir John Crawford, "The Significance of Recent Developments in Asia for the Economic Future of Australia," *Economic Record*, Vol. 37 (September 1961), esp. appendices pp. 291–292; Australian Industries Development Association. Committee on the European Economic Community, *Report on the Implications for Australia of the United Kingdom Becoming a Member of the European Economic Community* (Melbourne and Sydney: AIDA, 1962), esp. table 1, p. 14.

[5] Statement of February 24, 1960, in *SMH*, February 25, 1960.

tains a heavy duty against Australian wool. Meat and cheese are discriminated against. Surplus wheat disposals under Public Law 480, under which payments in hard currency are waived, have cut away large slices of potential markets for Australia's own wheat. Hence Washington's policies not only dampen Australian exports to America, but harm Australia's markets elsewhere. It would be a "wry paradox," according to McEwen, if Australia, an intimate friend who has never sought or received special aid from America, should find that U.S. surplus disposals "should, finally, seriously impair our natural trading opportunities, weaken us economically, and stultify our development." [6]

Regarding Europe, concern developed around the Common Market, either with or without Britain. The protective tariff wall of the European powers was unsettling to Australia, but the loss of preferences enjoyed in British trade would be a frightful setback, or so the Australian Government and a number of outside observers came to believe, and Australia fought hard to have Britain enter the Common Market on terms as "cushioning" to Australian exports as possible. Estimates of the harm that would befall the Australian economy if Britain joined a fully functioning EEC differed widely, but an average estimate was an £80 to 100 million annual loss—a shock not only staggering in its sheer size, but doubly pernicious because of the large number of Australian primary industries that would be dislocated with great economic cost to pro-

[6] *CPD,* HR 9, February 28, 1956, p. 301, and related discussion on pp. 296–302. Also see McEwen, *ibid.,* March 22, 1956, p. 1024; HR 23, April 30, 1959, pp. 1708–1711; "Australia and the U.S. Wheat Surpluses," *Industry Today,* Vol. 2 (June 1959), pp. 135ff.; Athol Townley, statement of September 23, 1958, in *CNIA,* Vol. 29 (September 1958), pp. 583–584; Casey, Michigan State University address of October 6, 1958, in *ibid.* (October 1958), p. 664; H. C. Menzies, Australian Trade Commission in New York, statement in Houston of June 8, 1964, in *SMH,* June 10, 1964.

ducers, their communities, and ultimately the nation.[7] In mid-1962, a junior minister, L. H. E. Bury, publicly denied any strong disturbance to the Australia economy should Britain join the Common Market. Not only was he dismissed from office, but indignant protests against him came from such sources as the general president of the United Farmers and Woolgrowers' Association, the president of the Australian Woolgrowers and Graziers' Council, the general manager of the Australian Wheat Board, the general secretary of the Australian Wheatgrowers' Federation, and the chairman of the Australian Dairy Produce Board.[8] French action barred British entry to the EEC, but Australia's concern about constricted opportunities within the Six remains.

### ADVOCACY AND INCENTIVE FOR CHINESE TRADE

IT IS in this setting that in the late 'fifties arguments and pressures were brought to bear for an expansion of Australian trade into newer markets, particularly Asia, and even more particularly into China. It was predictable that advocacy of a strong China trade should come from the Labor Opposition. There were, of course, the economic arguments whose advancement was by no means a Labor monopoly. Australia's welfare required trade expansion, China was a huge country, and all efforts should be pressed to explore market possibilities and then exploit them. But

[7] For representative predictions of the impact of British entry into the Common Market, see Australian Industries Development Association, *op. cit., passim; Australian Financial Review,* August 31, 1961; Crawford, "The Jolt of the Common Market," pp. 31–32; McEwen, statements of June 21 and July 12, 1961, in *CNIA,* Vol. 32 (June 1961), pp. 52–53, and *ibid.,* (July 1961), p. 23, respectively; McEwen, *CPD,* HR 35, May 3, 1962, pp. 1968–1969. For a general review of the controversy, see A. L. Burns, "Australia, Britain, and the Common Market," *The World Today,* Vol. 18 (April 1962), pp. 152–163.

[8] *SMH,* July 28, 1962.

Labor's attitude was also predictable on political grounds. If overseas trade were shown to be lagging, if the Government could be exposed as insufficiently vigorous in its trade promotion program, especially in untapped China, political capital could be gained. Both in the 1955 and 1958 electoral campaigns, Evatt stressed the need for pushing out into Chinese trade and tried to incriminate the Government for its laxity on this score.[9] In September of 1958, shortly before Parliament was dissolved to allow general elections, Labor instigated a debate in the House on a matter of "urgent public importance," aimed at the Government's alleged failure to take necessary steps to secure adequate overseas markets and prices. The debate immediately turned to the prospects of selling to China and the Government's failure to pursue this market strenuously.[10] Then again there was the ALP's disposition, following the 1954–55 split and the Hobart conference, to foster closer relations with China generally. The relationship between trade and Chinese diplomatic recognition will be examined in another context, but it is sufficient to indicate here that when Labor insisted that "we should not allow stupid, sentimental considerations" to interfere with Chinese commerce,[11] it was reflecting its general Chinese orientation.

Yet the ALP was by no means isolated in its advocacy of spurring the Chinese trade—evidence piled up that the country was thinking along parallel lines. From primary producing organizations and spokesmen came a spate of supporting comment. The presidents of the Australian Dairy Farmers' Federation and of the South Australian

[9] Evatt, statement and broadcast of November 30, 1955, in *ibid.*, December 1, 1955; Evatt, "Policy Speech of the Australian Labor Party" (Brisbane: ALP Federal Secretariat, 1958), delivered October 15, 1958, p. 23.

[10] The debate is found in *CPD,* HR 21, September 30, 1958, pp. 1731–1747.

[11] Alan Bird, *ibid.*, HR 11, May 30, 1956, p. 2621.

Stockowners' Association predicted that China offered major potential for dairy and wool sales, respectively.[12] An officer of the Monaro District Council of the Australian Primary Producers' Union suggested that a group of Australian women take knitting wool and needles to China to make the Chinese wool-conscious, for "if every Chinese person used one woollen article a year it would absorb the whole Australian wool clip." [13] The 1957 annual conference of the Farmers and Settlers' Association urged intensified trade with China.[14] At the 1958 Victorian Dairy Farmers' Association meeting a speaker who protested the sale of dairy products to China on political grounds was heckled and shouted down by most of the other 250 delegates, and the Association president announced that he was meeting a Chinese trade delegation then in Australia to discuss dairy product sales.[15]

Primary producers were joined by industrial and exporting bodies in the quest for Chinese trade. Various chambers of commerce organized committees to explore China trade possibilities. In a 1958 statement supporting Chinese trade expansion, the Associated Chambers of Manufacturers of Australia wrote that "in the export trade it is always well to remember—'If you are not there you may be sure that your competitors will'," [16] while the Export Development Council, the Associated Chambers of Commerce of Australia,[17] the Australian Industries De-

[12] E. G. Roberts (Dairy Farmers), in Melbourne *Herald,* August 2, 1957; R. Hawkes (Stockowners), in Sydney *Daily Telegraph,* October 8, 1958.

[13] C. E. O'Hare, in *Sydney Sun-Herald,* December 1, 1957. Also see report of the national organization's similar thinking in *SMH,* May 20, 1958.

[14] Sydney *Daily Telegraph,* July 31, 1957.

[15] *SMH,* May 28, 1958.

[16] Associated Chambers of Manufacturers of Australia, *Canberra Letter,* April 9, 1958. Also see *ibid.,* May 27, 1957.

[17] See Sir John Allison's address to the annual conference of the Associated Chambers of Commerce of Australia, Perth, April 20,

velopment Association,[18] and other bodies saw the matter in a similar light. Generally speaking, then, primary producers, manufacturers, and exporters all looked favorably on expanding trade with China, although there were differences of emphasis about how quickly and with what result the trade could be expected.

At the level of public opinion the pattern was much the same. The daily press was almost unanimous in its support for trading with China, many editorials on the subject appearing when the U.S. imposed lead and zinc quotas and when Britain attempted entry into the Common Market. Australian interests came first, it was frequently argued, regardless of how much revulsion the U.S. had about trading with her avowed enemy.[19] Even the general public showed early signs of supporting Sino-Australian commerce. In May of 1957 60 per cent were found to be in favor, and only 28 per cent opposed;[20] in September of 1958, as the second offshore island crisis was developing, the breakdown was 61 to 25 per cent, the remainder being undecided.[21] What made the 1957 poll especially interesting was that a greater proportion of Government than Labor supporters favored the China trade (64 per cent against 58 per cent), probably because Liberal-Country Party electors felt a greater economic stake in realizing

---

1959, in Melbourne Chamber of Commerce, *Commerce News,* May 1959.

[18] Australian Industries Development Association, *op. cit.,* esp. pp. 12 and 26. For a general statement from a private industrialist, see W. I. Miskoe, "Red China Trade 'A Matter of Time,'" *Australian Factory,* Vol. 13 (August 1, 1958), pp. 75–76.

[19] For representative expressions, see Melbourne *Age,* May 12, 1958, and John Hetherington in *ibid.,* September 29, 1958; Sydney *Sun,* July 8, 1958; "Onlooker" in *Sydney Sun-Herald,* September 28, 1958; Brisbane *Courier-Mail,* June 14, 1960; Denis Warner in Melbourne *Herald,* April 28, 1962; Adelaide *News,* October 11, 1962.

[20] *AGP,* nos. 1253–1263, June–July 1957.

[21] *Ibid.,* nos. 1347–1359, October–November 1958.

profits from primary or manufactured goods, possibly because of the apprehensions felt by ALP voters concerning the boomerang effect of Chinese imports on employment in Australia.

The sentiment on behalf of extending Australian trade with China was not simply based on vague hopes, since the experience of overseas countries and of Australia herself suggested that good business could in fact be done. The decision of the COCOM powers in 1957 to abolish the "China differential" in strategic materials lists was one indication of the willingness of committed anti-Communist states to broaden their Chinese trade. During the Korean War, China's trade with the West had fallen off to a dribble, but even before the 1957 Paris group decision there were signs that China was willing and able to buy outside the Communist bloc. Between 1955 and 1956 French exports to China doubled, Belgian and Luxembourg exports tripled, Danish trade increased eight-fold, and Norwegian trade nine-fold.[22] As the 'fifties advanced, even more favorable results were recorded by European states. The British, who especially since 1954 had been vigorously pursuing the China trade both through official and unofficial channels, made somewhat slower yet encouraging progress.[23] Among nations more comparable to Australia there also was hope and promising experience. In 1958 Canada's exports to China were ten times as large as in the previous year, and in December 1958 the Canadian trade commissioner in Hong Kong predicted a tripling of

[22] "China Trade," *Far Eastern Economic Review,* Vol. 22 (June 27, 1957), p. 824.

[23] See Luard, *op. cit.,* esp. pp. 140–141, 148–149; "F.B.I. Discussions on Expansion of Trade with China," *Board of Trade Journal,* Vol. 166 (June 12, 1954), pp. 1271–1272; "Prospects for Trade with China," Part 1, *Far Eastern Economic Review,* Vol. 19 (September 29, 1955), pp. 398–399; "A Look at the China-Britain Trade Situation," interview with F. J. Erroll, Parliamentary Secretary to the Board of Trade, *Far East Trade,* Vol. 12 (December 1957), pp. 1404–1405.

that amount within two or three years.[24] The general reaction in Australia was not only that if other countries were establishing beachheads in China, so could Australia, but indeed that some goods, especially wool, were unnecessarily being sold to Britain, then processed and resold at profit to China.[25]

The experience of the Australians themselves pointed toward the possibility of extended sales based on what they learned on commercial visits, what the Chinese themselves predicted, and ultimately based on China's own buying performance. During the three post-Korean trading years of 1953–54 to 1955–56, exports to China were relatively static, remaining well under £3,000,000 annually, consisted almost entirely of wool, and represented only .3 per cent of total Australian exports. But the immediately succeeding years showed marked improvement. The value of total exports rose to £6,438,000 in 1956–57, £9,768,000 in 1957–58, £13,567,000 in 1958–59, and £16,132,000 in 1959–60. The Chinese share of the Australian export market reached 1.7 per cent by the end of the decade, still not a great deal absolutely but considerably above the previous .3 per cent figure. Qualitatively too there was improvement, because the trade began to diversify. The first encouraging Australian wheat sale to Communist China, amounting to £233,000, was transacted in 1958–59. Chemicals began to show some promise, but the chief new category was iron and steel plate and sheet, which amounted to over £5,000,000 in 1958–59—still a record year.

[24] C. M. Forsyth-Smith, in Montreal *Gazette,* December 9, 1958. For the New Zealand position, see E. H. Halstead, Minister for Industries and Commerce, *EAR* (NZ), Vol. 7 (May 1957), p. 17, and P. N. Holloway, his successor, *NZPD,* Vol. 316, July 2, 1958, p. 390.

[25] For example, see Theo. Nichols, *CPD,* S 13, August 21, 1958, pp. 185–187; K. D. Gott, "Australian Trade with China," reprinted from *South Australian Farmer,* July 23, 1954, *passim;* ACMA, *Canberra Letter,* April 9, 1958.

It was no accident that sales jumped in 1956–57, for in that period Australians began to visit China to test for themselves the market opportunities. Several private traders went and reported favorably on trade prospects, both for primary and manufactured goods.[26] But perhaps the most celebrated visit at this time was made by H. C. Menzies, Australian trade commissioner in Hong Kong, who spent three weeks in various Chinese cities during March and April of 1956. Not only did he meet high Chinese trading officials, but no less a personage than Chou En-lai. His visit resulted in a helpful exchange of information on what might be bought and sold, clarification of earlier misunderstandings about procedures and payments, and a mutual pledge that trade missions would be welcome.[27] Menzies' impressions were confirmed the following year when an ALP Parliamentary delegation visited China. A number of trade unions apparently asked the delegation to inquire about trade prospects and the delegation leader, Leslie Haylen, agreed to do this; later in Peking, Chou expressed hope for increased commerce.[28] An ACTU delegation of the same year brought back a comparable report.[29]

In 1958 even stronger links were forged. This was the year of the U.S. lead and zinc quota decision. Shortly after the announcement was made, the Chinese commercial counselor in London told an Australian correspondent that Australia could find a "strong, if temporary," market in China for zinc and lead as well as wool and steel.[30] In point of fact wool and steel were to be much more sought

[26] See the reports of Marcel Dekyvere, William May, and Edward Dunn, in *SMH,* June 5 and September 6, 1956, and January 31, 1957, respectively.

[27] *Ibid.,* April 10 and 12, 1956, and *Canberra Times,* May 19, 1956.

[28] *SMH,* June 15, 1957; Haylen, *op. cit.,* p. 145.

[29] See statement by Albert Monk, in *SMH,* July 19, 1957.

[30] Ley Wang, interview of September 26, 1958, in *Sydney Sun-Herald,* September 28, 1958.

by China than lead and zinc, though the Chinese comment was warmly received. Likewise in 1958 the ship *Delos,* carrying an Australian trade promotion delegation to various Asian ports, docked at Shanghai for two days, allowing a rather concentrated exchange of views on Chinese import requirements.[31] Finally, 1958 witnessed the opening of what was to become a regular procedure in Australia's quest for an export outlet in China: representatives of the Commonwealth Trading Bank, a Government-owned but commercially operated and competitive institution, stopped in China for two weeks. A few individual bankers had apparently been to China before, but mainly to settle technical points. The Commonwealth men went primarily to promote business, the bank's customers earlier having given advice and endorsement to the project. While in China the Commonwealth men spoke to 13 Chinese state trading corporations and subsequently conveyed their findings to the bank's customers.[32] Similar banking visits have become a significant channel for trade promotion; in 1963, at least five separate banks dispatched missions to China.

Perhaps one more illustration is appropriate to underline the vigor and initiative of Australian interests. In 1958 Walter P. Heine, managing director of Heine Bros., Melbourne exporters, went to China and transacted a large-scale sale of steel products. The Chinese were then pressing for barter exchanges in their Australian trade—an especially difficult business arrangement due at least in part to existing Australian import licensing regultions. Heine produced an elaborate and ingenious arrangement. A barter deal was made possible, because Heine Bros. disposed of £6,000,000 worth of Chinese commodities—

[31] Australian Exporters' Federation, "Australian Trade Mission 1958. Report" (Sydney: The Federation, 1959), pp. 25–26; W. S. Johnston, "Australia's Floating Shop Window," *Etruscan,* Vol. 8 (March 1958), p. 27.

[32] See *Canberra Times,* July 3, 1958.

soybeans, grains, oils, and resins, among other things—through their connections in Europe. Hence Australia won a large steel contract, and no embarrassment caused by equivalent Chinese imports had to be faced.

### THE GOVERNMENT PARTIES' INTEREST IN CHINESE TRADE PROMOTION

IN THE final judgment, however, it was the Government's own approach that was crucial. In terms of a general trade expansion policy, the Government was and is consistently busy. Aside from attempting to negotiate favorable trade agreements, induce desirable international marketing and tariff systems, and the like, it has done much to foster a favorable export climate. An Export Payments Insurance Corporation was created to protect exporters against risks not commercially insurable. Various tax incentives and concessions are available to exporters. Trade fairs have been organized, trade display ships assisted, various forms of publicity and advertising sponsored, and trade commissioner services have been greatly enlarged. There is close collaboration with private exporters, and a special ministerial committee was formed seveal years ago to conduct a comprehensive and continuous examination of measures for export development. The Government's general trade promotion record is excellent.[33]

But what of China? This is a lengthy and fascinating story, and can best be introduced by noting the Government's publicly stated philosophy on the subject. Aside

[33] For descriptions of the Government's trade promotion, see "How the Department of Trade Aids Australian Businessmen," *Australian Grocer,* Vol. 52 (February 1963), pp. 94–99; "Australia Prepares Big Export Drive," *Far East Trade,* Vol. 16 (December 1961), pp. 1478–1479; A. J. Carmody, "Export Promotion," forum addresses delivered at the 58th annual conference of the Associated Chambers of Commerce of Australia, Hobart, April 2–5, 1962, esp. pp. 8–11; Bank of New South Wales, "An Australian Exporter's Guide," (Sydney: Bank of NSW, 1963), pp. 19–21; *SMH,* January 4, 1961, and July 15, 1963.

from strategic materials, the Government has expressed itself in favor of trade with China. At a press conference in October of 1958, shortly after the imposition of U.S. lead and zinc quotas, in reply to whether Australia should sell to China, McEwen replied "Most Certainly! In fact, if we don't sell to Red China we will find other countries selling to them and probably selling them Australian goods." [34] Paired with its declared support for Chinese trade has been a constant affirmation that the Government itself has no property to sell, that it does not itself promote trade with China, but that it does not obstruct private selling to the best advantage—its purpose being "to open further avenues wherever they can" for those engaged in trading transactions.[35]

Especially with regard to the Government's first point, namely that sales to China are desirable, it is necessary to remember that the Menzies Government has always been a coalition of Liberal and Country parties, not a single party bloc. Consequently, when one speaks of the "Government's" attitude on Chinese trade, it is an attitude that must take both parties into account. The Country Party, as its name implies, is a party based on rural interests and rural electorates. In South Australia it has blended with the Liberals. In Tasmania, after many years out of operation, it recently reappeared. It has flourished as a separate entity in the other states for many years, and presently supplies the Premier of Queensland. At the Federal level it has maintained remarkable representational stability. Between the 1949 and 1963 elections, while the Liberal fortunes fluctuated considerably, it steadily returned between 17 and 20 Members. It has supplied the Deputy

[34] Statement of October 6, 1958, in *ibid.,* October 7, 1958. Also see statement in Hong Kong of August 1 (?), 1963, in Melbourne *Age,* August 2, 1963.

[35] William Spooner, *CPD,* S 8, May 31, 1956, p. 1121. Also see, for instance, McEwen, *ibid.,* HR 35, May 3, 1962, p. 1905, and statement of July 22, 1957, in *CNIA,* Vol. 28 (July 1957), p. 559.

Prime Minister and has held other high offices; McEwen, the present Federal Leader of the Country Party, is also Deputy Prime Minister and Minister for Trade and Industry, while C. F. Adermann is Minister for Primary Industry. It is a party which fights hard for its survival against encroachment from either the ALP or Liberal side. When in the 1963 campaign Calwell suggested the abolition of preferential voting, which helps sustain the Country Party, McEwen replied that "this is not a fair go; this is not Australian"; under a first-past-the-post system only the major parties would survive, parties dominated by "either the Trades Hall or the financial centres of Sydney and Melbourne." [36] Yet when one speaks of the Federal Country Party working to preserve itself and the interests it reflects, one is really not speaking of a coherently organized group. The Country Party has virtually no Federal organization outside of Parliament. Within Parliament its delegation is dominated by the leadership, and particularly the Leader, at present McEwen. McEwen is clever, intelligent, and forceful, but most of his Country Party colleagues are parochial in the extreme and more than happy to follow their able Leader's guidance. No wonder that the other parties tend to sneer at the Country Party, and that the author has heard Liberal Parliamentarians refer to their Country Party compatriots on the Government benches as "peasants."

The Country Party's parochialism can be noticed in its China attitude. The Party is powerfully anti-Communist, having assumed a ban-the-Communist-Party policy before Menzies and the Liberals picked it up. But its anti-Communism tends to be of a rather crude, unsophisticated type. Even in its imaginative moments its anti-Communism is quaint. The Country Party's principal publicist, Ulrich Ellis, has spotlighted the terrible menace to Aus-

[36] Statement of November 25, 1963, in *SMH*, November 26, 1963.

tralia from militant, Communist China, a China with untold millions of people. If Australia is to protect herself against a Chinese threat she must not only have allies, but provide for self-protection. Self-protection implies population growth, not just in numbers, but through a better spread beyond the urban conurbations, especially in the South-East. New regions must therefore be developed and made attractive to settlement and self-sustenance. This becomes one of the arguments on behalf of the "new states" movement, a favorite Country Party plank which hopes to break off northern New South Wales, for one, into a separate state free of the control of sinister Sydney.[37] This argument may or may not be sophisticated, but it is typically Country Party. At the 1961 Country Party New South Wales annual conference, 174 resolutions were brought forward for discussion, but only two dealt with external affairs. One of the two resolutions called for the creation of a committee to investigate Peking's seating in the UN. There was great opposition to the motion, which was shouted and voted down by a huge margin—in part because of the horrible prospect of Communist China entering the UN, in part because some delegates believed that the conference knew too little about the subject; "let's leave it to the experts" seemed to be the reaction.[38] In Parliament, Country Party members are most conspicuous by their silence in foreign affairs debates, the author having noticed only one Country Party back-bench Parliamentarian from each house making any distinctive contribution in recent years.

But on Chinese trade the Party's anti-Communism has

[37] Ulrich Ellis, "New England. The Seventh State" (Armidale, NSW: New State Movement, 1957), pp. 3–8. Also see his "The Case for New States" (Canberra: 1950), pp. 2–4.

[38] Donald A. Aitkin, *The Organisation of the Australian Country Party (N.S.W.), 1946 to 1962,* Ph.D. thesis, Australian National University, 1964, pp. 248–249. Dr. Aitken added to his written comments in conversation with the author.

been amended to fit economic requirements. The Party, after all, is the champion of those very interests which wish to capitalize on primary goods sales abroad—wool, wheat, and the rest. This can easily be demonstrated with respect to wheat, now Australia's best-selling export to China. Fourteen Federal electorates have been suggested as falling within dominant or important wheat-growing areas.[39] After the 1961 Federal election, of 17 Country Party Members in the House, 8 sat within these 14 constituencies. After the 1963 election, 9 out of 20 sat in them. In New South Wales, the heaviest wheat-raising state, 5 of the 6 "wheat seats" are presently Country Party, as are 4 of the 5 wheat seats in Victoria, another large wheat-producing state. In an October 1962 postal survey of Country Party members in three New South Wales Party branch areas, 88.5 per cent answered that Australia should sell wheat to China, 7.4 per cent were opposed, and 4.1 per cent of the respondents gave no answer.[40] This was a higher favorable response than among the population at large in late 1962: 69 per cent in favor, 17 per cent opposed, and 14 per cent without an opinion as to whether wheat and wool sales should continue.[41] It is therefore not surprising that, once the wheat sales had begun in earnest, the New South Wales Country Party organ should have boasted that it would be impossible "to turn up a single statement of the Country Party declaring itself opposed to Communist trade." [42]

In the mind of the Country Party it has been possible to combine militant anti-Communism with practicality. On the one hand, the Party insists that while the ALP "invariably throws its weight behind policies likely to react to the

[39] Don Whitington, *Ring the Bells* (Melbourne: Georgian House, 1956), p. 120.

[40] Aitkin, *op. cit.,* p. 517.

[41] *AGP,* nos. 1653–1664, January–February 1963 (December 1962 poll).

[42] *New South Wales Countryman,* March 1961.

advantage of Communist countries, the Country Party has always been in the forefront of the forces supporting the defeat of Communist influences at home and abroad."[43] On the other hand—and the comment is representative—the Party claims that "when our bins are full and while we are still growing wheat and . . . [China and Russia] are prepared to pay for it, naturally we should sell it because after all their money is as good as anyone else's."[44]

The Country Party, therefore, or to be more exact the Country Party following McEwen, has been an enthusiastic supporter of Australia's China trade. The warmest China-trade Government comments have emanated from McEwen, not Menzies or any External Affairs ministers. Should this be interpreted to mean that the Country Party is in fact more determined to trade with China than the Prime Minister and his Liberal Party colleagues in the Government? Should it be inferred that the decision to favor an expansion of Chinese trade was the result of Country Party pressure, leveled against reluctant Liberals?

Only a week before McEwen's hearty endorsement of trade with China in October 1958, Menzies, speaking in the House to the ALP's charges in the "matter of urgent public importance" debate, reminded his listeners that the Chinese were at that moment using "naked aggression" against Quemoy. Disparagingly, he mocked Evatt's encouragement "to push out and make trade bargains with them, so long, of course, as the trade bargains involve only exports from us and no imports from them."[45] Consider too the 1958, 1961, and 1963 Federal elections. In the 1958 campaign, McEwen pointedly explained that the

[43] "We're Telling You!" (Sydney: Federal Council, Australian Country Party, 1961), pp. 8–9.

[44] Robert King, *CPD,* HR, October 30, 1963, p. 2475. Also see King, HR 33, October 30, 1961, p. 1595; Charles Anderson, HR 23, May 7, 1959, pp. 1960–1961; *New South Wales Countryman,* July 1960 and March 1961; *Victorian Countryman,* March 9, 1961.

[45] *CPD,* HR 21, September 30, 1958, p. 1734.

Government had always allowed the sale of nonstrategic goods to China.[46] In the days following, Menzies again ridiculed the ALP's demand for more trade with China, who was dropping shells on innocent offshore island civilians.[47] In 1961, addressing himself to the potential dangers facing Australia's economy if Britain were to join the Common Market, McEwen called attention to the existence of import earnings from wheat sales to China.[48] In 1963, after China had fattened the Australian money bags even more, Sir Garfield Barwick, Liberal External Affairs Minister, had the following unedifying exchange at an election meeting:

> *Barwick:* You know, I've heard the A.L.P. say we don't need a defence force. . . .
> *Interjector:* Bull!
> *Barwick:* Yes, my friend, that's what it is. We believe that the great threat to Australia is Communist China. . . .
> *Interjector:* What do you sell them wheat for? Why don't you starve them?
> *Barwick:* The Government doesn't sell the wheat. It's the farmers.
> *Interjector:* Weak, weak.
> *Barwick:* The real point of this election is, what is your foreign policy going to be? If this Government is defeated those 36 faceless men will run the A.L.P. for the Communists. . . .[49]

The imputation of Liberal-Country Party divergence also derives from press reports of a split between Casey, then the Liberal External Affairs Minister, and McEwen. Late in June of 1957 it was reported that at a stormy

[46] Speech of October 31, 1958, in *SMH,* November 1, 1958.
[47] See speeches of November 4 and 13, 1958, in *ibid.,* November 5 and 14, 1958, respectively.
[48] Speech of November 26, 1961, in *ibid.,* November 27, 1961.
[49] Cited in *ibid.,* November 23, 1963.

Cabinet meeting McEwen pushed for expanding Chinese trade while Casey "impassionately" disagreed, stressing the folly of alienating American feelings. Cabinet was reported to be divided and to have adjourned with no formal judgment being made.[50] In the immediately succeeding years, the *News Weekly* added to the impression of a McEwen-Casey dispute. In 1959, it intimated that McEwen was pressing extremely hard for wide Chinese trade because he wished to ingratiate himself with and dazzle the commercial community, which in turn would plump for him rather than some Liberal such as Harold Holt as successor to the Prime-Ministership.[51] Early the next year, when Casey resigned his office and was elevated to the peerage, *News Weekly* intimated he may have quit because he could no longer swallow the McEwen-preached line of Chinese trade and eventual diplomatic recognition.[52]

To the best of the author's judgment, the imputation of Country Party pressure against reluctant Liberals is unfounded. Wide coverage in interviewing among both politicians and officials revealed consensus that no arm-twisting was necessary. At all events, it stands to reason that Menzies and his Liberal colleagues understood both the economic and political facts of life. In a time of depressed prices and shortening markets, the earning of foreign exchange was useful to promote imports of benefit to city-dwelling consumers and manufacturers. Since the country was quite firmly behind the China trade, it would have been a brave Government indeed that could have faced with equanimity the stormy reactions which would have come had Chinese trade been seriously restrained. The differences in emphasis between McEwen and Liberal spokesmen are also explainable. McEwen spoke in essentially rural electorates, where he had to reassure growers

[50] Melbourne *Age* and Melbourne *Herald,* June 26, 1957.
[51] *News Weekly,* July 29, 1959. [52] *Ibid.,* January 27, 1960.

and graziers that his Government, or his Party, were not indifferent to their immediate welfare. Liberal spokesmen generally addressed urban audiences. But more significantly, Liberal comments were more designed to increase the pressure on Labor, to charge it with coddling evil Communist China, to smear the ALP with the now-familiar paint of far-leftism. As has been suggested before, it is a gambit that has worked splendidly in successive elections.

The McEwen-Casey disagreement imputation is false in substance but true to a slight degree. A report published only a day after the original revelations about a Cabinet crisis comes closer to the truth—there were differences, but no split.[53] Casey did for some time assume a more cautious attitude than McEwen, basing his reaction on American considerations. He was, however, urging a somewhat more phased development of the Chinese trade, which, in fact, he was able to bring about, rather than its prevention or even upward movement. The *News Weekly's* allegations should probably be dismissed as flimsy efforts to discredit the Chinese trade, which it has consistently and violently attacked. If Casey, for one, had difficulties with a colleague in the Government, that person was Menzies rather than McEwen, and the difficulty had nothing to do with Chinese trade.

## THE GOVERNMENT'S INVOLVEMENT IN THE CHINA TRADE

THE NEXT question requiring attention is how far and in what way the Government has moved in order to encourage commercial relations with China. The Labor Party has been especially incensed by what it regards as a monumental piece of Government cynicism. It claims that "the policy of this Government is power from the people at home by smearing the Australian Labour Party as the ally of Communism, and pounds from red China to bolster the

[53] *SMH,* June 27, 1957.

economy of the Australian farming community." [54] The Government is evading its responsibilities, and when it tries "to tell this Parliament and the people that it has not played some part in sponsoring and encouraging trade with Communist countries, it is sinking to the depths of hypocrisy. . . . By lifting a finger or the signing of a document it can prevent any goods going to red China at any time. But it is not doing that. . . . Either the Chinese and communism in China are a menace or they are not." [55] The remainder of this chapter will seek to uncover the extent of the Government's actual involvement in the China trade, and thereby test the validity of Labor's accusations.

First some consideration will be given to Government involvement in fostering trade promotion in China. The 1956 visit of Hong Kong trade commissioner H. C. Menzies was, of course, a visit by an official of the Commonwealth. The author understands that the Chinese had twice before issued an invitation to Menzies, but it had not been accepted. When the 1956 visit was arranged, naturally with Canberra's consent, the Australian Government advised, but did not consult, the U.S. Government on what was about to take place. While in China, Menzies talked of trade, not of politics and diplomacy, but he did meet with various ranking Chinese, including Chou En-lai. He was provided with social as well as business amenities, and himself gave a cocktail party for his Chinese hosts.[56] His report was later considered and evaluated by the Government, not simply released to interested private traders.

[54] W. C. Coutts, *CPD,* HR, March 19, 1964, pp. 698–699.

[55] Reginald Pollard, *ibid.,* HR 23, May 6, 1959, p. 1904. Also see Archibald Benn, S 15, September 30, 1959, pp. 908–910; Leonard Reynolds, HR 30, March 15, 1961, p. 163; James Cope, *ibid.,* March 16, 1961, p. 289; Charles Jones, HR 32, August 30, 1961, p. 675; ALP, "The Australian Labor Party. Speakers' Notes" (Brisbane: ALP Federal Secretariat, 1958), p. 6.

[56] *Canberra Times,* March 31, 1956.

Then there was the visit of the Australian trade mission on the *Delos* to Shanghai in late 1958. The idea of organizing a promotional trip of this sort to various Asian ports was largely the work of private exporters, not the Government. However, the Government did provide some technical and financial assistance. It was probably accidental that the mission went to Shanghai at all, since the principal Chinese trading contacts are found in Peking. But the *Delos* was not a chartered ship; the mission simply bought living and display space on her and went where the ship sailed, which happily was a commercially sound itinerary. Shanghai was a normal stop for the *Delos* (in this instance she was carrying Australian wool to China), so the mission included Shanghai on its promotional schedule. The Department of Trade did weigh the political implications of a China stop by a trade mission which carried official support, but decided not to interfere. Shortly before the ship was to sail from Australia, the Minister for Supply, Athol Townley, told the House that a skilled Trade Department officer was preceding the mission to its various intended ports of call, to arrange commercial advertising and generally carry out public relations operations. However, "returning to the proposition that has been put forward that the Australian Government is making an all-out attempt to woo Communists into trading, I point out that the very fact that the trade publicity officer is not going to Shanghai should be sufficient answer." [57]

But was it in fact a "sufficient answer"? There was the background of H. C. Menzies' 1956 Chinese visit. The Government was assisting the *Delos* mission in various material ways even without dispatching the publicity officer to Shanghai. Indeed, in preparation for the *Delos* visit to Shanghai, the Australian trade commissioner in Hong Kong notified Chinese officials there of the impending visit, and certain informal preparatory arrangements were

[57] *CPD,* HR 21, September 30, 1958, p. 1738.

discussed. This may not have been as ambitious an approach as sending the publicity officer to China, but it was sufficient. Only a few days after Townley's remarks in the House, McEwen stated that *any* trade delegation going to China would be accorded the normal Department of Trade assistance rendered to delegations going elsewhere.[58] It is absolutely plain that for years the Hong Kong trade commissioner and his staff have devoted a portion of their time to advising Australian traders interested in Chinese trade, and that the Australian Hong Kong establishment has dealt with the various Chinese trading corporations which are located in Hong Kong.

The Australian trade commissioner in Hong Kong has not, however, always carried out his Chinese trade functions through Hong Kong itself. In April of 1964, in reply to a question on notice, the Prime Minister stated that G. R. B. Patterson, Hong Kong trade commissioner, visited the Canton trade fair in May of 1961 and again in May of 1962, at a total cost to the Commonwealth of some £100.[59] Patterson's trips resulted from Chinese invitations, not Australian initiative, but they definitely were cleared and approved in Canberra. In 1963 the Government blocked the Hong Kong trade commissioner from going on holiday to China, but it is obvious that Canberra has used this office as a significant vehicle for exploring and facilitating Sino-Australian commerce.

Governmental contacts with Chinese coming to Australia either to buy or sell have also been established. Chinese trade delegations have ordinarily visited Australia under the invitation and sponsorship of private Australian concerns, but as far back as 1957 and 1958, when the missions first began to arrive, the Government publicly declared that it was prepared to provide information and

[58] Statement of October 7, 1958, in *CNIA,* Vol. 29 (October 1958), p. 666.

[59] *CPD,* HR, April 15, 1964, p. 1127.

to arrange contacts in much the same way that it handled non-Chinese trade delegations; the only reservation was that such contacts were not to be construed as intergovernmental.[60] In 1959, W. C. Wentworth, one of whose pet peeves is the China trade, produced a letter written to him the year before by the secretary of the Department of Immigration, which set out in some detail the Government's awareness of what sort of Chinese trade missions were arriving, what they wanted to discuss, and how the Department of Trade was prepared to assist them.[61] All of this suggested, and continues to suggest, Australian Government involvement. It also weakens if not destroys the claim that contacts are not "intergovernmental," since they are between the Department of Trade and Industry, a major department of the Australian Government, and Chinese who are officials of state trading corporations, which by definition are Chinese government instrumentalities, responsible to relevant Chinese Government Ministries. Canberra persists in abjuring intergovernmental relations, but in doing so it simply promotes a fiction.

This general review of the Government's role *vis-à-vis* promoting trade in China and facilitating the operations of Chinese missions in Australia can best be capped by examining related events in 1961 and 1962. In 1961, Dr. H. C. Coombs, Governor of the Reserve Bank of Australia, came to believe that because of the considerable movement of Australian goods to China, including wheat sales on credit, it would be desirable for him to visit his counterparts, the central People's Bank of China. The Australian bank already had exchanged visits with most reserve banks of countries with which Australia carried on trade of any size, and the visit to Peking was to be much

[60] For instance, see McEwen, statement of July 22, 1957, in *CNIA,* Vol. 28 (July 1957), p. 560, and *CPD,* HR 19, May 14, 1958, p. 1758; William Spooner, S 11, October 15, 1957, p. 549, and S 13, August 19, 1958, p. 55.

[61] *CPD,* HR 23, May 12, 1959, p. 2069.

of the same order, i.e., to clarify various technical points. While in China in October of 1961, Coombs did engage in valuable technical conferences, though the Chinese enlarged the discussion into the field of trade expansion opportunities generally.

As a matter of courtesy, Coombs told the Chinese bankers they would be welcome in Australia if they chose to come although, from the Australian standpoint, the 1961 talks had settled most of the technical matters and a reciprocal Chinese visit would have been superfluous. Nonetheless, the following year the Chinese advised Coombs they wished to avail themselves of his offer. In June of 1962 a three-man delegation arrived in Australia, headed by Tsao Chu-ju, President of the People's Bank. At the time the Chinese bankers came, the secretary of the Reserve Bank announced that "there is nothing abnormal about the visit. It is strictly a question of relationships between our Reserve Bank and the central bank of the People's Bank of China." [62] As it turned out, however, the Chinese bankers were much more interested in meeting people, obtaining information, and generally promoting trade than in engaging in technical shop talk with the Reserve Bank. They did not, in fact, even have a formal discussion session with Coombs.

What lessons about the Government's involvement can be drawn from the 1961 and 1962 exchanges? Prior to visiting China, Coombs consulted with the Treasurer, Harold Holt, under whose aegis the Reserve Bank functions. In 1962, prior to the Chinese visit, not only was Holt again consulted, as was admitted in the House,[63] but Coombs also spoke with Menzies, at the time External Affairs Minister as well as Prime Minister, and Sir Arthur Tange, the secretary of the Department of External

[62] A. C. McPherson, statement of June 14, 1962, in *SMH,* June 15, 1962.

[63] Holt, *CPD,* HR 37, November 14, 1962, pp. 2448–2449.

Affairs. Again, the Government did not interfere, although there were hints, based on the 1961 experience, that there would be little banking business to transact and that the Chinese were eager to engage in trade promotion as such. Once in Australia, the Chinese received some assistance from the Reserve Bank and from the Department of Trade, just as other Chinese missions had.

If the Government had been seriously interested in blocking either Coombs' trip or the reciprocal Chinese visit, it could have done so, despite the fact that Coombs is a very prominent and influential man, both because of the office he holds and for other reasons. Although the Reserve Bank carries considerable autonomy, it is theoretically possible for the Government to give it general instructions, which could have included a "cease and desist" order on either the 1961 or 1962 ventures. Moreover, the Government could have expressed its opposition to Coombs informally, in which case he probably would have called off the plan without waiting for a directive. Finally, as a last resort, the Government could have denied visas to the Chinese bankers in 1962, thus stopping their entry and at the same time avoiding the embarrassment of putting pressure on Coombs or the Reserve Bank. But it did none of these things, although those in the highest echelons of the Government knew what was transpiring. Commenting on the Chinese visit, the Canberra correspondent of the Melbourne *Herald* wrote that because the Government was sanctioning official banking links with China, despite the absence of diplomatic relations, "the Commonwealth Reserve Bank is taking the role the Department of External Affairs would have in normal diplomatic contacts," since both the People's Bank of China and the Reserve Bank were government instrumentalities.[64] While the banking link is not a substitute for ordinary diplomatic relations, Government involvement must certainly be at-

[64] E. H. Cox in Melbourne *Herald,* June 19, 1962.

tributed to the very high-level exchanges carried out in 1961 and 1962.

### THE GOVERNMENT AND THE WOOL TRADE

A FURTHER test of the Government's interest and involvement in the Chinese trade can be made by glancing at the position respecting wool and wheat, Australia's two heaviest-selling products to China. The Australian economy, it is sometimes said, rides on the back of a sheep. There are some 110,000 woolmen in Australia and about 160,000,000 sheep—roughly 15 times as many sheep as the total population. The sheep industry has long been Australia's principal foreign exchange earner, and despite a proportionate decline in recent years continues to supply about 40 per cent of export returns. The industry has, however, suffered from a dip in world wool prices, which by 1963 were 25 per cent lower than ten years previously, a problem compounded by the absence of subsidies. In this setting, the first important sales to China were especially welcome. In 1956–57, China's purchases of Australian wool stood at £6,153,000, up about two and one-half times from 1955–56. In 1957–58 sales reached well beyond £9,000,000, receded to £6,500,000 in 1958–59, and then jumped to £13,469,000 in 1959–60. But with declining wool prices, Australia found her total wool check skidding from £482 million in 1956–57 to £337 million in 1957–58 and a desperately low £295 million in 1958–59. Indeed, not only were larger wool sales to China welcome in this sense (plus the fact that additional wool buyers at auctions tend to raise final prices), but wool seemed to be the best single prospect in the China trade at large, amounting to 84 per cent of what Australia sold to China between 1951–52 and 1958–59.[65] In

[65] For some background, see Frederick Yu, "Prospects for Australian Wool," *Far Eastern Economic Review,* Vol. 30 (December

March of 1959, replying to a question on notice raised in the Senate, the Government not only praised the beneficial effects of the wool sales, but spoke with some confidence that China would continue to be a significant market, especially for greasy wool, as her textile industry expanded. Responsible economists were reaching much the same conclusion at this time.[66]

In 1961–62 and 1962–63 Chinese wool purchases from Australia continued to be strong but unspectacular—under £11,000,000 annually, representing about 3 per cent of Australia's wool export earnings. In 1963–64, China bought Australian greasy wool valued at £11.8 million. The sales have usually been made on standard terms—at time of sale (with nominated Australians acting as buying agents for China), the wool people are paid by private banks, the Chinese file a letter of credit and then pay the banks within 90 days with interest. The author is not aware that the Chinese have ever pressed for more lenient terms. The really significant aspect of the wool trade, however, has not been in the volume of wool currently being sold or the terms on which it is sold, but in increasingly strong projections of China's future needs for wool as her population bounds ahead, her standard of life gradually improves, and her emphasis on creating a textile industry becomes more and more apparent. It is understood in Australia that Chinese wool consumption is extremely low by world standards—only about .2 pounds *per capita,* and using only about 100,000,000 pounds of wool annually. Yet even a modest consumption increase

8, 1960), pp. 551–552, and financial editor, *SMH,* September 4, 1963.

[66] William Spooner, *CPD,* S 14, March 12, 1959, p. 349; Bureau of Agricultural Economics, *Wool in Communist Countries* (Canberra: 1960), Wool Economic Research Report no. 1, June 1960, esp. pp. 42–44, 63, and 74.

to .5 pounds would push China's wool requirements to 250,000,000 pounds, and some estimates have placed her 1970 wool needs as high as 450,000,000 pounds. This indeed is a glittering prospect for Australia, who already supplies a quarter of China's wool.[67]

In October of 1961, the Chairman of the Australian Wool Bureau (later the Wool Board), Sir William Gunn, announced that a major effort would be launched to induce China to buy more Australian wool. If necessary, he would personally travel to Peking to promote this end. His concern was a practical, economic one: "We have no politics. We will sell wool wherever we can sell it. We consider politics [to be] affairs for others to concern themselves with." [68] Within half a year, plans were announced for an even more elaborate mission to China. Not only was Gunn preparing to visit China to encourage sales, but also to offer technical assistance to the Chinese textile industry. He was to go in his capacity of Chairman of the International Wool Secretariat, of which Australia was and is the foremost member. The theory, of course, was that the faster Chinese textile resources could be put into operation, the quicker and larger would be China's call for wool, especially Australia's wool.[69] In November of 1962, close to the scheduled time for departure of the mission, the International Wool Secretariat's managing di-

[67] For representative literature, see M. J. Lawrence, "Wool in Mainland China," *Quarterly Review of Agricultural Economics,* Vol. 15 (October 1962), pp. 188–198; *The Times* (London), June 25, 1963; E. J. Donath, in Melbourne *Sun,* March 4, 1964, *Bulletin,* April 18, 1964, and "China—Australia's Fourth Best Customer," *Monthly Bulletin. Australian Institute of Export,* no. 24 (December 1963), p. 44; Colina MacDougall, "Australian Aid?" *Far Eastern Economic Review,* Vol. 36 (June 14, 1962), p. 551; *Bulletin,* November 7, 1964.

[68] Cited in *SMH,* October 27, 1961.

[69] See *ibid.,* March 28 and September 29, 1962; *Canberra Times,* July 25, 1962; MacDougall, *op. cit.,* p. 551.

rector announced that a postponement had been mutually agreed upon because of the pressure of business.[70] Fifteen months later Gunn made the Chinese trip, in company with a Secretariat official. He explained upon returning that contact had been made on a nongovernmental level and reiterated his indifference to politics. Three reasons had induced the visit. The first was the extension of a courtesy call in reply to an invitation from one of Australia's biggest wool customers (eighth-ranking, in point of fact). The second was to explain how Australia and the Secretariat also promoted wool sales abroad and assisted in the development of customers' manufacturing industries. The third—and crucial—reason was to inform China that the Australian Wool Board was prepared to render technical assistance to China's textile industry,[71] which included the bringing to Australia of Chinese textile people for consultation and advanced training.

There was small doubt that the majority of Australians took Gunn's mission in stride and even with much satisfaction. The graziers themselves had always approached the prospect of technical assistance to the Chinese textile industry with a minimum of political obstruction to their economic self-interest.[72] Press reaction was also favorable; close commercial relations with China had become quite natural and routine. As the Sydney *Daily Telegraph* wrote, "The technical aid to China does not imply that we embrace or approve her policies. But since we follow the realistic approach of Britain and France in trading with China, there is no point in trading halfheartedly. We must

[70] W. J. Vines, statement of November 1 (?), 1962, in *Canberra Times,* November 2, 1962.

[71] *SMH,* March 3, 1964.

[72] For instance, see *Muster* (organ of the NSW Graziers' Association), April 4 and October 10, 1962; D. von Bebra, of the Australian Wool Bureau, before NSW Graziers' Association, March 13, 1962, in *SMH,* March 14, 1962.

sell to survive, and China is an enormous—and growing—market for our most important primary products." [73]

The pivotal query, however, is the Government's own involvement in the Gunn project. When Gunn first publicly mooted the possibility of a technical assistance scheme for China, he *did not* consult the Government about its political or other reactions to the plan. His view has consistently been that consulatation is desirable only on the *principle* of whether to sell wool to China. Once this principle was established, technical assitance became a procedural matter. The Peking trip had been planned for late 1962. It was postponed and not undertaken for more than a year. Late 1962 was also the time of Chinese intrusion into India, and there has been widespread rumor in Australia that the China trip was halted either by Gunn acting on his own initiative or because of advice from Canberra, in order to avoid an indelicate situation. The author is prepared to state flatly that this is a false reading of the actual position. Gunn failed to make the trip on schedule because of Chinese-inspired complications raised about the proper role of the International Wool Secretariat as against the Australian Wool Board, because of problems arising out of South Africa's role in the mission (unrelated to the race issue), and because Gunn was especially busy at the time. The trip was not made in 1963 largely because of Gunn's preoccupation with difficulties at home over wool promotion subsidy payments. It was purely coincidental that the 1962 visit was postponed at the point of the Sino-Indian difficulties. It is further safe to assume that if the proposed technical assistance plan fails to materialize, it will be for reasons other than the Australian Government's interposition.

[73] Sydney *Daily Telegraph,* March 4, 1964. Also see Melbourne *Age* and Douglas Wilkie in Melbourne *Sun,* both of March 4, 1964. For favorable reactions to the 1962 announcement, see Adelaide *Advertiser* and Melbourne *Age,* March 29 and 30, 1962, respectively.

A fair question is whether the Government possesses the power to block such a technical assistance program, aside from its ability to deny visas to visiting Chinese technicians. A reading of the relevant Commonwealth legislation strongly suggests, although in the opinion of the author does not explicitly state, that it does. The Wool Promotion Act of 1953 authorized the old Wool Bureau to promote the use of wool in and outside of Australia. Other functions, such as improving wool production in Australia or encouraging research in or outside of Australia likely to be conducive to promotion were made "subject to any directions of the Minister." The Bureau could perform "such other functions for the benefit of the Australian wool industry as the Minister approves." [74] In other words, no special authority was granted enabling the Bureau to engage in "technical assistance"; if technical assistance were contemplated, the Government's permission (and therefore also its ability to veto) would be involved. The 1962 Wool Industry Act leaves the same impression. Promotion by the Wool Board may involve publicity, encouragement of research, and encouragement of improving wool production in Australia; "such other functions as are conferred on the Board by this Act, or, being functions conducive to the achievement of an object of this Act, are approved by the Minister." [75]

The extent of the Government's involvement in the projected technical assistance program can be assessed from another standpoint. The 1962 mission was to be an International Wool Secretariat enterprise. Some 64 per cent of the Secretariat's funds are contributed by the Australian Wool Board. The Wool Board itself, which is to be the sponsor of the 1964 technical arrangement, is underwrit-

[74] Wool Use Promotion Act, no. 23 of 1953, sec. 16, *Commonwealth Acts,* 1953, pp. 86–87.

[75] Wool Industry Act, no. 99 of 1962, sec. 24, *Commonwealth Acts,* Vol. 1, 1962, p. 442.

ten in part by the graziers themselves, in part by the Commonwealth Government—with the Government's contribution having recently been raised.[76] In other words, not only was Australian taxpayers' money used to finance the Gunn trip to Peking, but it will undoubtedly be applied toward expenses incurred by the Wool Board in training Chinese textile experts—though the question of who would pay how much for what was not raised during Gunn's stay in China.

Finally, there is public evidence that the Government not only condones, but in fact approves of what is in store. In 1963 the Wool Secretariat sent three technicians to Communist Poland on a textile-development mission,[77] although none were Australians. Regarding China, the Government has parroted the standard comment that the Wool Board is responsible for its own affairs and goes about its work in ways that it regards as most efficient. But almost in the same breath it has spoken of the advisability of diversifying and extending markets as widely as possible, and stated that it views the export of Australian apparel wool to China as a bright and desirable prospect[78]—which is what the technical assistance scheme is designed to accomplish. In late February of 1964, just as Gunn was about to depart for Peking, the Government, speaking through the Governor-General, said that "Experience shows that the establishment by marketing boards of processing plants overseas, especially in the lesser developed countries, will benefit the export of our primary products and also contribute to social and economic development in such countries. My advisers plan to facilitate the establishment of new plants of this sort."[79] The

[76] See *The Times* (London), October 15, 1963.

[77] W. J. Vines, statement of April 16, 1963, in *SMH,* April 17, 1963.

[78] See Harrie Ward, *CPD,* S, October 17, 1963, p. 1210, and William Spooner, *ibid.,* March 3, 1964, p. 115.

[79] *CPD,* HR, February 25, 1964, p. 12.

Wool Board is not a marketing board, but from what has been said earlier it certainly seems that the Government had in mind, *inter alia,* a favorable reaction to the type of project about to be negotiated by Sir William Gunn, even though it was to be with Communist China. After the Peking mission the Board addressed a letter to the Department of Primary Industry, setting out in general terms its hope for Government cooperation in any program devised with the Chinese. In the last analysis, the letter will probably prove superfluous. It is something of an asset to the Wool Board that Gunn is one of the most successful, influential, and respected business figures in Australia; the Government, however, inherently supports enterprises which yield results for Australia's commerce—and that is the purpose of technical textile aid to China.

### THE GOVERNMENT AND THE WHEAT TRADE

THE MOST rewarding and celebrated feature of Australia's sales to China, however, has been in wheat, Australia's second largest export earner. Prior to the late 'fifties, Australia's wheat sales to Communist China were virtually nonexistent. Then, in 1957–58, an incidental sale worth £52,000 was made, followed by a £233,000 sale in the following financial year. No sales were made in 1959–60, but then in December 1960 and January 1961 over a million tons of wheat were sold. It was the beginning of a truly remarkable trading achievement. Since the first large transaction, China has become Australia's best wheat buyer, taking 53.5 per cent of her wheat exports during the 1962–63 season. To mid-1964, Australia sold on the order of seven million tons of wheat to China, at a total figure of over £250,000,000—roughly the size of Australia's 1963–64 defense budget.[80]

[80] For instance, see E. J. Donath, in *SMH,* February 3, 1964, and "1961–62 Was Another Memorable Wheat Year," *Economic and Financial Survey of Australia. 1961–62* (Sydney: Birt, 1962),

Indeed, commensurate with the high Chinese sales, Australia's wheat production has been leaping ahead at record rates. Wheat acreage is more than twice as extensive as it was in 1957–58, nearly up to the 1930–31 peak of 18.2 million acres. Keeping pace has been the wheat yield itself. It was 247 million bushels for the 1961–62 season, 307 million for 1962–63, and about 331 million bushels in 1963–64. Since domestic Australian consumption—human, animal and reseeding—is only about 70 million bushels, quite clearly overseas buyers must be sought and won. The first large Chinese sale was made in the face of a prospectively embarrassing surplus, and subsequent sales have greatly eased the situation—indeed, they have even contributed to the enthusiasm with which new planting has moved ahead. Due largely to Chinese buying, by 1964 the overseas demand for Australian wheat became greater than available inventories.[81]

The reaction to the wheat sales has, understandably, been sympathetic throughout most of Australia. The growers themselves have not relished the thought of wheat piling up in silos and becoming infested with weevils. There has even been a shortage of silo space itself, although the grower cannot collect payment until he delivers his wheat to a silo. The grower community has likewise felt that Australia cannot rest on the laurels of her recent wheat sales, since Canada, France, and others are also heavily competing for the China wheat trade.[82] It is inter-

---

no. 15, esp. pp. 69–71; "Man on the Land," in *Bulletin*, December 14, 1963; Australia-China Society, Victorian Branch, "Our Fourth Best Customer," special statement, April 1964.

[81] See "The New Wheat Stabilisation Scheme," *Trends* (Rural Bank of NSW), Vol. 6 (December 1963), pp. 6–7; E. J. Donath, "Australia's Wheat Sales to China," *Far Eastern Economic Review*, Vol. 37 (August 30, 1962), p. 387; Donath, in Melbourne *Age*, January 7, 1964; J. V. Moroney, chairman of the Australian Wheat Board, statement of March 4, 1964, in *SMH*, March 5, 1964.

[82] *Muster*, November 14, 1962; T. C. Stott, general secretary, Australian Wheatgrowers' Federation, statements in *SMH*, Janu-

esting to notice the reaction in Queensland country districts prior to the 1963 state elections. The campaign was waged against a setting of fresh large shipments of wheat to China from Queensland ports. The Queensland Labor Party, Queensland version of the DLP, was preparing to assault the ALP by associating its support for the China trade with a sell-out to Chinese imperialism, but local papers, whatever their politics, only took notice of these complaints to rebut them. The Toowoomba *Chronicle,* for instance, wrote that "the massive wheat sales to Red China, whatever criticism they may evoke in certain quarters, must be accepted as one of the most important planks of our trade programme"; Australia must exploit the Chinese market "if we are to survive in what may be a new world trading set-up," and the recent shipments from Queensland were "on a scale vitally beneficial to our economy, particularly in 'Common Market year.' "[83] The public generally has approved of the wheat sales, an August 1963 poll disclosing 78 per cent in favor and only 13 per cent explicitly opposed to continuing the large wheat sales to China.[84] Furthermore, while few analysts are prepared to cast exceptionally long-range predictions, there is a general feeling that China will continue to require large amounts of wheat. She has in some part recovered from the natural disasters and the fiasco of the "great leap forward" of a few years ago, which originally prompted heavy grain buying. She is, however, finding it economical to export domestically grown rice and to import wheat for

ary 16, 1963, and *Victorian Wheat and Woolgrower* (organ of the Victorian Wheat and Woolgrowers' Association), February 8, 1963; K. McDougall, statement of July 12, 1963, in *SMH,* July 15, 1963.

[83] Toowoomba *Chronicle,* January 14, 1963. Also see Bundaberg *News Mail,* January 4, 1963.

[84] *AGP,* nos. 1698–1710, September–October 1963. For some early favorable metropolitan press comments, see Melbourne *Herald,* February 7, 1961, and *SMH,* February 8, 1961.

home consumption. Australians who have visited China have been told that Australian soft wheat is well liked (it apparently does well in Chinese steamed bread and noodles), and that Australia can look ahead to a continuing market. In sum, the wheat trade has captured Australia's imagination.[85]

The Government's role in the Chinese wheat trade requires special and careful exposition from several angles; its involvement, as will be seen, has been considerably more prominent than in wool sales and promotion. The legal position has always been clear. The Australian Wheat Board, unlike the Wool Board, is a marketing oganization, deriving its authority from a combination of Federal and state statutes. All Australian wheat sold at home or abroad is actually sold by the Board. Growers do not hold an option to sell privately. Growers in New South Wales, Victoria, and South Australia each select two members, the Queensland and Western Australian Wheat Boards nominate two each, and there are five Commonwealth-appointed members, including a chairman. The most recent Federal wheat legislation, which recapitulates an established situation, reads that "the Minister may give directions to the Board concerning the performance of its functions and the exercise of its powers, and the Board shall comply with those directions." [86]

As early as 1954 the Wheat Board made inquiries through official sources in Canberra about the Government's reactions if wheat were to be sold to China, and was

[85] See International Wheat Council, *Review of the World Wheat Situation 1962/63* (London: The Council, 1963), pp. 44ff.; Sir John Crawford in *Australian Financial Review*, October 8, 1963; articles in *Commonwealth Agriculturalist*, Vol. 33 (December 1963), by J. V. Moroney, "The Wheat Industry Today. The Marketing Outlook for Australian Wheat," p. 6, and by P. B. Leach, "The Wheat Industry Today. A Grower Reports," p. 7; *SMH*, September 4, 1964.

[86] Wheat Industry Stabilization Act, no. 83 of 1963, sec. 13, *Commonwealth Acts*, 1963, paper issue, p. 8.

told there was no objection. In the years that followed Wheat Board men, passing through Hong Kong on other business, contacted the Chinese Resources Company and made general queries about Chinese interest in Australian wheat, but were advised that none was needed. The relatively minor Chinese purchases of 1958 were made through a private source who had bought the wheat from the Board. The Board felt that, in part, these early purchases were intended to establish the principle of Chinese interest in Australian wheat. Then came the first impressive sales, transacted by the Wheat Board in Hong Kong in December 1960–January 1961 for a sum of about £27,000,000. Although these were cash sales, it seems plain that the Government was consulted and gave approval. Attacked from certain right-wing quarters, Wheat Board Chairman Sir John Teasdale replied that the Board was a commercial organization of a trustee character and not concerned with political ideologies. While its operations were guided and sanctioned by legislative enactments, the Board was responsible for disposal of the wheat it controlled. There had been no "sinister political implications" connected with the secrecy in which the deal had been negotiated. It was normal practice to withhold information about the size of sales lest shippers conspire to raise transport rates. "Beyond any doubt," said Sir John, "the huge sales benefit the wheat industry in particular and also the whole of Australia." [87] Speaking retrospectively in late 1963, after a number of other and larger wheat sales had been concluded, the Trade Minister's deputy in the Senate reflected the same attitude: the Wheat Board had performed admirably, especially in reducing wheat surpluses to the absolute minimum.[88]

However, selling wheat to China on a cash basis was

[87] See his remarks in *SMH*, February 7, 1961, and *Victorian Countryman*, February 9, 1961.

[88] Harrie Wade, *CPD*, S, August 29, 1963, p. 301.

one thing, while selling it on extended credit was something quite different. In March of 1961, fast on the heels of the cash sales, the Wheat Board was approached about a further sale, this time on credit. There was a relevant precedent to consider. Wheat had been sold on credit to Communist countries before—to Poland in 1955 and to Rumania in 1956.[89] China was, however, quite special. She was Communist, just as Poland and Rumania are, but occupied a unique position in terms of Australia's external relations; furthermore the East European sales had been minor by comparison with what China was preparing to buy.

Early in April Teasdale admitted that an approach had been made by the Chinese for wheat on credit, but showed no spontaneous enthusiasm, carefully pointing out the need to keep sound commercial considerations in mind as well as the general state of international conditions. Since credit sales to overseas countries touched on the national interest, the Wheat Board had always followed the practice of referring the matter to the Government in advance.[90] In the same month a Wheat Board delegation journeyed to Peking. The Chinese were willing to buy about a million tons, but only on credit. The Board was almost evenly divided, with Teasdale leading the anticredit faction. Although Teasdale himself was strongly anti-Communist, he and his supporters were opposed largely on economic grounds, such as the danger of overdependence on the Chinese market and to some degree uncertainty about China's ability to honor her commitment in the face of no available insurance to cover risks. It was, incidentally, an uneasiness shared by a number of growers.[91] When the sale was effected, the Wheat Board explained

[89] C. F. Adermann, *ibid.*, HR 32, August 29, 1961, p. 301.
[90] See *Muster,* April 5, 1961.
[91] In public sources, see E. J. Donath, "Australia's Wheat Sales to China," pp. 387–388; *News Weekly,* February 21, 1962.

that it preferred not to sell on credit, but that an exception had been made because of the volume of the present sale as well as the previous cash transaction; about the same time, the Wheat Board rejected a minor request by Bulgaria for £1,750,000 of wheat on credit.[92] There were, however, other stimuli to the Chinese credit deal. For one, Canada was in process of negotiating an extremely large credit sale with China, and Australia could not afford to forfeit the quickly expanding Chinese market to a more flexible competitor. In fact, the Australian terms were more attractive. She awarded 10 per cent cash, 40 per cent in six months, and 50 per cent in twelve months, while the initial Canadian credit sale was 25 per cent cash and the remainder nine months after shipment.[93]

Teasdale's own comment that the Government was "not implicated in the deal in any way" [94] was only partially correct and certainly misleading. It was true that the Government did not guarantee the sale against Chinese default, for at that juncture there was no suitable machinery for such a guarantee. But it is obvious that the Government knew of the impending credit sale and gave its consent, although it resorted to its usual defense of no involvement. In a small masterpiece expressing the satisfaction of having your cake and eating it too, Senator Harrie Wade, Country Party, representing the Country Party Minister for Primary Industry, said, "it is not for the Government to approve or disapprove of such a transaction, but in any event the Government does not disapprove of a big sale such as this, which will earn us a substantial amount of export income. I do not think the Government has the

[92] C. J. Perrett, general manager of the Australian Wheat Board, statement of June 19, 1961, in *SMH,* June 20, 1961.

[93] See Colina MacDougall, "Agreement of 'Intent,'" *Far Eastern Economic Review,* Vol. 32 (May 18, 1961), p. 317. Comparative Australian and Canadian terms are available in *CPD,* S, October 8, 1963, p. 922.

[94] Statement of May 11, 1961, in *SMH,* May 12, 1961.

power to prevent the transaction, but I say quite plainly that the Government does not disapprove of it."[95] In the first place, of course, it was absolutely untrue that the Government lacked power to halt the credit deal. In the second place, in March, Wade himself had said that any sales contemplated on other than commercial terms would be carefully scrutinized by the Government to protect both the wheat growers and the Australian public at large, and he was defining "commercial" as being distinct from credit.[96] Later, however, McEwen explained that the Wheat Board had reported to the Government its intention to pursue credit negotiations with the Chinese, and had been advised that it was free to pursue whatever commercial transactions it thought desirable.[97]

What emerges from all this contorted reasoning is that the Government decided that a commercial transaction was one which did not involve prices substantially below world levels. The Department of Trade had apparently studied the picture and reported that the Chinese were good credit risks. At any rate, no special political complications were envisaged. Therefore, according to Country Party sources, on the advice of McEwen and Adermann, the Government decided not to interfere—which meant, in practical terms, that it approved.[98] In substance, this coincides with what the author has been able to learn privately. The Country Party ministers did not need to press and plead to convince their Liberal colleagues, but they certainly were keenly interested in moving ahead with the experiment. The Government's attitude was without question a decisive factor in leading the majority on the Wheat Board to pursue the deal. Afterward, the Government asked the Wheat Board for "an opportunity to comment"

[95] *CPD,* S 19, May 16, 1961, p. 1006.
[96] *Ibid.,* March 21, 1961, p. 378.
[97] *Ibid.,* HR 31, May 2, 1961, p. 1360.
[98] *NSW Countryman,* June 1961.

on any wheat sales on terms in excess of six months.[99] Since all subsequent sales to China have been on terms longer than six months, it is clear that there has been routine consultation following the first credit deal. From such consultations emerged the only known instance of a Governmental directive being delivered to the Wheat Board regarding sales to China.

In 1963, first France and then Canada extended credit on wheat sales to China on an 18-month basis. Canada in particular was anxious to match the Australian Wheat Board's growing reputation as a slick and effective salesman so as to maintain her own healthy sales of hard, somewhat more expensive wheat. Competition had been lively, and a "survival of the fittest" climate was coming to be understood in Canada.[100] In mid-1963, at the time the Canadians were about to complete their generous deal of 25 per cent down and the balance in 18 months, the Chinese insisted on comparable terms from Australia. When the Government learned of this, it in effect instructed the Wheat Board people to return to the conference table and not yield beyond the established 12-month practice. After hard bargaining, the Chinese relented and accepted a 12-month contract. It is impossible to say if the Government would have allowed 18 months had the Chinese issued a "no buy" ultimatum. Some plausible reasons for the Government's original order are, however, discernible. The author understands that the Government, and perhaps to a degree the Board itself, were not too happy with the prospect of entering a race with Canada to allow increasingly

[99] Adermann, *CPD,* HR 35, April 4, 1962, p. 1259. Also see E. J. Donath, in *Bulletin,* April 21, 1962, and "Australia's Credit Wheat Sales to Communist China," *Australia's Neighbours,* 3rd Series, nos. 126–127 (April–May 1962), p. 8.

[100] See Charles Taylor in Toronto *Globe and Mail,* July 4 and 19, 1963, and Bruce MacDonald in *ibid.,* August 3, 1963; Frederick Nossal, "Wheat Diplomacy," *Far Eastern Economic Review,* Vol. 41 (July 18, 1963), p. 151.

liberal terms, not knowing when and how such concessions could be stopped. Also—and this was an argument stressed with the Chinese—the Australian economy, and especially the technicalities of payments to growers, would have been unduly disrupted through the extension of over-generous payment terms.

An 18-month contract, concluded with the Government's knowledge and approval, could have spelled real electoral trouble. The Menzies Government was then limping along with a bare 62 to 60 advantage in the House. It had escaped defeat in 1961 by the skin of its teeth, and only a relatively strong performance in Victoria had made even this victory possible. Now it was considering another election, which in fact was held on November 30 of 1963. It was generally agreed that such an election would also be tight, and the Government could not afford a bombardment from the DLP or its own right-wing in such crucial times. If Victoria slipped, where the DLP was especially active, R. G. Menzies and his colleagues might be retired into opposition. The Government's attitude was, of course, a calculated risk. If the Chinese had not agreed to 12 months and had refused to buy Australian wheat, that too could have caused alarm in Australia, together with political repercussions. Perhaps the Government's only cushion would then have been the comfort of a generally improving overseas wheat market, assisted by Soviet purchases of Australian wheat.

Another consideration which may have prompted the Government to refuse 18 months of credit was the position of the United States—a theme which will be examined more closely in the next chapter. Extensive queries by the author among both Australian and non-Australian sources confirmed a background of U. S. discussions with Australia about the China trade. It would appear that these were discussions as such, not protests or representations in the ordinary sense of those words, but they included contacts at the highest levels—perhaps as high as Kennedy and Menzies, certainly as high as Rusk and Barwick. What the U. S. seemed to have done was to stress the wheat credit aspect of Australia's trade with China, underscoring the dangers of overdependence on a Communist buying source and likewise mentioning that credit was really a form of foreign aid to a "near-enemy" country.

Related to this has been the issue of wheat sold to China which was diverted to other, particularly Communist countries. In 1962 and 1963 some people began to suspect that this was going on, and questions were raised in and out of Parliament.[101] The Government was very evasive. Publicity had not been given to this phenomenon, and ministers were inclined to render ambiguous and unsatisfactory answers, or to admit that it existed but to play it down.[102] In actual fact, as the Government finally stated in April of 1964, China had bought wheat from Australia and consigned 61,000 tons to Albania, 57,000 tons to North Korea, and 12,000 tons to Cuba. The Government also explained that in such transactions with the Chinese it was understood that they "should in no way prejudice sales of Australian wheat to such of the countries as may purchase directly from the Board." [103] What it did not reveal, however, was that the Wheat Board had always known in advance that these Chinese wheat purchases were destined for direct shipment to Albania, North Korea, or Cuba. It did not mention that such sales had started in late 1960, to Albania, even before the first

[101] George Hannan, *CPD,* S 22, August 23, 1962, p. 455; Beazley, *ibid.,* HR 37, December 6 and 7, 1962, p. 3176; Statements of December 5, 1962, by J. Riordan, federal secretary, Federated Clerks' Union and by New South Wales Deputy Premier J. B. Renshaw, in *SMH,* December 6, 1962.

[102] For instance, Menzies, *CPD,* HR 37, December 6 and 7, 1962, p. 1376, and William Spooner, S 23, April 9, 1963, p. 18.

[103] Adermann, *ibid.,* HR, April 8, 1964, p. 885.

large Chinese cash sale had been concluded. It did not explain that there had been several Albanian and North Korean sales in the early 1960's, and that the Cuban shipment was arranged *after* the Cuban crisis of late 1962. Nor, finally, did it admit that once again the U.S. had talked to Australia, this time about the Cuban sale. Although America was not herself prohibiting the shipment of food and medicines to Cuba, she obviously was upset about any precedent being laid down for a prospective Austral-Cuban commercial link.

Indeed, in 1963 the U. S. was still making disparaging remarks about free world trade with China, particularly as it affected Japan and with special reference to credit. In May 1963 Franklin D. Roosevelt, Jr., U.S. Under Secretary of Commerce, said in a Japanese interview that it was Japan's choice to trade or not to trade with China, but that China wished for trade on credit, on long terms and with low interest, and that could only be construed as economic aid rather than trade.[104] In August, there were more reports of U. S. annoyance with Japanese extension of credit to China.[105] Roger Hilsman, then Assistant Secretary of State for Far Eastern Affairs, stated in an interview of the same month that trade for China was more a political than an economic function. The rather garbled thought he was trying to convey reads as follows: "So I think that whereas certain nations like Canada and Australia have very large wheat surpluses and that it is in their—and deals have been worked out here, in terms of long-run trade, and the potentialities, it seems to me that I just wonder how much Communist China has got to offer on this." [106] What was plain was that the U. S. was not looking favorably on her allies' propensity to trade with

[104] "Japan-U.S. Trade Problems," interview in *Oriental Economist,* Vol. 31 (May 1963), p. 267.

[105] *NYT,* August 10, 1963.

[106] Washington interview with Japanese NHK correspondent, cited in *Japan Times* (Tokyo), August 31, 1963.

China on credit, and the Australian Government could well have had this in mind when weighing the 18-month credit request.

Still another plausible consideration which could be attributed to the forming of the Government's attitude is essentially economic, to wit, that the Chinese request for 18 months of credit was a sign of their weakness, evidence that China was running short of foreign exchange, and that it would therefore be *unsafe* to enter into an exceptionally long-term contract. To test this assumption a few steps backward are necessary. When the Wheat Board was conducting its first credit sale to China, it approached the Export Payments Insurance Corporation (EPIC), about the prospects of insuring the deal. EPIC had originally been created by statute in 1956 to encourage exporters to make certain risk sales. It stood prepared, after examining the suitability of a request for insurance, to write insurance against various risks of default by the buyer. By general guiding principle, but not by legal compulsion, EPIC was prepared in 1961 to insure raw materials, consumer goods, and miscellaneous general commodities shipped on terms up to 180 days. Manufactured goods and capital equipment sold on credit of up to five years was also acceptable for insurance. The Chinese wheat sales, which entailed 12 months of credit, did not fall under either of these guidelines. But even if they had, or an exception had been made, so very much money was at stake that EPIC could not risk its limited capital. EPIC was required to secure sufficient revenue over a period of years to meet all expenses properly chargeable to revenue. To accomplish this it needed to follow fairly orthodox insurance principles, which included an acceptable spread of risks between and among markets. These factors have been reflected in EPIC's record over the past few years. After almost six years of operation, shipments totaling £80,000,000 had been insured, the large majority of policies being issued to exporters who were insured for tens of thousands of pounds, not millions.[107] In this context it is not surprising that the Wheat Board was told that EPIC was unprepared to write insurance for millions of pounds worth of wheat. But the decision was definitely not political. Both before and after the Wheat Board query, EPIC had insured corrugated iron and flat steel sheet sold to China on credit. By the close of 1963, the value of these goods bound for China so insured exceeded £8,000,000.

When the first credit deal was consummated, a special "national-interest" clause was being written into law. It was not available in time for this sale, but EPIC advised the Board that it might explore it for future reference. In substance, the national-interest clause was designed for transactions which fell outside the normal spread of EPIC's risks and operations. Henceforth, requests of an unusual type would be handled by the Government itself. It would decide if insurance should be granted, would collect premiums, pay claims, etc. Its decision to underwrite a national-interest request would be conditioned by whether the proposition held promise of opening up worthwhile new export markets, whether an industry with high export potential would be stimulated, whether the transaction was important to the development of a particular Australian area or industry, or whether obvious and significant benefits for Australia's trade relations with the country concerned would be conferred.[108] Plainly, the Chinese wheat sales would have qualified under these criteria.

[107] See Export Payments Insurance Corporation, *7th Annual Report and Financial Statements, 1963* (Sydney: 1963), *passim;* A. D. P. Martin, "The Role of Export Credit Insurance in Australia's Export Drive," The Economic Society of Australia and New Zealand, Economic Monograph no. 252, June 1963, mimeo., *passim.*

[108] See McEwen, *CPD,* HR 31, April 13, 1961, pp. 823–824, and May 11, 1961, p. 1758; Export Payments Insurance Corporation (Amendment) Act, no. 14 of 1961, sec. 16, *Commonwealth Acts,* 1961, pp. 89–90.

The Wheat Board took EPIC's advice and approached the Government. No credit deal with China was imminent, and the query was therefore a general one, asking how the Government felt about insuring Chinese sales. A reply was received in September of 1961, indicating that the Government *would not* be willing to underwrite. As in the 18-month controversy in 1963, the Government in 1961 may well have had political considerations in mind, even though the Wheat Board did not have an immediate sale in motion, one which would have taken place before the end of the year, when elections were scheduled. Then too there may have been uneasiness about American reactions. This would be an exceptionally plausible explanation, since the West Irian dispute was then climbing toward its peak and Australia was very much concerned about Washington's attitude. But an explanation based on Government fears that the Chinese would renege on payment and force the Government to pay on the Wheat Board's claims does not make sense. As seen above, early in 1961 the Government already had advice that the Chinese were prompt payers. By September, China was paying on her Australian and Canadian credit transactions, always on time.

From this analysis a connection can be made with the 1963 Government decision to balk at 18 months of credit. If by late 1961 the Chinese payment record was sound, by mid-1963 it was firmly established as excellent in every respect. The Chinese were paying not only on time, but often in advance of prescribed deadlines. The Wheat Board itself has tended to look back on 1961 with relief that no credit insurance had been obtained, since it has in no way been needed. Indeed, as matters stand, the Wheat Board (and therefore the growers) is realizing a profit beyond the cash value of wheat sales to China. The interest rate, whose exact figure is a secret, is known to be larger than the interest paid by the Board when it borrows commercially in Australia to pay advances to the growers long before the Chinese have paid fully on their credit transactions. If insurance had been taken under EPIC's national-interest clause, payment of premiums would undoubtedly have wiped out the present "extra" dividend and in fact cut into the basic return to growers. The occasional charges that the Chinese have been quietly excused from paying interest[109] have been flimsily argued and at all events can categorically be said to be false.[110] In December of 1962, when a new credit sale was announced, a Wheat Board member claimed that the Board's decision had been unanimous.[111] By then, to be sure, Teasdale was dead and had been replaced, but the solidarity of the Board at large was a far cry from the days of early 1961, and one powerful reason was the meticulous payments record of China.

What has emerged from the wheat trade discussion so far is that the Government has not interfered and in fact has sanctioned credit sales. It has refused to offer insurance coverage and intervened when the Chinese asked for 18 months of credit, but found itself in marvelous luck both times, since China did not default on uninsured purchases and accepted a 12-month contract in 1963 rather than creating an impasse. As of mid-1964, the Chinese had not repeated their request for 18 months of credit of a year earlier. Yet the Government has been continuously involved in the China wheat trade in still another way, however unobtrusive on the surface, and one which supplies a few more insights.

[109] For instance, Peter Samuel, "Australian Economic Aid," *Australia's Neighbours,* 4th series, nos. 15–16 (May–June 1964), p. 8; Santamaria, as cited in *News Weekly,* May 6 and 14, 1964.

[110] For a denial available in public sources, see E. G. Hoy, before United Farmers and Woolgrowers' Association, July 20, 1964, in *SMH,* July 21, 1964.

[111] T. Shanaha, statement of Dec. 30, 1962, in *ibid.,* Dec. 31, 1962.

Continuously since 1948 Australia has operated under wheat stabilization programs which are relegislated every five years. Reduced to its pertinent essentials, the legislation has provided that when a fund contributed to by growers themselves runs dry, the Commonwealth, through ordinary revenue sources, will guarantee payment on exported wheat to a given price per bushel for a given number of bushels. The guaranteed price, readjusted annually, is based on a generous estimate of cost of production. In other words, should world prices fall beneath the guaranteed price, the difference will be covered by the Government, to the limit legislatively provided. For many years no Government subsidy was required, but beginning in 1959–60 the overseas price of wheat began to fall, the growers' own fund did not suffice, and the Government began to honor its legal obligations. It was also about this point that heavy selling to China began. Although exact per bushel prices have not been announced, it is clear that the Chinese, among others, have paid lower prices per bushel than the guaranteed "cost of production" level. Putting these developments together yields the conclusion that the Australian taxpayer has, in effect, been subsidizing the China wheat sales, perhaps to the extent of about £11,000,000 through the 1962–63 growing season. For the three wheat pools of 1960–61, 1961–62, and 1962–63, almost £27,500,000 was paid into the wheat fund from consolidated revenue. Since the Chinese bought an average of about 40 per cent of Australia's wheat over this period, the figure of some £11,000,000 is reached.[112]

In late 1963 the guaranteed export price per bushel was

[112] See Josef Wilczynski, *Australia's Trade with the Communist Bloc,* M.Ec. thesis, Australian National University, 1963, p. 228, and his "Dilemmas in Australia's Trade with the Communist Bloc," *Australian Quarterly,* Vol. 36 (March 1964), p. 15; McEwen, *CPD,* HR 33, Oct. 12, 1961, p. 2076; Adermann, HR 37, Nov. 8, 1962, p. 2203; Australian Wheat Board, Annual Report, Season 1962–63 (Melbourne: 1964), p. 22.

lowered, but the number of bushels guaranteed was raised considerably, from 100 to 150 million, a decision, as the Government admitted, which took into account "the increased export capacity of the wheat industry and its significant contribution to our overseas income." [113] To this tendency China has contributed mightily, since she now absorbs over 50 per cent of Australia's wheat exports. Since world prices appear to be rising again, this will not necessarily commit the Government to greater expenditures, but in fact would reduce payments to the stabilization fund. At all events, the Government had no qualms (nor did the Labor Opposition) about relegislating in a way that at least opened the road to further subsidies resulting from sales to China more than to any other source.

The Government's role in the stabilization program may have one final lesson to teach. Chinese default on wheat credit payments could, and for political reasons in relation to the Country Party and the growers probably would, induce the Government to take nonpayment into account in assessing the average export price obtained for determination of the amount payable under the Wheat Industry Stabilization Act(s). The author's discussions with people very close to Australian wheat politics and economics produced a majority opinion that the Government would interpret and apply the legislation in this way. In fact, when the Polish credit sale was made, Cabinet decided—*without* the Wheat Board's knowledge—that default would bring about such action. This decision was never rescinded when the Chinese credit sales appeared, and McEwen for one would surely have insisted on its implementation had the Chinese defaulted. Put another way, the stabilization legislation may have, in the background, served as a very special kind of "Government insurance" for the Chinese credit sales. In the light of this interpretation, the Government's refusal to entertain formal insur-

[113] Adermann, HR, Oct. 24, 1963, p. 2266. See also Ian Allan, *ibid.,* Oct. 30, 1963, p. 2475.

ance writing under EPIC's national-interest clause in 1961 becomes more understandable. Although the Government's 1961 position was based on legislation enacted in 1958, when few contemplated the bountiful Chinese market which later emerged, it was a great convenience to have this shock-absorber available, and to escape the political and/or diplomatic damage that formal insurance might have carried. Again the Government was in luck, and in large part was able to maintain the fiction that it did not itself engage in or actively assist the China trade.

The ALP's criticisms have therefore been well placed. The Government has been hypocritical in denying implication in the China trade, or denying that it can halt it, but it has gotten away with it as the exports have grown and the hard Chinese foreign exchange has rolled in. The Government has, in fact, become almost carelessly cocky in piously denying the facts of the matter. In March of 1964, a Parliamentary queston was answered. The question asked if any Australian trade delegations had visited China during the past five years. The reply was carefully considered, since the question had been submitted in advance, on notice. The reply was given in one word, "No." [114] Various private individuals had been to China, including Heine, who returned there after his 1958 barter deal. Trading bank delegations—five in 1963 alone—had been to China to promote trade for their customers. Promotion authority men (Wool Board) had gone. Marketing organization men (Wheat Board) had gone. Officials of a quasi-autonomous Government enterprise (Reserve Bank) had visited China. A full-fledged Commonwealth official (Patterson) had gone. Surely somewhere in this catalogue an "Australian trade delegation" could be uncovered. Perhaps the next chapter can in some degree unravel the Menzies Government's hypocrisy, if not outright prevarication, on Chinese trade.

[114] Adermann, *ibid.*, March 18 and 19, 1964, p. 648.

# VII

# THE CHINA TRADE: CRITICISMS AND DIPLOMACY

WHILE THE preceding discussion emphasized the stimuli and results of Australian exports to China, some hint was given that Australian-Chinese trade has not been a simple, open and shut proposition, free of criticism and complication. Criticism and complication there have been, however, and it is necessary to explain their source and impact, beginning perhaps with the strategic embargo, the most visible Governmentally induced restraint on trade with China.

## THE CHARACTER OF THE CHINESE STRATEGIC EMBARGO

AS WAS SEEN, the Korean War induced the Western powers to establish a special strategic embargo against China, a more restrictive list than applied to other Communist countries; the Paris-based COCOM and CHINCOM groups became the coordinating agencies. Until almost mid-1957, despite the passage of several years since the end of the Korean War, the Chinese embargo list remained basically unaltered—only a handful of items was added and subtracted. This was not to the liking of a number of Western governments, particularly the British. The "China differential" was seen as pointless because the Chinese could acquire prohibited goods from Russia, for whom the embargo was lower, and because many of the categories still defined as strategic no longer seemed to fit that definition. Furthermore, powerful pressures were accumulating among British businessmen, who sensed that the special China embargo was harming their trade prospects—the Chinese themselves were indicating that the embargo was heavily responsible for retarding Sino-British trade. Finally, the Government in London was concerned about the inability of certain colonies to sell their products to China, for example, Malayan rubber, which resulted in marked economic loss. By 1956 Britain began to back out of the China embargo by invoking the "exceptions procedure." This method allowed occasional departure from the standard prohibited list, but was slow and cumbersome to administer and at all events failed to dent the established proscribed goods list; it was, as its name implied, an "exceptional" arrangement.[1]

By May of 1957 pressure in Britain and elsewhere to remove the extraordinary embargo on materials shipped to China had become intense. Complete agreement among all COCOM members to make the adjustment was not possible because of U.S. opposition. The British, however, threatened to alter their own practice unilaterally, if necessary. But this was not necessary. Other countries quickly joined Britain in equalizing the Chinese and East European lists. As early as July 1957 Japan, so closely dependent on the U.S., followed the parade.[2] In the months and years which followed, sales to China were further facilitated through the scaling down of the now unified strategic list operating against Communist nations. By the second half of 1958 items such as civil aircraft and engines, many machine tools, vehicles, and almost all electrical motors could be freely exported to China. Quantita-

[1] See Luard, *op. cit.*, pp. 141–142; Eden, *op. cit.*, p. 332; *The Times* (London), June 5, 1956; "Pressure to Ease China Embargo," *Far East Trade*, Vol. 12 (April 1957), p. 392; "China Trade," *Far Eastern Economic Review*, Vol. 22 (June 27, 1957), p. 823; Kayser Sung, "The China Trade Riddle," *ibid.*, Vol. 29 (September 1, 1960), pp. 504ff.

[2] For a discussion of the changes effected, see "Relaxed Restrictions on China Trade," *Oriental Economist*, Vol. 25 (September 1957), p. 478.

tive restrictions were disposed of, although a "watching list" of intermediately strategic materials was established.[3]

So far as Australia was concerned, even as early as the 1957 European equalization step, there had been signs of closer commercial contacts with China. H. C. Menzies and several private individuals had been to China and had returned with favorable estimates, the trade itself was beginning to move upward, and so on. On hearing of Britain's decision to equate the Chinese and East European strategic lists, McEwen offered a guarded reaction. Australia would not immediately follow Britain's example. The British action would need to be assessed against the actual composition of a new China list. Once the new list was available, further Australian measures would be considered.[4] As the months passed, no further statement came from the Government. Business circles, however, were becoming impatient. They were eager to enter the Chinese market, but ran into obstacles. In September of 1958—almost a year and a half after McEwen had promised to review the position—evidence began to accumulate that in fact little or no change had been effected. At least two Australian firms that tried to sell copper wire, sheet, and tubing to China had been barred from doing so; they then discovered that British interests had sold the same materials in a contract worth £750,000 sterling.[5] Then the Government began to admit that the China differential had in fact been retained—though it did so casually. Late in 1958, in the supplement to his electoral policy speech,

[3] See *NYT*, August 15, 1958; Sir David Eccles, President of the Board of Trade, press conference statement of August 14, 1958, in *The Times* (London), August 15, 1958.

[4] Statement of May 31, 1957, in *SMH*, June 1, 1957.

[5] See *ibid.*, September 27, 1958. For other expressions of Australian business community displeasure, see *ibid.*, June 27, 1957; *Australian Financial Review*, June 19, 1958; Sir John Allison, in *Commerce News* (Melbourne), May 1959.

Menzies said that his Government's policy had been a "steady one," conducted "in close harmony with that of our allies." Australia did not sell strategically significant goods to China. She had a control list for this purpose, had "made no change in this policy for a long time, and . . . [had] none in contemplation." [6] Clearly, the "allies" were not the NATO powers and Japan, but the U.S., who did not trade with China at all. "No change in policy" meant no change in the pre-1957 position. About a year later McEwen sharpened the point. Australian export policy to China was "Substantially more restrictive than is the policy of the United Kingdom Government." [7] He reversed his claim that the prohibited list had never been modified, but only to the extent of saying that there was some scope to move goods from an absolutely prohibited to a discretionary list.[8] Since then the Government has been loath to discuss the China differential, though comprehensive checking by the author has made it entirely plain that a differential continues. Indeed, the Government has been reluctant to discuss strategic trade generally, and has worked itself into some embarrassing corners.

What is clear is that Australia employs three categories of goods when she determines strategic content. There is a list of selected yet fairly representative items which may be exported freely to all destinations. This list, which runs to two foolscap pages, typed double space, is issued periodically by the Department of Customs and Excise. A list issued on January 25, 1961, contained such obviously strategically neutral items as beeswax, earthenware, kitchenware, sulpha drugs, toys, and wheat. Agricultural machinery and implements were also on the list, including tillage, seeding, and harvesting items, but *not* tractors.

[6] R. G. Menzies, "Federal Election 1958. Joint Policy Speech" (Canberra: Federal Secretariat, Australian Liberal Party, 1958), delivered October 29, 1958, supplement, p. 27.

[7] *CPD,* HR 24, September 3, 1959, p. 880.

[8] *Ibid.,* August 26, 1959, p. 564, and August 27, 1959, p. 635.

This is the only relevant list published by the Government, and even it is not strictly a guide to what is or is not strategic. Customs regulations absolutely prohibit the export of various narcotics, for instance. With special permission only, it is possible to export such similarly nonstrategic items as birds of paradise and their plumage, and skeletons, or parts of skeletons, of Australian or Tasmanian aborigines.[9]

Aside from items freely exportable to China, there are two strategic control lists. One is a list of goods absolutely barred from shipment to China. The other is an intermediate list, very large in scope, for which an export license must be sought and on which the Government decides what may or may not be shipped depending on circumstances. While the Department of Customs and Excise administers the licensing system, the Department of External Affairs is responsible for policy, i.e., determining what may or may not be shipped. The Department of Trade and Industry is also brought in for consultation on frequent occasion.[10] According to Government spokesmen, the absolute embargo list, while not published by Australia, is easily accessible, as it follows the list issued by the British Board of Trade and is periodically published, with revisions, in the *Board of Trade Journal.*[11] McEwen's 1959 statement that the absolute embargo and intermediate lists were modifiable between one another at the discretion of the External Affairs Department probably does not contradict the above practice if viewed in

[9] For instance, see Regulations Under the Customs Act 1901–1957, *Statutory Rules,* 1958, no. 5, 17pp.

[10] McEwen, *CPD,* HR 19, May 14, 1958, p. 1758; Casey, *ibid.,* HR 25, November 24, 1959, p. 3061; Gorton, *ibid.,* S, October 10, 1963, p. 1030, and Spooner, May 5, 1964, p. 905.

[11] McEwen, *ibid.,* HR 31, April 27 and 28, 1961, p. 1290, and Gorton, *ibid.,* S, October 17, 1963, p. 1243. For a sample list, see "Consolidated List of Goods Subject to Embargo for Soviet Bloc and China," *Board of Trade Journal,* Vol. 183 (September 28, 1962), supplement.

large perspective. Since Australia maintains a China differential, obviously the Board of Trade list is excessively lenient and insufficient by itself. Within the intermediate, or discretionary, category are items which in practice are never released for sale to China. Still other commodities are only rarely released. Hence there is flexibility, but flexibility within a tighter framework than the British, for one, utilize. Australia has, for example, shipped iron and steel plate and sheet to China—over £5,000,000 worth in the peak year 1958–59—and as early as mid-1957 a second-hand rolling mill was sold. These items had to be cleared by External Affairs because they fell on the intermediate list, just as the forbidden copper deal had.

It is probably in this vein that another seeming inconsistency in the Government's public position can be cleared up. On the one hand, the Government has been steadfast in refusing to publish "the names of goods that come broadly within the category of strategic materials which may not be exported to mainland China." [12] What the Government appears to mean is that it will not release, *in addition* to the basic list of items obtainable in the *Board of Trade Journal,* those goods which fall into the intermediate category but are in fact barred, or those which are almost invariably barred. Late in 1961 McEwen was asked, on notice, which of eight specified items fell on the strategic list. McEwen answered precisely—zircon and uranium oxide.[13] However, among the other six items were copper and plate steel, *both* on Australia's intermediate list, but with *dissimilar* history of export entitlement from the Government. McEwen had simply delivered a reply based on the absolute list. It certainly helped to create confusion as to what the Government was willing to disclose and what it wished to conceal, but at bottom no

[12] Gorton, *CPD,* S, October 17, 1963, p. 1211.
[13] *Ibid.,* HR 32, September 6, 1961, p. 934.

statement has ever been released with an enumeration of which items within the intermediate list are, in fact, at a particular time considered to be exportable or not. The secrecy extends so far that the Australian trade commissioner in Hong Kong, who deals with Australians wishing to sell to China, is not shown any embargo lists, can only guess what is on them, and must refer all questions to Canberra. An officer in the External Affairs economic section, which manages the strategic embargo, was by far the most tight-lipped official encountered by the author in any government department in Australia.

Two questions therefore require attention: why Australia persists in maintaining a China differential, and why she administers her China embargo as she does. These questions can probably best be answered when seen against not only the pressures which have been directed against strategic trading, but also against trade with China at large.

While Britain, other European countries, Japan, and Canada all cut back their Chinese embargo lists years ago—some with considerable enthusiasm—Australia has held out, standing somewhere between the majority and the total trade-ban approach of the United States. The point is that the U.S. has not only refused to conduct commercial relations with China, but has resisted such practices by others in various ways. Before mid-1957 Britain especially, under both Eden and Macmillan, had made appeals for an equalization of Communist nation embargo lists. Washington, however, responded with delayed replies and unsatisfactory compromises.[14] Finally, when after almost a year and a half of fruitless negotiation Britain declared she would proceed alone if necessary, the State Department huffed and puffed, declaring it was "most disappointed" and that free world security interests

[14] See especially Eden, *op. cit.,* pp. 332 and 364; *NYT,* April 21 and May 7, 1957.

would be best served if prevailing restrictions were maintained against China.[15] Further reductions of the embargo against Communist states have been received grudgingly and under pressure. In 1961–62, when Britain arranged to sell civil aircraft equipped with navigational radar to China, America again expressed her pique publicity.[16]

## AMERICAN AND DOMESTIC CRITICISMS OF CHINESE TRADE

BUT THE U.S. has not confined its opposition to strategic trade alone. In a major policy address of September 1958, J. Graham Parsons, Deputy Assistant Secretary of State for Far Eastern Affairs, produced a set of unvarnished criticisms of trade with China. He repeated the injunction about strategic goods—whose denial should be stepped up rather than curtailed in the interests of free world security. He embellished the point of Chinese trickery by recounting the 1958 suspension of trade with Japan for political reasons and other evidence of misbehavior. China used trade not for commercial but for political gain, he insisted; trade with non-Communist nations was for China "simply another form of warfare," and all nations would need to be vigilant.[17] While Sino-Japanese commerce was later restored, and indeed has risen promisingly, U.S. officials have persistently—and not infrequently in public—lectured the Japanese about the mistake of heavy Chinese trade. Japan is seriously dependent on the U.S., who is Japan's best customer and best supplier. There is also a strong American investment and technical stake in Japan. Therefore, according to one correspondent writing late in 1963, "in view of the enormous power the U.S. still has to make or break the Japnese economy, warnings [not to

[15] *Ibid.,* May 31 and June 1, 1957.

[16] *Ibid.,* December 9, 1961, and January 16 and 18, 1962.

[17] J. Graham Parsons, "Foreign Trade: Welfare of Warfare," *Department of State Bulletin,* Vol. 39 (October 13, 1958), pp. 566–570.

overdo trade with China] must be considered as threats, and warnings are being issued thick and fast." [18]

In Canada, the China trade attitude of the U.S. has for years left an especially disagreeable imprint. Under American law, parent companies in the U.S. are expected to prevent their overseas affiliates from exporting materials to proscribed destinations just as they themselves must. In 1957 and 1958 Canadian affiliates were prevented from shipping ball bearings, pharmaceuticals, and passenger cars to China—the ban on shipping Ford motor cars being the most prominent example of this practice. These revelations entered into the 1958 Canadian electoral campaign, and ultimately produced a discussion between Prime Minister Diefenbaker and President Eisenhower, at which the President promised to relax the regulations when they seemed to bring special adverse effects to Canada's economy.[19] But this promise was somehow shunted into a drawer, for within the year there were additional exposures of blockage against aluminum and rubber products.[20] In 1961 Washington embargoed the sale of grain suction pumps which Canada needed to buy from the U.S. to expedite her wheat shipments to China, and again

[18] "Trade Triangle," *Far East Trade,* Vol. 18 (September 1963), p. 939. Also see "China Trade Lures Japan—II," *ibid.,* Vol. 16 (June 1961), pp. 693–694; Robert Paul, "China and Japan—The Mutual Attraction," *Far Eastern Economic Review,* Vol. 37 (September 27, 1962), pp. 582–584; S. Griffin, "China Trade Issue," *Eastern World,* Vol. 17 (August 1963), pp. 14–15; Premier Ikeda's statement of June 3, 1962, in *Nation* (Rangoon), June 4, 1962; Ambassador Reischauer's Tokyo television interview, in *Japan Times,* May 19, 1961.

[19] See Montreal *Gazette,* March 22, 25 and 26, 1958; Diefenbaker's speech of March 28, 1958, in *ibid.,* March 29, 1958; Diefenbaker, *Canadian Parliamentary Debates,* HC, Session 1958, Vol. 2, July 11, 1958, p. 2142; Fred Alexander, *Canadians and Foreign Policy* (Melbourne, London and Wellington: F. W. Cheshire, 1960), p. 20.

[20] *Canadian Parliamentary Debates,* HC, Session 1959, Vol. 1, January 27, 1959, pp. 394–395.

Canadian representations were required for an exception to be made.[21] As late as September 1963 reports appeared of further parent-affiliate difficulties, this time over the sale of auto parts to China.[22] The acme of absurdity, however, was reached in early 1959. Canadian trucks carrying Chinese imported goods from the port at Vancouver were halted at the U.S. frontier and prevented from proceeding over American roads on their way to other Canadian destinations. According to U.S. sources, this was justified under a clause in GATT which specified that, in times of emergency, free transit provisions over a country's territory could be blocked if such transit threatened national security. In point of fact, the goods which were deemed to constitute this threat to American security were entirely foods—frozen shrimp, herbs, soy sauce, and the like. The U.S. relented in the face of this diabolical Communist conspiracy, but again only after vigorous Canadian representations.[23] So far as Australia has been concerned, it has already been shown that there have been very high-level admonitions from the U.S. about the heavy credit trade in wheat.

Within Australia, expectedly, the Chinese trade has created a great furor in certain quarters, particularly among the DLP-NCC and among right-wing Liberals, the most visible and vocal of whom are the band of backbenchers in the Federal Parliament. While the Government parties and the ALP are officially committed to the Chinese trade and enjoy the support of most of the press

[21] Toronto *Globe and Mail,* June 7 and 9, 1961; Diefenbaker, *Canadian Parliamentary Debates,* HC, Session 1960–61, Vol. 6, June 8, 1961, p. 6016.

[22] *Ibid.,* HC, September 30, 1963, p. 3020.

[23] Montreal *Gazette,* May 2 and 5, 1959; Diefenbaker, *Canadian Parliamentary Debates,* HC, Session 1959, Vol. 3, May 4, 1959, p. 3278, and Vol. 4, May 25, 1959, p. 3967. For general comment, see "China-Canada Trade," *Far Eastern Economic Review,* Vol. 26 (June 4, 1959), p. 774.

and the public at large, the opposition minority has raised objections which, as they reflect on both domestic and external affairs, require comment and analysis.

As might be suspected, the vociferous China trade critics feel that a serious moral issue is involved. As fervent anti-Communists, they are discomfited by any relationship which enhances China's power and thereby adds to the durability of a wicked regime. As Killen once put the point rather flamboyantly, Australia will have reached a most sorry state of affairs if she lets "pennies flow in our blood instead of corpuscles, if we are going to put pounds before principle."[24] They see the Government's technically passive role in the Chinese trade as a fraud, an attempt to masquerade, a shameful sellout which is morally reprehensible. Even before the first large wheat credit sale was consummated, the DLP Federal president charged that the Government had "betrayed its trust by openly adopting the policies of the Evatt Party for the recognition of Communist countries [i.e., re-establishing diplomatic relations with the Soviet Union] and trade with China, but the reason is not [the same as] the desire of the Evatt Party to embrace the Communist ideology, but pure selfish greed and inhumanity."[25] The Government's own right-wing critics are somewhat more timid in saying this sort of thing in public, but they do in fact share the DLP's conviction.

But moral considerations aside, the China trade critics have from time to time produced what they think are

[24] *CPD,* HR 19, May 8, 1958, p. 1635. Also see Hannan, *ibid.,* S 19, March 16, 1961, p. 245; Kent-Hughes' letter to the Melbourne *Age,* February 2, 1961; *News Weekly,* March 29, 1961.

[25] "Address by R. Joshua, Federal President of the Democratic Labor Party, to Third Commonwealth Conference," delivered in Canberra, August 8, 1959, mimeo., p. 7. Also see *News Weekly,* June 20, 1962, and B. A. Santamaria's television program remarks of March 8, 1964, in *ibid.,* March 12, 1964.

tangible, hard-headed reasons for being wary of selling to China in quantity, and especially on credit. The principal net of criticism which they have spread concerns Parsons' own evaluation of 1958—that China employs trade for warfare, not welfare. Incidents such as the Japanese experienced in 1958, have long been a favorite target of reference for these Australian critics: China broke recently signed contracts with Japan, virtually suspended trade, tried to defeat the Kishi Government by offering a restoration of trade only if suitable foreign policy reorientation were undertaken by Japan, and later resumed commercial relations only with selected "friendly" Japanese companies.[26] They have found confirmation of China's sordid intentions in other related ways: Chinese spokesmen have mentioned that trade with Britain would flourish only if "unnatural" obstacles were removed—among them being British support for various aspects of U.S. China policy, such as not backing Peking's admission to the UN prior to late 1961.[27]

[26] For discussions of this Sino-Japanese problem, see "Sino-Japanese Economic Severance," *Oriental Economist,* Vol. 26 (June 1958), p. 29; "Re-Start of Sino-Japanese Trade," *ibid.,* Vol. 28 (November 1960), p. 625; Leng Shao-chuan, "Japanese Attitudes Toward Communist China," *Far Eastern Survey,* Vol. 27 (June 1958), pp. 81–89; *Far Eastern Economic Review,* Vol. 26 (April 23, 1959), special supplement on Japan, pp. 571–572; "China Trade Lures Japan—I," *Far East Trade,* Vol. 16 (May 1961), pp. 575–576; Kazuo Takita, "Tough Trade," *Far Eastern Economic Review,* Vol. 33 (September 14, 1961), p. 650. For descriptions of pre-1958 Chinese efforts to use trade politically, see Leng, *Japan and Communist China,* pp. 90–105, and C. Martin Wilbur in Council on Foreign Relations, *Japan Between East and West* (New York: Harper for the Council, 1957), pp. 203–217.

[27] See interview with Chou En-lai, in *The Times* (London), November 9, 1960; interview statement by Chi Chao-teng, general secretary of the China Committee for the Promotion of International Trade, in Stuart Gelder, "Britain *Can* Do More Trade with Us, Say China's Leaders," *Far East Trade,* Vol. 16 (January 1961), p. 55.

What the critics in Australia have cautioned about is, first of all, that China has no scruples about turning off or diverting the trade faucet when it pleases her. Apart from any political leverage which might be attached, substantial Australian trade with China therefore is hazardous. The fact that for some years now the Chinese have been buying in volume and paying their debts promptly has, in its way, only sharpened the cries of alarm. Since Australia sells huge quantities of wheat and a great deal of wool to China, a sudden Chinese halt would have disastrous effects. Dependence has been developed, wheat acreage enlarged, and the penalty may yet have to be paid—together with a Chinese default on credit, which in any event is regarded as a form of foreign aid to China.[28] These considerations, it should be remembered, are the ones which the U.S. has raised with Australia since substantial trading with China began.

But the argument quickly and almost invariably shifts to politics. There is the expected contention that, given Australia's dependence on her alliance with the U.S. and America's unhappiness with Chinese trade, Australian trade with China on a formidable scale weakens the tie and in addition subtracts from the ability of the U.S. to provide credible leadership in the unending contest with militant Communism.[29] The DLP-NCC group has in fact evolved a systematic analysis of how the trade plays into China's hands for her program of aggrandizement. The Chinese master plan may require a quarter century to

[28] For typical comment, see Bruce Wight, *CPD,* HR 20, August 19, 1958, pp. 484–485; Kent-Hughes, *ibid.,* August 28, 1958, pp. 922–923; Francis McManus, *ibid.,* S 14, April 28, 1959, pp. 1067–1068; *News Weekly,* February 20 and March 19, 1964; DLP, "A New Conception in Australian Politics" (Melbourne: 1961), p. 8; Australia-Free China Association, "China. Free . . or Red?" p. 7. For a non-DLP caution on overdependence, see *Bulletin,* January 12, 1963.

[29] For instance, Kent-Hughes, *CPD,* HR 34, March 28, 1962, p. 1083, and remarks in *SMH,* December 29, 1962.

realize, it is admitted, but come it will unless naïve Australia wakes up and takes notice. As Santamaria has explained, there will be successive stages in which the free, Western, anti-Communist Australian salient will be dissolved. "In each of these periods, Red China will offer Australia increasing amounts of trade, firstly in return for diplomatic recognition, the next in return for the ending of Australia's American alliance, and finally for bases off the Australian coast, for a "friendly" government in this country." [30] The various DLP-NCC people to whom the author has spoken all agree that China undoubtedly has some sinister motive up her sleeve, or will shortly find one, and will convert the present punctilious trading relationship with Australia into a diplomatic weapon, which Australian Governments would have the greatest difficulty in resisting. They automatically attribute such susceptibility to a Labor Government, and feel that the Country Party element in the present coalition would be easy prey as well.

It is valid to ask what in practice the critics would like to do about the China trade. The Government's own fringe group supporters have little to offer. At the time of the U.S. imposition of lead and zinc quotas, Wentworth went so far as to say that if a friendly country mistreated Australia to this extent, it stood to reason that China would be infinitely more crass in her dealings, and if necessary Australian lead and zinc should not be sold at all rather than having Australia court China as a substitute for the American market.[31] Some years later, he asked the Government to arrange a conference of wheat export-

[30] Remarks in *News Weekly,* November 25, 1959. Also see Santamaria, "China's Plans for Australia," *Observer* (July 12, 1958), pp. 331–332; NCC, "Conflict. A Nation Faces the Challenge" (Melbourne: NCC, 1961), pp. 28–30; J. Tehan, "Trade with Communist Countries," *Pastoral Review,* Vol. 72 (April 18, 1962), pp. 350–351.

[31] *CPD,* HR 21, September 25, 1958, p. 1627.

ing countries. Such a conference would discuss the possibility of insuring that no wheat sold to China would in any way be used to sustain the Chinese armed forces. If China would not give such a promise, all countries should agree to halt sending her wheat.[32] Kent-Hughes' suggestion after the first wheat sale on credit amounted to much the same thing. If the Chinese were starving, the wheat should be sold for cash or supplied *gratis* through the International Red Cross.[33] Since at the time—and more certainly in later deals—the Chinese were unwilling to buy for cash, the net result would have been no realization of any profit for Australia.

The DLP-NCC line began in even stricter fashion. DLP Leader George Cole said in the Senate in November of 1960 that his party did "not believe in trade of any kind with red China, Russia or any other Communist country." [34] Early the next year, Santamaria was urging that Australian wheat be given to China as a humanitarian gesture. In his phrase, "for the government—nothing; neither recognition nor admission to the United Nations. For the people—everything; they are our brothers and they will need our aid in 1961." [35] By the end of 1961, with an election approaching, the DLP seemed undecided. The officially authorized speakers' notes issued to DLP candidates in Victoria stated that "Democratic Labor is completely opposed to political or trade relationships with Communist China," [36] while Cole's own policy speech stated that the DLP was "utterly opposed to credit [*sic*] trading with Communist countries." [37] Beginning in

[32] *CPD,* HR, August 12, 1964, p. 116.
[33] Statement of May 11, 1961, in *SMH,* May 13, 1961.
[34] *CPD,* S 18, November 9, 1960, p. 1446.
[35] Television remarks, in *News Weekly,* January 18, 1961. Also see his statement of June 19, 1961, in *SMH,* June 20, 1961.
[36] DLP, "Speakers' Notes—Part 2," p. 76.
[37] G. R. Cole, "Joint DLP-QLP Policy Speech," delivered in Melbourne, November 8, 1961, mimeo., p. 13.

1962, public DLP pronouncements achieved consistency, and certain ground rules have been offered for trade with Communist states. The people of the Communist country involved must actually be in need of the goods supplied. Australia must be able to inspect the distribution of such goods to insure that they are not diverted elsewhere or otherwise misused. All sales must be on a cash basis. Naturally, nothing resembling a strategic item could be shipped.[38]

It seems perfectly apparent that these conditions, while on the surface falling short of the earlier "no trade" position, amount to counseling no trade. The Chinese are not prepared to pay cash for their substantial wheat purchases—and indeed have been seeking longer terms of payment. Furthermore, it is unthinkable that China would for a moment tolerate Australians snooping around the country, satisfying themselves that wheat was not being transshipped, or that wool was not being used to clothe soldiers posted on the Indian frontier or on the Korean armistice line, or that iron and steel were not being incorporated into militarily useful vehicles or apparatus. During interviews the author gained an admission from more than one DLP-NCC person that this shift from the earlier position was a tactical maneuver. The DLP remains almost unalterably hostile to Chinese trade, but realizes that for the moment the trade is flourishing and has gained public acceptance. Hence the "change" has been made, however much it represents a set of impossible conditions.

However, the DLP-NCC also realize that in prevailing circumstances some outlet must be found—or at least commended—for goods now moving to China. This is where the Pacific Confederation scheme fits in. As was

[38] See DLP federal executive decision, in *SMH,* August 13, 1962; Australian Democratic Labor Party, *Policy Decisions of the 5th Commonwealth Conference,* at Canberra, July 1963, mimeo., p. 5; memorandum entitled "Trade with Red China," from DLP Victorian executive office, 1963.

noted before, the Confederation plan envisages extremely close economic relations among a number of explicitly anti-Communist nations. In arguing the economic features of the Confederation, its proponents disparage and warn against trade with China and promise that the Confederation would handily absorb exports now winding up in China.[39] It is striking that a ranking DLP figure told the author that a dominant if not the central inspiration behind the presentation of the Confederation plan was a wish to divert attention away from Australia's trade with China and toward a fresh set of markets. It will be remembered that DLP-NCC spokesmen have admitted that the Confederation was planned for a misty future, with no close prospect of realization. These people are so antagonistic to Chinese trade, so paranoid about the catastrophe that will befall Australia through it, that they will go to extraordinary lengths to counter it—even if it means advertising a substitute market solution which is as impractical as it is ingenious. It has already been shown that at the start of heavy Australian trading with China the *News Weekly* inserted stories about McEwen's ambitions and spats with Casey. This shock-treatment approach was probably meant more to incriminate the trade itself than John McEwen personally.

People of wider range than the DLP and right-oriented Government back-benchers were able to "make common cause" on particular occasions: first, when Tibet was absorbed, and then when the Sino-Indian border fighting broke out. For some time prior to these events, argument had been advanced that even commodities such as wheat and wool could be utilized for strategic purposes. Since an army, in this instance Chinese, can only be effective if it is properly fed and clothed, Australian nonstrategic exports were in fact being converted to strategic uses. It is prob-

[39] DLP, "Speakers' Notes—Part 2," pp. 69–70, 98; Caine, *op. cit.*, pp. 40–43.

ably necessary to differentiate between the sources responsible for this form of criticism. The Labor Party has, as was shown before, tried to score points by pressing the inconsistency between the Government's military and diplomatic quarantine of China and its persmissiveness on trade. In regard to what may or may not be a strategically useful commodity, it has also twitted the Government for several years, beginning before the Sino-Indian troubles and continuing on to the present. In February of 1964, for example, Calwell tried to "expose" the Government for having denied explicitly strategic materials to China, but "in the context of the cold war, who can draw a line between strategic and non-strategic materials?" [40] In December of 1962, the New South Wales Labor Council endorsed a resolution condemning wheat credit sales to China while the border war continued,[41] and the then-Deputy Premier of New South Wales, J. B. Renshaw, voiced the same opinion.[42] It is fair to say that not all these criticisms from ALP sources have been entirely sincere. Certainly a man like Beazley made his objection from conviction, and some others have as well. But it must be remembered that Labor has been agitating for trade with China for a considerable time, that it has never discontinued its commitment to the trade, and that when it, like Calwell, has spoken of the strategic applications of otherwise innocuous materials, it has not suggested that their export be eliminated, curtailed, or even, in the case of wheat, shifted from a credit to a cash basis. Interviews with ALP men of both right and left-wing shades, front

[40] Statement of February 1, 1964, in Melbourne *Age,* February 2, 1964. Also see Calwell, *CPD,* HR, March 19, 1964, p. 678; James Cope, HR 30, March 8, 1961, pp. 78–79, and March 15, 1961, p. 212; Beazley, HR 24, September 2, 1959, p. 854, and HR, March 19, 1964, p. 685; Charles Jones, HR 38, April 4, 1963, p. 388.

[41] *News Weekly,* December 5, 1962.

[42] Statement of December 5, 1962, in *SMH,* December 6, 1962.

and back-bench Parliamentarians alike, made it absolutely clear that had Labor been in office over the past several years it would not have interfered with the trade, regardless of what has been said for public consumption about Chinese soldiers eating noodles made of Australian wheat or marching into Tibet or India in the dead of winter, warm and snug in their Australian wool clothing. On the surface, of course, the impression was left, particularly in late 1962 and early 1963, that there was a strong protest about neutral commodities serving strategic purposes, since the expected right-wing Liberal and DLP-NCC criticisms [43] were fortified from other quarters.

### THE GOVERNMENT'S STRATEGIC TRADE POLICY IN PERSPECTIVE

AGAINST the background of American opposition to Chinese trade and criticisms within Australia, the Government's own behavior on both strategic and nonstrategic trade becomes more intelligible. The Chinese differential on strategic materials involves a mixture of causal factors. The crucial period when a choice needed to be made on whether to conform to the European decision of 1957 was in 1957 and 1958. Australian business circles were keen on entering the China market and were upset with the temporizing going on in Canberra. The DLP was still pretty much an untested quantity in Australian politics, and its criticisms of a change of policy in conformity with European states and Japan would not have then been weighed too seriously. However, although in 1957 and early 1958 there was no major crisis in Asia, the Government's decision was almost certainly affected by fears of offending Washington. The bitter fight by the U.S. to pre-

[43] For instance, see Kent-Hughes, *CPD,* HR 24, August 20, 1959, p. 479, and HR 37, November 15, 1962, pp. 2538–2539; Hannan, *ibid.,* S 19, March 16, 1961, p. 245; McManus, statement of October 30, 1962, in *Canberra Times,* October 31, 1962; *News Weekly,* December 19, 1962.

vent the equalization of East European and Chinese strategic lists was an indication of sentiment in Washington. The outspoken attacks on Chinese trading motives and tactics only added to Australia's perception of how her major ally felt, and the SEATO annual report of March 1957 contained a passage, undoubtedly instigated by the United States, which underscored the dangers of trading with an unscrupulous China.[44] The author has been told on very competent authority that there were U.S. representations in 1957–58, urging Australia not to equalize strategic lists. At all events, it is useful to consider an episode that took place in late July and early August of 1957. A Farmers and Settlers' Association conference discussed Chinese trade, endorsed its expansion, and even recommended the installation of an Australian trade commissioner in China.[45] The guest speaker, William McMahon, the Minister for Primary Industry, said his Government agreed with the principle of Australian primary product exports to China, but on the matter of a trade commissioner he urged that Australia should "hasten slowly," and added that "The United States has, in effect, said to us, 'If anyone attacks you, we will consider it an attack on us.' We must not endanger our future, our interest, or our security through this question."[46] It has already been shown that in 1957–58 Casey applied a soft brake to the flow of nonstrategic materials to China. This being so, it was reasonable for Australia to elect not to jeopardize American goodwill on the far more sensitive subject of strategic goods, even if some Chinese contracts were lost to countries which had lowered their embargo lists.

The reasons governing the continuation of a China

[44] Report of March 5, 1957, in *CNIA,* Vol. 28 (March 1957), esp. p. 225.

[45] Sydney *Daily Telegraph,* July 31, 1957.

[46] Address of August 1, 1957, in *SMH,* August 2, 1957. Also see report in *Canberra Times,* August 2, 1957.

differential are somewhat but not entirely different. It is still considered important to maintain excellent relations with the United States, not only for support where special Australian interests are involved, as in New Guinea or Malaysia, but also in those instances where Australia wishes to preserve *entré* and influence with respect to wide international issues such as the offshore islands and Laos. The fact that high American officials have spoken to Australia about the pitfalls of nonstrategic trade surely has served as a warning signal concerning what reaction would follow a reduction of the Chinese strategic embargo.

The DLP's criticisms of the China trade *in general* probably have some bearing on the handling of *strategic* trade. In 1959, Francis McManus, then the DLP's Deputy Parliamentary Leader, intimated that if the Government persisted in condoning such atrocious practices as commerce with China, his party might need to reconsider its policy of urging DLP electors to cast second preferences for the Government parties.[47] For practical purposes this was and remains pretty much an idle threat, since the only alternative to the Government parties is the ALP. Indeed, despite huge leaps in the China trade since 1959, the DLP has never retaliated in this way, and there is no prospect that it will. If there is an impact on the Government generated by DLP criticisms of Chinese trade, it lies elsewhere. If the Government were to switch its embargo policy at this late date, its solo action would stand out most prominently. The DLP would surely pound away with all its might, and right-wing Liberal critics would be vocal as well. The net result might be that the Government's carefully cultivated image of strong anti-Communism would be rendered less credible, and it would be accused of violating the sacred friendship with the great Pacific ally. The Government thrives on its own use of slurs and imputations of softness on Communism against

[47] Statement of July 12, 1959, in *SMH,* July 13, 1959.

Labor, and it prides itself on being the true friend of the United States. If the right-inspired charges were to be made loudly and often, they could induce voters to cast first preferences for the ALP instead of the DLP or the Government parties. In a close contest such as 1961, a few thousand lost votes could spell a lost election.

Another reason for not changing strategic goods policy is undoubtedly that the nonstrategic trade has been so successfully executed. In the first instance, it is plausible to suppose that among the reasons that Australia has been able to trade so heavily with China in nonstrategic materials is that American objections have been so subdued and private, and have therefore not created embarrassment. Yet the U.S. may have soft-pedalled the nonstrategic trade *because* Australia has been so cooperative and considerate in sticking by a China differential in strategic materials while America's other allies have climbed on the embargo equalization bandwagon.

In the second instance, the experience of heavy and profitable nonstrategic trade with China has deflected attention away from proposals to sell more clearly strategic items. The earnings from wheat and wool have been so considerable that, taken in the large, it has not been necessary for the Government to worry about what "strategic" goods are not being sold. There certainly is no organized campaign in Australia to lower the strategic list now imposed on China. There have been cases in recent years of export licenses being rejected, but even the business community suffers no serious discomfort over standing policy. Nor, to the best of the author's knowledge, have there been unseemly incidents over parent company vetoes, although from time to time the Department of Trade and Industry has been approached for advice by affiliate firms interested in selling to China. There is considerably more U.S. control over Canadian than Australian industry, especially in goods that might be considered for export to China. Australian manufacturers have met with rather surprising success in selling in Asia outside of China. At all events, there were the Canadian precedents to keep in mind.

Aside from what appears to be a self-imposed restraint by Australian manufacturers on any temptation to lift the cover of the discretionary embargo list a bit higher, two factors should be noticed. One is that Australia does not have a great many products to sell which are truly strategic in nature. It was understandable that in the mid-'fifties industrial Britain and Japan were far more eager to lower the Chinese embargo than was Australia. The other factor is that, within controlled limits which still preserve a China differential in practice as well as theory, goods of a quasi-strategic character have been allowed for export to China. Although China has never duplicated the amount of iron and steel product purchases she transacted in 1958–59, she has continued to buy smaller amounts of plate, bar and rod castings, and the like. By the close of the 1962–63 trading year her iron and steel product purchases from Australia had reached £8,678,000.[48] Furthermore, in reply to a 1958 question on notice, McEwen indicated that during the calendar year 1957 Australia had sold to China motor cars worth £14,781 and aircraft engine parts valued at £5,013.[49] In other words, Australian manufacturers, despite the China differential, are not completely shut out from the Chinese market. It is possible to assume that here lies a substantial explanation for the Government's caution and secrecy about revealing strategic lists. The present policy not only facilitates flexibility, but also leaves room for an occasional, unpublicized infraction of what might otherwise be a hide-bound embargo list.

Otherwise, of course, the nonstrategic trade proceeds

[48] See *CPD*, HR, May 6, 1964, p. 1630.
[49] *Ibid.*, HR 18, March 20, 1958, p. 594.

smoothly. The earnings continue, and the public at large is pleased. The Government's own outward dissociation from the China trade is useful because results are achieved and a certain amount of political backlash avoided, despite the well-placed accusations of hypocrisy. Note for instance the position during the Sino-Indian border crisis. Australia expressed her sympathy for the Indian cause, duly reprimanded the Chinese, contributed over £2,000,000 in military and other assistance to India and joined in the Indian-Commonwealth-U.S. air exercise and training scheme.[50] What the Government did not, however, do was to heed criticisms and curtail trade with China, a trade which most certainly was contributing to feeding and clothing Chinese soldiers intruding into India. It is understood that the Government saw the conflict as serious but not a genuine war between India and China. For instance, the author has been reminded by responsible persons that India and China did not even break off diplomatic relations. There is evidence that the Indian High Commissioner in Ottawa and External Affairs Minister Howard Green discussed Sino-Canadian trade during the crisis,[51] but apparently no comparable talks were held in Canberra —certainly not with Barwick. There is an intimation that if the fighting had remained severe for a longer time, Australia would have reappraised her position, though events made this unnecessary. Nonetheless, the Sino-Indian episode probably was a useful illustration to the Government that its treatment of Chinese trade had been sound: allow the trade to continue, but without involving the Government directly or assuming responsibility. The public also had few qualms. An August 1962 opinion survey asked if continued wheat and wool sales to China were

[50] See Barwick, statements of March 10, 1963, in *CNIA,* Vol. 34 (March 1963), p. 22, July 23, 1963, in *ibid.,* (July 1963), p. 61, and August 16, 1963, in *SMH,* August 17, 1963.

[51] Howard Green, *Canadian Parliamentary Debates,* HC, Session 1962–63, Vol. 3, December 10, 1962, p. 2488.

favored. The reply was 72 per cent, "yes," 17 per cent "no," and 11 per cent "no opinion." In December, during the crisis on the Indian frontier, the same query broke down to 69, 17, and 14 per cent.[52] Explicit opposition was no stronger during than before the difficulties.

In point of fact, Australian opinion has not only approved of Sino-Australian trade, but has become increasingly amused by what it regards as silly rigidities and inconsistencies in the trading polcies of the U.S. as applied to the Communist world. In late 1963 the U.S. authorized a giant sale of wheat to Russia. Molnar, the *Sydney Morning Herald's* cartoonist, did a splendid piece of satire. A business-executive type was shown pointing to a chart labeled "U.S. Wheat for U.S.S.R.," and saying to his approving colleagues, "We'll show these goddamn Australians and Canadians that we can be as competitively humanitarian as anybody." [53] When the Johnson Administration kicked up dust about the sale of British buses to Cuba, Australian opinion was again amused and even annoyed, especially against the backdrop of the Soviet wheat sales. In a caustic editorial, the Melbourne *Age* wrote:

> Sending English buses to Cuba . . . is no more a matter of military strategy than is Australian wheat to China. America's own policy gives her little right to stand in judgment, particularly when her own economic interests are concerned. She is providing many of the arms which are shooting British troops on the Borneo frontier. . . . It would be a good thing, all the same, if America examined her own position before asking Britain for action which no great trading nation could afford to take.[54]

[52] *AGP,* nos. 1653–1664, January–February 1963.

[53] Molnar, in *SMH,* October 11, 1963.

[54] Melbourne *Age,* February 12, 1964. Also see Melbourne *Herald* and Sydney *Daily Mirror,* February 10, 1964.

Conceivably, if this climate of opinion persists, the Australian Government might, if it chose to proceed, find the equalization of strategic embargo lists to be more politically palatable than before.

### TRADE AND SINO-AUSTRALIAN POLITICAL RELATIONS

AND WHAT of dire predictions that the Chinese trade would lead to political blackmail by Peking? The Government was fully aware of the seriousness of China's action against Japan, and Casey made a public reference to it in a 1959 Parliamentary statement.[55] The Sino-Australian relationship, however, has proceeded almost flawlessly. There have been no Chinese pronouncements to the effect that the development of Australia's exports to China was in any way dependent on curbing "hostile" behavior such as support for Chiang on Formosa or voting against Peking's seating at the UN. Chinese trade delegations visiting Australia have not made pleas for diplomatic relations. Australians traveling to China, on business or otherwise, have had no intimations that continuing trade would depend on the gift of recognition, or a reduction in the strategic embargo, or what not, although some business delegations have been told that an exchange of diplomatic representatives could improve the *efficiency* of trade. Indeed, the author has been told time and again by people who have dealt in Chinese commerce that the Chinese were hard bargainers, but spotless in their demeanor, with no intrusion of politics. On more than one occasion the Chinese have been referred to as "gentlemen," and their conduct has been assessed as better than that of representatives of a number of non-Communist states with whom Australia conducts commercial relations. In 1964 C. J. Perrett, who the previous year had retired as general manager of the Wheat Board, was invited to China as a private individual. His fares to and from Melbourne were

[55] *CPD,* HR 23, April 23, 1959, p. 1519.

paid, his accommodations in China arranged, and he spent several delightful weeks touring the country. It is true that Perrett remains a consultant to the Wheat Board, but only that. The Chinese may have felt that he could still be useful to them but that is doubtful. Perrett had always been a leading advocate of the wheat trade with China, had developed excellent rapport with the Chinese, and undoubtedly was invited because the Chinese wished to extend grateful hospitality—probably without knowing where he stood on recognition, the UN, Formosa, SEATO and the rest.

The only remote instance of the Chinese mixing trade and politics came to light in the first half of 1964. In the House, Wentworth and Kent-Hughes charged that Chinese trading corporations had recently sent cables to 1,700 firms around the world, including Australia, which had recently dealt with China. The cable spoke of the detention by Brazilian authorities of nine Chinese journalists and businessmen, and said that "any act of upholding justice by your company will be appreciated with heartfelt thanks." This appeal, according to Wentworth and Kent-Hughes, was really blackmail—a threat to cut relations with firms which failed to oblige.[56] Some weeks later a letter to the *Bulletin* quoted an April 22 Radio Peking broadcast which had indicated that Australian firms had been among those responding, and this to the letter writer was evidence not only of Chinese blackmail tactics, but of Australian susceptibility.[57] Yet in time even the *News Weekly* was led to confess that responding firms had done nothing but send courtesy replies—acknowledging the receipt of the Chinese cables.[58] The author is not aware that any retaliation was undertaken by China against non-

[56] Wentworth and Kent-Hughes, *ibid.*, April 23, 1964, pp. 1469–1470 and 1472–1474, respectively.

[57] James Tehan, letter to *Bulletin,* June 6, 1964.

[58] *News Weekly,* June 25 and July 9, 1964.

cooperating firms and export groups. The cables were sent to firms in 70 countries, with whom China has large to small trading contacts, and which represent a variety of political complexions. The liberation of nine Chinese from Brazilian custody hardly seemed a sufficient stake to endanger commerce with individual firms or even whole countries.

Indeed, there appear to be excellent reasons why, respecting Australia, China has not used political leverage and probably will not in the foreseeable future. Brave Australian Government promises that any attempts at political blackmail will not be tolerated [59] are not apt to be put to a test. First, to be blunt, Australia is not as great a prize as Japan, who has suffered Chinese pressures. If China wishes to run the various international risks, i.e. forfeiting her commercial reputation, which would accompany political blackmail, she would probably aim at a more significant target. Second, Australia's political scene is such that she is far less susceptible to pressure, contrary to what the DLP-NCC might say, than a country with Japan's politics. Not even an ALP Government, both because of conviction and an eye on public reaction, could be expected to surrender to political threats. Third, China continues to find Australia's goods useful. She has various shortages of her own, her trade with the Soviet bloc has declined substantially, and any conscious halting of primary products commerce with sellers such as Australia or Canada would be much like cutting off her nose to spite her face.

While Australian right-wingers have for years been flying storm signals about Chinese political leverage through the trade nexus, another stream of comment has emanated from people who have seen a necessary and/or desirable

[59] C. F. Adermann, statement of Oct. 1, 1964, in *CNIA*, Vol. 35 (Oct. 1964), p. 22; Hasluck, statement of Dec. 13, 1964, in *SMH*, Dec. 14, 1964.

connection between diplomatic recognition and trade. In the late 'fifties, as exports to China were beginning to move upward but had not yet approached the proportions of later years, argument was made that Australia could not expect to realize any sizeable gains from the Chinese market unless she recognized China—either because the hostile implications of nonrecognition would be resented by the Chinese, who would keep their buying to a minimum, or because diplomatic relations would markedly facilitate commercial contacts and transactions. Comments of this nature came from the ALP,[60] press sources,[61] and certain business circles.[62] In some instances, as it continues to be, it was difficult to assess how much of this pressure was based on strictly commercial considerations and how much was the result of just another argument being advanced by people who were first and foremost interested in recognition, or in improved relations with China generally. Indeed, within the Labor Opposition, there surely was no regret if the Government could be politically embarrassed by the "inconsistency" of trade promotion combined with reluctance to recognize China in order to win a greater market there.

The connection between trade and recognition seemed to be a very real one, judging by the course of relations between Australia and another Communist nation, the Soviet Union. In the trading year 1953–54, Australian exports to Russia reached the gratifying total of £26,146,-

[60] E. J. Ward, *CPD,* HR 9, March 8, 1956, p. 674; Leslie Johnson, HR 21, Sept. 25, 1958, p. 1624; Calwell, HR 24, Aug. 13, 1959, p. 203.

[61] Sydney *Sun,* Aug. 12, 1958; Sydney *Daily Mirror,* June 1, 1959.

[62] See comments of K. L. Ballantyne, a member of the *Delos* mission, in *SMH,* December 22, 1958, and in Sydney *Daily Telegraph,* December 23, 1958; discussion of remarks by A. M. Simpson, federal president of the ACMA, in *News Weekly,* October 8, 1958. Also see remarks in "More Australian Trade with China," *Far East Trade,* Vol. 14 (April 1959), p. 498.

000, largely in wool. But in April-May of 1954 came the Petrov affair. The Russians withdrew their diplomatic mission from Australia, and then Australia followed by withdrawing from Russia. When the Russians pulled out, they also announced their departure from the wool auctions. The results were immediately and depressingly apparent. In 1954–55, the Soviet bought goods worth only £154,000 from Australia; in the years that followed, Soviet trade vanished almost to the zero mark. While the *exposé* of Soviet espionage was by no means welcome, there was a steady stream of displeasure that trade and politics had somehow been allowed to clash. The Russians may have been wrong to allow politics to affect trade, but Australia should now work for a restoration of diplomatic relations and not "allow stiff-necked pride to complicate dealings with a major potential customer." [63] Early in 1959 diplomatic ties were finally restored. While the Menzies Government denied that its decision to resume relations had been primarily governed by commercial calculations, it admitted that the step was bound to encourage a revival of trade,[64] and that in fact was the result.

The Government did not, of course, take the hint to alter its view of diplomatic relations with China—either from the explicit pleas of those who urged Chinese recognition, or the experience of revived trade with Russia after relations had been restored. The theme of recognition at large will be fully examined in another context. Here it is sufficient to indicate that the Government has simply explained that its recognition policy is being and will continue to be dictated by noncommercial considerations. If there should ever be a switch in Australia's recognition posture, "it will have no relationship whatever to trading

[63] Adelaide *News,* May 1, 1956. Also see Brisbane *Courier-Mail,* December 7, 1955; Sydney *Daily Telegraph,* December 29, 1955; *SMH,* February 6, 1956; Melbourne *Age,* May 23, 1956.

[64] Spooner, *CPD,* S 14, April 22, 1959, p. 949, and McEwen, HR 24, August 27, 1959, p. 629.

circumstances or how many bales of wool are sold." [65] Or, in Barwick's words, recognition was "completely divorced from the question of trade or of any other relations. You do not need to recognize a country in order to trade with it and you do not necessarily trade with a country because you have recognized it. They are two independent actions." [66]

The extent of Australia's Chinese trade in recent years has, of course, been an answer to earlier pleas that recognition would be the magic key to a Chinese treasure market. Marvelous things have happened to Australia's wheat and wool without recognition. Requests for recognition based on the trading factor continue, but most sound hollow and even naïve. To some extent the press and the ALP, now realizing that a prosperous Chinese market has been opened minus recognition, have turned their earlier argument around and are saying that *because* the trade has gone so far recognition should be extended—in the interest of consistency. If Australia is willing and able to be on such cordial terms with China at the commercial level, why not end the hypocrisy of anti-Chinese rantings and rationalize the relationship diplomatically? The U.S. neither recognizes nor trades with China, Calwell has said, but the Menzies Government has a "bob each way," [67]—it has hedged its bets. Going even farther, on the occasion of French recognition of China, Calwell declared that because Australia had developed such a dependence on the Chinese trade, Peking might attempt to make recognition

[65] McEwen, *ibid.*, HR 28, September 28, 1960, p. 1404.

[66] *Ibid.*, HR 36, October 3, 1962, p. 1122. For other recent expressions, see Menzies, HR 37, November 27, 1962, p. 2614, and press conference statement of October 12, 1963, in *SMH,* October 13, 1963.

[67] Statement of November 26, 1963, in *ibid.*, November 27, 1963. Also see his statement of February 1, 1964, in Melbourne *Age,* February 2, 1964. For press comment, see Sydney *Daily Mirror,* June 11, 1963, and January 24, 1964; Melbourne *Age,* January 17, 1963.

a condition of continuing its heavy imports; then recognition, which could have been an act of free will by Australia, could turn into surrender in the face of commercial blackmail. If China did this, Menzies would need to eat every word he had said on the question.[68] This, in part, was a DLP argument, and Calwell was clearly clutching at the nearest political straw, however fragile. Perhaps the most interesting answer came, ironically, from Santamaria. China would buy from Australia only as long as she needed the wheat and other products. The grant of recognition would have no effect on her commercial policy. And, in addition, "The Chinese Communists, reminded by Mr. Calwell of the opportunities which their imports offer for political blackmail, may well place the pressure on this country to accord recognition in order to force a further division between Australia and the United States." [69] This prospect is hardly likely, but neither is Calwell's prophecy. If there is any eating of words in store, it is unlikely to be by Sir Robert Menzies.

But if recognition seems irrelevant to the trade as such, or at least to Australian exports to China, is it relevant to facilitating the contacts and negotiatons connected with it? So far as wheat and wool are concerned, the two most prominent commodities sold to China, definitely not. The Wheat Board has been able to operate efficiently with the Chinese both in Hong Kong and in China. Since it carries sole responsibility for the disposal of Australian wheat, no diplomatic establishment could replace it. The contacts are so firm that an event such as Perrett's invitation to China can take place. Wool is somewhat different. The Chinese use designated Australian agents to attend auctions and buy. Perhaps it would be easier for the Chinese

[68] Statements of January 28, 1964, in *ibid.*, January 29, 1964, and of February 9, 1964, in *SMH,* February 10, 1964.

[69] Address of February 10, 1964, before the Constitutional Club, Melbourne, cited in *News Weekly,* February 13, 1964.

to use their own, Australian-based people, but even this is most doubtful. Auctions are held in many localities, and an inordinately large number of trained individuals would be required to make the rounds. At all events, it is understood that the Australian agents represent their clients honestly and well, and that the Chinese have thorough confidence in them. When general wool promotion is involved, Sir William Gunn and his associates can manage very nicely without the trappings of formal diplomatic ties.

The position regarding other commodities is somewhat less definite. A recent work by J. Wilczynski suggests that nonrecognition has obstructed the trade in "some minor ways." First, Wilczynski asserts, private traders have found it more difficult to arrange business travels. Second, trade officials and missions to China "are not officially invited and do not receive official hospitality, encouragement and valuable contacts which otherwise would be extended as a matter of course."[70] The Australia-China Society has argued that recognition would facilitate contacts with Chinese Government agencies, expedite visa arrangements, provide a steady stream of trade information, and the like.[71]

The author's discussions with Australian traders interested in the Chinese market only partially confirm this conclusion concerning the usefulness of diplomatic relations, and not necessarily for the given reasons above. Since the Chinese buy not through a myriad of private firms and individuals but through official agencies, dealings are simplified. The accessibility of these agencies might be improved through permanent on-the-spot Australian representation, but not by much. Visas for Australians traveling for business purposes have not been

[70] Wilczynski, *Australia's Trade with the Communist Bloc,* p. 233.

[71] ACS, "Our Fourth Best Customer."

impeded. The author has failed to encounter anyone who has reported that his hospitality in China has been so poor that business affairs have suffered. On the contrary, the Chinese are usually most accommodating. Market information, trends in industrial and consumer needs, etc., would probably improve with representation, but ways have been found to circumvent the absence of representation. For example, the constant movement of trading bank delegations to China to perform survey and promotional work is a reasonably satisfactory substitute. The personal contacts effected by the banks are appreciated by the Chinese and in their way serve to fill the gap resulting from no diplomatic links. Technical problems can also be disposed of without recognition, as the Coombs mission suggested. In short, Australian trade is by no means hamstrung by lack of diplomatic relations. Substitute methods have been devised and operate well.

The appointment of a trade commissioner to China is a different proposition, but the ability to do without one is explicable in much the same terms as is the ability to function without diplomatic representation. The posting of a trade commissioner, while politically tender, would nonetheless be less incriminating than diplomatic recognition, and the Government actually had the matter under active consideration in the late 'fifties—and admitted to it publicly.[72] At all events, the Australian trade commissioner in Hong Kong, even though he goes into China very rarely, deals with competent Chinese commercial representatives frequently within Hong Kong itself, thus accomplishing at least part of what he might achieve if stationed in China. The Government's defense that trade has moved satisfactorily without benefit of trade-commissioner representation in China [73] is essentially true.

[72] Spooner, *CPD,* S 12, April 12, 1958, p. 617.
[73] Barwick, *ibid.,* HR, April 14, 1964, p. 1064.

## PROBLEMS OF CHINESE IMPORTS

THE DISCUSSION of Sino-Australian trade has so far turned almost exclusively on Australian exports to China. However, the reverse side of the coin—exports from China to Australia—has raised some special issues in its own right, though exports and imports have not operated as distinct functions in the trading relationship. In the financial years between 1949–50 and 1952–53, the value of imports from China exceeded Australian exports. For the next three years there was a slight trading balance advantage for Australia. But beginning in 1956–57, the disparity began to widen, not because Australia was buying less, but because exports to China were climbing. In 1956–57 and 1957–58 exports stood three times higher than imports, and in 1958–59 and 1959–60 they were four times as great—all of this before the heavy wheat sales had opened.

The Chinese were not pleased with this imbalance and frequently mentioned it to Australian traders. If possible, China was interested in barter deals, i.e., exchanging goods with Australia with about the same value moving in each direction. But the Government did not accommodate the Chinese. It has never regarded a barter relationship as suitable for Australia. The reasons have been plain enough. First, Australia is an inordinately heavy exporter. Second, given the differential in population and commodity requirements by value between China and Australia, it simply is not reasonable to expect as much buying as selling, or exchanging, by the latter. Third, the character of China's principal export goods is not exceptionally suited for heavy Australian acquisition. Also, the character of Australia's foreign exchange regulations, tied as they are to Australia's membership in the sterling bloc, renders barter trading extremely difficult to manage. Finally, for a number of years and until February of 1960 import licensing prevailed in Australia. Importers were allowed licenses for limited amounts only. They could buy from wherever they chose, but preferred to deal with more traditional markets, and with goods in greater demand in Austrialia than those China was offering. China was not the only country aiming for special concessions on import licensing, but so far as is known the Government allowed an exception to only one such petitioner, New Zealand. To have allowed special import-licensing privileges for Chinese goods would have opened a Pandora's box, and probably undermined the whole import restriction program.

From 1960 onward two changes occurred. In the first place, Australian exports to China soared, making China a truly valuable customer and perhaps suggesting that if the market were to be preserved, Australia on her part would have to buy more. Second, once import licensing was abolished, the legal impediment to large-scale buying from China was removed. But the results have not been encouraging to China. In 1963–64, exports to China were over ten times greater than imports. The import figure of £8,331,000 was still not much of an absolute gain over the £4,419,000 imported in 1959–60, the last year in which import licensing operated. It is perhaps useful to note the results of a parallel development in Canada. In 1962, Canada's exports to China stood at $137,000,000, but imports were a niggardly $4,500,000. The Chinese strenuously complained. Canada wished to maintain her large grain sales to China. The result was an agreement in mid-1963 under which Canada promised to relax certain inhibitions on the entry of various reasonably priced Chinese goods, while China promised to tread carefully so as not to upset the Canadian textile industry.[74] In other words,

[74] See Charles Taylor in Toronto *Globe and Mail,* June 7 and July 4, 1963 and December 4, 1964; Bruce MacDonald in *ibid.,* August 3, 1963; Mitchell Sharp, Minister of Trade and Commerce,

Canada made explicit concessions to China for the express purpose of maintaining her substantial exports.

In September of 1963, replying to a question in the House as to whether China had been applying pressure on Australia to buy more from her, McEwen said that "there is no foundation whatever for any such suggestion." [75] If by this McEwen meant that the Chinese had not gone so far as to threaten explicitly a sharp cut in their Australian purchases unless the trade balance were somewhat redressed, then he was correct. But without doubt in 1963 the Chinese increased the tempo of their pleas to Australian traders to arrange for greater imports. Late in June, for instance, a member of a recent Wheat Board mission which had negotiated with the Chinese recounted the rising Chinese discomfort with the import situation,[76] and similar evidence has come to the author's attention in a number of other ways. Furthermore, the Chinese have from time to time asked Australian business and trading groups to speak up for them in tariff hearings, to emphasize that high duties on Chinese goods could lead to an unacceptable trade imbalance. The point has been raised in tariff hearings—as recently as October of 1963 [77]—but not necessarily because of Chinese prompting. Australian importers of Chinese products are, for their own good reason, opposed to unduly steep tariffs.

What factors are responsible for the fact that Australia

---

*Canadian Parliamentary Debates,* HC, Session 1963, Vol. 3, August 2, 1963, p. 2984; Frederick Nossal, in *Australian Financial Review,* August 6, 1963; Richard Hughes in Melbourne *Herald,* July 20, 1963.

[75] *CPD,* HR, September 10, 1963, p. 742.

[76] E. G. Hoy, before executive committee of the United Farmers and Woolgrowers' Association, Sydney, in *The Land* (Sydney), June 27, 1963. Also see Ronald Anderson in Melbourne *Herald,* June 4, 1963.

[77] "Tariff Board's Report on Pillow Cases," October 14, 1963. *Parliamentary Papers,* paper edition, no. 10952/63, p. 4.

continues to purchase little from China, causing predictable Chinese unhappiness? One set of reasons—although certainly minor—is of the Australian Government's own making. First, it has been learned that in the late 'fifties the Chinese, through Australian trade contacts, made known their wish to participate in a trade fair in Australia. The idea was passed on to the Government, and the Government passed back word that it would not consent. The Chinese apparently have not again made a similar approach, probably because they know the answer in advance. Still, a public exhibition of Chinese goods could stimulate interest and eventually buying. Second, as has been seen, the Government has considered but rejected the exchange of trade commissioners. If there were a Chinese trade commissioner in Australia, his contact and promotional work might very well enlarge the volume of Chinese imports to Australia. The Government's reasons have been both political and economic. The political reasons require no elaboration. The economic reason, at base, has been that Australian *exports* have managed to flourish without benefit of trade commissioners, and the Chinese have never issued a "buy more" ultimatum which could have included a trade commissioner in Australia as a *quid pro quo* for preserving the sizeable Chinese purchases.

Another explanation for the absence of heavy Australian buying is that, as in the late 'fifties, there is not a great deal that China has for sale that Australia finds overwhelming reason to buy. Consider the character of the goods bought from China in recent years. In 1958–59, the top five commodities imported from China were, in order, bristles and bristle substitutes, silk, bleached cotton piece goods, chemical, medicinal, and pharmaceutical products, and tung oil. In 1962–63, the order was printed cotton piece goods, bristles and bristle substitutes, towels and towelling, tung oil, and handkerchiefs, napkins, and tablecloths. Because Australia is a small country, because she has other and more traditonal import sources, because her own industry produces a wide range of goods, it is no wonder that there is no wild scramble to buy from China.

The final and related reason for limited Australian purchases is the impact of Chinese imports on native Australian industry. As far back as 1957 and 1958, right-wing sources such as the *News Weekly,* which were interested in discrediting trade with China generally, predicted terrible consequences from the entry of underpriced Chinese goods.[78] In point of fact, while Chinese goods represent barely one half of one per cent of Australia's imports, there have been complaints from time to time about specific items, and some analysis is required.

Consider footwear imports from China. In 1962–63, nearly 100,000 pairs of Chinese shoes were imported into Australia, China being the third largest overseas source of women's leather soled shoes, second largest source of men's leather soled shoes, and the largest source of "other leather soled" footwear. Much of the imported Chinese footwear is an imitation of Australian styles. Quality varies from fair to excellent, and retail prices are attractive. In 1964 Chinese-made dress shoes were selling in Sydney for only £2 a pair. This was a "special" price, to be sure, but even the regular price would have been reasonable. Anguished cries have been coming from the Boot Trade Federation that, with the local industry operating beneath capacity, the Chinese imports constitute a danger to Australian workingmen.[79] Clive Stoneham, the Leader of the ALP Opposition in Victoria, has expressed con-

[78] For example, *News Weekly,* June 19, 1957, and July 23 and November 5, 1958.

[79] See remarks of J. P. Condon, federal secretary of the Boot Trade Federation, in *ibid.,* August 1, 1962, and in *Fact* (Melbourne), August 29, 1963. Also see remarks of W. T. Hoburn, NSW secretary of the Federation, in Sydney *Daily Telegraph,* July 27, 1962.

cern.[80] The Footwear Manufacturers' Association has shown its own agitation.[81] But in 1962, when application was made for temporary tariff protection, "it was found that the value [of Chinese footwear] was so small that it did not even warrant a reference to a 'Special Advisory Authority,'" [82] a body which screens tariff applications before full Tariff Board consideration is given.

Other Chinese goods have also met with complaints. In 1962, for instance, Stoneham attacked Chinese tea-towel imports, claiming they were flooding the Australian market and selling at ridiculously low prices, and indicted Victorian Premier Henry Bolte for his weakness and failure to "stand up and fight for justice for this State." [83] Stoneham's proclivity to attack Chinese imports probably should not be magnified to assume any serious, politically significant proportions. It is understood that once, after meeting some Chinese trade officials and getting on with them splendidly, he assailed footwear imports in an electorate that contained a fair number of shoe industry employees. Afterward, he apparently was asking if these remarks could not be explained away for the benefit of the Chinese whom he had recently met. The author asked a large number of members of the ALP whether Chinese imports had become an embarrassment to their Party, which stands for selling to China and the protection of workingmen's interests. The answer was invariably and quickly in the negative, regardless of the ideological orientation of the person replying, and there is no external evidence to the contrary. A day of embarrassment may yet

[80] See *News Weekly,* August 1, 1962.

[81] N. H. Mack, federal president of the Footwear Manufacturers' Association, remarks in Sydney *Daily Telegraph,* July 27, 1962. Also see *SMH,* July 27, 1962.

[82] Wilczynski, *Australia's Trade with the Communist Bloc,* p. 165.

[83] Cited in *Canberra Times,* July 27, 1962.

come but, for the moment, despite its protectionist tradition, the ALP can subscribe to Cairns' observation that "so it is pillow cases versus wool and wheat. Which is likely to win? I would have my money on wool and wheat any day"; if Australia expects to sell, she must expect to buy, despite occasional hardships on local industries.[84]

But complaints against Chinese imports should not be treated frivolously. For example, while dumping complaints against cotton piece goods were rejected, complaints against handkerchief, towel and towelling, and pillow case imports from China have been upheld and additional duties levied. Local manufacturers have been pleased to get this relief, but are not completely satisfied. Since Chinese goods often arrive at irregular intervals rather than in a steady flow, bringing a complaint before tariff authorities and then receiving a judgment may take a very long time. There is dissatisfaction also with the technique of protection now favored by Australia, who uses tariffs almost exclusively rather than quantitative restrictions.[85] Then too, since tariffs are assessed by category of goods rather than against individual source nations, any special Chinese undercutting of prices or other deplored practices can become tangled in consideration of similar goods entering from elsewhere.

In recent years, despite complaints of underselling, the Chinese seem to have learned some lessons. They apparently no longer try to sell to Australia at absurdly low levels, for when some retailers have capitalized by selling to consumers at extremely low prices, there have been howls of protest. Not wishing to jeopardize their imports to Australia entirely because of tariff retaliation, the Chinese have raised their own prices, though they remain attractively low. Additionally, while practices vary, some retailers, perhaps most of them from among the larger

[84] *CPD*, HR, March 11, 1964, p. 451.
[85] See ACMA, *Canberra Letter*, March 15, 1962.

concerns, are circumspect in their retailing of Chinese goods. Myer's is the largest chain of retail department stores in Australia, with over 20 branches in all states save Western Australia. Only about 8 per cent of the goods sold by Myer's is imported: of these 4 per cent are Japanese, and China ranks far down on the list. The Myer organization consciously keeps its Chinese goods low in volume, and would be averse to staging a special "China day" or elaborate Chinese display, though there has never been any public pressure or outcry against these items. The store prefers not to make "killings" on cheap Chinese goods in the interest of avoiding controversy and adverse publicity, to avoid tariff retaliation, and to maintain an alert and aggressive rather than compacent sales staff. In fact, while quite obviously exorbitant tariffs are unwanted, the store's philosophy seems to be that inordinately low tariffs are also undersirable, for they would subtract from rather than stimulate native industries which contribute to national growth and promote greater purchasing power.

In the last analysis, while Chinese goods represent but a tiny fraction of Australia's total imports and abuses have not been rampant, there has been some concern and enough instances of duty impositions or voluntary retail sellers' restraint to limit the volume of incoming Chinese commodities. This accounts, in part, for the continuing massive imbalance in Sino-Australian trade.

## AUSTRALIAN TRADE WITH FORMOSA

AUSTRALIAN-FORMOSAN trade, while showing considerable improvement over the scale on which it moved in the late 'fifties, continues to constitute but a fraction of Australia's overseas commerce in general and of Chinese mainland trade in particular. In 1963–64 Australian exports to Formosa reached £3,627,000, certainly a healthier figure than 1957–58's £503,000, but still only about .2 per cent of the goods sold by Australia overseas. Imports from Formosa have also gone up; between 1958–59 and 1963–64 they increased many times over, but absolutely they are still meager, the 1963–64 figure of £1,435,000 being just over one-third of exports to Formosa. Put another way, in 1963–64 the value of Australian goods sold to China was about twenty-three times greater than to Formosa, while imports from China were some six times larger.

The Nationalists have been exerting themselves to increase their Australian trade. For a number of years high-level Formosan trade delegations have been visiting Australia, both to buy and to sell. The Nationalists have participated in trade fairs in major Australian cities and in 1963 a decision was taken to appoint a permanent commercial counsellor in Australia, who since has established headquarters in Sydney.[86] In other words, the Formosan drive for more Australian trade is a determined one, and in certain ways does not suffer from the problems that the absence of relations raises for Sino-Australian commerce.

And yet trade between the two countries remains at a comparatively minor scale. At bottom, as with China, Formosa does not have the sorts of goods which Australia is eager to buy in volume. In 1962–63, the single largest import item was textile piece goods, while other commodities included essential oils, head-gear, cements, undressed feathers, and wool, presumably carpet wool. Nonetheless, despite the easy movement of traders back and forth, Australian exports to Formosa, which have been dominated by wool, have not been sensational either. Various restrictive policies observed by the Formosan authorities until

[86] For comments on Formosa's drive to trade with Australia, see *SMH,* May 12, 1958, April 2, 1959, June 13 and October 21, 1960, June 28, 1962, and March 24, 1964; *China News* (Canberra), November 2 and December 14, 1960, September 6, 1961, and September 26, 1962; "Trade with Australia," *Far Eastern Economic Review,* Vol. 36 (April 12, 1962), p. 54.

the late 'fifties held down imports from Australia. Predictions of a greater Formosan market made in 1959 and 1960[87] proved partially accurate, but it is now widely believed in commercial circles and in Canberra that exports to Formosa will not be substantially raised in the near future.

This appraisal leads to some comment on Australia's perception of what kind of commercial representation is needed on or for Formosa. Until mid-1956, Australian trade promotion in Formosa was handled from the Hong Kong trade commission. Then the Formosan responsibility was removed from Hong Kong entirely and transferred to the newly created trade commissioner in the Philippines, who was to be based in the Philippines but would make periodic visits to Formosa. This practice has continued ever since. Additionally, in May 1959 a trade correspondent was engaged in Taipei. The present incumbent, who is British rather than Australian, is paid a part-time salary to look after Australian trading interests in an on-the-spot manner. This is as far as Australia has gone. There is not now nor has there ever been a full-time trade commissioner in Formosa.

Why so? There are two schools of opinion on this subject. The official explanation is that expert analysis of the Formosan market situation offers little hope for a major expansion of exports, and therefore no commercial representation above the present level is warranted. The 1956 transfer of responsibilities is explained as an efficiency move. The Hong Kong trade commissioner was already heavily burdened (increasingly with Chinese trade, *inter alia*), while the new Phillippines post was a lighter assignment and would permit more thorough at-

[87] See D. L. Crawford, "Prospects in Taiwan for Australian Exports," *Overseas Trading,* Vol. 11 (May 6, 1959), pp. 174–175, and Crawford, "Direct Shipping Opens up Taiwan Market," in *ibid.,* Vol. 12 (August 19, 1960), pp. 364–367.

tention to Formosa. The trade correspondent performs his work satisfactorily and apparently requires no extra assistance or up-grading in his responsibilities. The second school of thought does not deny the above explanations, but it adds a political interpretation of its own. A few months before the shift of Formosan responsibilities was effected, H. C. Menzies, the Hong Kong trade commissioner, had gone into China and returned with a report of strong trading possibilities. There were also other indications that increased Australian trade with China seemed likely. Therefore, some allege, the Formosan responsibility was moved out of Hong Kong so as not to compromise commercial contacts and eventually trade with China. Moreover, it is alleged that despite the improvement in Australian exports to Formosa during the past several years, Australia has not seen fit to install a trade commissioner there—a sign that Canberra has no wish to upset China, who is buying such large quantities of Australian commodities. In the choice between slightly increasing exports to Formosa and maintaining the present level of shipments to China, Australia opts for the latter.

Since there is almost universal agreement that a major improvement in Australian exports to Formosa is not in store, it should straight away be concluded that this has been a major consideration in the handling of commercial representation. But has there *also* been a political motive? In the first instance, it would appear that not only was Formosa upset about the prospect of a strong Sino-Australian trading bond from 1956 onward, but that her feeling was expressed to Australia. After H. C. Menzies had visited China, the Nationalist Embassy in Canberra made representations to the Government, sounding the conventional noises about how unreliable, ephemeral, etc., Chinese trade in fact was. Then, in 1958, Liang Yung-chang, leader of a Formosan trade union delegation to Australia, whose visit coincided with a Formosan trade mission's presence, said that any Sino-Australian trade agreement was apt to have Communist strings attached; in any event, wages were higher and goods cheaper in Formosa than in China, where wages were low and discontent widespread.[88] These were, in their way, deliberate intrusions in Australia's wish to develop commerce with China at a time when the foundations of that commerce were not yet solid. It is plausible that Nationalist interventions followed by the placing of a trade commissioner on Formosa could, in Canberra, have been construed as undesirable—a provocative step as far as China was concerned. The early 1958 Chinese employment of trade as a political weapon against Japan surely did not go unnoticed in this context.

Yet the author is satisfied that the Trade Department's relocation of Formosan responsibilities in 1956, and its failure to suggest to Cabinet the installation of a separate trade commissioner in Formosa prior to the arrival of large wheat sales, were entirely guided by an economic assessment of Formosa, not by fear of endangering the Chinese trade. It is conceivable that had Trade recommended a trade commissioner, Cabinet would have produced political reasons for rejecting the recommendation, but the matter never advanced that far. Once Australian selling to China had expanded substantially, there was more incentive to avoid its forfeiture. But on the other hand, Australia also realized that China was buying her wheat in 1960 and 1961 because she desperately needed it. By 1962, when China's immediate food needs had somewhat been corrected, the Chinese continued to buy, and their conduct was impeccable. They paid their bills on time or in advance, they did not try to squeeze Australia politically, and they were even dissuaded from an 18-month credit wheat arrangement in 1963 without any threats of curtailed buying arising. In other words, Aus-

[88] Statement of May 11, 1958, in *SMH,* May 12, 1958.

tralia's export experience with China has been uniformly satisfying, regardless of the anti-Chinese character of much of Australia's security and diplomatic policy. The placement of a trade commissioner in Formosa—an action not as politically sensitive as the installation of a formal diplomatic mission—would probably not disturb the Chinese trade. Since heavy selling to China opened, the Department of Trade has continued a periodic review of the Formosan question, and has never found any economic justification for a bolstering of trade representation. The possible impact on the China trade has apparently occurred to those responsible for these trade commission assessments, but has not in any way been conspicuously featured. In the last resort, both experience and prediction in Australia stress that while China is an impressive customer, Formosa most definitely is not.

# VIII

# THE MOVEMENT OF PEOPLE

IT HAS been seen that commercial assignments have frequently taken Australians to China, and have brought Chinese to Australia as well. But larger questions arise. How has the Government regarded the movement of persons between the two countries generally? What kinds of people have gone to and from China, and under what auspices? What special domestic repercussions, if any, have resulted in Australia? Does the traffic between Australia and China have any bearing on other aspects of Sino-Australian relations, or on relations between Australia and other states?

## THE GOVERNMENT'S PASSPORT POLICY

THE GOVERNMENT'S own approach to passports and travel to China needs to be clarified first. Following the Government's 1952 decision to disallow passports for persons wishing to attend the Peking Peace Conference, there was a period of complete permissiveness. Between the Peking Conference episode and April 1954, no Australian was debarred from travel to any Communist country for any reason. But in April 1954 the screws were tightened again, not only against Communist countries, but against Communist-inspired congresses held outside of the Communist bloc—though the denial of passports became selective rather than comprehensive. A delegation of Australian unionists wishing to attend a conference organized by the All-China Federation of Trade Unions and to attend May Day celebrations in Peking, was denied passports. Holt, still the Immigration Minister, explained that the Government had certain information about the scheduled Peking congress. It was also taking into account recent developments in Indo-China and the Petrov case disclosures; the Royal Commission investigating the Petrov case might require the presence in Australia of certain individuals scheduled to attend the Chinese congress. He continued to stress that the Government's legal powers were not entirely adequate, but that under the defense power vested constitutionally in the Government a restrictive passport policy was being imposed.[1]

In April 1955, one year later, Holt announced a return to leniency. He repeated the reasons which had prompted severity in 1954, and proceeded to denounce Communist-inspired peace congresses as instruments of Communist policy that are designed to divide the people of the West and to distract their attention from Communism's aggressive and subversive intentions. Special and subtle appeals had been fostered by such congresses covering special groups such as women, youth, and trade unionists, and Australian Communists who traveled to Communist countries had been responsible for furthering opposition to Australia's foreign and defense policies. Still, while the Government reserved the right to reimpose a passport ban as general or particular circumstances required, it remained "dedicated to liberal principles" and was therefore now loosening up.[2]

The restrictive policy of 1954–55 had produced some situations which had not reflected well on the Government. A journalist, Alec Robertson, apparently had his passport privileges removed because he was thought to be on his way to the 1954 Peking trade union conference—though he disclaimed any such intention.[3] Neil Glover, a

[1] See Holt's statements of April 14 and May 10, 1954, in *SMH,* April 15 and May 11, 1958, respectively.

[2] Statement of April 6, 1955, in *ibid.,* April 7, 1955.

[3] Alec Robertson, letter to *ibid.,* May 14, 1954.

Melbourne Anglican clergyman interested in attending a peace conference in Berlin, had his passport blocked. Holt's muddled explanation was that clergymen could attend such conclaves only if they carried the sponsorship of their church superiors. In this instance, Glover did have the permission of his superior, but the trip was not regarded favorably by his superior. Therefore the Government felt justified in withholding Glover's passport.[4]

Glover's situation also highlights the Government's unconvincing legal position. It will be remembered that the Government claimed legal disability short of invoking the dubiously applicable defense power in stopping Burton's delegation in May of 1952. Three months later it blocked those who had wished to travel to the broader Peking congress, but without indicating that it was employing the defense power. In 1954 Holt said the fresh restrictions were being taken under the defense power, although the Government was uncomfortable about operating under this clause. It had good reason to be. The constitution states that Parliament shall have power to make laws for the peace, order, and good government of Australia with, among other things, respect to "the naval and military defence of the Commonwealth and of the several States, and the control of the forces to execute and maintain the laws of the Commonwealth."[5] The High Court has allowed very wide play for the Government under this clause in times of war, but not at other times. By coincidence, just before the Government lifted its restrictive policy in 1955, Glover had been blocked from attending still another peace congress in Europe. He appealed to the High Court for a writ to compel the issue of a passport. The writ was denied, Mr. Justice Taylor claiming that ministerial discretion under the Passport Act was extremely wide, and that

[4] Holt, statement of May 14, 1954, in *ibid.,* May 15, 1954, Also see *ibid.,* May 14, 1954.

[5] *Commonwealth Constitution,* Part v, Section 51 (vi).

in any event, in Glover's case, Holt had not exercised his discretion on grounds extraneous to the Act.[6] In other words, the Government had power to block passports on general political-international grounds without recourse to the defense power. Yet for years the Government had protested that its own best legal advice suggested the contrary. As a result it had worked itself into some foolish and inconsistent predicaments, and had exposed itself to political exploitation by the Labor Opposition.[7]

The Government also failed to make a respectable defense of its policies when announcing the new lenient approach in April of 1955. The old excuses for severity, namely Indo-China and the Petrov hearings, had, to be sure, ended. But Holt's elaborate denunciation of peace congresses suggested that this also had played a part in the restraint imposed on Australian travel overseas. Yet Communist peace congresses were no different in 1955 than they had been in 1954; if they had been inimical to Australian interests before, why not now? The author understands that the Government was being set upon by various cross-pressures. The international situation had a habit of moving from crisis to crisis—e.g., from Indo-China to the offshore islands. At home there were assorted pressures from powerful union organizations on behalf of a permissive policy. The ALP could also be expected to set some trip-wires under the Government. It seemed anomalous that Australia should have officially entertained the British Labor Party delegation which had just returned from a visit to China in view of the fact that Australians would not have been permitted to make the trip. Indeed, an opinion survey indicated that more than twice as many Australians had reacted favorably to the Attlee mission's

[6] *SMH,* April 6 and 7, 1955.

[7] See Calwell's statement of April 14, 1954, in *ibid.,* April 15, 1954

China trip rather than unfavorably.[8] Within the Government some ministers were more liberally disposed than others. Holt had always been among the principal exponents of liberality, and he threw off the restrictions of 1954–55 as quickly as he could. His explanations were frequently unconvincing, probably as a result of the uncertainties besetting his Government. At all events, discounting the improvement in the international situation in 1955, it is proper to say that with the new policy of leniency the Government was relieved to liberate itself from its previous and largely self-imposed difficulties. At least a liberal passport policy would not create indefensible and anomalous situations resulting from passport denial. If and when strictness needed to be restored, legal barriers no longer were a worry.

How in practice has passport policy been implemented since April 1955? Until July 1, 1964, Australian passports contained a statement that they were valid for travel anywhere except to *all* Communist countries, which were itemized by name. Furthermore, the official passport application form continues to include questions concerning which countries the applicant proposes to visit, how long he expects to be absent from Australia, where he expects to embark from Australia, and by what means he intends to travel. There is a conspicuous warning on the form that any false statement renders the applicant liable to a fine of £50 or imprisonment for three months. But the distinction between appearance and reality has been complete. Persons wishing to visit China or other Communist nations prior to July 1, 1964 were asked to prepare a written application stating the reasons they wished to go as well as where. In practice, permission was given *pro forma* regardless of what reasons were submitted. Respecting China, the word "China" was scratched from the list of prohibited coun-

[8] *AGP*, nos. 1036–1046, September–October 1954.

tries on the passport, and on another page a rubber stamp was affixed reading, "Endorsement. China Deleted from Reference on Page 4. . . . Australian Migration Officer." The author is not aware of a single instance since April 1955 of an exception not having been allowed. Indeed, even if a person chose to lie on his application form and did not indicate he was going to China, he could easily avoid penalties. He could later claim he had not *intended* to visit China, but had changed his mind. Furthermore, the Chinese have been very obliging with their visas, often providing a separate slip of paper rather than leaving any trace on an Australian passport that its carrier had entered and then left the country. It would therefore be relatively simple to visit China without detection—though it was generally pointless to do so, since permission was automatically available.

It is not entirely apparent why these cumbersome procedures were retained in the face of a policy of absolute permissiveness. Perhaps in the first years after April 1955 it was felt that there might come a time when stringency would have to be reinvoked. Yet, despite many international crises abroad, it never happened. Records were kept, however, of all requests for exemption from the theoretical bar on travel to Communist destinations—perhaps for general statistical reference but probably directed more at security.

However, on July 1, 1964, all mention of prohibited countries was eliminated from Australian passports, in itself testimony of the leniency with which policy had been administered. While it is still theoretcally possible to withhold or confiscate a passport, the old procedures were paying no dividends. They were unnecessarily time consuming for all concerned, while the value of exemption application records faded as well, given the volume and variety of the traffic from Australia to China. Perhaps too, the lengthy prohibited list on the old passports was thought to leave a false and poor impression with foreigners who were unaware that the list was meaningless.[9]

## THE EXTENT OF AUSTRALIAN TRAVEL TO CHINA: THE AUSTRALIA–CHINA SOCIETY

THE PRECISE number of Australians who have visited Communist China is most difficult to gauge, though it is surely many hundreds, perhaps over a thousand. In 1956 alone, one writer has calculated, six separate Australian multi-member delegations went to China, [10] and that was a low year for Chinese travel by comparison with later years. Perhaps the best illustration of the government's passport liberality comes from the movement of Australian Communists to China. As was seen, Australian Communists were going to China even during the Korean War. After April 1955 the traffic widened. There have been visits by Australian Communists in various capacities, including organized tours in which they were included and as part of trade union or other delegations. More strikingly, however, Australian Communists have been going to Chinese congresses, May Day celebrations, and the like, and have sometimes gone for lengthy periods of training and indoctrination. When the Sino-Soviet dispute occurred, members of the Communist Party of Australia shuttled back and forth between Moscow and Peking for consultations with top figures. In 1963 the CPA split: the majority holding to the Moscow line, and the minority, concentrated in Victoria under the leadership of E. F. (Ted) Hill, formed a new, hard-line, Peking-oriented party—the Communist Party of Australia (Marxist-Leninist). In mid-1963 Hill spent a month in China in conference not only with Chinese officials, but presumably with

[9] See the brief comment by S. D. Paltridge, *CPD*, S, November 9, 1964, p. 1515.

[10] Evron Kirkpatrick, ed., *Year of Crisis* (New York: Macmillan, 1957), Table 39, p. 365.

leaders of the Peking-oriented Communist parties of New Zealand and Indonesia. The linkage between the Hill group and China has moved ahead vigorously. For instance, "Peking has already made a significant contribution by appointing one of Hill's supporters, Australian correspondent for the Hsin-Hua Press Agency. It is generally believed that this person, in moving about the country ostensibly on Agency business, will also have the task of fostering and maintaining contact with a network of potential pro-Peking party members."[11] There is no political organization in Australia which identifies itself more intimately with militant Communism and with China, both of which are anathema to the Menzies Government, than the Hill group. Yet no obstruction has been placed before it, either in Australia or in its attempts to establish connections with Peking. It is no harder for Hill or his associate to enter China than it is for the Governor of the Reserve Bank of Australia or any ordinary person—at least from the Australian Government's standpoint.

Aside from Communists and commercial people, whose desire to visit China can easily be explained, what kinds of Australians have gone to China, and under what auspices? Much of the stimulation for Australian visits to China has come from the Australia-China Society, the principal pro-Chinese interest group in Australia. The Victorian branch of the ACS was established in 1951, followed in early 1952 by a branch in New South Wales. Another branch has since been established in Queensland, and a subbranch operates in Newcastle, New South Wales. The branches are virtually autonomous, though their aims and organization are comparable, and they are loosely linked by a Federal organization of which

[11] "Between Moscow and Peking—the C.P. of Australia," *Current Affairs Bulletin,* Vol. 34 (June 22, 1964), p. 46. For a brief review of Australian Communist movements to China, see Passin, *op. cit.,* pp. 65–66.

Professor C. P. Fitzgerald of the Australian National University is President. The constitution of the Victorian branch, typical of the ACS at large, lists the Society's objectives to be the strengthening of cultural, commercial, and peaceful relations with China, Australian recognition of China, and a seat for Peking in the UN.[12] The Society has no use for a two-China formula. It believes that Formosa is an integral part of China, and that she has no claim to separate UN representation.

While the ACS bars no one because of his political party outlook or affiliation, its composition is naturally slanted. Apparently a handful of Liberals have joined the organization, and possibly one or two Country Party members have belonged. In Victoria and New South Wales (the two largest branches with about 200 members each), it is believed that about 25 per cent of the members are card-carrying Communists—either of the Moscow or Peking faction. Ted Hill himself has been enrolled in the Victorian branch. How many others are Communist voters is not definitely known, though it is almost surely true that the bulk of the Victorian and New South Wales membership would be ALP voters. The proportion of Communists on the executive committees of the two is about the same—one quarter of the total. The exact influence of the Communists in the ACS cannot be stated with full certainty. The *News Weekly,* predictably, has written that the ACS is "probably the most thinly disguised 'front' organization now operating." [13] The Australian contributors to the Australian–New Zealand section of Professor Passin's recent book on *China's Cultural Diplomacy* have emphasized the faction-fighting within the ACS over "revisionism." [14] The author has spoken to officers of

[12] "Draft Constitution of the Australia-China Society (Victoria)," mimeo., p. 1.

[13] *News Weekly,* June 13, 1962.

[14] Passin, *op. cit.,* pp. 57–58.

both the Victorian and New South Wales ACS branches. They have admitted previous troubles over revisionism of the Titoist sort, but have said that the Moscow–Peking strife has not created turmoil in the Society. Furthermore, they have denied any Communist attempts to "take over" the organization, and have indicated that any such maneuver would be successfully resisted. Indeed, they have pointed out that there is no need for Communists to attempt any packing or other domination of the ACS. For one, the non-Communist membership already shares a pro-Chinese view with the Communists. For another, any blatant Communist take-over might frighten off present and prospective non-Communist members and weaken the influence of the ACS within the general community.

On the other hand, former ALP Senator J. J. Arnold of New South Wales, President of the Newcastle group, tells another story. The Newcastle ACS has some 100 members, of whom Arnold estimates about 20 to be card-carrying Communists. For the record, he told the author he believes the subbranch to be Communist inspired, and that the Communists find his name and position useful. A. W. James, ALP MHR for Hunter, New South Wales, is another Newcastle ACS officer, and presumably is "used" in the same way. The people who really run the ACS there are the vice-secretary and her husband, both of whom are Communists. Again, however, Arnold says that he continues on because he believes in the ACS's cause, and because the Communists in Newcastle have not attempted a formal and obvious take-over.

The ACS, especially the larger branches, carries out a variety of activities. At least in Victoria and New South Wales the ACS has for some years been approaching school teachers and libraries with Chinese-produced mateparials, and has found a reasonably interested response, particularly in primary schools, for which the literature has minimal political content. The secondary schools have been a tougher nut to crack, because the materials are far more politically slanted, and Australian students below university level are not sufficiently discriminating to use them properly. The Society also tries to interest the public at large in such Chinese publications as *China Reconstructs* and *Peking Review*. It meets no official resistance in this. While Australian censorship—Federal, state and local—of alleged smut lies somewhere between laughable and disgraceful, censorship of political materials is next to nonexistent. Sex rather than Marxist socialism, the authorities seem to believe, is the real menace. "Radical" book shops flourish in the major cities, and Chinese materials are imported, displayed, and sold without hindrance, much to the ACS's relief.[15]

ACS sponsorship has also been given to publications in newsletter form, public lectures on China, films on China, displays of Chinese art, and so on. Visiting Chinese have been provided with ACS hospitality. The New South Wales branch sponsors an annual summer school at Newport. At the 1962 school, for instance, various individuals who had visited China participated by delivering lectures on Chinese art and modern education, showed films, and held book review discussions.[16] Two months later the ACS sponsored a forum in Newcastle. Delegates from a number of interested organizations attended. Among the themes raised was support for more trade with China, recognition and a UN seat for Peking, and a debunking of alleged starvation conditions in China. Among the featured speakers were two left-wing Parliamentarians from New South Wales, Leslie Haylen and Tom Uren, a lecturer from the Australian National University, and a

[15] For Government expressions on imported Communist literature, see Frederick Osborne, *CPD,* HR 11, June 21, 1956, p. 3518, and John Gorton, S 18, October 6, 1960, p. 932.

[16] See ACS (NSW Branch) *Bulletin,* May 1962. For the 1964 summer school program, see ACS (NSW Branch), special announcement.

representative of the Anglican Bishop of Newcastle, James Houden, who has a strong pro-China bias.[17]

But perhaps the major function of the ACS has been the facilitation of Australian visits to China. The Chinese have always been ready to accept ACS members as visitors, particularly in groups. When non-ACS members have indicated a wish to visit China, the ACS has often tried to supply information on them to the Chinese authorities. In the past few years, the ACS has received invitations from China to send delegations from its ranks. Early in 1963, for example, word came that a party of approximately 18 would be welcome for a tour starting in August, which would include 20 days in China and 5 in Hong Kong. The itinerary was given. Interpreters were promised. Participants would need to pay, but at reduced rates: "Anyone wishing to join the group must have been a member of the Australia–China Society for six months prior to the date of travel. Immediate relatives are eligible if travelling with a member." [18]

Some illustration of the ACS's pervasive role in Australian visits to China would be useful. In 1956 the ACS received an invitation from the Chinese People's Association for Cultural Relations with Foreign Countries, asking that an Australian cultural mission be dispatched. Fitzgerald, in his capacity as ACS Federal President, invited ten Australians from various academic, artistic and professional ranks, though he chose largely from names recommended by the New South Wales and Victorian branches. While the people selected were not necessarily pro-Chinese, so far as is known none went with a special animus against China. At all events, arrangements, delegate selection, and leadership devolved on the ACS in one manner or another.

[17] ACS (NSW Branch) *Bulletin,* June 1962.

[18] *Ibid.,* April 1963. For the report of the delegation which visited China, see *ibid.,* November–December 1963.

In 1957 one B. Burgoyne Chapman wished to visit China with his wife. He later reported that his own attempt to secure a Chinese visa had been disregarded by Peking, though not intentionally, he thought. Then he wrote a fresh appeal to the Chinese Foreign Office, and was backed by a letter from the ACS. The visa then promptly materialized.[19]

In early 1957 eight Australian university students, in part representing the National Union of Australian University Students, visited China. The group had in no way been preselected or screened by the Chinese or the ACS, and represented a cross section of political outlooks. When the group returned to Australia the ACS, at least in Victoria, invited some of the delegation members to address them. It is understood that because the students' remarks were found to be unduly critical of China in certain respects, the ACS then staged a set of fresh follow-up meetings at which "corrections" were made by ACS members.

In 1958 the National Women's Federation of China directed a letter to ACS branches asking that an Australian women's group be assembled for a Chinese trip. The women were selected on the basis of their accomplishments rather than political views. One was the women's editor of the *Sydney Morning Herald*. Another was the women's session editor of the Australian Broadcasting Commission's "country hour" and a former officer for women's affairs in the New South Wales Agriculture Department. A third was the principal of the University Women's College, Melbourne, and a director of the Elizabethan Theatre Trust. Another was deputy commissioner of Girl Guides. The fifth was a member of the Western Australian state Executive of the ALP. None was then an

[19] B. Burgoyne Chapman, "China Revisited" (Sydney: ACS, NSW Branch, 1957), mimeo., p. 2.

ACS member, though arrangements were in the ACS's care.[20]

One of these women, Myra Roper of Melbourne, shortly thereafter joined the ACS's Victorian branch, and there hangs an interesting story. In 1963 Miss Roper and John Dixon of Melbourne agreed that they would like to take television pictures in China for later screening in Australia and if possible elsewhere in the world. The ACS wrote to Peking in advance and was assured that such a film team would be welcome. Then Dixon was advised that he would need to join the ACS if he were to make the Chinese trip. He agreed, though it was generally understood he was doing so purely to gain entry into China. Roper and Dixon then proceeded to China in conjunction with a larger ACS tourist group. Once there, they were told by the Chinese that before the film could be released in Australia it would first have to be viewed by two ACS members, and the two designated persons were members of the ACS tour then in China. Dixon and Roper gave consent. The Chinese apparently did not make the showing of the film over Australian television conditional on the two ACS members' approval, but it did not matter. The film was shown to them, only one or two minor alterations were requested in the commentary, and Dixon made them gladly, feeling the criticisms were well taken. But when the film was publicly screened, in two hour-long installments, Miss Roper and the ACS in Victoria showed displeasure. The scriptwriter who had worked under Dixon's supervision had botched the job, they thought. It was "an unfortunate commentary, made apparently against the wishes of Miss Roper, so blatantly and mistakenly aimed at hostile sponsors [and it] weakened what was, in many respects, a pictorially interesting film." [21]

In the China television film episode as in a variety of

[20] See *Canberra Times,* September 20, 1958.

[21] ACS (Victorian Branch) *Bulletin,* April 1964.

other situations, then, the ACS has been involved in the movement of Australians to China. Whatever its political composition and various other activities may be, and whatever indictment is possible of its occasionally bumptious behavior, it is clear that it has served a useful purpose in facilitating Australian travel to China. According to one ACS officer, the Society is called upon by the Chinese to perform its yeoman work in the travel business because, mistakenly he thinks, the Chinese honestly believe it to be an essentially Communist organization!

### THE CHINESE ATTITUDE TOWARD AUSTRALIAN VISITORS

WHILE the ACS has assumed a fair share of responsibility for arranging Australian travel to China, not by any means has it been the sole and necessary intermediary between China and Australian visitors. The Chinese themselves, while quite generous in admitting Australians, have on occasion thrown up restrictions. As far as is known no Australian who has wished to enter China for business purposes has been blocked, regardless of his private politics, his absence of ACS connections, and the like. Prior business trips to Formosa have not complicated entrance into China for similar purposes. Nancy Buttfield, *Liberal* Senator from South Australia, entered China as a private traveler in 1963 without difficulty, despite being a Government Parliamentarian and having visited Formosa in the past. The Australian contributors to Passin's book intimate that Peter Russo, an Australian correspondent who is relatively well disposed toward China, was refused a visa some years ago,[22] but in 1956 Selwyn Speight, on behalf of the *Sydney Morning Herald,* and Reg Leonard, representing the Melbourne *Sun* and the *Herald,* entered China and filed lengthy reports. Australian delegations of students, women, unionists, artists, doctors, Churchmen, and so on have been to China, and within these delega-

[22] Passin, *op. cit.,* p. 63.

tions have been people who either had little political interest, or were skeptical about the Chinese experiment, but the Chinese have seldom if ever chosen to interfere in the composition of such groups.

When the Chinese have evinced stringency in admission policy, it has usually been against individual applicants for entry. Instances of this clustered some years ago, and apparently for reasons especially important to China. Professor Fitzgerald himself, the Federal ACS President but by no means an uncritical student of the present regime, seemingly had some preliminary visa trouble before his second trip to China, in 1957–58. It has been suggested that the difficulty arose because the Chinese did not wish knowledgeable people to enter so soon after the closing down of the "hundred flowers" period.[23] This view is partially sustained by the experience of Lord Lindsay, then still connected with the Australian National University. During the war Lindsay escaped from the Japanese and spent nearly four years living in Chinese Communist areas with his Chinese wife. In mid-1949 he visited north China once again. In 1954 he accompanied the British Labor Party delegation to China as interpreter, but his impressions afterward were not wholly favorable.[24]

In February of 1958 Lindsay completed a visit to Formosa, and his reactions were most complimentary. He spoke admiringly of economic progress there, declaring it to be the best evidence to dispel the illusion that Communism was the answer for underdeveloped areas. Nor was he critical of political progress on the island, and compared Formosan elections favorably with those conducted in Australia and Britain.[25] Then he tried to enter China. He was stopped at the border and without further cere-

[23] *Ibid.*, p. 60.

[24] See "China's Policy Towards Far Eastern Countries," *Far Eastern Economic Review*, Vol. 25 (August 14, 1958), p. 194.

[25] *China News* (Canberra), February 13, 1958.

mony was advised that entry permits for the entire Lindsay family had been canceled. His own explanation of the incident was that the Chinese had just completed an anti-rightist campaign. He was not the sort of person who would accept a conducted tour, and the Chinese did not appreciate having outsiders "find out what the real situation is." Dogmatism, superstition, and suppression of freedoms were closing in on China, and the leadership was in no mood to advertise its mistakes.[26] Evatt himself intervened on Lindsay's behalf with the Chinese Foreign Office on grounds that Australia should know all there was to be known about China, but the Chinese did not relent. Leslie Haylen, who had visited China earlier, subsequently wrote that Lindsay's exclusion had been unfortunate, "but the sword in the heart of China is Formosa. It is a touchy subject"; the Chinese had found Lindsay's Formosan impressions "too enthusiastic." [27] There was much truth in this evaluation. It seems clear that the coincidence of the state of affairs in China with Lindsay's acclaim for Formosa were the factors responsible for his exclusion.

And yet, as has been suggested, many types of Australians, including those not sympathetic to the regime, have entered China, and while there have not been bombarded with flagrant propaganda or kept on a leash. When Australians have sought out Chinese officials, they have found them accommodating. Australian correspondents,[28] the 1956 cultural delegation,[29] and the ALP delegation of 1957 [30] held interviews with Chou En-lai. The Roper-Dixon television team filmed an interview with Chen Yi,

[26] See *SMH,* February 10 and 11, 1958.

[27] Haylen, *op. cit.,* pp. 10–11. Also see comment in Melbourne *Herald,* February 11, 1958.

[28] Leonard's interview in Melbourne *Sun* and Melbourne *Herald,* August 6, 1956; Speight's remarks in *SMH,* April 28ff., 1956.

[29] C. P. Fitzgerald and P. H. Partridge, "Report to the Council of the Australian National University on the Visit to China of the Australian Cultural Delegation," mimeo., pp. 30–32.

[30] Haylen, *op. cit.,* pp. 143–145.

China's Foreign Minister.[31] Senator Buttfield was able to talk to Chinese officials during her two-week visit, and Miss Roper, who carried a special letter of introduction from Perrett, talked about agriculture and Sino–Australian trade with the vice-director of the Chinese import-export cereals organization.[32] Generally, the Chinese have avoided political discussions unless invited to do so by Australians themselves. Professor P. H. Partridge of the Australian National University, a member of the 1956 cultural delegation, stated flatly that "the Chinese did not try to talk politics at us or to extract from us expressions of approval or support. If we wanted to talk politics, as I did, we had to take the initiative." [33] The 1957 student delegation had a bit of a row with officers of the All-China Student Federation about China's resistance to Australian participation at the 1956 Bandoeng Afro-Asian Student Conference, but the debate was inspired by the Australians themselves.[34]

There, of course, has been a Chinese effort to show "the best face" of the country. The Chinese have tried to avoid outright refusals of requests by Australians to see or do this or that, but rather have used less obvious methods. Dixon attempted to film certain back-street scenes in Peking, but the Chinese deliberately set schedules and itineraries which made this impossible. Still, not only was film taken of a variety of Chinese scenes in 1963, but the 1957 student delegation also took films which had been commissioned by the ABC and were later screened on Austral-

[31] Interview reproduced in *Sydney Sun-Herald,* November 17, 1963.

[32] Myra Roper, "China Revisited—1," in Melbourne *Age,* November 20, 1963.

[33] P. H. Partridge, in Australian Cultural Delegation, "Report on China" (Sydney: ACS, NSW Branch, 1956), p. 26.

[34] "Students in China. Report of a Delegation from the National Union of Australian University Students to the People's Republic of China" (Melbourne: 1957), esp. pp. 41–43.

ian television. The student delegation was subtly prevented from having dinner with a Reuters correspondent then in Peking and an interested member was unable to gain access to the People's University, but a very revealing conversation with a member of the Chinese "national bourgeoisie" in Shanghai was not stopped—though the interviewee was very bourgeois. Elaine Haxton, an Australian artist who visited China in 1956 with the cultural delegation, reported that not only was the group allowed to raise whatever questions it liked, but that if an English-speaking Chinese were being questioned, the Chinese interpreter would retire.[35] Selwyn Speight covered over five thousand miles while in China and spoke to hundreds of people of all types and grades. In nearly every instance, the personal hospitality of the Chinese toward their Australian guests has been excellent.

## AUSTRALIAN IMPRESSIONS OF CHINA AND THEIR RECEPTION AT HOME

THE ACTUAL impressions carried out of China by Australian visitors have, expectedly, varied considerably. On the one hand, there have been such transparently sycophantic reports as that of one Pete Thomas, who after his 1958 visit wrote a pamphlet which opened with a comment by a teen-age Chinese girl who, with her family, was alleged to have suffered mightily before the Communists took over: "Please tell all Australians how happy we are. Before, I could only cry. Now I smile and laugh all the time." [36] Thomas went on to praise the remarkable enthusiasm and progress of the Chinese people, derided the malevolence of the discredited Chiang regime, and concluded his panegyric by exclaiming, "People's China threatens no one.

[35] See *Sydney Sun-Herald,* June 10, 1956.

[36] Pete Thomas, "As We Saw it . . . China's Great Leap" (Sydney: Current Book Distributors, 1958), p. 7.

The slogan 'Long live world peace!' inspires and directs her deeds."[37] Still others, sympathetic to China but by no means apologists for her, have not only seen progress there but have felt it necessary to alert Australia to the importance of China, and to the need for more constructive thinking and policy, as they have seen it. Professor Partridge felt that the interchange of persons between the two countries, and especially of Australians to China, could bring only gain and understanding. Beyond acquainting herself with China, Australia should do what she could "to bring China into full contact with the Western liberal world."[38] After her 1963 Chinese visit, Miss Roper advocated continuing trade, recognition, and a UN seat for Peking—which, once the Chinese people achieved a higher standard of living, would that much sooner "soften the more rigid, doctrinaire aspects of the regime."[39] Sir Mark Oliphant, professor, distinguished physicist, and President of the Australian Academy of Science, went a step farther upon returning from China late in 1964. He had become convinced that the release of Formosa to China would measureably calm Peking's external behavior.[40]

Even from sources of more moderate reputation than these have come reactions which cannot be construed as hostile. In 1958 J. D. Kenny, assistant secretary of the New South Wales Labor Council and junior vice-president of the ACTU, returned from China. He was a Roman Catholic and widely respected as a trade union moderate. He attended mass in Chinese Catholic churches as well as attending the All-China Federation of Trade Unions Congress. In the balance, he felt it would be "suicidal" for

[37] *Ibid.*, p. 53.

[38] P. H. Partridge, "Opportunities for Close Relations," *Voice,* Vol. 5 (July–August 1956), pp. 11–12.

[39] Myra Roper, "China Revisited—2," Melbourne *Age,* November 27, 1963.

[40] See his remarks in *SMH,* October 22, 1964.

Australia to disregard China's friendship, and hoped for the rapid conclusion of diplomatic relations.[41] Although Kenny had relatively little to say about the state of religion in China, an earlier Australian delegation had much to say. In 1957–58 a group of ranking Anglican churchmen spent time in China. Among those who went on record speaking favorably of religious freedom and advancement generally were the Bishop of Tasmania, the Archbishop of Perth, and Dr. H. W. K. Mowll, Primate of Australia, who had lived in China for ten years between the wars.[42] Consider finally Nancy Buttfield's reactions. In April of 1964 she addressed the Senate on the subject of her Chinese journey. Generally, she found Chinese life depressing, but she considered the trip valuable. Without meaning to urge a fresh Australian diplomatic approach to China, she said, she thought that more Australian visits to China would enable Australia in particular and the West more broadly to become better known in China, and thereby possibly weaken official Chinese anti-Western propaganda within the country.[43]

It is true that one will find a considerably higher proportion of individuals sympathetic to China among those who have visited the country than exists in the population at large. Yet few if any Australians who have gone to China have regretted doing so. Nearly all have encouraged their countrymen to come and see for themselves. Many have returned with proposals for a reconstruction of Australia's China policy. Others, even if they have found much that was undesirable in China, have felt that the free movement of Australians to China might yield beneficial long-term results, for China herself or for the cause of peace and amity with the non-Communist world. In a

[41] See his remarks in *ibid.*, January 16, 1958, and the praise given him by the Sydney *Daily Telegraph*, January 17, 1958.

[42] See *SMH*, November 30, 1956, and January 3 and 7, 1957.

[43] *CPD*, S, April 9, 1964, pp. 571–578.

fashion, the Chinese have achieved their aim. Professor Fitzgerald has remarked that those who already "believe" will have their faith refreshed by a visit to China. Some will go with a relatively open mind and then undergo conversion. Still others will enter and then leave unconvinced, but will in honesty need to recognize the reality and scope of the changes brought on by the regime, and their "evidence will have all the more value as coming from an ideological opponent." [44] Furthermore, for countries which have no diplomatic relations with Peking, "there is an undoubted advantage in permitting unofficial delegations and groups representing various professions to visit China and gather first-hand information on the nature and scope of the changes now transforming that country." [45]

The conduct of the Australian Government would suggest that Fitzgerald's characterization fits Australia. The complete leniency on passports is certainly one indication in itself. In 1957 Casey said that the Government neither encouraged nor discouraged travel to China, but left the matter to the good sense of the individual visitor.[46] Casey was apparently underplaying his own and his Government's attitude. It is true that when in 1958 Miss Roper approached Casey and asked his view of her projected China trip she was given the same reply. But before the student delegation left for China, Casey, who had been similarly approached, gave explicit encouragement and support. Before going to China Senator Buttfield informally approached some of the Government ministers for advice. Her trip would, after all, be the first by a Federal Parliamentarian on the Government side. The advice tended toward dissuasion. But when she consulted a higher source in the Government, she was told to proceed if she liked, and this she did. After he had resigned from

[44] C. P. Fitzgerald, *Flood Tide in China* (London: Cresset Press, 1958), p. 197.

[45] *Ibid.*, p. 42.

[46] *CPD*, HR 15, May 20, 1957, p. 1560.

his position and left Parliament entirely, Casey himself became interested in visiting China. He applied for a visa through the Chinese mission in London, but did not pursue the matter when no reply was forthcoming. There can be small doubt that intrinsically the Australian Government, always careful about its public pronouncements, agrees with what Sydney Smith, Canada's former External Affairs Minister, said on the subject. Personal contacts with China were useful. The people who went learned something. Through their writings and by word of mouth they informed the Canadian public. By developing relations in limited sectors, Canadians could "break down some of the political distrust which unavoidably exists between Canada—and indeed, the whole western world—and the Peking government." [47]

As Fitzgerald suggests, travel by Australians to China compensates also for the lack of formal diplomatic ties. Relations generally are helped along by the traffic, but there is another angle to the matter. The Government follows a selective policy of interviewing individuals who have returned from China. In most instances, those interviewed have been asked to appear for a chat. In other cases, as with Myra Roper after both her 1958 and 1963 trips, returned Australians have themselves offered to talk about their impressions. Both explicitly pro-Chinese Australians and others have been interviewed. Most of these interviews are conducted by External Affairs officers in Australia, or by the External Affairs officer attached to the Hong Kong trade commissioner's office. In one instance the trade commissioner gave a dinner for two Australians just out of China, the discussion taking the form of an interview. In one known instance, with Mr. Perrett, the interview was conducted by the Australian security service. Thus the Australian Government learns something of

[47] *Canadian Parliamentary Debates,* HC, Session 1959, Vol. 2, February 26, 1959, p. 1407.

China without committing itself to recognition. Travel leniency is therefore not just a gesture of liberality, but a way of strengthening relations and obtaining information, however unsystematic the process and fragmentary the information. Domestically, freedom of movement to China tends to neutralize some of the demand for recognition, cutting away at the argument that only through recognition can Australia, or Australians, learn something of China and enjoy personal contacts. Obviously, a lenient passport policy allows something to be learned of China without the necessity of offending the United States by granting diplomatic recognition.

Among Australians of far-right political persuasion the traffic to China has not been a congenial phenomenon. Rather than thinking that the success of travel has knocked out one of the pro-recognition arguments, they are afraid that a reverse effect is actually being produced. They feel that the easy movement of Australians to China, and the hospitality they are accorded there, serves to make Australia complacent about the Chinese threat generally. They see people of various political shades returning from China with at least some kind words, and perhaps with proposals for changes in Australia's China policy, and they think this creates a climate of opinion which is fraught with danger. One of their favorite people is American Professor Richard L. Walker, who several years ago wrote a review article entitled "Australians in Wonderland," a blistering attack on the alleged naïveté of three books written by Australians who had visited China.[48] In Walker's opinion, these books "illustrated only too effectively the wide range of talents which can be recruited for telling a story in a manner which will serve the interests of

[48] The three books were Haylen's *Chinese Journey*, Fitzgerald's *Flood Tide in China*, and Dymphna Cusack's *Chinese Women Speak* (Sydney, London, Melbourne and Wellington: Angus and Robertson, 1958).

the Mao regime today, as presumably respectable writings served that of Stalin in the nineteen-thirties." [49]

The Walker article drew a rejoinder which illustrated the excitement which Chinese travel can generate on both fringes of political opinion. Elizabeth Wolf (Vasilieff), herself a China sympathizer and former visitor there, tore into Walker by claiming he was no authority on China, that "you certainly need to be pretty smart to be an authority on something you don't recognise the existence of," and that it was people of Walker's sort who "advised" a reactionary U.S. foreign policy which a sycophant Menzies Government had made its own.[50] At bottom, the debate between the exponents and critics of Chinese travel is not an edifying one. Those who go to China with prior pro-Chinese convictions accuse their critics of ignorance—as Elizabeth Wolf does. The critics of Chinese travel claim most Australian visitors are gullible, since they swallow the Chinese line and fail to recognize the pitfalls beneath the red carpet laid out for them. Yet the detractors of Chinese travel have largely been disarmed. According to a right-wing Liberal critic, Australia should convince the Chinese to open their entire country to inspection, especially slave labor camps. But he admits this is unlikely. A ranking DLP figure says his party opposes Chinese travel, for reasons already described, but conceded that the Government and public alike are now accustomed to easy movement into China and nothing would be gained by giving the issue political prominence.[51] As far back as November 1957, before travel to China had become as extensive and well established as it is now, an opinion poll indicated that while 57 per cent favored the acceptance of

[49] Richard L. Walker, "Australians in Wonderland," *Quadrant,* Vol. 4 (Autumn 1960), p. 3.

[50] Elizabeth Wolf (Vasilieff), "No-Hopers in Never-Never Land," *Overland,* no. 18 (Winter–Spring 1960), pp. 43–45.

[51] For an early DLP attack on Chinese travel, see Francis McManus, *CPD,* S 10, May 1, 1957, p. 522.

invitations *by the Peking Government* to visit China—which loaded the question slightly—only 22 per cent were expressly opposed.[52]

### AUSTRALIAN TRAVEL TO FORMOSA: THE AUSTRALIA–FREE CHINA ASSOCIATION

IF AUSTRALIAN travel to China stirred up uneasiness among anti-Chinese Australians, it also upset the Formosan authorities. Until 1956 Australian travel to Formosa had been a rarity. When it occurred, it tended to be by individuals rather than delegations, and most of those who went, like early Australian visitors to China, were heavily predisposed toward the regime—people such as Goddard and Kent-Hughes. In 1956 the Nationalist Embassy in Canberra began a long-term program designed to counter the growing China traffic. Twelve Australians of stature were issued invitations to visit Formosa at the expense of the Nationalist Government. Deliberately, there was a heavy emphasis on political persons. Deliberately, both Government and Opposition supporters were invited. Eight Parliamentarians went, including ALP Senator Donald Willesee and Charles Morgan, ALP MHR. The delegation was led by Sir John Latham, former Chief Justice of the High Court of Australia. The group spent ten days on Formosa. On departing, Latham said on behalf of the delegation that the facts on Formosan social, economic, and political progress had been sorely distorted in the past. It would be desirable for increased trade and cultural exchanges to develop between Australia and Formosa. While it was for the Australian Government to make the decision, the group favored Australian representation on Formosa.[53]

[52] *AGP,* nos. 1288–1298, December 1957–January 1958.

[53] See *SMH,* July 28, 1956; *China News* (Canberra), August 24 and 30, 1956; P. E. Lucock, Country Party MHR delegate, in *NSW Countryman,* September 1957.

The Formosan authorities were encouraged by this successful Australian visit, and stepped up their efforts to interest Australia in Formosa, and at least indirectly tried to distract Australia from China. Shortly before the Australian student delegation left for China, an invitation was received from the Formosan student organization, suggesting a visit to Formosa before the Australians went on to China. The offer was rejected, for it was properly interpreted as a tactic designed to anger the Chinese and lead to a cancellation of the China trip. In mid-1957 a group of Australian trade unionists visited Formosa on the invitation of the National Federation of Labor in Formosa. This was roughly the time when ACTU delegations were beginning to visit China intensively. The Australian visitors to Formosa were given an excellent reception, including a meeting with Chiang Kai-shek, and returned to write a highly laudatory report.[54] The following year the Nationalist Government extended an all-expense-paid invitation to Greg O'Dwyer, who had been to China as deputy leader of the 1957 student delegation. O'Dwyer became the first Australian observer to visit both China and Formosa.[55]

Starting in 1958, the Formosan cause was given a lift by the founding of the first chapter, in Victoria, of the Australia–Free China Association. The Association has since established branches in New South Wales, Queensland, and Western Australia. Inspiration for the AFCA did not come from the Nationalists themselves, but indirectly the Nationalist efforts to stimulate Australian visits from 1956 on were responsible. By 1958–60 there were people in the several states who had visited Formosa, were impressed, and believed that for far too long Australia had neglected the country and knew too little about it. What

[54] J. P. Maynes, compiler, "Report of the First Delegation of Australian Trade Union Officials to Visit South-East Asia," 1957, mimeo., Formosan account on pp. 4–9.

[55] See *SMH,* September 4, 1958.

information came through, either in the press or from intellectual-academic sources, was badly slanted. The ALP had since 1955 adopted a relatively pro-China policy, there was a strong flow of Australians to China, and some corrective was needed. Interestingly, however, the formation of AFCA branches was not stimulated by a wish to counter the ACS, which had been operating for some years.

The AFCA does, nevertheless, resemble the ACS in several respects. First, it is organized on a state basis, with virtually no Federal bond among the branches. Second, like the ACS, it is not by any means a study group. The AFCA is an explicitly pro-Formosan organization, and simply reverses the main objectives espoused by the ACS. It is interested in exposing the domestic and international wickedness of China. It wishes to emphasize the progress taking place on Formosa. It resists all attempts to recognize China or seat her in the UN, and wishes to preserve the *status quo* in these respects, plus urging the placement of an Australian diplomatic establishment on Formosa. It naturally encourages travel to Formosa.[56] Although its branches do not publish newsletters, the reading of *China News,* the Nationalist Embassy's newsletter, is promoted. Occasional booklets are issued, not just to members but to influential persons at large. The New South Wales branch, probably the most active of the four chapters, produced a brochure in 1963 entitled "China . . . Free or Red?" This publication was distributed among all Federal Parliamentarians, all state legislators in Australia, and many academicians, newsmen, and so on. In November of 1959, on the invitation of the Victorian AFCA, Dr. Ku Cheng-kang, president of the board of directors of the Asian People's Anti-Communist League, visited Australia to speak at a Melbourne "freedom rally," a counter to the Melbourne Peace Congress. The New South Wales branch

[56] See "Australia-Free China Association [NSW Branch] Constitution," mimeo., objectives listed on p. 1.

in particular maintains close relations with the Embassy in Canberra, which is useful in the exchange of ideas, but structural ties between the Association and Nationalist diplomatic or consular bodies are intentionally avoided.

As is true with the ACS, the AFCA imposes no restrictions on the political affiliation of its members, though in practice it too is slanted in its composition. Communists obviously do not join. There are ALP electors in the Association, but almost no prominent and formal ALP members, since ALP's policy contradicts AFCA policy. Kenneth Gee, the New South Wales President, was at one time an ALP candidate for political office. A number of Federal Parliamentarians from the Government side belong to the AFCA. In Victoria, this has included Senator John Gorton, a Liberal minister, and ex-Senator George Hannan. Hannan is President of the AFCA and the Asian People's Anti-Communist League in Victoria, where the two groups are identical in membership, and is also national President of the APACL. Broadly speaking, the AFCA branches are predominantly Liberal in membership. Resident Chinese also belong, to a much wider degree than obtains in the ACS and certainly in greater proportion than their numbers in the general population would suggest. The New South Wales branch, which has enrolled some 100 members, has about 30 Chinese. At one time Nationalist officials in Australia probably made efforts to recruit local Chinese into the AFCA, though the Association and the Nationalists believe that the AFCA can do its job best if it remains basically non-Chinese Australian in composition.

The presence of the AFCA has helped to stimulate Australian travel to Formosa, though the Association has played a smaller part in this task than the ACS has exercised regarding movement to China. Because there are Nationalist diplomatic and consular missions in Australia, travel arrangements in general can by-pass the AFCA.

Then too, the Nationalists, who feel they cannot afford poor publicity or be particular in other ways, impose next to no conditions on who may come to Formosa. It is a completely hypothetical point, but Dr. Chen Chi-mai, the Ambassador in Canberra, assured the author that Ted Hill would not be debarred from visiting Formosa. Hence whatever "screening" function the ACS may serve for Australian movement to China, no counterpart effort by the AFCA is required.

The flow of Australians to Formosa has gone on apace. Apart from visits by Australian Government personnel, which will be analyzed in the next chapter, a variety of people have gone—Parliamentarians from both sides, businessmen, unionists, athletes, correspondents, and so on. In January of 1961, at Taipei, a Sino-Australian Cultural and Economic Association was formed, whose functions include sustained Australian interest in all aspects of Nationalist China, including the exchange of visitors.[57]

## THE ALP: TRAVEL TO FORMOSA AND CHINA AND RELATIONS WITH THE AFCA AND ACS

TRAVEL to China and/or Formosa, plus associated matters, have caused special problems for two significant Australian bodies, the Labor Party and the ACTU. Since 1955, the ALP has officially favored Australian diplomatic recognition and a UN seat for China, which by definition clashes with the stated objectives of the AFCA. It is not therefore possible for Labor Parliamentarians to take out formal membership in the Association. Nonetheless, there is a group within the Parliamentary ALP, perhaps 12 to 15 strong, which on balance prefers the AFCA's position on recognition and UN seating to its own party's policy. The AFCA is aware of the situation. It does not encourage ALP men to force the issue by joining the

[57] *China News* (Canberra), July 4, 1962.

Association. It feels instead that these Parliamentarians are perhaps even more useful allies outside the AFCA than if they were in it. Because these ALP personalities do not actually belong to the AFCA and no direct conflict of interests arises, the ALP has not faced a disciplinary problem.

However, some of these ALP men have acquired their convictions on Chinese questions as the result of visits to Formosa. There is nothing in the ALP's program which forbids travel to any country. A visit to Formosa by Evatt, Calwell, or Whitlam would not have contravened Party policy, but it would have exposed the party to serious internal strife, since a ranking member's presence would have been construed as an indirect betrayal of policy. The author is able to say that one of these three men at one time almost visited Formosa, but reconsidered. With lesser figures in the party the story has been different. Willesee and Morgan, both ALP Parliamentarians, went to Formosa with the 1956 delegation at the Nationalist Embassy's invitation. Sir John Latham's parting remarks in Taipei, with which all delegates agreed, included a call for Australian representation on Formosa, which meant that Willesee and Morgan were attaching themselves to a China policy even *more* pro-Formosan than the Menzies Government's. It is understood that the Willesee–Morgan trip, to say nothing of the favorable conclusions reached by the delegation, attracted the attention of the ALP's Parliamentary Executive. No effort was made to punish them—contrary to one current story, which has it that Evatt was pushing for expelling them from the party. But there were murmurs of displeasure. Perhaps in part because no sanctions were attempted against Willesee and Morgan, other ALP men have subsequently gone to Formosa. In 1960, Francis Stewart of New South Wales, at a press conference on Formosa, expressed his wish for an early recovery of mainland China from Communist rule, and spoke impressively of his Formosan experience.[58] In 1963 Fred Daly, another New South Wales Labor Parliamentarian, not only made an extensive tour of Formosa, but also went to Quemoy,[59] which the ALP officially regards as part of China and whose transfer to China's rule it preaches. Appraisal of this situation's impact on the ALP's China policy will be deferred until the next chapter. What stands out for present purposes is that ALP trips to Formosa have contributed to sympathetic reactions, and that the AFCA enjoys the spiritual adherence of ALP individuals who have no formal or even informal contact with it.

ALP visits to China herself have not, of course, created any conflict with ALP policy. There has been only one official ALP delegation in China, that of 1957, which comprised Haylen, Percy Clarey, Charles Griffiths, and Senator Arnold. A number of others have gone since, but never an ALP Parliamentary Leader or Deputy Leader—a consideration which also can more conveniently be treated in a later context. There is, however, one special sidelight of the 1957 visit which should be mentioned here. Shortly before the ALP delegation was scheduled to leave Australia, Arnold was approached by a U.S. Embassy official in King's Hall, the spacious foyer of Parliament House. Arnold was urged not to go to China. If he changed his mind, a round-the-world trip and an expenses-paid holiday in America would be provided for him. If he persisted in going, he would not in future be welcome in the United States. The story comes from Senator Arnold himself, who spoke for the record. It is doubtful that such an approach could have been the work of an individual operating without official backing, for if Arnold had accepted the offer

[58] *Ibid.,* October 13, 1960. Also see *ibid.,* October 6, 1960.
[59] *Ibid.,* September 2, 1963.

money and arrangements would have been needed to fulfill the other end of the bargain.

The 1945 ALP Federal Conference resolved that no member of the Labor Party in any state of Australia could officially represent the Party on the platform of a Labor demonstration or function at which Communists were officially represented. This did not debar ALP Union officials from attending industrial gatherings such as the ACTU Congress.[60] The China policies of the ALP and the ACS are sufficiently close to avoid troubles of overlapping membership. But the ACS is full of both Laborites *and* Communists. Arnold, until 1965 an ALP Senator who is President of the ACS's Newcastle subbranch, has openly described his group as Communist managed. The apparent conflict between ALP rules and the ties of members of the ALP with the ACS has already created some disturbance, and could easily produce more. In August of 1959 Haylen and two ALP New South Wales state Parliamentarians were scheduled to appear at an ACS-sponsored discussion on Sino–Australian relations. It was reported that because two prominent Communists appeared with the Labor people, a complaint had been lodged with the New South Wales ALP state Executive.[61] In response, the ALP Federal electorate of Parkes, the constituency represented by Haylen, announced its unqualified endorsement of both his presence at the meeting and the remarks he expressed.[62] The following Friday the state Executive was scheduled to consider the complaints. Perhaps it failed to take any action because of the sudden death the day before of one of the accused, Gertrude Melville.[63] Perhaps it discarded the complaint because, just as the ACS meeting

[60] Excerpt supplied by courtesy of Mr. C. S. Wyndham, General Secretary, ALP.

[61] *Sydney Sun-Herald,* August 16, 1959.

[62] *SMH,* August 17, 1956.

[63] Sydney *Daily Telegraph,* August 22, 1959.

was about to begin, one of the Society's officers moved the two Communists off the platform and into the audience. The Communists did speak at the meeting, but technically were not on the same platform with the three Laborites. Equally plausible is the explanation that the state Executive found the whole matter of ALP-Communist contacts too explosive. If Haylen and his friends had been disciplined, what would come next? Would it have been necessary to purge all ALP people out of the ACS, including prominent figures such as Arnold and James in Newcastle?

Technically, state Executives are responsible for disciplinary measures in such cases, even though it is a Federal ALP regulation which is at stake. If Federal regulations are flaunted but the flaunting is condoned by state Executives, the Federal Executive has authority to interpose its own discipline. The author asked a wide range of ALP people whether they thought that joint organizational participation in a context such as the ACS, of common platform appearances with Communists in discussions revolving around China policy, were illegitimate. One replied that it was a question of common sense; joint membership in parent-teacher groups and joint platform appearances in such contexts had no political overtones and were quite in order—but the ACS situation was different. Another suggested that joint appearances of *any* kind were legitimate so long as Laborites and Communists debated on separate sides, rather than simply speaking to an audience as individuals.

The consensus of opinion was that, basically, the ALP–Communist nexus in the ACS is a clear violation of party rules. Abolition of the nonmingling clause, to bring theory into consonance with practice, is out of the question. The rule does inhibit mixing with Communists in many non-ACS situations and is favorably regarded by many Laborites. Also, the rule's abolition would be grist for the DLP's mill, a perfect target at which to fire charges that the ALP had completely sold out to the Communists. As matters stand now, the DLP snipes at Labor both for its ACS connections and because of Labor's alleged hypocrisy and inconsistency; [64] the rules bar mixing, but the mixing is tolerated. An ironic feature of the whole picture, as the author has been given to understand, is that the ALP rule on joint participation and appearances is not more rigidly enforced—even by "moderate" state Executives such as in New South Wales—because the ALP resents the DLP's constant carping and thinks it a matter of pride not to acquiesce!

### THE ACTU AND PROBLEMS OF RECIPROCAL VISITS

WHILE the ALP has faced some special problems arising out of visits to China and Formosa and AFCA and ACS relations, the ACTU nearly split over the question of reciprocal visits. In 1957, ACTU President Albert Monk and three other ACTU officials spent eleven weeks in China at the invitation of the All-China Federation of Trade unions. They attended the ACFTU Confederation, went to Peking's May Day festivities, and moved about China fairly extensively, concentrating their attention on social and industrial developments. Upon return, both Monk and the delegation at large issued reports of impressions, which were strongly favorable.[65] Nonetheless, the official explanation of the trip's inspiration needs to be noticed. There was the natural wish to learn about China and Chinese conditions. But it was also stressed that prior to the trip various individuals and groups of unionists, often with marked Communist leanings, had gone to China and had returned with flattering reports which were not

[64] For instance, *News Weekly,* September 2, 1959, and June 13, 1962. For a defense of ALP participation at the 1959 ACS meeting, see *Century* (Sydney), August 21, 1959.

[65] Both the Monk and ACTU reports are reproduced in *A.C.T.U. Bulletin,* Vol. 3 (December 1957), pp. 67–71.

always believed. The ACTU Executive therefore decided to accept the 1957 invitation in order to send an official, non-Communist, and respected group to China. One of those who went in 1957, Alex Macdonald, was a Communist, but he was only one in four, and would have been one in five had J. D. Kenny, who visited China some months later, been well enough to undertake the journey with his colleagues.[66] At all events, other ACTU trips followed. By the second half of 1959, three ACTU delegations had gone to China, and one to the Soviet Union. At the ACTU Congress held in August–September 1959, Monk moved a resolution recommended to Congress by the Executive, which would empower the Executive "to arrange visits to and from other countries including those countries from which the ACTU has accepted invitations." [67] In the course of his remarks, Monk made it clear that the resolution was meant to include trade union delegations from China and Russia, and estimated that the cost of importing visiting unionists, from whatever source, would average out to some £753.[68] An amendment designed to limit reciprocal visits to unions affiliated with the International Congress of Free Trade Unions, and empowering the ACTU Executive to carry out necessary arrangements, was defeated 79 to 307.

In this unsuccessful amendment lay the seed of serious trouble. Its challenge had been directed at Chinese and Russian visits, which were not encouraged by the ICFTU, a body with which the ACTU was affiliated. In 1955, the ICFTU Executive Board had resolved that international labor solidarity and the interests of freedom and world

[66] Monk, statement before ICFTU executive board, Brussels, December 1959, in ACTU, *Executive Report 1961,* p. 76; Clement Ridley (one of the 1957 tour members), *CPD,* S 18, November 9, 1960, p. 1471.

[67] ACTU, *Congress Minutes 1959,* at Melbourne, August–September 1959, p. 35.

[68] *Ibid.,* pp. 35–36.

peace "require that no free trade union organization should exchange delegations" with any nation which, in effect, was authoritarian in its treatment of human and especially trade union rights. The resolution further stated that the ICFTU general secretary should be informed of any invitation for such visits received by affiliated groups, so that these groups could be fully apprised of the dangers which lay behind "this Communist strategy of confusion and disruption of the free world labor movement."[69] Monk appeared before the ICFTU Executive Board in December of 1959. He explained that the ACTU had wished to reciprocate the courtesies already shown it, especially by the Chinese, who were close and important to Australia generally. Then too, the decision to arrange visits to Australia had been taken democratically at an ACTU Congress; while the ACTU subscribed to the ICFTU and recognized its decisions, it reserved the right to determine its own policies.[70] Later, at the 1961 ACTU Congress, he explained that, after hearing his statement, an ICFTU subcommittee deliberated and returned a report which repeated the terms of the 1955 resolution, but also indicated that this resolution had termed reciprocal visits with Communist countries *undesirable* though not necessarily *forbidden*.[71] In1960 nine ACTU-affiliated unions wrote to the ICFTU complaining about a Chinese union visit to Australia. The ICFTU Director replied at length that his body disapproved of such visits, and gave reasons. But he did not say that such visits were impermissible.[72] From all indications, therefore, the ACTU was knowingly breaking the spirit but not the letter of the ICFTU's position on reciprocal visits.

During 1960 the situation brought increasing signs of

[69] Text in *A.C.T.U. Bulletin,* Vol. 3 (May 1957), p. 37.

[70] Remarks in ACTU, *Executive Report 1961,* p. 77.

[71] ACTU, *Congress Minutes 1961,* at Paddington, NSW, September 1961, Appendix B.

[72] See *SMH,* November 4, 1960.

crisis to the ACTU. Early in the year the ACTU Executive decided to implement the 1959 Congress decision by assessing a levy on ACTU members of 2d. per adult male and 1½d. for females or juniors. This levy was designed to encourage visits by foreign unionists in general, but it was generally understood that delegations from Communist countries, and especially China, were to be included. The Executive then received a number of letters from member unions on the subject. Some supported the decision. Others took sharp exception, arguing that the levy was unconstitutional since it had not been endorsed by a majority of state branches; the Executive has no authority to impose such a levy. But at its August meeting the Executive determined that the 1959 Congress resolution had been plain. It had empowered the Executive to arrange reciprocal visits, and without distinction as to the political character of the countries to whose trade union bodies invitations could be directed. The Executive then set down a program of invitations. The order adopted was the General Secretary of the ICFTU, the ACFTU, the Asian regional organization of the ICFTU, the Soviet trade union movement, and the British TUC. The ICFTU General Secretary advised he would be unable to visit Australia. The ACFTU was asked and accepted, and the fat was in the fire.[73]

Whatever merit the constitutional argument of the ACTU dissidents may have carried, it is clear that they were far more incensed about ACTU sponsorship of Chinese unionists than they were about the legality of the move. At the 1959 Congress, it is recalled, the lost amendment had hoped to eliminate Communist countries from a reciprocal visits program, but included words identical to those in the passed resolution about executive authority to make needed arrangements—which at least by

[73] See the summaries in *A.C.T.U. Bulletin,* Vol. 4 (October–November 1961), p. 1, and *SMH,* August 19, 1960.

implication suggested the raising of funds. The attack against the Chinese visit also contained references to the inconsistency between ICFTU and ACTU policy, but was weakened by the fact that the ICFTU had not moved to bar the Chinese visit or otherwise discipline the ACTU; it simply was unhappy. Some of the unions which opposed the Chinese visit were essentially ALP in composition, though conservative. Others were in DLP hands. In any event, Monk and the ACTU faced a double problem. In the first instance, the opposing unions threatened to withhold their assessed levies. In doing so they risked not just censure but disaffiliation from the ACTU—a difficulty which Monk fielded by calling it hypothetical and that in any case no action could be contemplated until the ACTU Congress of September 1961 [74]—almost a year after the scheduled Chinese visit and in ample time, or so he thought, to patch up the cracks.

Secondly, a bitter campaign was undertaken against the Chinese and the effects that their visit would have on Australia. In Parliament, the proposed visit of two Chinese delegates and an interpreter was denounced by Liberal right-wingers as an invitation to spying and the forging of links between pseudo-unionists and genuine unionists.[75] The DLP and the NCC, who had started their vilification of a possible Chinese visit some time before, now shifted into high gear.[76] The Federal Secretary of the Clerks' Union, J. Riordan, noticed that the leader of the Chinese delegation was to be Liu Chang-sheng, Vice-President of the ACFTU. It was Liu, Riordan protested, who as recently as June 1960 had said that war could not be elimi-

[74] Statement of August 30, 1960, in *ibid.*, August 31, 1960.

[75] Especially Wentworth, *CPD*, HR 28, August 25 and 26, 1960, p. 500.

[76] Australian Democratic Labor Party, Victorian Central Executive, *Information Bulletin*, no. 29/1959 (May 22, 1959); *News Weekly*, May 13, 1958, May 25, 1959, and February 24, August 31, September 7 and September 28, 1960.

nated while imperialism existed—there were "just" wars and "unjust" wars, and Communists must be prepared to support the former. It therefore was unthinkable to countenance the presence of such a man, from such an aggressive country, in Australia.[77] When in defense Monk declared that the Australian visit could open the Chinese' eyes to the way of life in the free world, one editorial writer scoffed, and asked how anyone in his right mind could believe that "seasoned Communist gangsters . . . will change their minds by having a cup of tea with Mr. Monk or visiting an Australian glass factory?"[78]

The Chinese stayed in Australia from October 10 to November 5, and a hectic visit it was. The day after their arrival the Chinese were scheduled to attend a reception at the Sydney Trades Hall. Demonstrators appeared, among them DLP supporters, Nationalist-oriented Chinese Australians, and members of the right-wing Clerks' Union. They carried placards with messages such as "Phony Unionists" and "Release Enslaved Chinese Workers." Some skirmishing and exchange of blows occurred with "loyal" unionists. When the Chinese showed up, heavily built union officials had to form a human cordon to get them out of the taxi and into the Hall.[79] Then on to Brisbane for the Chinese. At the airport more skirmishing between rival unionists broke out, and one man was knocked unconscious.[80]

Next came Adelaide, together with inordinate precautionary measures by the ACTU hosts. The Chinese were placed on a "changed" incoming flight, and while in Ade-

[77] See *SMH,* September 28, 1960. For another union's objections, see the Ironworkers' protests in *ibid.,* July 7 and August 20, 1960.

[78] "A Cup of Tea with Mr. Monk," *Observer,* October 15, 1960.

[79] *SMH,* October 12, 1960. For a DLP version of the event, see *News Weekly,* October 19, 1960.

[80] *Sydney Sun-Herald,* October 16, 1960.

laide they were barely exposed to the public.[81] But if Adelaide was a tame experience, Melbourne most certainly was not. Melbourne was ACTU headquarters and also DLP country, with predictable results. When the Chinese landed at Essendon airport, fights immediately erupted between rival unionists.[82] But the worst was yet to come. Before the Chinese were scheduled to visit the Melbourne Trades Hall, about 500 angry persons of each persuasion milled around the area. The anti-Chinese demonstrators massed their forces and raised their banners. The pro-Chinese faction charged and ripped down the banners. "Men reeled from struggling, punching groups with bloody faces and ripped clothing. Banner poles were used to bash yelling groups who ripped the slogans." Peak hour traffic in Victoria Street, where the Trades Hall stands, was thrown into chaos. Forty police originally on duty had to be heavily reinforced before the contestants could be separated.[83]

Both sides accused the other of having instigated the ugly scenes around the country. Monk and the ALP generally said the demonstrations and fights had been the doing of the DLP, acting on Santamaria's instigation, who in fact had gone on a Catholic television program in Melbourne on October 23 to urge a "nation-wide tide of protests" against the Chinese.[84] It was also pointed out that among those seen on the anti-Chinese side at the Melbourne Trades Hall were men in clerical dress.[85] Santamaria told the author (it was also reported in the *News Weekly*) that the DLP and NCC felt they had to protest the Chinese visit. People were brought together to picket, but this was a democratic privilege. They were orderly but

[81] *News Weekly,* October 26, 1960.
[82] *SMH,* October 25, 1960. [83] *Ibid.,* October 28, 1960.
[84] *Ibid.,* October 24, 1960.
[85] See *Labor,* November 1960. Also see Monk's accusations in *SMH,* October 25, 1960.

were attacked by pro-Chinese thugs, not *vice-versa*.[86]

The visit of the Chinese had therefore been a frightening experience for the ACTU. The ACTU had been abused for its violation of the ICFTU spirit and for its reception of men who were bogus unionists in the first place and enemies of Australia in the second place. The Chinese visit had been a nightmare of riots and street fights. Many unionists had stayed away from receptions, so that dining-rooms and halls stood half-empty before the Chinese. Now the ACTU was confronted by the prospect of being pulled apart by the refusal of 19 unions to pay their levies. A February 1961 poll indicated that only 11 per cent of Australian trade union members and their wives, against the background of the Chinese visit, believed that unionists should meet the costs of Chinese and Russian labor officials invited to Australia.[87] But on the side of the obstreperous unions there also was reason to seek accommodation. Disaffiliation from the ACTU would deprive them of considerable advantages and influence, not the least being the wish of DLP unions to maintain a foothold in the ACTU and to fight Communism there. Since Labor had split at the political level, retention of the remaining union ties was especially important.

By slow and unsure steps a *modus vivendi* began to emerge. In May of 1961 the ACTU Executive decided to postpone any further visits either way until consideration could be given to the question by Congress later in the year. The Executive threw out a peace offering to the dissident unions. If they paid their past and current reciprocal visits levy, such money would be applied exclusively to underwriting the visits of unionists from ICFTU countries. They would also be able to enjoy full representation at the 1961 Congress. But the offer did not satisfy. The unions failed to pay, and the ACTU had no choice

[86] *News Weekly,* November 2, 1960.

[87] *AGP,* nos. 1515–1530, March–May 1961.

under its regulations but to deny them representation on account of their "non-financial" status.[88]

This threw the ball back into the ACTU's court. By August of 1962 it was reported that a compromise had been achieved. The hold-out unions would pay their owed levies and would be restored to good standing, while the ACTU promised not to invite Communist unionists in the future.[89] The final decision on visits had to await the 1963 ACTU Congress in September 1963. The right-wing unions paid their obligations and were seated at the Congress. Two related resolutions were passed. One declared that while Congress *was not* departing from its 1959 position, it was now allowing visits by union *observers* to overseas countries (without restriction on country), but without the right of such observers to commit a sponsoring union to policy declarations or to vote on any specific questions. The second resolution empowered the ACTU Executive to carry out a pragram of reciprocal visits with "particular attention" being given to the Asian region. Money for such invited unionists would be draw from the previous unexhausted levy, or by any levy struck in future by Congress, i.e. *not* the Executive.[90]

To the words of these resolutions must be added the informal understandings which were attached to them. There is no specific bar on Chinese being invited to Australia by the ACTU, but it was agreed that emphasis on the "Asian region" would mean non-Communist countries in Asia. At the 1963 Congress a right-wing union moved an amendment which would have expressly excluded China from the countries eligible for such visits, but it was

[88] *A.C.T.U. Bulletin,* Vol. 4 (October–November 1961), p. 1; J. D. Playford, *Doctrinal and Strategic Problems of the Communist Party of Australia, 1945–1962,* Ph.D. thesis, Australian National University, 1962, pp. 373–374.

[89] *SMH,* August 15, 1962.

[90] ACTU, *Congress Minutes 1963,* at Melbourne, September 1963, pp. 26–27.

voted down. In practice, the amendment was superfluous, but the ACTU leadership had saved some face by not allowing the exclusion of China or other Communist countries to be mentioned in the resolution. The ACTU won a point by extracting the unpaid levy, but it was clear that this or future money for reciprocal visits would not be applied to Communist unionists. The first resolution, in fact, was a reversion to the pre-1957 position. Individual ACTU unions may send members to Communist countries, but only as observers and without any commitment of policy or outlook falling either on the sponsoring union or the ACTU. An attempt by a right-wing union to preclude observers traveling to Communist countries was defeated. The right-wing thereby won something in that no more official groups were to visit Communist countries, but the ACTU leadership salvaged observers. It is early to tell how long and successfully these understandings will survive. In February of 1963, considerably before the Congress, the ACTU Executive declined a Chinese invitation to May Day celebrations.[91] In 1964 unionists did go to Peking, but as observers and no more.[92] A few years ago the ACTU was drifting toward a split. Neither side wanted this, and satisfactory repairs were made. Perhaps neither side will again wish to allow visits to and from China to serve as a great and divisive wedge.

## GOVERNMENT POLICY ON THE MOVEMENT OF CHINESE TO AUSTRALIA

WITHIN the story of the ACTU-sponsored Chinese visit stood the fact that, despite heavy criticism of the trip, the Government issued visas. Was this typical of Government policy? Has there been a generally liberal trend in visas for Chinese as well as in passports for Australians wishing to visit China? Official policy has never been stated with any

[91] *SMH,* February 15, 1963.
[92] *Sydney Sun-Herald,* March 29, 1964.

precision. The available statements have been brief indeed. One came from Barwick in 1962. Essentially, he said, Australia allows visas for Chinese who wish to enter for commercial purposes, but draws a distinction with the "attendance by Chinese Communist propagandists at gatherings of the Australian Communist Party or its fronts, for which visas are courteously but firmly refused."[93]

Regarding the first category of Chinese, namely traders and bankers, the record of visa awards has in fact been liberal. There was an instance in 1958 when a Chinese trade delegation, which had come for two months, asked for a two-month extension but was granted only one month, without official explanation.[94] The author is not aware of any refusals of visas to commercial persons. The factor of length of visit may have been cleared up after 1958 because the Chinese themselves have not tried to overstay their business time.

Instances of Chinese visitors to Communist or Communist front group functions are more difficult to judge. In 1958 the Government denied visas to two Chinese who had hoped to attend the triennial Congress of the CPA. It was intimated by Immigration Minister Alexander Downer that had the Chinese asked to enter for about two weeks, sufficient time in which to attend the Congress, they would have been let in. But they applied for six-week visas, which suggested some "ulterior motive."[95] On the occasion of the next CPA Congress, in 1961, news that Soviet Party officials had been denied entry was first learned in Australia through a Radio Moscow broadcast. Government officials would not comment, but unofficial sources in Canberra confirmed the report, and indicated that Chinese and Italian as well as Russian delegates had

[93] Barwick, "Australian Foreign Policy 1962," p. 12. Also see Hubert Opperman, *CPD*, HR, August 25, 1964, p. 591, and his comment in *ibid.*, October 22, 1964, p. 2206.

[94] John Hetherington in Melbourne *Age*, July 7, 1958.

[95] *CPD*, HR 18, March 27, 1958, p. 746.

been denied visas. In any case, no Chinese attended the Congress.[96] In 1964 the Moscow-inclined CPA invited to its Congress delegates from various foreign Communist parties. The Chinese were not invited, understandably. But of the nine delegations invited from various countries, only three—British, Canadian, and New Zealand—were allowed entry. It would stand to reason that a Chinese delegation would have been kept out, just as the Russian, Italian, Mongolian, Indian, Cypriot, and Ceylonese were.[97] It would appear that Chinese have on occasion come to Australia for what have been more "front" than explicitly Communist functions, though in general a tough Government policy, plus Chinese foreknowledge that entry is discouraged, has kept political visits from China down to a trivial point.

The admission of Chinese trade unionists has not followed any steady pattern. Perhaps put more accurately, there have been two phases in visa policy toward such visitors, through 1960 and after 1960. In 1956 both Chinese and Russian unionists were invited to Australia by the Boilermakers' Union, which was under Communist direction. It was the first important Chinese group to enter Australia. The Chinese remained in Australia a little over a month. They toured various states, looked in on workshops, mines, building jobs, farms, and schools. They generally hobnobbed with left-wing unionists, but also met Albert Monk. There apparently was some heckling against them in Newcastle, but their visit was largely uneventful.[98]

It is difficult to imagine that the relative peace, quiet, and uneventfulness which surrounded the 1956 Chinese visit inclined the Government to award visas for the 1960 trip. After all, strong controversy was already brewing by

[96] *SMH,* June 8 and 9, 1961. [97] *Bulletin,* July 4, 1964.

[98] See accounts in *SMH,* March 3, April 18 and May 8, 1956; editorial comment in *ibid.,* May 4, 1956, and in Brisbane *Courier-Mail,* May 3 and June 7, 1956; a summary of the Chinese' own impressions is in *Labor,* May 1957.

the time the Government needed to make its decision on visas. Probably, however, the Australian Government had no idea of how raucous the four-week visit of the Chinese would be. More than likely, the Government was reluctant to deny visas to people officially sponsored by Australia's largest and most influential trade union body. It maintained that the visit was the ACTU's own internal concern.[99] The extent of the Government's intervention was the promise that the Chinese would not be permitted to inspect defense and related industries, which was natural enough.[100]

But six months after the 1960 visit the Government blocked visas for two Chinese unionists who had been invited by the Boilermakers and other metal unions, and by some building trade unions. F. Purse, Federal Secretary of the Building Workers' Industrial Union, claimed that an Immigration Department official had telephoned him with the news that "the decision is in the negative for reasons that cannot be disclosed." [101] It is not normal practice for the Immigation Department to announce reasons for visa refusals, so nothing special should be read into this comment. What is plain, however, is that the Immigration Minister personally handles visa applications from Communist countries, and that very definitely this was so in the 1961 case. Most likely, the Government was not anxious for a repetition of the 1960 experience—a visit which the *News Weekly* later claimed would have brought on demonstrations "three or four times higher" than those of the previous year.[102] The Communist paper *Tribune* claimed that Monk was seeking a reversal of the ban,[103] but at all events this invitation was minor league in comparison with 1960, and could therefore more readily be stopped by Canberra. The

[99] William McMahon, *CPD,* HR 28, September 23, 1960, p. 1486.

[100] Menzies, *ibid.,* August 31, 1960, p. 585.

[101] *SMH,* April 28, 1961. [102] *News Weekly,* May 3, 1961.

[103] *Tribune* (Sydney), May 3, 1961.

fact that an election was expected within the next half year was surely another factor which Downer and his colleagues counted when weighing the advisability of another controversial Chinese visit. Under the ACTU's new policy on visits, the Government may not need to face the choice of admitting or blocking Chinese unionist entrants for some time to come.

In the field of cultural-artistic visits by Chinese, the Government's record has been spotted by some truly dismal behavior. Olympic Games were scheduled to be held in Melbourne starting on November 22 of 1956, a grand event for small yet sports-minded Australia. The Chinese Classical Theatre Company, some 80 or 90 strong, had originally been billed to perform in Australia during August and September, and the Government had allowed visas. Then the Chinese asked for a rescheduling of their Australian tour. Arrangements were made with the Australian management and, so far as everyone was concerned, the Company was to open at Melbourne's Princess Theatre on November 11, shortly before the Games were to start.

In mid-October Menzies rose in the House and said that the Company would be free to perform in various Australian cities, including Melbourne, but could not perform in Melbourne at the time planned. Considerable controversy might be aroused, given the strong feelings of various people about Communist China, and it was inappropriate to allow the Games to be poisoned by acrimony of this or any other kind.[104] It was reported in the press that the Company, then on tour in New Zealand, had been asked for a written guarantee that it would not appear in Melbourne just before or during the Games. If no such guarantee were forthcoming, the Company could not come to

[104] *CPD,* HR 13, October 18, 1956, p. 1601. Also see the prior announcement in *SMH,* October 17, 1956.

any Australian city until the Games had finished, and perhaps would be debarred entirely.[105]

Politely and without recrimination, the Chinese consented to rearrange their Australian itinerary. But the Government had no peace from its critics, of whom there was an abundance. Evatt's reply to Menzies was brief and to the point. The Government's decision was foolish and poorly rationalized. A Chinese team was going to perform at the Games, and a Chinese artistic group should not be singled out for punishment. The Government's decision would bring Australia into contempt and ridicule just as the world's eyes were turning on her. "The Government," said Evatt, "should be ashamed of itself!" [106] The press, especially in Melbourne and Sydney, could not have agreed more with Evatt. The decision was termed an "extraordinary blunder" which would surely make Australia a laughingstock abroad, for the Chinese actors were no more liable to provoke unmannerly demonstrations than the various Communist athletes in the Games.[107] The *Sydney Morning Herald* wrote mockingly that no Games item had been canceled because a Nationalist Chinese might chase a Communist Chinese athlete around Melbourne with a javelin.[108] The conservative *Bulletin* argued that the decision only testified to Australia's provincialism; such an incident would be unthinkable in sophisticated cities abroad, and probably the Company would even pass muster with Senator McCarthy.[109] The Melbourne *Age* had its own brand of sarcasm: "If we are so sensitive that we cannot allow . . . [the Company] in Melbourne during the Olympics, then why not ban Beethoven because we have had a couple of wars with

[105] Melbourne *Argus,* October 18, 1956.
[106] *CPD,* HR 13, October 18, 1956, pp. 1601–1602.
[107] Melbourne *Herald,* October 19, 1956.
[108] *SMH,* October 19, 1956. [109] *Bulletin,* October 24, 1956.

Germany in recent years? It all makes the same kind of nonsense." [110]

One of the few public voices of approval was raised by the Chinese Nationalists. Tien Fang-cheng, consul-general in Wellington, greeted the decision with the claim that the Company had been sent to Australia and New Zealand to extend China's bogus peace offensive.[111] The Nationalists had more reason to rejoice when, on November 6, the Chinese withdrew from participation in the Games, not because of the Opera Company incident but because the Nationalists were being allowed to compete. But a few days earlier the Chinese had their own laugh at Nationalist expense. At the official opening ceremonies of the Olympic Village, the Chinese Communist instead of the Nationalist flag was raised as the Nationalist contingent came on. It was a human mistake, but the Nationalists were furious, the Nationalist consul in Melbourne, K. Y. Leng, claiming that they would walk out of the Games entirely if Nationalist China and Australia were not such good friends.[112] Poor Leng. Four years later he attended a ceremony in the Mural Hall of Myer's department store in Melbourne. Big and bright, a Chinese Communist flag was hanging in the room. No one had any notion of how the flag had been put there.[113]

The question of what actually prompted the Government to prohibit the Company's appearance in Melbourne just before and partially during the Games remains unsettled. It cannot be answered with certainty, but some clues are available. One press report suggested that American sources had urged the rescheduling of the Company's appearance.[114] Saying is not proving, but it might be relevant to remember that in the following year the U.S.

[110] Melbourne *Age,* October 19, 1956.
[111] See Melbourne *Herald,* October 19, 1956.
[112] *SMH,* October 30, 1956. [113] *Ibid.,* October 22, 1960.
[114] Melbourne *Herald,* October 19, 1956.

tried to bribe Senator Arnold into not going to China, and that the U.S. was actively working to dissuade Australia from equalizing her Chinese and East European strategic embargo lists. Hence the report about advice rendered on the Opera Company is not entirely implausible. When Senator Neil O'Sullivan, a member of the Cabinet, was asked late in October of 1956 whether the decision had originated in Cabinet or had resulted from overtures made to Australia by a foreign power, his reply was evasive: "I am not in a position to answer the honorable senator's question in detail, but the decision was made by Cabinet after full consideration of all the circumstances involved."[115]

Another intimation is that DLP–NCC sources put pressure on the Government to block the Company's appearance. The correspondent Peter Russo saw something peculiar in what he asserted was NCC foreknowledge that the ban would be imposed.[116] Indeed, the *News Weekly* published a short item written at least a week *before* the ban was announced that the Government had decided to proceed in this way.[117] It is difficult to imagine that the Government would have taken its drastic step just because the DLP–NCC were displeased. But if right-wing elements of this sort in Victoria had let it be known to Canberra that mass demonstrations would be staged, which could have created chaos and untold embarrassment at the Olympic Games, the Government would have been disposed to listen carefully. Whether right-wingers in Victoria would have gone ahead with demonstrations, assuming they threatened such action to the Government, is of course problematical. In hindsight, however, there is the evidence of the 1960 protests against Chinese trade union visitors and the 1961 claim that another such visit would

[115] *CPD*, S 9, October 25, 1956, p. 897.
[116] Peter Russo in Melbourne *Argus*, October 19, 1956.
[117] *News Weekly*, October 10, 1956.

have been greeted by three or four times as many protesting demonstrators.

When the Government originally imposed the restriction, the explanation was that it was unwilling to court a situation in which harsh criticism and perhaps other troubles could arise, since the Company was Communist Chinese. In May of 1957 Sir Arthur Fadden told the House that one factor leading to the decision had been a request by Olympic authorities that as far as possible the associated dramatic entertainment should be Australian in origin.[118] More than two years later, Kent-Hughes, who had been Australian chairman and principal organizer of the Games in Australia, repeated the above point. He added that an Italian opera company had expressed a wish to perform at Games time, but since so many countries were participating in the Games, it was unfair to show preference to anyone. Therefore the Chinese Company was excluded for the same reason, and Kent-Hughes was "prepared to take full responsibility for having put that request to the Government on that basis." [119]

The first and apparent difficulty is that the original explanation by Menzies clashes with Kent-Hughes' version. The second difficulty is of a different nature. Kent-Hughes was and is an established critic of China and a supporter of the Nationalists on Formosa. As far back as February of 1955, while in Formosa, he said at a press conference that an investigation ought to be made to determine whether Chinese Communist athletes were truly amateurs, and whether the true spirit of the Olympiad was properly respected in China.[120] The author has also learned that at some point, despite his official Olympic capacity, Kent-Hughes urged the Nationalist team to arrive in Melbourne

[118] *CPD,* HR 15, May 22 and 23, 1957, p. 1885.

[119] *Ibid.,* HR 24, September 1, 1959, p. 755.

[120] Statement of February 13, 1955, in *China News* (Canberra), February 25, 1955.

very early, to beat the Chinese to the spot in the hope that China would be induced to withdraw from the Games entirely. Furthermore, it is firmly understood that Kent-Hughes himself believes the ban was imposed for political reasons, and that his own fear that the Chinese were carrying agents with them prompted an appeal to Menzies to block the Company's appearance. Firm conclusions are therefore hard to come by in the Chinese Opera Company fiasco. What is plain, however, is that not a single official explanation of what happened should be accepted at face value. A bad decision was made worse by evasiveness and contradiction.

Some years later arrangements were made by the Australian Elizabethan Theatre Trust to bring another Chinese theatrical group to Australia in late 1962. But this was also the period of armed Chinese encroachments on the Indian frontier. The Trust itself temporized a bit as to the propriety of bringing in the Chinese at such a delicate time. Then an official intimation came from Canberra that the Chinese would not be welcome. This settled the matter. The Trust advised the Chinese that their visit would need to be postponed. The Government was allowing extensive wheat and wool sales to China to continue, and it did not try to interfere in Gunn's proposed visit to Peking. But of course trade is valuable, and in any event the Government has consistently alleged that it neither sells anything nor promotes sales in the manner of the Wool Board. The Elizabethan Trust situation was different. The Trust enjoys a substantial financial contribution from the Government. Then too, there was the unhappy memory of what happened when the Chinese trade unionists arrived in 1960. In a period of international tension, even an artistic Chinese group would have met with demonstrations. Surely, too, the Government was not insensitive to political reverberations. It was then struggling along on a hairline majority, and was not prepared to face any more embarrassment than it could possibly avoid. But this time, in 1962, word was passed to the Trust in strict secrecy. The complications of 1956 were therefore avoided—no public debate, no entanglement in a web of rationalizations and contradictions, and so on.

The final point in this vein must be made with caution. In 1963 the New South Wales branch of the Australian Institute of International Affairs began to promote the idea of a "Living with China" symposium which would be staged in Australia in 1964 under the Institute's auspices. A number of foreign speakers were to be invited, including Chinese. Barwick was approached and asked if the scheme had his support, and he replied that it did. It is not known whether he was speaking for himself alone or had also consulted his colleagues in Cabinet. At all events, some preliminary contacts between the AIIA and the Chinese produced difficulties—the Chinese wanted to have every opportunity to rebut any unfavorable comments, etc. Certain persons in the Institute expressed scepticism about inviting Chinese. At point of writing, the symposium has been postponed for at least a year. It is not known what Barwick's successor, Hasluck, thinks about allowing Chinese to enter for such an event, nor are the views of the Government-at-large known. But Barwick's reply at least suggests that the Government is not inflexible. In the past it has been most generous with passports to China. It has been considerably less generous with visas entitling Chinese to enter Australia, and in the process has not always acquitted itself well.

# IX

# AUSTRALIA'S CHINESE DIPLOMATIC POLICY

MANY FEATURES of the Australian Government's China policy have reflected pliable policy positions. Active efforts to erect security barriers against Chinese influence in Asia have been coupled with a falling back from provocative or disdainful gestures. A stiff strategic embargo against China has not impaired lucrative trade relations. The movement of people between the two countries has been relatively free of official harassment. Pro-Chinese voices and writings in Australia, ranging up to the Peking-oriented Communists, have been scorned but not persecuted. At the diplomatic level, however, Australian policy has outwardly evinced tightness. Australia continues to recognize the Republic of China, and no overt gesture has ever been made to Peking to establish relations. In the UN the Australian vote has consistently been cast against the substitution of Communist for Nationalist China. To what extent has this posture represented an inconsistency in the total picture of Australia's China policy? Has the diplomatic policy been in fact as unyielding as might appear? Have the Government's critics produced sensible alternatives? What reasoning, in the last resort, has prompted the Menzies Government to proceed as it has? All these points require elaboration.

## THE EVIDENCES OF FLEXIBILITY

THE KOREAN WAR created special reasons for Australia not to shift her diplomatic policy toward China. But once the war had ended, there was widespread feeling in many quarters that the non-Communist world would need to learn to live with China. Menzies' own reaction to the closing of hostilities continued to be that he did not discuss recognition with enemies. No one knew whether the armistice would be honored, and how Chinese behavior would evolve.[1] These remarks were cast against a September 1953 ANZUS Council Meeting, at which the ministers had formally agreed to oppose a seat for Peking in the UN or diplomatic recognition by the three signatory powers.[2] Although Casey had been party to this declaration, it was reported that Australia and New Zealand both felt that prevailing circumstances could be altered as the result of the forthcoming political conference on Korea.[3] About this time, it will be remembered, Arthur Calwell was claiming that at the recent Commonwealth Prime Ministers' Conference Menzies had been talked into recognizing China. The *News Weekly,* temporarily the Labor Party's ally, was trumpeting the same accusatory language.[4] Following the ANZUS meetings, Casey undertook a tour of Asia, during and immediately after which these allegations of a forthcoming shift on China policy assumed more plausibility. Casey's remarks hardly corresponded to those of his own Prime Minister. Serious consideration must be given to Communist China's entry into the UN when she "demonstrates her bona fides," by which he meant her attitude in the coming three to six months on the situations in Malaya and Indo-China. If the UN were to perform as a world forum, it "must include all world ideologies." [5]

[1] *CPD,* HR 1, September 9, 1953, p. 10, and September 24, 1953, p. 652.

[2] See relevant text in *CNIA,* Vol. 24 (September 1953), p. 525.

[3] *New Zealand Herald,* August 5, 1953; *SMH,* September 11, 1953.

[4] *News Weekly,* August 5 and 19, 1953.

[5] Statements of October 17 and November 1, 1953, in *SMH,* October 18 and November 2, 1953, respectively.

But no agreement was reached on Korea, and in early 1954 Asia was beset by the crisis in Indo-China. Both T. Clifton Webb, New Zealand's External Affairs Minister, and Casey, worked toward a realistic settlement of the crisis. Both held interviews with Chou En-lai. Webb's conclusion was that Western nonrecognition of China and a bar to UN entry were inimical to a Far Eastern *détente.* He understood the depth of American feeling against China and realized that China would need to offer some evidence of pliability before a Western *volte face* could be taken toward her. But interested governments ought to edge the U.S. into a new and necessary posture, for there was danger "that by cold-shouldering China we drive her more firmly into the Russian orbit and defeat our own object." [6] This was the opinion of a New Zealand National—not Labor—Party External Affairs Minister, spoken in public view in Parliament. Casey, Australia's Liberal Government Minister, was just then stopping off in New Zealand. His reaction to Webb's statement was essentially noncommittal,[7] but in an interview which appeared a week later in *U.S. News and World Report,* repeating the requirement of some tangible evidence of Chinese good intentions, his meaning was close to Webb's. Casey did not think of himself as one who believed that "at no time and no circumstances should Red China be recognized diplomatically or admitted to the United Nations." [8] Later in the year, the UN once again invoked the moratorium on discussing the Chinese representation issue. Henry Cabot Lodge was content to declare that "the United States will not engage in a discussion of the substance of the question." [9] Casey cast Australia's vote on

[6] *NZPD,* Vol. 303, July 6, 1954, pp. 212–213. Also see *ibid.,* July 8, 1954, pp. 300–303.

[7] Statement of July 8, 1954, in *SMH,* July 9, 1954.

[8] "New Plan to Defend Southeast Asia," p. 53.

[9] UN General Assembly, *Official Records,* Ninth Session, 473rd Plenary Meeting, September 21, 1954, p. 4.

behalf of the U.S.-sponsored moratorium, but added that if the Chinese corrected their behavior "the day on which most of us might find it possible to accept the presence of its representatives in this Organisation might come sooner rather than later, at least so far as the Australian delegation is concerned." [10]

Then came the offshore island crisis of 1954–55. But 1955 was also the year of Bandung, the year of the "Geneva spirit" of goodwill, and generally of Chinese sweet reasonableness. Australia was not invited to participate in the Afro-Asian conference at Bandung, but she sent observers, including her Ambassador to Indonesia, and openly kept fingers crossed for a fresh, honest and relaxing dialogue by Chou En-lai.[11] Continuing his role of peacemaker, Chou returned home from Bandung and called for a grand nonaggression pact in Asia and the Pacific, and sweetened the pill by promising to negotiate the "peaceful liberation" of Formosa with local authorities there.[12] Casey did not ignore the offer. Chou's suggestion was "clearly worth exploring," and Casey hoped that progress at the forthcoming Sino-American discussions in Geneva could open the way to an exploration of wider questions [13]—presumably including recognition and UN seating.

Late in August of 1955 Canada's Lester Pearson said his country must soon take another, "searching look" at her China policy. It was "unfortunate" that Sino-Western conversations on outstanding issues had to be held outside the UN's councils, and it was unreasonable to demand "positive proof or utter purity from this or any other regime before we consider giving it formal diplomatic

[10] *Ibid.*, p. 7.
[11] Casey, statement of April 15, 1955, in *SMH*, April 16, 1955.
[12] Statement before National People's Congress, July 30, 1955, in *ibid.*, August 1, 1955.
[13] Statement of July 31, 1955, in *CNIA*, Vol. 26 (July 1955), p. 495.

recognition." [14] Casey happened to be in Canada several days later, much as his New Zealand visit of 1954 had coincided with Clifton Webb's remarks. Again Casey hedged, rather than risking an indiscretion. Australia was not thinking about the Chinese matter quite as positively as Canada, but it was "one of the matters on which we are doing a certain amount of thinking." [15] Speculation about Australia's intentions persisted. Australian diplomats in Asia and officials in Canberra were said to be disturbed about the *status quo* position. Menzies and Casey had not been fully communicative, but they were operating behind the scenes to bring about normal diplomatic relations with China as soon as it could be judiciously carried off—or so it was imagined.[16]

The year 1956 was more than the year of Suez and Hungary. It was still another season for speculation about Australia's Chinese intentions. Agreement that Australia was nearing a new position appeared among strange bedfellows. On the one hand, the *News Weekly* leveled its traditional accusation that Menzies had never ceased flirting with the idea of recognizing China, and that his pilgrimage to the London Commonwealth Prime Ministers' Conference was in part designed to find means to achieve this end.[17] Apparent confirmation arrived from quite different sources. *The Times* quoted one conference delegate as saying that a remarkable degree of open agreement had been reached; the Far Eastern situation was "incongruous" and "cannot last," and even more conservative Prime Ministers, namely Menzies and Strydom of South Africa, were reported to share this view. Menzies and St. Laurent of Canada, however, advised that little could be done to ease the situation until after the November elec-

[14] Statement in Vancouver of August 25, 1955, in Montreal *Gazette,* August 26, 1955.

[15] Statement in Ottawa of September 9, 1955, in *Sydney Sun-Herald,* September 11, 1955.

[16] *SMH,* August 9, 1955. [17] *News Weekly,* June 27, 1956.

tions in the U.S.[18] The Melbourne *Age,* one of Australia's most respected papers, said much the same thing; not even Menzies or Strydom were purported to believe that China's exclusion from the UN made any sense.[19]

Prior to the 1958 Australian elections, the author has been told, Casey informally sounded out the DLP on what its reaction would be should Canberra recognize Peking. He also wondered aloud in front of the person being questioned whether there were not certain elements in the U.S. State Department which might like Australia and other countries to extend recognition, as a bit of healthy arm twisting *vis-à-vis* the United States.

In 1959 came a series of public statements from Government ministers which again hinted at flexibility, and perhaps willingness to strike out along a fresh course. In a carefully prepared statement on China delivered to the House, Casey listed various obstacles to a change in Australia's Chinese diplomatic stance. But toward the close of his remarks he made it explicit that the prevailing position should *not* be interpreted as "a slamming of the door for all time. The world does not stand still." [20] Even Menzies himself, usually less adventurous than his External Affairs ministers have been in the handling of the subject, acknowledged that "there was no doubt the case for recognition was tremendously strong." [21] But the most controversial observation came from John McEwen. He remarked in a television interview that if the present Chinese regime remained in power—and it certainly seemed it would—"then in due course, at some point in time, the fact would be recognized by all countries as it has already been recognized by the United Kingdom and most great powers." Though McEwen later denied that any shift in

[18] *The Times* (London), July 3, 1956.
[19] Melbourne *Age,* July 9, 1956.
[20] *CPD,* HR 24, August 13, 1959, p. 199.
[21] Radio broadcast in London of June 25, 1959, in *SMH,* June 27, 1959.

Australian policy was being contemplated,[22] Santamaria attacked him with full force, alleging in particular that McEwen's desperate bid for Chinese trade was obscuring his vision on the terrors which Australian recognition of Peking held for the country.[23] The year 1959 was also the last full year in which Casey was External Affairs Minister. In Casey's last years in office, ministerial statements before the Joint Parliamentary Committee on Foreign Affairs left the unmistakable inference that Australia was seriously considering the recognition of China—according to an opinion supplied by a member of that committee. Casey lent credence to this view in a comment he made about a year after resigning office. He was pleased that the Kennedy Administration stood prepared to review the China problem. Menzies was about to visit the new President in Washington, and Casey hoped that the Prime Minister would probe the subject. It was becoming increasingly difficult to maintain the UN's quarantine against China. If only China had been more disposed to be less of a nuisance, things might now be different, for "a number of countries have been on the verge of rethinking the China problem, only to see Red China commit some devilish aggression against Korea, Vietnam, Burma, India or Laos." [24]

The search for clues and their meaning has never really disappeared, although it probably reached its recent crest in early 1961. As the year opened and the Kennedy Administration assumed office, Homer Bigart of the *New York Times* flatly asserted that Australian political leaders were convinced America faced certain defeat if she persisted in maintaining the moratorium on the Chinese seating question at the UN. These leaders were counting on a

[22] For McEwen's original and later explanatory statements, see *CNIA*, Vol. 30 (June 1959), p. 328.

[23] See Santamaria's statements in *News Weekly*, June 2 and 10, 1959.

[24] Statement of February 20, 1961, in *NYT*, February 21, 1961.

new two-Chinas line evolving in Washington, and themselves were wavering on the issue of Australian diplomatic recognition of China—though for the moment Menzies had promised not to break the line.[25] Menzies did visit the President. Although no official hint about the Chinese aspects of the discussion were made public, it was understood that the subject of China had been broached. The Nationalist Communications Minister, Dr. Shen Yi, then visiting Australia, went out of his way to recite the calamitous consequences of admitting Peking to the UN.[26] After Washington, Menzies moved on to London for a Commonwealth Prime Ministers' Conference. A dispatch to the Melbourne *Herald* insisted that *all* Prime Ministers had agreed that world tensions would be moderated only if China entered the UN, while Menzies was reported to have branded as "ridiculous" any Russo-Western disarmament agreement which lacked China's participation.[27] The *Canberra Times* wrote that the Prime Ministers in London had further agreed to unseat the Nationalists from the UN entirely if that became a condition of seating Peking.[28] Douglas Wilkie, writing in the Melbourne *Sun-Pictorial,* insisted that "inspired leaks" had recently been floated that Australia had joined the new U.S. Administration in marching ahead toward a fresh attitude on China.[29]

Sir Garfield Barwick, both before and during his tenure as External Affairs Minister, did not always dispel such conjectures. At the 15th UN session in 1960 he declared that the principle of universal representation in the UN was ultimately necessary.[30] In his appearance before the

[25] Homer Bigart in *ibid.,* February 2, 1961.
[26] Cited in *Sydney Sun-Herald,* March 5, 1961.
[27] Trevor Smith in Melbourne *Herald,* March 9, 1961.
[28] *Canberra Times,* March 10, 1961.
[29] Douglas Wilkie in Melbourne *Sun-Pictorial,* March 13, 1961.
[30] UN General Assembly, *Official Records,* Fifteenth Session, 894th Plenary Meeting, October 8, 1960, p. 544.

January 1964 conference of the Australian Institute of Political Science, he pointedly endorsed Casey's "no slamming of the door" axiom and urged Australian foreign policy to look ahead to the day when China (not necessarily a non-Communist China) would resume a full role among the nations.[31] When France announced her recognition of Peking, Barwick stressed the interest with which his Government would examine the terms of the final arrangement,[32] presumably to judge whether France could succeed in developing a two-China formula.

It is from this last point that further inference about the Government's view of the Chinese diplomatic problem might be drawn. Over the years the Government has found many occasions on which to state its reasons for not recognizing Peking or supporting its seating in the UN. Most of these reasons had an early origin and have generally been retained in the Government's lexicon, but since the late 'fifties one reason has tended to be the first mentioned in any recitation, or the one most heavily underscored. That reason, plainly stated, is that Peking has been intractable on a two-China solution. It has been unwilling to enter into relations with governments which deny Peking's automatic claim to Formosa, or to consider a UN seat while the Nationalists remain. The inference in point is that if the priority given this factor by Canberra matters, it means that Australia does not intrinsically oppose relations with China, or a Chinese UN seat, but is unwilling to contribute toward the sacrifice of the people and possibly the security value of Formosa. A two-Chinas attitude is therefore not unwelcome, and if Peking would consent to two Chinas other considerations inhibiting nonrecognition and UN seating might be disregarded.

[31] Barwick, "Australia's Foreign Relations," p. 23.
[32] Statement of January 28, 1964, in Melbourne *Age,* January 29, 1964.

THE EVIDENCE OF RIGID BEHAVIOR

DESPITE this record of apparent plasticity, of abundant hints and inferences that Australia was not happy with the diplomatic isolation of China, she has not deviated from the "hard-line" promoted by the United States. At the UN, she consistently voted in support of the Chinese moratorium. When in late 1961 Washington decided to yield to pressures from various governments and consented to the appearance of the Chinese seating question on the General Assembly's agenda, Australia followed—as did nearly everyone else, both the friends and critics of Red China. Once the decision to remove the moratorium had been taken, however, Australia joined with Colombia, Italy, Japan, and the U.S. to cosponsor a draft resolution, later adopted, which stipulated that any proposal to alter Chinese representation was an "important question" under the terms of Article 18 of the UN Charter, and therefore required a two-thirds majority. This naturally was designed to make a decision favorable to Peking more difficult to achieve. Then and henceforth, Australia has voted against seating Peking. The question immediately arises whether the press reports about the 1961 Commonwealth Prime Ministers' Conference contained any validity. The author has learned on excellent authority that nearly all these reports were fanciful. Menzies did not lead or even join any Commonwealth Prime Ministers' celebration to place Peking in the UN and perhaps to oust the Nationalists. Barwick's retort that the early reports were "highly imaginative" [33] was almost an understatement. The only accurate feature of the reports was that Menzies had urged on his colleagues the necessity of including China in any meaningful disarmament scheme—but it did not necessarily follow, as he later explained, that this would require

[33] Statement of March 9, 1961, in *SMH,* March 10, 1961. Also see Menzies, *CPD,* HR 30, April 11, 1961, p. 656.

China's presence in the UN, or widespread Western diplomatic recognition.[34]

Consider also the behavior of the Australian government delegates (there being also employer and employee delegates) at the International Labor Organization sessions when Chinese questions arose. Starting in 1950, challenges were raised by East European states against the presence of the allegedly bogus Nationalist delegates. The ILO's Credentials Committee just as consistently rejected the complaints, as of 1951 basing its ruling on the General Assembly resolution of December 1950 that UN specialized agencies should adhere to the Assembly's own views on representation in the event of a contest. Under ILO rules a unanimous ruling of the Credentials Committee is binding on the plenary body and is not debatable. Therefore the issue was not tested among the membership at large. But very quickly the Nationalists faced another complication. They had fallen behind in the payments of their ILO assessments and were in danger of forfeiting their vote. They pleaded special circumstances and eventually requested concessions on contributions. For several years the question was debated in plenary session. Most delegations argued the subject purely on the technical ground of whether the Nationalists were making a reasonable effort to pay, and therefore were entitled to concessions. India and Burma, to select two examples, injected explicit political overtones into their arguments; they were interested in voting against the Nationalists largely because the Nationalists had no standing as the representatives of China. The British trod an uneasy line between procedural and political argument and wound up voting against allowing the Nationalists to retain their vote. Australian government delegates consistently supported the Nationalists. Their arguments tended to stress the technical side of the question, but at the 1954 ILO session

[34] *Ibid.*, HR 32, August 15, 1961, p. 97.

Ralph Harry of Australia spoke some revealing words. He said that while this was not a debate on credentials as such, it had consequences for credentials. If the Nationalists were denied their vote because of financial arrears, China would be left without a voice in the ILO—yet the General Assembly had requested its specialized agencies not to follow a course different than its own.[35] Implicit in his remarks was the fear that a denial of the vote to the Nationalists might be just the kind of breach of the General Assembly's advice that could in future lead the Credentials Committee, and then the conference in plenary session, to remove the Nationalists and replace them with delegates dispatched by Peking. Indeed, in the same year at the ILO, Australia cosponsored a resolution to allow the Nationalists to retain their vote. This was also the year—1954—when Casey had much to say about the need to draw Peking eventually into normal diplomatic contacts with the international community. However, it is understood that on all important ILO questions, and certainly on the Chinese issue, the Australian government delegates were in close touch with Canberra, to the extent that their behavior in Geneva reflected Cabinet-level judgments.[36]

What stands out, therefore, is that while Australian spokesmen have time and again intimated a wish for a flexible diplomatic approach to China, their Government has invariably stopped short of any overt breach of a rigid line. In fact, it has seemed particularly disposed to demonstrate an unfailingly anti-Chinese posture in certain showdown situations. Among these could be counted the

[35] International Labour Conference, *Record of Proceedings,* 37th Session, June 17, 1954, p. 245.

[36] For partial confirmation, see Harold Holt's remarks in "Reports of the Australian Government, Employers' and Workers' Delegates to the Fortieth Session of the International Labour Conference, Geneva, June 1957," *Parliamentary Paper,* presented November 1957, p. 14.

cosponsorship of the 1961 "two-thirds majority" resolution in the UN, as well as the contribution of a specially constructed argument and cosponsorship of a resolution at the ILO designed to retain the Nationalists' vote but indirectly aimed at warding off eventual Chinese Communist representation. But has Australia operated behind the scenes on behalf of a more relaxed Chinese diplomatic policy? It is known that at London in 1961 Menzies definitely did not organize or join any "seat China" movement. The author's own crosschecking among various well-placed politicians and officials in Australia made it almost equally certain that Australia *has not* endeavored to talk the United States into a different Chinese diplomatic policy, or to receive American blessings for a changed Australian position. Australia has definitely remonstrated with Washington about other Chinese issues—such as the conduct of the Korean War and the disposition of the offshore islands—but almost surely not on diplomatic policy.

## SOME EXTERNAL FACTORS AFFECTING AUSTRALIA'S CHINESE DIPLOMATIC POLICY

THERE is an assortment of explanations which has dictated a preservation of the Government's Chinese diplomatic policy. Among these explanations, and the one which has served as a foremost public excuse for no overt shift, has been China's reluctance to accept a two-China solution. The Government's defense has been straightforward on this point. It is wrong to barter away the fortunes of Formosa's eleven or twelve million inhabitants, and inadvisable to forfeit Formosa's strategic value and political impact on Chinese communities elsewhere in Asia. Since Peking will not accept a two-China formula, support for its representation in the UN or Australian recognition are precluded.[37]

[37] For instance, see Casey, *CPD,* HR 24, August 13, 1959, pp. 196–197; D. O. Hay, before UN General Assembly, October 16,

The evidence of China's unwillingness to consider a two-China formula is decisive. When the ALP delegation visited China in 1957, Chou En-lai told the Australians that Sino-Australian diplomatic relations would be welcomed. But he frankly added that it was pointless for anyone to press for a two-Chinas arrangement in the UN. China would never consent to sit in that body with the Nationalists, and " 'If our friends forget this we are just not friends any more.' "[38] The inescapable inference was that diplomatic relations were likewise unacceptable with any government which would not enter into them unconditionally, i.e. without stating any reservations about Formosa. The following year Chen Yi made the same observations to Canadian sources,[39] while Chou went out of his way to scold Britain—who had recognized Peking years before—for not supporting China's seating at the UN. Only if Britain abandoned this mistaken, unfriendly, and American-leaning position could fully accredited ambassadors be exchanged.[40] By the close of 1964, flushed with success respecting her nuclear detonation, China imposed fresh conditions if she were to accept a seat at the UN. Not only would the Nationalists need to be removed from the General Assembly and the Security Council, but from all UN specialized agencies as well.[41]

Early in 1964 France expressed her intention to enter into relations with China. The joint Paris-Peking declaration made no mention of Formosa, whom France then recognized and with whom she had diplomatic relations. It simply spoke of the decision to establish relations, and of the agreement to designate ambassadors within three

---

1963, in *CNIA,* Vol. 34 (October 1963), p. 46; Barwick, "Australia's Foreign Relations," p. 23; Hasluck, *CPD,* HR, August 19, 1964, p. 352; Gorton, *CPD,* S, October 22, 1964, p. 1199.

[38] Haylen, *op. cit.,* p. 145.

[39] Interview in Toronto *Globe and Mail,* July 29, 1958.

[40] Interview in *The Times* (London), January 11, 1958.

[41] *NYT,* December 5, 1964.

months.[42] According to Barwick, France had advised Australia of her intentions in advance of the formal step, and had given assurances that no prior commitment had been made with Peking respecting France's relations with Taipei, France's future conduct on the Chinese question at the UN, or anything else. Australia would examine the development of the conditions on which French recognition would be carried out, Barwick added, since Peking's previous attitude had been a "principal impediment" to its wider acceptance by the international community.[43] But immediately afterward the Chinese produced their own gloss. The "spirit" of the agreement with France had been such as to preclude French relations with both Chinas, or to admit that the two Chinas could share UN representation.[44] In due time the Nationalists themselves severed relations with France. Had they not done so it is almost certain that Peking would not have exchanged missions with France until the Nationalists had been evicted from Paris. This surely was Australia's interpretation, and strengthened even further the conviction that it was hopeless to plot policies on a two-Chinas assumption.[45] Indeed, the Chinese reactions on Formosa have been so stubborn that American wishes in 1960 and again in 1961 to exchange correspondents with China were frustrated by Peking's insistence that the U.S. first renounce its "military occupation" of Formosa.[46]

This state of affairs has perplexed much if not most of Australian opinion. The press has for many years tended

[42] *The Times* (London), January 28, 1964.

[43] Statement of January 28, 1964, in *SMH,* January 29, 1964. Also see his remarks in *CPD,* HR, March 11, 1964, p. 473.

[44] *The Times* (London), January 29, 1964.

[45] Barwick, *CPD,* HR, March 11, 1964, p. 474. The difficulties inherent in a two-China approach are raised in B. D. Beddie, "Australia and the Recognition of China," *Australian Outlook,* Vol. 13 (June 1959), pp. 129–134.

[46] *NYT,* September 9 and 14, 1960, and Kennedy's news conference of March 8, 1961, in *ibid.,* March 9, 1961.

to back the principle of Australian recognition of China and a UN seat for Peking, but so often it has admitted that Formosa cannot be unceremoniously jettisoned.[47] The Labor Opposition, which since 1955 has favored recognition and UN representation for China, has quite consistently said the same thing. Its leadership openly supports self-determination by the Formosan people and leans toward two Chinas coexisting at the UN [48]—although the Party's official platform simply urges a "sympathtic and informed attitude . . . to the problem of Formosa." [49] In 1964 the ACTU Federal Executive moved beyond the stated Party platform. It adopted a resolution making the recognition of China explicitly conditional on the Formosan people's right of self-determination.[50] Australian public opinion has been inclined to react similarly. On the UN question, surveys have shown nearly even division between those who favor and who oppose Chinese seating, with a slight advantage to the former. But even among those who have favored Chinese seating, by far the greatest number have been disinclined to continue their support for Peking if its entry would entail eliminating Formosa from the UN. A November 1961 poll, for instance, yielded 42 per cent "for," 40 per cent "against," and 18 per cent "undecided" on Chinese UN seating. But after the 42 per cent had been asked if they were prepared to scrap Formosa to get Peking in, the adjusted total of Australia-wide backing for admission on such terms was

[47] For instance, Adelaide *News,* April 21, 1955; *Canberra Times,* August 4, 1958; Melbourne *Herald,* June 30, 1959; Melbourne *Age,* December 18, 1961.

[48] For instance, Evatt, *CPD,* HR 9, February 22, 1956, p. 121; Calwell, HR 29, December 6, 1960, pp. 3579–3580, and "Labor's Policy," pp. 21–22; Whitlam, "Australian Foreign Policy 1963," p. 18.

[49] ALP, *Proceedings of the 24th Commonwealth Conference,* p. 35.

[50] See *News Weekly,* April 2, 1964.

only 9 per cent.[51] The surveys on recognition have failed to raise a comparable question, i.e., if support for Peking would be desired at the expense of no concessions to Formosa. By inference, however, a feeling of public uneasiness can be detected. While there has tended to be a slight advantage for those favoring Australian recognition of Peking, the number of persons with "no opinion" has been extremely large since 1955—between 25 and 40 per cent. This is a greater number of "undecided" responses than has appeared on most foreign policy questions, and undoubtedly reflects uncertainty over what the recognition of China would imply for Formosa.[52]

Australian opinion, official and otherwise, has not been alone in regarding Peking's inflexibility on Formosa as a serious stumbling block to establishing normal diplomatic contacts. Although Canada and New Zealand have usually spoken out with less inhibition than Australia about reaching a *modus vivendi* with Peking, all major parties in both countries—Liberals and Progressive-Conservatives in Canada, National and Labor parties in New Zealand—have held office in recent years but have invariably found the impossibility of some two-Chinas arrangement to be a crucial deterrent to shifting their respective China policies.[53] It is a deterrent bound to affect Australia and a number of her friends and associates for some time to come.

[51] *AGP,* nos. 1558–1580, November 1961-January 1962.

[52] The latest available survey (December 1962) yielded 36% for recognizing Peking, 36% against, and 28% without an opinion. See *ibid.,* nos. 1653–1664, January-February 1963.

[53] On Canada, see Howard Green, *Canadian Parliamentary Debates,* HC, Session 1960–61, Vol. 4, April 26, 1961, pp. 4028–4029; Diefenbaker, *ibid.,* Vol. 8, September 20, 1961, pp. 8591–8592; Paul Martin, HC, October 22, 1963, pp. 3848–3849. On New Zealand, see Holyoke, statement of January 1, 1962, in *EAR* (NZ), Vol. 12 (January 1962), p. 27; Nash, statement of December 30, 1959, and March 23, 1964, in *ibid.,* Vol. 10 (January 1960), p. 33, and *SMH,* March 25, 1964, respectively.

Aside from this stumbling block, however, the Menzies Government has given other, somewhat more substantive reasons for retaining its present policy. It has argued that recognition of China—even if carried out by Australia alone—or Australian support for seating Peking at the UN, would produce undesirable repercussions in Asia. This, it has been intimated, might be true even if a two-China formula could be pieced together. It is almost gospel among most Australians that their country must be on strong, cordial, and if possible influential terms with Asia and Asians. One reading of this notion has convinced some that Australia's nonrecognition policy and behavior at the UN has antagonized Asian opinion. The Nationalist regime on Formosa is said to be notoriously unpopular among many nations in the region, and Australia's refusal to switch from Formosa to the "reality" of the regime in China is asserted to undermine the credibility of Australia's professions about eschewing colonialism and standing ready to cooperate with Asia's aspirations for a relaxation of international tensions. As Professor Macmahon Ball has put it, "The Asian image of Australia is shaped not only by what we do in the Colombo Plan but by the policies we follow on international issues to which Asians attach the deepest significance. Our policies towards 'colonialism' and 'racial discrimination' as well as our policy towards China and Formosa are likely to impress Asians more than anything we may do under the Colombo Plan."[54] More particularly, a reconsidered Australian China policy has even been recommended on grounds that

[54] W. Macmahon Ball, "Australia's Political Relations with Asia," in John Wilkes, ed., *Asia and Australia* (Sydney, London, Melbourne and Wellington: Angus and Robertson for the AIPS, 1961), p. 75. For other illustrations, see Percy Clarey in *Labor,* October 1957, and Justin O'Byrne, *CPD,* S 21, February 22, 1962, p. 87; C. P. Fitzgerald, "China and the United Nations," lecture before the Australia-China Society, Victorian Branch, September 16, 1961, mimeo., p. 3.

since Indonesia, whose behavior has proved to be so critical to Australia's interests, has decided to favor China, Australia's only sensible option is to ingratiate herself with Indonesia by recognizing China! [55]

It would be inaccurate to attribute insensitivity to the Government regarding the relationship between its Chinese diplomatic policy and Asian opinion. The Government has worked earnestly to maintain close relations with nonaligned as well as committed anti-Communist states in Asia. It is a fair surmise that one reason—though surely not the sole reason—why Australian spokesmen have highlighted Peking's truculence on a two-China formula has been the relative respectability of such an argument before neutralist Asian eyes. It has made the Austrialian position appear more reasonable, more constructive, more tied to the welfare of people as such, in this instance Formosan, than if the argument had been disregarded or downgraded.

It is in this connection that the course of Australia's relations with Nationalist China assumes special relevance. Australia has still not established any kind of diplomatic mission on Formosa. Criticisms of this policy have been frequent and sharp, both from certain Government supporters [56] and from the DLP-NCC.[57] The burden of these criticisms has been that since Formosa is strategically located and an influential political counterfoil to

[55] Gordon Byrant, *CPD,* HR, September 10, 1963, p. 771.

[56] See Kent-Hughes, *ibid.,* HR 17, December 5, 1957, p. 2945, HR 18, April 15, 1958, p. 882, HR 23, May 12, 1959, p. 2028, and statement of December 7, 1962, in *SMH,* December 8, 1962; Bruce Wight, *CPD,* HR 20, August 27, 1958, pp. 784–785; E. M. Fox, HR, October 1, 1964, p. 1738; Wentworth, HR 24, September 3, 1959, p. 940; Hannan, S 20, October 17, 1961, p. 1190, and S, April 29, 1964, pp. 592–593.

[57] For instance, Cole, *ibid.,* S 10, March 21, 1957, p. 114, and April 3, 1957, pp. 321–322, and S 16, November 12, 1959, p. 1459; McManus, *ibid.,* S. 15, September 30, 1959, p. 903; DLP, "Our Platform" (Sydney: DLP Federal Secretary, 1963), p. 19.

the Communist regime, at least among overseas Chinese, Australia should do nothing which hints of faint, half-hearted backing for the Nationalists. Asia is Australia's principal area of interest, yet while diplomatic missions have been established in various parts of the world, no mission has been placed on Formosa, a crucial country and a handy listening post. Indeed, it is known that in protest over Australia's indifference toward them, respecting a diplomatic establishment, the Nationalists did not elevate their head of mission in Canberra to rank of ambassador until 1959. It is also understood that from time to time the U.S. has urged Australia to establish a mission in Taipei.

The Menzies Government has, however, invariably avoided volunteering comment and explanation on this subject. When pressed by its critics, it has repeated its sentiments of support for Formosa, indicated that the matter of a mission on the island has been kept under review, but has plead that lack of trained personnel and funds prevented immediate action.[58] Furthermore, high-level Australian visits to Formosa have reflected a similarly cautious posture. Not until October of 1957 did the ranking External Affairs official, Sir Arthur Tange, arrange a trip to Formosa. Not until November of 1960 did any Australian minister pay an official call, and then it was a junior minister of the Government, Senator John Gorton. Not until mid-1962 did a Minister for External Affairs visit Formosa, when Barwick went. Shortly after his installation as External Affairs Minister, Paul Hasluck announced his intention of acquiring first-hand contacts with leaders in various Asian captials, but the Republic of China, among other nations, was left over for a "subsequent" time.[59] The Tange, Gorton, and Barwick visits were given

[58] Casey, *CPD*, HR 23, May 12, 1959, pp. 2028–2029; Spooner, *ibid.*, S 16, November 12, 1959, pp. 1461–1462; Barwick, statement cited in *News Weekly*, May 29, 1963.

[59] Hasluck, statement of May 15, 1964, in *CNIA*, Vol. 35 (May 1964), p. 38.

extremely little publicity, and barely reported on. So far as is known, Barwick made only one reference to his trip, and even that was brief and raised almost in passing.[60]

The behavior of Chinese Nationalist diplomatic and consular officials in Australia has been correct and has given no cause for Canberra to show its disapproval diplomatically. A few illustrations will suffice. In the first place, Nationalist representatives in Australia have been quite circumspect in their relations with the Australian Chinese community. Most Australian Chinese lack strong ideological convictions and are not active in politics on behalf of either China.[61] The Nationalist Chinese posted in Australia support those organizations which favor the KMT, although their endorsement is not carried out with ceremonious publicity. The Nationalists oppose the principle of remittances to Communist China, but informally realize that there is a tradition of such money being sent, and that it is difficult to dissuade Chinese from contributing toward the welfare of their families. Several years ago the Peking authorities wrote carefully framed letters to certain well-to-do members of the Australian Chinese community. The point of the letters was that relatives would be allowed to leave China if the Chinese in Australia would, in a "constructive spirit," contribute toward paying for 15 tons of fertilizer per person let out. A fair amount of money was involved, but the Nationalists did not rise in indignation or try to discourage the approached individuals.

Another illustration of circumspect behavior by the Nationalists concerns illegal Chinese migrants to Australia. For some years persons of Chinese extraction have been slipping into Australia, sometimes under the aegis of

[60] Barwick, "Australian Foreign Policy 1962," p. 10.

[61] A useful résumé of the politics of the Australian Chinese community is contained in a memorandum prepared by the Communist Party of Australia for the information of a visiting Chinese delegation in 1956. A transcript of this memo was made available to the author by courtesy of Peter Coleman of the *Bulletin*.

smuggling rings. In 1962 Australian authorities apprehended one Willie Wong, who had entered Hong Kong from China to seek employment, and then illegally entered Australia, where he lived undetected and in virtual seclusion for several years. A deportation order was issued. Kent-Hughes and Wentworth intervened on behalf of Wong, claiming he would probably be killed by the Chinese if he were placed in their hands. The Department of Immigration rescinded its order too late, and Wong was handed over to the Chinese at the Hong Kong border. The Nationalist Embassy in Canberra made no public protest, but indicated its willingness to arrange asylum in Formosa for any Chinese who might in future be scheduled for deportation to China.[62] Furthermore, despite their contacts with the Australian Chinese community in Australia, the Nationalist diplomatic and consular staffs have not tried to arrange for illegal migrants to be sheltered from the Government's searches, or otherwise to influence the Government's decisions.

At the nonpolitical level, the Nationalists have made efforts to portray themselves in the best light. In 1958 they arranged for Chinese Nationalist participation in an Asian film festival in Perth. In 1961 a "Chinese Art Week" was staged in Canberra by the Nationalist Embassy in conjunction with the School of Oriental Studies at the Australian National University. Exhibits, films, and lectures were assembled.[63] The Nationalist Embassy and Government have been making gifts of historical, literary, and artistic interest. Among the recipients have been the University of Sydney, the Australian National University, and the School of Oriental Studies at the University of Melbourne, which in 1962 was presented 1,600 volumes

[62] See *Sydney Sun-Herald,* April 15 and May 6, 1962; *SMH,* October 27, 1962; Alexander Downer, *CPD,* HR 36 August 8, 1962, p. 170.

[63] *China News* (Canberra), January 25, 1961.

through the Institute of Chinese Culture, Taipei.[64] The Australian Government has reciprocated some of these favors. University scholarships designated for Nationalist Chinese students have been sponsored by the Government, and in recent years—at the suggestion of Ambassador Chen—the Department of External Affairs has been sending its Chinese language students to Formosa rather than Hong Kong.

Why then, in the light of criticisms from domestic and American sources, good behavior by the Nationalists in Australia and otherwise friendly Nationalist-Australian relations, has Canberra been so politically bashful about a country which it recognizes and whose diplomats and visiting dignitaries it hosts? A frequent reply to this question given to the author by political persons not in the Government was that Menzies is so much an Anglophile that he has found it emotionally necessary to bring his Chinese diplomatic policy at least in small part in line with that of the British, and the farthest that he has been able to go has been by keeping Formosa at arms length. This is surely a fanciful interpretation. Menzies is indeed an Anglophile, but he makes his assessments of Chinese policy on far more concrete grounds than this. At all events, refusing to place a mission on Formosa is hardly a balance for reluctance to recognize China or to support her seating in the UN. Whether Menzies is or is not sentimental, he certainly is not näive.

For several years after the Korean War Australia's refusal to establish a mission in Taipei was probably conditioned by her uncertainty over whether a general Western shift on Chinese diplomatic policy might take place, eventuating in the recognition and UN seating of Peking. Also, incidents such as one that occurred in 1955—when the Nationalists in the Security Council vetoed the admission of Outer Mongolia and spoiled a "package deal" with the

[64] See especially *ibid.*, September 12, 1962.

Russians under which Japan was to be admitted—placed them in an unusually unfavorable light.[65] In 1957–58 Canberra probably came as close as it ever has to placing a mission. A major position paper was prepared by the Department of External Affairs, and there is some—though not conclusive—reason to believe that Tange's visit to Formosa late in 1957 was designed to provide an on-the-spot evaluation of the situation. Nothing, however, has happened. The contingency of a general Western diplomatic reversal on China has faded with the years. What has increasingly come to concern Australia has been that an outward sign of cordiality by Canberra toward Taipei would be misunderstood in much of Asia. After so many years of refusing to establish a mission, a sudden about-face would puzzle nonaligned Asians, who might impute a hard, freshly conceived, uncongenial attitude to Australia. This interpretation, which is almost certainly accurate, would also explain the infrequent and unpublicized nature of official and political Australian visits to Formosa. These visits, according to one very responsible source, have in fact been more designed to appease the right-wing critics in Australia than to promote serious dealings with Formosa. Presumably, had such "appeasement" of the critics not been found prudent, such visits would have been even further restricted in the interest of not offending Asian opinion.

In any event, quite aside from the reluctance to run the risk of Asian misunderstanding, Australia has lost little if anything from her Formosan diplomatic policy. There have been American complaints, but Australia's faithful observance of Washington's line on the really significant features of Chinese diplomatic policy has certainly avoided any damage to U.S.-Australian relations. Com-

[65] See adverse Australian press reactions in *Newcastle Morning Herald* and Perth *West Australian,* December 13, 1955, and in *SMH* and Brisbane *Courier-Mail,* December 15, 1955.

merce between Australia and Formosa has not suffered through the absence of a mission in Taipei. Political contacts are available through the Nationalist Embassy in Canberra. The number of Australians on Formosa has been small: about 20 according to 1958 figures. Included was a small contingent of Australians employed by a local airline and a few people connected with a religious mission who have been registered with the British consulate on Formosa, which provides whatever services are needed. Hence, without actually impairing her interests on Formosa or in Washington, Australia has convinced herself that her Formosan policy can be of use, however indirect, in maintaining the trust and confidence of her sensitive Asian neighbors.

But even neutrals may have their own reservations about Chinese diplomatic success and consequent extension of Chinese influence. There is reason to believe that the Australian Government thinks some of the nonaligned states would privately prefer to see China kept out of the UN for the time being, regardless of how they actually vote on the subject. There is in fact a rising feeling, shared by Asians, that China may not be especially interested in a UN seat, or a diplomatic *détente* with individual anti-Communist governments.[66] But Australia is also very much concerned about the willingness and ability of anti-Communist South-East Asian states to preserve their posture. Australia is deeply committed to the integrity of such states as Malaysia, Thailand, and Vietnam. Directly or indirectly their health and survival insulates Chinese Communist influence and thereby assists Australia. A switch in Australia's Chinese diplomatic policy, carried out after years of speaking and acting otherwise, could weaken the morale of what remains of the alliance system in the region, encourage Peking to earn propaganda

[66] See K. V. Narain in *Hindu Weekly Review,* September 14, 1964.

capital from a shift by a traditional anti-Communist nation, affect the balance of allegiance among overseas Chinese, or cause other repercussions.[67] While the degree of such an impact is impossible to prophesy, French recognition of China—although undertaken by a nation which has virtually disengaged from Asia—was uncomfortably received in Australia for just these reasons. Comparable action by Australia, a country with a deeper commitment in Asia, would only compound the embarrassment to the security system and complicate life for Australia's Asian friends and allies.[68]

A little known, indirect, but rather illuminating illustration might shed some light on Australia's apprehensions about the loyalties of Asians, Chinese, or others. Since 1956, Radio Australia has been beaming Mandarin language broadcasts, two hours of which now occur daily, seven days a week. In 1964 a Cantonese service was established. The Chinese language broadcasts cover all of South and South-East Asia and can be heard in most parts of China herself, though they are first and foremost aimed at the former audience. There is a high entertainment content—music and the like—though news about Australian and foreign affairs, Australian newspaper editorials and news commentaries are included. Radio Australia's musical presentations are adapted to the language served—hence Chinese music is transmitted on the Chinese service, Indonesian music on the Indonesian service, and so on. The spoken portions of Radio Australia's various language broadcasts tend to be alike. They are first written in

[67] See Menzies' London radio appearance of June 25, 1959, in *SMH,* June 27, 1959, and his remarks in *CPD,* HR 28, September 8, 1960, p. 987; Casey, address of June 29, 1959, in *CNIA,* Vol. 30 (June 1959), p. 338; Alexander Forbes, *CPD,* HR, September 10, 1963, p. 763.

[68] Barwick, *CPD,* HR, March 11, 1964, p. 474; Adelaide *Advertiser,* January 20, 1964; *SMH,* January 23, 1964; Brisbane *Courier-Mail,* January 27, 1964; Melbourne *Herald,* January 28, 1964.

English and then translated into and beamed in the various foreign languages as well as English. However, the very fact that there is an active Chinese service underscores the interest Australia maintains in the overseas Chinese population.[69]

But the content of the commentaries is perhaps even more revealing, regardless of the languages of transmission. The news commentaries, usually of 400–500 word length, are commissioned from among a group of academicians and journalists. The author examined the texts of all commentaries for the period from June 1963 to February 1964 which had bearing on China. A large number dealt with the Sino-Soviet dispute. Other themes included Chinese reaction to the nuclear test-ban treaty, the issue of Chinese representation at the UN, and French recognition of China. While there was little blatant slanting, the tone of the commentaries was decidedly conservative, and never favorable toward China. Australian policy was never criticized. On October 25, 1963, discussing the UN's recent decision not to seat Peking, one commentator concluded his remarks by citing the speech of Australia's UN delegate—that portion which pointed to China's misbehavior as a large factor in making her admission undesirable. On January 24, 1964, another commentator, noting France's intended recognition of China, wrote that "In Australia, which does not recognise the Peking Government, the fate of Formosa and its peoples is not something to which Australian opinion would be indifferent. . . . Any French recognition of Communist China will not reduce the need for support of national independence in Asia against Communist pressures: and Australia will continue to make her contribution." On February 3, still another writer was openly critical of France's suggested

[69] For a review of Radio Australia activities, see "Batman" in *Bulletin,* December 19, 1964; Harry Cox, "The Ear of the World," *People,* October 23, 1963, pp. 19–21. Regarding Chinese language broadcasts, see Casey, *CPD,* HR 13, October 10, 1956, p. 1300.

neutralization of South-East Asia.[70] Commentaries with such inflections were typical of the period reviewed by the author.

It is understood that at one time the Department of External Affairs required all such commentaries to be cleared by its own officers prior to broadcasting. Extremely close External Relations-Radio Australia liaison is still maintained, though the screening of commentaries has come to devolve on Radio Australia itself. The people whom Radio Australia now commissions to write scripts are by now old hands and "safe" in the first place. There are certain persons, such as journalist Peter Russo or Professors Macmahon Ball or Fitzgerald who would simply not be invited. Secondly, from time to time even the "safe" commentators have found their scripts rejected. The explanation proffered for the conscious failure to balance the commentaries is the fear that listeners would associate "left-wing" broadcasts with the Australian Government itself, rather than with individual authors. In the interest of safety, broadcasts must be kept roughly within the Government line. Australia has no wish to unsettle the population of South-East Asia, to raise questions about her anti-Chinese Communism, or to plant doubts about the course of her Chinese diplomacy.

The Peking regime is apparently somewhat impressed with Australia's broadcasting efforts, especially as they reach overseas Chinese in South-East Asia. Radio Australia broadcasts have been intermittently jammed by Peking. It started with Radio Australia's French language service in 1953, and later revolved around the Mandarin broadcasts. While Australia regards some of this jamming as unintentional, the major part of it is thought to be deliberate.[71]

[70] Scripts supplied by courtesy of Radio Australia, Melbourne.

[71] Regarding jamming, see *SMH,* March 27, 1954; Charles Davidson, *CPD,* HR 28, August 24, 1960, p. 321; statement by

Australian attention has also turned toward the related controversy of whether China's presence in the UN would enhance the prospects for a quieter and safer Far Eastern scene. The subject has engaged governments and commentators the world round, but some special Australian angles have been added. The argument for fostering China's admission to a place in the UN is clear enough. Much of it has simply been an extension of what was advanced during the Korean War. An isolated China is a suspicious China, yet Chinese behavior determines the course of Asian developments. *Ad hoc* conferences are not enough. What is needed is a permanent, international context in which China would have to justify herself and presumably would be chastened by the weight of world opinion. Her presence in the UN would not only facilitate the settlement of local and special disputes, such as Vietnam or the Sino-Indian border conflict, but also her participation in and subscription to long-term de-escalation agreements, as over nuclear and/or general and complete disarmament. The logic of this position is not, it is claimed, overturned by persistent Chinese extravagances. On the contrary. When the Chinese misbehave, that only freshens the need for incorporating them into the UN, and does not justify glib pretexts for keeping them out. This line of argument has enjoyed considerable currency in Australia, both during and between crisis periods. Press comments to this effect have been legion,[72] as have com-

---

Sir Charles Moses, general manager of the Australian Broadcasting Commission, December 3, 1963, in *SMH,* December 4, 1963.

[72] For sample comment, see Melbourne *Argus,* July 28, 1953; *SMH,* October 24, 1953; Sydney *Daily Telegraph,* July 26, 1955; Brisbane *Courier-Mail,* August 1, 1955; *Bulletin,* April 23, 1958; Hobart *Mercury,* October 9, 1959; Launceston *Examiner,* February 26, 1960; Adelaide *News,* April 27, 1960; Melbourne *Herald,* October 10, 1960; *Canberra Times,* August 7, 1961; Melbourne *Age,* July 18, 1962; Adelaide *Advertiser,* October 18, 1963; *Australian,* December 11, 1964.

ments from the ALP—both by the leadership[73] and others, be it from the left or moderate quarters.[74]

The thrust of the Australian Government's reply to these pleas has quite definitely not been to deny the principle that China's presence at the UN would be a positive step forward. Much the opposite, as has been shown. Australian statements on the subject have frequently alluded to the desirability, and even inevitability, of Chinese representation at the UN. Quite aside from the vexing question of Formosa's position, however, Australia has repeated her anxiety over promoting Peking's admission before the Chinese had demonstrated some willingness to comport themselves in a civilized manner. Unlike most of its critics, then, the Government has regarded Chinese-inspired or abetted crises as reasons for postponing rather than hastening the time of UN representation. While it has not believed that extra-UN contacts between China and the West are a permanently suitable substitute for association in the UN, it has scrutinized China's conduct in such probationary settings and has found it wanting. The Sino-American talks at Geneva and then Warsaw have gone on for years, but have produced no major achievement. The Chinese violently assailed the nuclear test-ban treaty, although they could have associated themselves with it outside the UN's framework, and then proceeded to set off their own nuclear test. The UN's own peace-keeping efforts have been derided by China. In the absence of any tangible proof of her goodwill, Canberra has concluded, China's seating in the UN might create more harm than

[73] Evatt, *CPD,* HR 23, April 30, 1959, p. 1718; Calwell, HR, March 19, 1964, p. 678; Nicholas McKenna, S 19, April 12, 1961, p. 437; Patrick Kennelly, S 21, May 16, 1962, p. 1425; Whitlam, statement of September 9, 1962, in *SMH,* September 10, 1962.

[74] For instance, E. J. Ward, *CPD,* HR 24, September 23, 1959, p. 1280; Charles Griffiths, HR 26, March 16, 1960, p. 272; Clyde Cameron, HR 30, April 13, 1961, pp. 880–882; Thomas Uren, HR, September 12, 1963, p. 947; Allan Fraser, in *Canberra Times,* October 28, 1963.

harmony. While scoring the diplomatic victory of being admitted after all these years, she would lessen the UN's stature and effectiveness because she had entered without even remotely meeting the qualification of being a peace-loving state. She could also disrupt the UN's work beyond the point that the Russians have, especially at a time when Soviet conduct has become more mellow than the Chinese.[75]

The Government's explanations should probably be taken as genuine. Australia herself has certainly not abjured contacts with China, witness travel, trade, Casey's conversation with Chou in 1954, the dispatch of observers to Bandung, Casey's refusal to reject Chou's Pacific security scheme out of hand, and the Government's promotion of Chinese participation in disarmament plans. It is recalled that early in 1961 Casey said that if only China had not repeatedly become involved in serious breaches of international conduct, many governments would have been prepared to reconsider their diplomatic stance. This remark, it is clearly understood, was intended to *include* Australia. It is almost certain that Australia has never urged Washington to revise its Chinese diplomatic policy, or to ask for consent to proceed on her own. If, however, there had been a suitable period of international quiescence, with China remaining relatively orderly, the guess is that Australia's diplomacy would have moved in that direction. A successful probationary period would have dispelled some of Australia's apprehensions about China, and would also have permitted a less risky intervention by the U.S. Indeed, it is the American factor which, more than any other, has inhibited more vigorous Australian activity in this sphere.

[75] For recent expressions on this theme, see James Plimsoll, before UN General Assembly, October 26, 1962, in *CNIA,* Vol. 33 (October 1962), p. 77, and D. O. Hay, before UN General Assembly, October 16, 1963, in *ibid.,* Vol. 34 (October 1963), pp. 46–47; Menzies, *CPD,* HR, November 9, 1964, p. 2609.

## THE "AMERICAN FACTOR" IN AUSTRALIA'S CHINA DIPLOMACY

ARTHUR CALWELL has written that the Menzies Government has been guilty of "complete dependence on the United States," and he underwrites his point by reciting Australia's policy on the recognition and UN seating of China.[76] The adjective "complete" is overdrawn, but the gist of Calwell's charge is correct—and it has been admitted by the Government. The Government has said that if Australia wants her friends to support her, she has to support them, and one way to accomplish this is by standing up and being counted in the UN.[77] It has explained its nonrecognition of China by confessing that Australian recognition "would create avoidable differences" with the U.S.,[78] and that American policies of containing Chinese Communism, so far as they would be subverted rather than fortified by an act of Australian recognition, "would clearly affect profoundly Australian-American relations."[79]

It is significant to notice that Australia has not needed to guess at how the U.S. has regarded the recognition and UN seating of China. The evidence has been varied and impressive. Both houses of the American Congress, of whose political influence Australia is not unaware, in 1948 began the ritual of deploring the recognition or UN admission of China through resolutions adopted by overwhelming majorities. At the time the Indo-Chinese crisis was winding up and widely scattered persons and govern-

[76] Calwell, *Labor's Role in Modern Society,* p. 175.

[77] Casey, broadcast of October 3, 1954, in *CNIA,* Vol. 25 (October 1954), p. 732.

[78] R. G. Menzies, "Joint Policy Speech. Federal Election 1958" (Canberra: Federal Secretariat, Liberal Party of Australia, 1958), Supplement, p. 24.

[79] Casey, *CPD,* HR 24, August 13, 1959, p. 197.

ments were beginning to contemplate the possibility of a different posture opposite China, William Knowland was declaring that if China entered the UN he would quit the Senate leadership to lead a movement for U.S. withdrawal from the organization, and also announced the formation of a bipartisan Senate bloc which was studying radical U.S. actions should China gain admission.[80] Rather than repudiating Knowland unconditionally, President Eisenhower then launched a slashing attack against China, saying he could not understand how any state could in good conscience vote for China's admission at that stage, and Dulles was reported to have advised Eden that "cataclysmic consequences" would follow Peking's seating.[81] The same year, the U.S. Information Service in Sydney was issuing an elaborate six-part booklet on "The China of Mao Tse-tung," which was not an explanation of America's China policy as such, but an unadulterated denunciation of various aspects of Chinese Communist rule, including China's foreign policy.

Two years later, in 1956, Eden was told by U.S. officials in Washington that if China were admitted to the UN, the U.S. might be expected to resign, and that such action would not be confined to the special circumstances of an election year.[82] Later in the year, according to a person who was privy to the event, an all-male dinner was arranged at the U.S. Embassy in Canberra. Most of the Australians invited were senior officials and politicians. After dinner the group retired to the smoking room. The guest of honor, Walter Robertson, U.S. Assistant Secretary of State for Far Eastern Affairs, immediately sailed into a fierce tirade against China, and how wicked it was to deal with her. The gathering then adjourned without further delay. According to the author's informant, the

[80] *NYT,* July 6, 1954.
[81] *Ibid.,* July 8, 1954.
[82] Eden, *op. cit.,* p. 333.

whole affair resembled a set piece, a staged demonstration by America's foremost official China-baiter to leave no doubts in Australia about how the U.S. felt.

In 1957, a SEATO Foreign Ministers' Conference was held in Canberra. Secretary Dulles did not confine himself to the business at hand. Quite out of context, and in the presence of two SEATO members who already recognized China, Dulles inveighed against Chinese recognition and tried to rebut the arguments which commonly were presented on behalf of such a course.[83] A few months later, W. J. Sebald, the newly appointed U.S. Ambassador to Australia, made his maiden speech in the country. He spoke to a Sydney audience on "Our China policy." The speech was a rather stale recitation of the official American position and an indictment of all the standard vices—recognition, UN seating, trade with China, etc.—precisely those topics which were then under serious discussion in Australia.[84] Leslie Haylen then fired off a 350-word telegram to Sebald, protesting his alleged effort to lecture Australians as if he were "issuing a directive to a subject people." Casey's reaction was that the Haylen protest had been "out of place and impertinent." He described Sebald's remarks as a "logical and entirely understandable outline of American policy"—though he did not say he agreed with the substance of the Ambassador's remarks.[85] It was also in 1957 that a U.S. Embassy official, according to Senator Arnold, tried to bribe him not to visit China with the ALP delegation.

In the following year, the State Department made pub-

[83] Dulles' statement of March 12, 1957, in *Department of State Bulletin,* Vol. 36 (April 1, 1957), pp. 531–532. For some uncomplimentary reactions to Dulles' performance, see Geoffrey Sawer, "Problems of Australian Foreign Policy, June 1956-June 1957," *Australian Journal of Politics and History,* Vol. 3 (November 1957), p. 12; *SMH,* March 13, 1957; Evatt, *CPD,* HR 14, April 2, 1957, p. 426; Alan Bird, *ibid.,* April 4, 1957, p. 568.

[84] Address of July 26, 1957, in *SMH,* July 27, 1957.

[85] *Ibid.,* July 29, 1957.

lic a memorandum on the nonrecognition of China which it had just distributed among American diplomatic missions. Included was a reference to the requirement of containing Chinese Communism in Asia by means not confined to military deterrence alone, i.e., nonrecognition and non-seating at the UN. If the combined measures to contain China failed, the consequences for Australia and New Zealand would be especially serious; they would be isolated and strategically exposed, argued the memorandum.[86]

At the June 1960 SEATO Council meetings, attended by Menzies himself, New Zealand's Walter Nash suggested that China's admission to the UN might help to ease tensions in the Pacific. It was more a comment than a full exposition, unlike Dulles' lecturing remarks in 1957. But it was met with a lengthy and forceful retort by Secretary Herter, who openly referred to China as an outlaw.[87] Two months later, at the University of Sydney, Acting U.S. Ambassador William Bolton amplified the Dulles-Herter-Sebald position with a blast against "treacherous" China.[88]

With the election of John F. Kennedy in 1960 and the removal of the Republicans from the White House, there was widespread hope in Australia that Washington might be ready for a fresh look at its China policy, and that Australian policy might therefore be at last and easily adjusted.[89] There was in fact some substance to this feeling. Spokesmen of the new Administration stressed the inevitability of getting along with China, including in the UN, and talk of American withdrawal from the world

[86] See *CNIA,* Vol. 29 (August 1958), p. 513.

[87] *SMH,* June 3, 1960.

[88] Address of September 15, 1960, in *ibid.,* September 16, 1960.

[89] For instance, Melbourne *Age,* November 14, 1960; Douglas Wilkie in Melbourne *Sun-Pictorial,* November 15, 1960; Sydney *Daily Mirror,* January 23, 1961; Melbourne *Herald* and Hobart *Mercury,* both of February 8, 1961.

body was gone.[90] An attempt was made to revive prospects for an exchange of newsmen, but the Chinese reacted with disdain and no improvement in relations was achieved.

By May 1961 Vice-President Johnson had visited Formosa on behalf of Kennedy, and pledged the U.S. would not recognize Peking and would continue support for the Nationalists in the UN and through defense commitments.[91] But it was also the time when various nations, including Britain, Japan, and Pakistan, decided that they would no longer support the ancient ritual of imposing the UN's moratorium on the Chinese representation issue.[92] The U.S. worked strenuously to win at least one more year for the moratorium, but in time yielded. It had become persuaded that the best way to avoid resentment against itself and the Nationalists, and to insure a heavy vote against Chinese seating, was to shift course and allow—in fact encourage—a lifting of the moratorium. It is understood that the U.S. tried to collect several middle powers, all America's friends and/or allies, to cosponsor the lifting of the moratorium. All save one hesitated to take on the job. Its purpose was not, as formally painted in the UN, to allow for a constructive discussion of Chinese seating, but to ward off the forces of resentment that might accumulate against the Nationalists and bring on Peking's seating. Among the invited cosponsors of the resolution, only New Zealand consented, but with qualms.[93]

[90] See statements by Rusk, Harriman, and Stevenson, in *NYT,* January 13, 16 and 19, 1961, respectively.

[91] See *ibid.,* May 15 and 16, 1961.

[92] See Sheldon Appleton, *The Eternal Triangle?* (East Lansing: Michigan State Univ. Press, 1961), p. 155. Also, especially, the statements of British Foreign Secretary Lord Home, *UKPD,* HL, Vol. 228, February 8, 1961, col. 438, and of Japanese Prime Minister Ikeda, in Japan *Times,* September 30, 1961.

[93] For New Zealand's explanations of her vote, see the memorandum accompanying instructions to the New Zealand delega-

What stands out for present purposes is that Australia *had not* been invited by the U.S. to cosponsor the moratorium removal, though New Zealand and Canada had been. The reasons for this are conjectural, but some reasonable inferences can be extracted. An election was fast approaching in Australia, and Washington probably did not wish to impose any avoidable political burden on the Menzies Government. Indeed, as has been shown, Australia cosponsored the resolution which called for a two-thirds vote on the substantive question of Chinese seating. As will be seen, the Menzies Government has received excellent mileage from its established Chinese diplomatic policy. Australia had only recently begun her controversial credit sales of wheat to China, and active participation in the moratorium cancellation could have deprived the loyal Liberal-Country Party coalition of its useful anti-Communist image, despite the fact that the moratorium lifting was ultimately designed to frustrate rather than facilitate China's seating. Conceivably too, in long-run terms, the U.S. did not wish to plant the seed in Australia that Australia's involvement in the game of moratorium raising might be a precedent for something quite different in the future—such as flirting with such dangerous notions as actual backing for a Peking UN seat, or diplomatic recognition. On these matters Australia had long remained more circumspect than New Zealand or Canada, and perhaps it was best to insure that she stayed that way. The U.S. probably sensed—and wished to honor—the Australian leaders' feeling that while Western recognition and a UN seat would ultimately reach China, "they have added,

tion, in *EAR* (NZ), Vol. 11 (September 1961), p. 27; McIntosh, UN General Assembly, *Official Records,* Sixteenth Session, 1014th Plenary Meeting, September 25, 1961, p. 78; "The Representation of China in the United Nations," *EAR* (NZ), Vol. 12 (April 1962), esp. p. 8.

privately, that Australia should not be the first of America's allies to break the line." [94] At all events, there is no tangible evidence in recent years of additional heavy-handedness on the part of the U.S. regarding Australia's Chinese diplomatic policy. While in the post-Eisenhower years the U.S. has raised its doubts about the Chinese trade conducted by Japan, Canada, and Australia, among others, the Australians have heard of such doubts in private, never in public. In part, this may be because the Kennedy and Johnson Administrations have simply been more tactfully disposed than the former Administration. More likely, the answer lies in Australia's failure to evince tendencies toward an alteration of policy, or an attempt to persuade America to change.

Among the Government's publicly stated reasons for not amending its Chinese diplomatic policy has been its wish to preserve excellent relations with the United States. But it has not been just another of several reasons. It has been the foremost reason. The other explanations are not sheer fabrications, but are subordinate to the American factor. China's haughtiness about two-China formulas has been awarded top billing in public pronouncements because, in the main, it has been found to be a useful explanation of an apparently insoluble dilemma; and it is thrown back at the large army of political, journalistic, and academic critics that have badgered the Government. These are not the author's personal speculations, but the candid admissions of exceptionally qualified persons.

The reason for the dominance of the American factor is not hard to come by. In so very many ways Australia has convinced herself that her interests require American assistance. The U.S.'s presence is needed in the whole security network of the region. America must be encouraged to stay on, not waver and possibly withdraw from her commitments, and this implies rendering Washington

[94] Melbourne *Age,* January 29, 1964.

every bit of support and genuine friendship available. Since American feelings on China run so high, it would be self-defeating to spoil Washington's pleasure with its sympathetic Pacific ally. Then again, there are special Australian interests, as in New Guinea and Malaysia, where Canberra has needed to exert itself especially hard to win and hold Washington's interest, and then steer Washington along Australian-defined policy courses. This has been a delicate operation, and again not worth bungling through a change in Chinese policy. Then there have been the occasions when Australia has wished to calm Washington, when the senior partner has seemed to push too hard, too swiftly, too impetuously, for the good of peace and order in Asia. This has suggested that Australia must have access and influence in Washington. But she has quite decidedly always been the junior partner, with limited leverage. Offending the U.S. through a change of China policy would have lessened, not enhanced, what leverage has existed. Trying to shove America into surrendering her China policy might *per se* have been resented, and depleted Australia's diplomatic leverage with America. Australia continues to reason that such leverage must be kept in reserve for the large and pressing issues—Indo-China, the offshore islands, Indonesia's confrontation on Malaysia, and the like.

In the meantime, Australia realizes some real advantages without recognition both because of and despite her respectful attitude toward Washington. Without recognition, she trades handsomely with China, and the kicks and pricks from America are probably far less potent than if Australia's behavior on Chinese diplomacy ran counter to America's. Australia has no diplomatic relations with China, but her people visit China in many connections, and from this the Government learns something. The Australians have no mission in Peking, but conveniently the British do. When Australia has a representation to lodge with China, Britain does it for her, as she did with the imprisoned civilian airmen. The few Western missions in China are handicapped in various ways, but much of what the British are able to learn and interpret is passed on to Australia. This includes not only the annual reports placed before the Foreign Office by the mission in Peking, but also the more detailed and revealing fortnightly reports. Canberra, it would seem, knows about as much about China as London.

These considerations are not new. Calculations which dictate present policy are often traceable to the earliest years of the Liberal-Country Party Government. Australia believes them to be as valid today as they were in the Korean period. The pervasiveness of the Chinese factor in Australia's policy framework is truly impressive, and at nearly every turn relations with the United States are manifest.[95] For some years Australia's ambassadors in Washington have been on special instruction to keep a watchful eye on any shift in America's mood and conduct toward China. It is easy to appreciate why this is so.

## CHINESE DIPLOMATIC POLICY AND DOMESTIC POLITICS

WHILE the Government has concluded that there are compelling international considerations which demand no alteration in the established Chinese diplomatic policy, the political scene in Australia has also been conductive to preserving the *status quo*. The forces behind the DLP-NCC have, of course, been violently antagonistic to Australian recognition of China, or support for installing her in the UN. They have gone so far as to denounce the admission of China into international disarmament discussions even outside the UN, because of their suspicion of Chinese motives and trustworthiness and their apprehen-

[95] See Henry S. Albinski, "Australia and the American Alliance," *Australian* (Canberra), July 16, 23 and 31, 1964.

sion that even innocent contacts can lower the West's guard and encourage more formal contacts.[96] At the slightest Government hint by word or deed that a milder Chinese diplomatic policy might be in preparation, as has been seen, they have exploded with wrath and screamed the dishonor of sellout. When their apprehensions about a turn of policy have been particularly acute, they have sponsored, or helped support, or given grand publicity to, any public demonstrations of protest.[97]

On recognition, as on most foreign and defense issues, the Government understands that in the present political climate the DLP is in no position to retaliate against an unwelcome official policy. DLP advice that its electors should transfer their second preferences from the Government parties to the ALP would be utterly self-defeating. The Menzies Government has extended vast trade credits to China, allowed visits by Australians to China and some Chinese visits to Australia, declined to post a diplomatic mission in Formosa and resumed diplomatic relations with Russia. The DLP resented all these policy movements, but could do nothing. Even in the most unlikely—almost inconceivable—event that the Government should amend its Chinese diplomatic policy in the face of American displeasure, the DLP could still not afford to recommend second preferences for Labor.

But with recognition and the UN, as with other Chinese-related issues, the Government has found the DLP-NCC militancy politically helpful, since the DLP is far more interested in raking Labor than the Government over the coals. Continuing a firm Chinese diplomatic policy presents the Government with assets which lie beyond the international field. It can persist in its highly profitable ex-

[96] For example, Cole, *CPD,* S 19, April 12, 1961, p. 449, and McManus, *ibid.,* April 13, 1961, pp. 490–491.

[97] See *News Weekly,* September 9 and October 21, 1953; September 10, 1958.

ercise of branding Labor as a villain, and the assist which it gets from the DLP helps. Fire against the ALP from the Government *and* the DLP is more overpowering than if it emanated from the Government parties alone. Of course, the very existence of the DLP, as it pulls votes from Labor and delivers second preferences to the Government coalition, is welcome. As explained before, the greater the seepage of DLP second preferences to Labor, the less the Government's advantage. Remaining differentiated from the ALP on a sensitive Communist issue such as Chinese diplomacy is therefore good politics—not just good foreign policy.

During electoral campaigns, the Government has forsaken its usually moderate voice on recognition and UN seating and has reverted to noises of righteous indignation. For instance, at a 1961 Brisbane electoral meeting, Menzies bellowed to the crowd: "No one in Communist China would say thank you for any recognition which did not recognise that Formosa belonged to it. You cannot recognise Communist China without handing over Formosa. How many Australians would agree to sell Formosa into slavery as the A.L.P. proposes to do?" [98] Again, in the 1963 campaign, he declared that nothing could be more fatal to the resistance of anti-Communist states in Asia than Labor's proposal to hand China an immense diplomatic victory.[99]

The irony, as on other foreign and defense issues, is that the Government has succeeded in making the ALP appear dangerous and irresponsible on China policy despite the fact that Labor would not do anything materially different from the Government. It has already been noted that the official ALP platform and the ACTU Executive have made provision for a sympathetic consideration of the Formosan population, and that Labor's own leaders

[98] At address of December 4, 1961, in *SMH,* December 5, 1961.
[99] Address of November 25, 1963, in *ibid.,* November 26, 1963.

have called for self-determination on the island and have not asked for Formosa's expulsion from the UN. There are some in the ALP's Parliamentary group who think China should be given recognition by Australia and backed in the UN regardless of the consequences for Formosa, but they are at least matched in numbers and influence by a right-wing element, composed of men such as Beazley, Willesee, and Stewart, who in fact have small use for *any* sort of diplomatic support for Peking, even on a two-China basis. Men of this stamp have generally been to Formosa, come home impressed, and have, the author understands, had fair impact on the middle-ground majority among the Party's Parliamentarians, among whom one should count the leadership. Furthermore, the leadership itself is not unaware of the repercussions which a falling out with Washington could bring for Australia. Both Calwell and Whitlam have been to America, and carry a personal admiration for what America represents. They are not by any means America-baiters.

The ALP leadership has also been alert to the political damage that a chest-beating, unconditionally pro-Peking diplomatic policy could bring. Even Evatt, despite his often bewildering behavior, saw it this way. After Haylen and his ALP colleagues had returned from China and presented a highly complimentary report, Evatt praised it.[100] But despite a long-standing invitation, which was repeated, Evatt refused to lead the Party's delegation to China, and in fact never went. Evatt delighted in travel, but he clearly was afraid of what would be said if he, as Leader, visited China. It has been learned that while the New Zealand Labor Party was in office during 1957–60, Evatt personally wrote to Nash and urged New Zealand to proceed with recognition. But it is understood on equally strong authority that in the 1958 electoral campaign he rebuked a Senator of his own Party for a pro-recognition

[100] Statement of July 25, 1957, in *ibid.,* July 26, 1957.

speech. Calwell, unlike Evatt, has never had much enthusiasm for travel, especially to Asia. Nonetheless, for essentially politically pragmatic reasons, neither he nor Whitlam has ever visited China. The internal evidence is almost totally conclusive that had Labor won the 1963 election, as many expected, Calwell would have been his own External Affairs Minister, in large measure to insure that foreign policy, including Chinese diplomatic policy, would be kept in safely moderate hands.

In operational terms, what would an ALP Government do about recognition and UN seating for China? Whitlam has said that Australian policy would move off its stationary position and the U.S. would be urged to change its own stance. If this worked, Australia and others would then gladly proceed in tandem. He believes that some *quid pro quo* ought to be offered to Peking; for instance, if it consented to some two-China arrangement, it would be awarded the offshore islands in return. But in the same breath he has confessed the near impossibility of persuading the Chinese to accept any such compromise.[101] Even James Cairns, widely regarded as a left-winger but a Labor front-bencher with undoubted leadership ambitions, has declared that "It does not matter whether Australia recognizes China or not, but it is important that the United States of America should do so, and it is important that Australia should do everything possible to encourage the United States along those lines." A Labor Government's first step would be to send its External Affairs Minister to Washington to reason with America; it would not

[101] Whitlam, "Australian Foreign Policy, 1963," p. 18. For some academic recommendations that Australia test Chinese intentions on two Chinas, even with a high expectation of failure, see Michael Lindsay, "Australia, the United States and Asia," *Australian Journal of Politics and History,* Vol. 3, (November 1957), pp. 41–42, and his remarks in *Observer,* August 22, 1959; Leslie H. Palmier, "Recognition of the Chinese Governments," *Australian Outlook,* Vol. 12 (December 1958), esp. pp. 39–40; Macmahon Ball, "Australia's Political Relations with Asia," pp. 78–79.

be to undertake unilateral action.[102] If Calwell were Prime Minister, he would without question resist anything short of a two-China recognition and UN seating formula. There is also evidence that he would *welcome* any opportunity to *avoid* switching from the incumbent Government's line on China, i.e., not to recognize China at all. Shortly before the 1963 election, he told Nationalist Ambassador Chen Chi-mai that Chen should harbor no anxieties about a Labor victory. Not long after settling into office, Calwell would probably tour Asia and stop off in Formosa. There would probably be some faint gesture toward Peking regarding recognition on a two-China basis. Since the Chinese would be expected to say no, and since on the strength of personal experience Calwell could report favorably about Formosa's progress and importance, nothing would change in Australia's policy—while the advocates of a new China line would in part have been appeased.

This is not the kind of language Calwell has ever used publicly, and he might be reluctant to admit having used it at all. The idea that Australian recognition of China, or support of her UN seating, is in fact almost out of the question under Labor is also not broadcast, despite its truth. Why then does the Party, and especially Calwell, continue to invite the political attacks which contribute to the "soft on Communism" image? The organizational features of the Party are certainly in part responsible. The recognition of China and her seating in the UN are imbedded in the Party's official program. The Conference membership, more left-wing and less attuned to political realities than the Parliamentary Party, would not rescind these clauses. The organizational wing of the Party has also had its share of powerful yet embarrassingly irresponsible individuals. In 1961, F. E. Chamberlain, the ALP's Federal Secretary, told a correspondent that the U.S.

[102] *CPD,* HR, March 19, 1964, p. 725.

should save face on China by quietly fomenting a revolution on Formosa against Chiang. It had, after all, conspired in this way to eliminate Syngman Rhee in South Korea![103] But among many figures in the Parliamentary Party, regardless of the formal requirement to support the official program, stands a genuine devotion to the Party, a sense of solidarity, and therefore a reluctance to dispute openly what has been decided by prescribed means. Calwell would surely be a prime example of this tendency. Whatever his reservations about this or that aspect of Party organization or policy, he believes in the Party very much as in an article of faith.

Continuing electoral setbacks and an unnaturally lengthy residence in opposition have also left their mark. Labor has become over-quick in its reactions, too transparently clever, too prone to grasp for meaningless debating points, and Calwell has been among the prime offenders. His reaction on the relation between trade with China and recognition has already been noted. Labor's reaction to French recognition of China is another case in point. When France's intentions were first announced, Calwell immediately volunteered that without any doubt de Gaulle's action would encourage other nations to follow suit, though he charged the Australian Government with having lost virtually all power of initiative.[104] Later, when it turned out that no two-China formula had evolved from French recognition and other nations were not falling all over themselves to emulate Paris, Calwell tried a fresh tack. He scolded Barwick for having drawn the allegedly false inference that Peking was to blame for having blocked a two-China solution. After all, according to Calwell, was it not the Nationalists' own withdrawal of their Paris embassy that had foiled French hopes for a two-

[103] As reported in Sydney *Daily Telegraph,* March 1, 1961.

[104] Statement of January 28, 1964, in Melbourne *Age,* January 29, 1964. Also see *Fact,* February 20, 1964.

China arrangement?[105] Nothing was said by Calwell about the quite obvious Chinese reluctance to exchange missions while the Nationalists remained in Paris, or of France's impatient desire that in the face of Chinese intransigence on two Chinas the Nationalists would depart gracefully.

It was in one of those moments of striving to "expose" the Government's inconsistencies that Calwell came upon a perspicacious characterization of the politics of Chinese recognition. Early in 1959 he wrote a short piece entitled "Bob and Krush Now 'Buddies.'" He predicted that Soviet-Australian diplomatic relations would shortly be restored, and intimated that this might be followed by recognition of China. A sneaky man, that Bob Menzies, Calwell was trying to say. But, Calwell complained, if it were a Labor Government that was about to deal with the Russians, or tinkering with recognizing China, the Liberal-Country Party group would stamp this with some such epithet as un-Australian or Communistic.[106] Here Arthur Calwell spoke a great truth. The Government defines trade with China as a-political realism but brands the ALP's recognition policy as treacherous. Be that as it may, it is certainly a handsomely effective political gambit.

[105] *CPD*, HR, March 19, 1964, p. 677.
[106] *Labor*, February 1959.

# X

# THE RELEVANCE OF THE CHINA PROBLEM

THE POSTWAR condition of Asia has been one of rapid and often troubled change. As a relatively isolated, underpopulated yet Western country, situated on the edge of this unstable setting, Australia has naturally taken a keen interest in appraising the developments to her north and in devising appropriate policy measures. Within her perception of the Asian context the presence and influence of Communist China has been a central concern, perhaps even a preoccupation. She has felt that various military, diplomatic, and economic antidotes must be applied to contain China's ability to exert direct or indirect pressure on her Asian neighbors, whose sociopolitical integrity is linked to Australia's own well-being. Nevertheless, Australia has never felt that her attitude and policies toward China should be governed by absolutist principles. She has appreciated the risks which attend a posture of unreserved hostility toward China, believing that an aroused and provoked China is a dangerous China.

The "China problem" in Australia has therefore been a problem not simply of identifying the importance, the character and the strength of Chinese power. It has also turned on the proper balance which must be struck between resisting the circulation of this power and creating conditions in which accommodation can be achieved. It has not been an easy task, especially for a nation whose material and diplomatic resources are not of the first rank. Nor, in this setting of balancing and weighing alternative positions, has Australia escaped the inevitable internal debate about what should be done, and how, in particular circumstances. The area of agreement, however, has always been that there is a China problem, that it intimately affects Australia, and that it needs to be reckoned with seriously.[1]

## LOOKING OUT ON THE CHINA PROBLEM

THE PERVASIVENESS of the China problem is apparent. It has not simply entailed an anticipation of overt Chinese encroachments in Asia and eventually perhaps against Australia herself. Most Australians have agreed with the Menzies Government that the survival and viability of South and South-East Asian states serves to buttress Australia's own security. Most have agreed that Chinese policy has been exerted to accomplish the reverse. Most Australians have also shared the perception that a number of disputes which outwardly appeared detached from the Chinese factor—such as West Irian and Malaysia—have carried overtones which related them to China's presence and ambitions.

Australia's reaction to China has aimed at observing an outwardly straightforward formula: to resist the spread of Chinese influence while avoiding provocation—and if possible conducting "business as usual" in the process. By nearly every standard Australian society is Western—by race, language, religion, tradition, and attachment. But because of geographic position Australia has found herself not only removed from Western centers, but nearly in the midst of an Asian milieu. She has perforce had to deal with Asia and Asian problems intimately, while striving to engage and maintain the interest of her Western allies in what she, Australia, has convinced herself to be the essen-

[1] Drawn from Henry S. Albinski, *Australia and the China Problem During the Korean War Period* (Canberra: Dept. of International Relations, ANU, 1964), p. 1.

tials of her security. Hence a delicate balancing act has constantly been in progress. Chinese aggression in Korea could not be countenanced, for its success could have endowed her with renewed boldness and dislocated the fledging countries in the region. But bluster and bombs against China could have prolonged and even widened the war, so Australian diplomacy worked for sense and restraint. A permanent security arrangement with the United States was indispensable. Yet winning American participation required conscious efforts to please her. Reservations about the UN aggression resolution and the strategic embargo against China ultimately had to be withdrawn and a façade of Western unity patched up, while diplomatic recognition of China was taken beyond the reach of active consideration.

Aggravation of the fighting in Indo-China was seen from Canberra as self-defeating. But collective security arrangements were also imperative. China had to be blocked from further adventures by the example of a united coalition, yet she must not be egged into protracting the conflict. A negotiated settlement was the only realistic answer to the Indo-Chinese troubles, but an ill-timed effort to build a security pact would destroy such prospects, and drive from its ranks the very nations which required protection most.

Formosa could not be made a sacrificial offering to China, but neither should Formosa, nor surely the offshore islands, be allowed to serve as harassing thorns in China's tender side. Priorities mattered; the offshore islands were liabilities, not assets, for the cause of peace and order in the area, and they only complicated cooperation in the infinitely more significant prize of Formosa.

Anguished choices of policy were brought on by Indonesia's behavior. The interested hand of China was recognized, but alternatives of placation as against frontal resistance to Indonesia's blustering opposite West Irian and

Malaysia remained. If possible, an irreparable Australian-Indonesian breach should be averted. If possible, Indonesia should not be driven into Communist arms. If possible, a frontal clash with her ought to be avoided, but if it became inevitable, it should not increase China's hold on Indonesia, or precipitate China's intervention.

Australian material welfare called for exploring and exploiting the Chinese market. Without exception, however, security considerations in Asia required an Australian policy which would result in precisely the right mix of strength and restraint by the United States. So the trade has been disguised as not officially sponsored, and has carried at least the theoretically strict limitation on strategic materials.

So too with diplomatic policy. Contacts with China have never been deprecated. Contacts induced by the trading relationship, at the level of noncommercial exchanges of visitors, or at informal diplomatic occasions as in the Casey-Chou conversations, have at least tacitly been encouraged, with concrete and not just idealistic motives in mind. But circumstances have never been propitious for formal diplomatic ties or the pursuit of a UN seat for China. The reasons have been many, but have centered on considerations of not offending the United States. Indeed, by adhering to the substance of America's wishes, Australia has found more space for maneuver in such areas as trade, the exchange of persons, and even the nonplacement of a mission on Formosa.

Despite all its stated misgivings about Chinese intentions, the Government for an inordinately long time put on a poor show respecting the country's defense establishment. By any legitimate yardstick, Australia seemed embarrassingly undressed. Until late 1964, she devoted under 3 per cent of her gross national product to defense. Her army was scheduled for expansion, but only to 28,000 by 1967–68. Since 1959, she had lacked any form of compulsory service. She simply chose to invest as much as possible in her quasi-welfare state and to allow a maximum of spending for consumer goods and civil development projects, in order to become the affluent society of the South-West Pacific.

Academic critics, the press, the ALP, the DLP, the Returned Servicemen's League, the Indonesians, even *Time* magazine, all poured scorn on Australia's military weakness. In Professor J. D. B. Miller's words, Australia's position in the world looked very much like humbug.

> We support the United States and Britain, presumably because this seems the best way of deterring an ultimate Chinese attack on Australia or Chinese moves which would isolate Australia and leave it defenceless. We practice diplomacy which leads us to express this support in definite terms which include or imply military support. But we do not provide the military support. What we do provide is no doubt welcome in its place, but it did not assist the British troops in Borneo or provide more than token help in Vietnam. Yet our Government speaks in terms which suggest that both these causes are just; not only just, but also closer to Australia's interests, because of its geographical location, than to either Britain's or the United States in the long run. Does this not look like humbug? It is not meant to be, but our associates abroad can be forgiven if they describe it as such. Perhaps we should put up or shut up.[2]

[2] J. D. B. Miller in *Bulletin,* June 20, 1964. For some other recent criticisms, see T. B. Millar, "Australia's Defence Needs," in *Australia's Defence and Foreign Policy,* pp. 69–89, and R. I. Downing, "The Cost of Defence," in *ibid.,* pp. 101–118; Returned Servicemen's League, *48th Annual Report 1963* (Canberra: RSL National Executive, 1964), pp. 19–24; *Bulletin,* October 26, 1963; *Time,* May 29, 1964.

There was validity in such attacks. The Government was aware of the criticisms, but it wanted affluence *plus* security—in the manner that it conducts the Chinese trade. It helped itself by deploying the country's meager resources far and wide. Malaya proper, Malaysian Borneo, Thailand, and Vietnam represented only token contributions (as Miller notes), but they are placed to achieve maximum visibility and conspicuousness. When the Americans look around Asian trouble spots, some Australians usually are about. There may not be many, but they reassure Washington that Australia is not hiding them in the interior of Tasmania. It boosts the American spirit, which after all is what counts. It gives Australia a claim to participate in planning and decisions, which also counts. To a degree, the North West Cape establishment can be read in a similar light. To America, the station is worth more than an extra Australian squadron, frigate, or batch of instructors, in South-East Asia. Chinese nuclear preparations only served to raise the station's value. To Australia, it was a painless, and indeed a dividend-bearing, means of keeping the boys on the job at home rather than under the colors abroad, while drawing America closer to Australian foreign policy interests, both general and particular.[3]

But by the close of 1964, these substitutes for an increased military establishment were at last seen as insufficient. The fighting in Vietnam was becoming increasingly critical. Indonesian pressures against Malaysia were assuming frightening proportions. The Chinese were continuing their truculence, and had exploded their first nuclear device. Therefore, the Prime Minister announced, defense expenditures were to rise sharply, military equipment and facilities were to be improved, the army was to be enlarged to over 37,500, and conscription was to be re-

[3] See Henry S. Albinski in *Australian,* July 23, 1964.

introduced, with compulsory service overseas for conscripts if the Government so wished to deploy them.[4]

In sum, respecting the Chinese problem, while Australia does depend on her American alliance in many and crucial ways, she does not do so in a blind or unthinking manner. The picture has many, often subtle facets, and to date the Australian Government had managed to juggle its component parts skillfully. There was considerable truth in Barwick's observation:

> We need allies with whom we can co-operate for defence and on issues of major concern to the Western World. We retain complete freedom to express, within the conclaves of such alliances, our own viewpoint in relation to such causes. At times it is appropriate that we should, and we do, express these views publicly. We decide for ourselves whether it is in our interests to support, criticize or reject proposals on which others have taken the initiative. This is the exercise of responsibility and common sense independence. In truth, the fact of the matter is that Australian foreign policy is as independent as that of any nation on earth. We stand firmly on our own feet, but not alone.[5]

### LOOKING IN ON THE CHINA PROBLEM

THE SIGNIFICANCE of China for Australia has in large and small ways been noticed and acted upon well beyond the level of foreign policy execution. There is an organized group, the Australia-China Society, which fosters a pro-Chinese position, while the Australia-Free China Association exerts itself against China and on behalf of Formosa and the Nationalists. The author has also been told—but without being able to confirm—that organized enclaves of

[4] Menzies, *CPD,* HR, November 10, 1964, pp. 2715–2724.

[5] Barwick, "Australian Foreign Policy 1962," p. 9. For a comparable comment by Menzies, see his broadcast of July 30, 1958, in *SMH,* July 31, 1958.

democratic socialists exist in several states. These people are opposed to all forms of authoritarianism. They try to expose and discredit the Chinese regime by means which include the distribution of appropriate materials in schools and elsewhere. But the group's principles dictate distaste for the allegedly reactionary Formosan regime as well, which by one of the member's admission complicates the job of selling a plausible China policy line. The membership is drawn almost entirely from among politicians, trade unionists, and academicians of Labor Party persuasion. Because of the explicit anti-Chinese tone of the group, the members, and especially the politicians, do not advertise this connection.

Special concern has manifested itself over the "neutralist" tendencies found in the country, particularly as expressed by the ALP's left. Hence, the Australian Association for Cultural Freedom has persuaded its parent organization headquarters in Paris to help underwrite the Melbourne journal *Dissent*. *Dissent's* credentials as a progressive organ are impeccable, but it has assumed an antineutralist line and exposed "peace movements" in Australia. It therefore is being encouraged in its appeal to an intelligent, socially forward but hopefully anti-Communist, and especially anti-Chinese Communist, audience. Far more boldly, in their own obsession with the Communist threat and Australia's vulnerability, the Returned Servicemen's League and the DLP are on record as supporting nuclear arms and sufficient delivery systems for Australia.

Then, of course, there is the polarity of political opinion on China. Considerations arising out of Communism, and of Chinese Communism in heavy measure, have created a schismatic Peking-oriented Communist Party on the far left, and have nourished the DLP-NCC's propaganda on the right.

From the political standpoint, however, it has not been so much the mere appearance of diametrically opposed groups as the affect on the party struggle that has counted for most in the context of the intramural Australian dialogue on China. As has been argued above, the Liberal-Country Party coalition has with much electoral profit hammered at ALP foreign and defense policies associated with China, often with exaggeration and even distortion. The purpose of this has not explicitly been to invoke Chinese policy *per se* as a dominant campaign issue, but to incriminate the Labor Party as confused, misguided, alien to Australian interests, and even susceptible to Communist blandishments. The affect of the DLP as an inhibitor of ALP electoral success has also been welcomed, and in some degree has stiffened the Government's need to distinguish itself more from the ALP, both in word and deed, than might otherwise have been.

It goes without saying that criticims of Labor's foreign and defense policies have only partially explained why the Liberal-Country Party Government hangs on election after election, the ALP continues to lose, and the DLP maintains its decisive Labor-defeating role. In 1963, for instance, the country had emerged from the trying economic conditions which had almost cost Menzies power in 1961. Also in 1963 the Government parties pledged aid to parochial schools, which pleased Catholics and contrasted sharply with the ALP's own confusion on the subject, particularly in the pivotal state of New South Wales. But in 1963 the Government bore down especially hard on foreign and defense policy, and the DLP ran its own chamber of horrors, including a sensationalist television portrayal of despicable Red China, complete with pictures of human skulls. Santamaria, for one—though probably mistakenly—described the verbal beating administered to Labor on external policy as the single most potent factor in the electoral campaign.[6] The DLP's *intent* in the cam-

[6] B. A. Santamaria, "The Federal Election, 1963, and the American Alliance," *Twentieth Century,* Vol. 18 (Autumn 1964), p. 247.

paign, as Senator Cole later explained, had expressly been first "to alert the electors . . . to the threat to Australia posed by Communist China, and secondly, to ensure that we had in Canberra a government that would maintain our alliance with the United States of America."[7] At any rate, the association of Labor with policies presumed to favor an unspeakably wicked China did the ALP no good.

The succession of electoral defeats and the continuing split in the political labor movement has had its own repercussions on the ALP. It has already been seen that Labor's leaders have shied away from visiting China and that ALP official policies have been revised or softened for public presentation—as in the instances of the terms of Chinese recognition, the nuclear-free zone proposal, and the presence of Australian forces in Malaysia. Also, there is fairly convincing evidence that even the formal statements of policy have been made less doctrinaire by Conference because of an eye on public reactions. Hence, regarding recognition, there is a clause respecting the interests of Formosa's inhabitants; regarding the North West Cape center, the Party does not explicitly advocate its dismantling; regarding overseas troop commitments, in 1963 it rejected the Hobart declaration and stated that troops could be placed in Malaysia or elsewhere, though under certain conditions.

However, Labor's extended political dry spell has had its reverse affects. The very fact that a block of right-wing Laborites departed from the Party during the split left the ALP more left-oriented than if the split had not occurred. Quite aside from the sense or nonsense of one programmatic position or another, had Labor remained undivided not only would there not have been a DLP to snipe at Labor and deprive it of votes, but the Party would undoubtedly have had a more conservative foreign policy—and therefore one less susceptible to electoral exploitation by the Government. The Party's leadership is, at all

[7] *CPD*, S, March 4, 1964, p. 195.

events, prepared to follow a mild, relatively conservative line if elected to office. It cannot be blunt about making these admissions, in part because the left-wing would strongly complain. But by not making these admissions it exposes the Party to what amounts to Government and DLP engineered misrepresentations. The ALP leadership's choice is hardly enviable. It either risks shaking the Party to its foundations, or it gets violently shaken by its political opponents. Very nearly, it is a matter of damned if you do and damned if you don't. Furthermore, Labor's long occupancy of the Opposition benches has operated to render it more irritable and irresponsible. As has been shown, Calwell among others has increasingly resorted to all sorts of transparent, too-clever-by-half, unconstructive snapping at the Government's China policy.

Some observers have interpreted Labor's inability to win elections as being the result of faulty party organization and leadership. In a postmortem election report to the NSW Executive which leaked out in April of 1964, Gough Whitlam said precisely this. He complained about the poor liaison in the party structure, the tendency of groups and individuals to quarrel rather than cooperate, the undue weight given to the trade union element in the Party's decision-making organs, i.e., the Conference and National Executive, and the restrictions placed on the freedom and influence of the Parliamentary group.[8] Whitlam himself maintained that the Party was not suffering from inferior or unattractive policies, but from undesirable organizational and leadership practices. Others, however, have insisted that the two are inseparable. Confused or mistaken policies, they have claimed, have been brought on by the shackles which bind the relatively realistic and moderate leadership in Canberra. On this point rests much of the debate over a possible reunification of the Labor Party.

[8] Text reproduced in Sydney *Daily Telegraph*, April 14, 1964.

Time and again the DLP has insisted that the widest substantive issue which keeps it apart from the ALP is foreign policy, and especially perceptions of China and how to handle her. DLP spokesmen have not directly tried to impute left-wing radicalism in foreign policy to Calwell. They regard him as a well-intentioned weakling, a man who is the captive of his party and of its policy enormities. They claim that the only way for Labor to clean up its foreign policy is to assume a direct hand in scrubbing the Communist influence out of the trade unions, since the ALP Conference and the Federal and certain state executive organs are dominated by left-wing union nominees. Unless labor overhauls its foreign policy, there can be no reconciliation; unless it is willing to fight the Communist influence in the unions, it would not be able to achieve this change.[9]

The DLP's views on the Labor Party's formal decision-making structure are ambivalent. It delights in slapping at the ALP for being managed by the "36 faceless men" of the Conference. It wants "Communist-inspired" influences purged out of the Federal and state level conferences and executives, and believes that Communist influence in the un unions, in part perpetuated by Labor's laxity on enforcing a ban on unity tickets, should be fought. But some elements in the DLP also remember that their own leaders—such as McManus and Cole—once were Conference delegates, and had no objection to the system of decision-making as such. Additionally, to maintain a base of influence in the trade union movement, DLP unionists, and DLP-controlled unions, have generally remained within the ACTU, participated in its proceedings, and been subject to

[9] For example, Cole, "D.L.P. Policy Speech [1963]," pp. 7–8; Frank McManus, "DLP Deal Terms," *Dissent,* Vol. 4 (Autumn 1964), pp. 10–12; Santamaria, letter to *SMH,* October 23, 1963; NCC, "Conflict," pp. 31–43; J. P. Maynes, "Conquest by Stealth" (Melbourne: 1961?), pp. 12–13; *News Weekly,* September 10 and November 5, 1958; September 25, 1963.

its authority, if one allows for tensions such as developed over the ACTU's invitation to Chinese unionists. It is perhaps of interest that Santamaria, who has always operated from without rather than within political parties, who never sat in the councils of the "pre-split" ALP, insists that structural alterations in the Labor Party would be an indispensable feature of any merger.[10]

But within the ALP there is very, very little sentiment on behalf of merger with the DLP, regardless of what alterations in party organization or even tamperings with official policy might be advocated by ALP men themselves or by the DLP. This sentiment is by no means limited to left-wingers in the Party, be they Parliamentarians or otherwise. In the first place, the ALP is increasingly convincing itself that the DLP is losing the character of an ALP splinter and is being converted into a conservative, essentially Catholic party. Many DLP supporters were too young to be ALP or any other kind of electors prior to 1955; they have achieved their seniority and political identification entirely in the "post-split" era. Some other, older DLP voters are recent migrants from Europe, "New Australians" who were not in the country before 1955, or who lacked voting eligibility before then. One responsible DLP prediction given to the author was that if the Party should break up, rudderless, probably over half of its electors would vote Liberal. But if the DLP leadership gave careful guidance, some 80 per cent could be persuaded to lay their allegiance before the ALP. The ALP believes that if by some mysterious process the DLP should vanish, or deliberately rejoin the ALP, most of its electors would gravitate into the Liberal camp, no matter what advice were forthcoming from the DLP's leadership. Hence reunification loses its relevance.

Then too, the ALP is suspicious that any sweet talk of

[10] B. A. Santamaria; statement cited in *ibid.,* August 6, 1964.

merger possibilites which emanates from DLP quarters represents not a genuine wish to resume coexistence, but a blatant grab at power. The DLP says that should the ALP and DLP ever come together, "obviously . . . there would need to be provision for reasonable representation of each element in the Party's machinery and in Parliament."[11] So far as Labor is concerned, this means the DLP wants control, not compromise, and that would be intolerable.

But an even stronger bar to merger is the deep and bitter resentment held by so many ALP members against the DLP for what it did, and what it does, and what it represents. The simple fact that the DLP has been so long a thorn in Labor's flesh, has succeeded in keeping it out of power in Canberra, and has destroyed and prevented the return of ALP regimes in Victoria and Queensland, has been hard to disregard. Any tendencies at seeking reunion on practical grounds are at least matched by feelings that a deadly and effective enemy was being invited into one's home. It no longer matters that many present DLP men at one time did not resign from the Party but were expelled.

Also, Labor men of various left-right shadings, Catholic and Protestant alike, profoundly deplore the DLP's Catholic identification and associations. Again and again the author heard voices raised against the alleged confessional character of the DLP, especially in Victoria but elsewhere as well. Two days before the 1958 election, Archbishop Mannix of Melbourne praised the DLP's stand against Communism and warned that "every Communist and every Communist sympathizer wants a victory for the Evatt party,"[12] and he later went on to abuse Labor in every conceivable way, including condemning the recogni-

[11] McManus, "DLP Deal Terms," p. 12.

[12] Statement of November 20, 1958, in *SMH,* November 21, 1958.

tion of China as "morally reprehensible and politically mistaken." [13] Mannix gave aid and comfort to the DLP-NCC in various ways. The *News Weekly* was sold in many Victorian churches on Sundays. Santamaria delivered a regular television broadcast under the Victorian hierarchy's sponsorship until Mannix's death late in 1963. The ALP also has seen the DLP as the handmaiden, if not the creature, of Santamaria and the NCC. Although nearly everyone respects Santamaria for his intellectual gifts, the ALP despises him as an authoritarian personality, a power behind the DLP's throne, manipulating the levers by dint of his own driving energies and the exclusively Catholic NCC over which he presides. There are, incidentally, some DLP people who are also quite uncomfortable about Santamaria and his sway.

If anything, the ALP's Catholics are more antagonistic toward the DLP than are their Protestant colleagues. They see the sectarian features of the DLP as an enormous disservice to Australian Catholicism, which should confine itself (as Cardinal Gilroy in Sydney does) to spiritual efforts. They see the split as a tragedy because Catholic-Protestant suspicions have been severely advanced, to the detriment of the entire society. They also feel a personal hurt. They resent the insinuation that to belong to and fight for and with the ALP is a contribution to Communism and a disservice to Catholicism. They recall some of the incidents which have plagued them and their families. One Catholic ALP Parliamentarian was so mercilessly jeered at his own parish that he had to attend services elsewhere. Another had to withraw his child from a Catholic school because of sneers and ostracism about his father's ALP ties. Another recounts an incident when, at the time of the split, Santamaria visited his home and promised him the Premiership of his state if he would bolt

[13] Address before National Catholic Rural Movement, in Albury, cited in *News Weekly*, April 22, 1959.

the ALP. Accompanying Santamaria during the visitation was a Catholic priest. The intended inference was unmistakable to the politician—breaking with the ALP was not only politically wise, but wise and necessary by the standards of the Catholic Church.

Consider Calwell himself. Nothing could be farther from the truth for Calwell than to think of himself as party to a Communist conspiracy. He may wheel and deal, compromise with left-wingers, and utter dubiously valid statements, but he is a sincere and devout Catholic who attends mass daily. On the desk of his office at Parliament House is a miniature Australian flag. With Calwell, this is not a show of ostentation. The author has heard him described by a close friend and colleague as a "fanatical Australian," and that would seem to be an uncommonly accurate characterization. When he suffers official DLP or public Catholic abuse because he leads a party which is defiled as unworthy of the devout and patriotic man's support, no wonder he cannot stomach the thought of clasping the DLP's hand. A revealing incident occurred after the December 1964 Senate election. DLP candidate McManus was declared elected in Victoria, beating incumbent Liberal Senator Hannan by a slim margin. Hannan requested a recount which McManus tried to block by applying to the High Court. Appearing in court was Victorian Labor Senator Sam Cohen, QC, who made a submission which argued that McManus' application should be rejected and Hannan's bid for a recount allowed. The Court did in fact rule against McManus, though the resulting recount still gave him the seat. What stands out in the present context is that Calwell had been so intent on having a DLP candidate from his own state defeated that he saw to it that Cohen made his submission. It did not seem to matter that Hannan was a Government man, that he stood right of center in his own party, or that the ALP's intervention before the Court might bring it political embarrassment. In Calwell's estimation, the highest priority was to move heaven and earth to whip the DLP.[14]

Finally, the Labor Party believes that the DLP, despite its professed spirituality, patriotism, and opposition to the mailed fist of Communism, is a pack of rascals—of cheats and liars and distorters who stop at nothing to smear the Labor Party. "Misrepresentation," many ALP figures feel, is the DLP's middle name, and they point especially to the ugly electoral barrages which they claim are the DLP's stock in trade. Many Labor persons of all faiths would endorse the sentiments of an editorial written after the 1963 election in the *Catholic Worker,* a lay-owned and operated paper. The *Worker* wrote:

> The role of the D.L.P. in this election was one that we hope will never be repeated in Australian politics. Its campaign had a simple message—that a victory for Labor would mean ultimately a Chinese Communist takeover. And they put it over with piles of skulls and hordes of Chinese troops marching across the television screen.
>
> Its advertisements were designed to shock the simple. No doubt they succeeded. But they shocked others in perhaps a different way—causing revulsion that allegedly responsible Christian citizens could so calculatingly set out to generate fear and hatred. The DLP has made a gigantic contribution to the sowing of bitterness and distrust among people in a country which is fundamentally united.[15]

Given the strength of feeling in most ALP circles that this is in fact what the DLP creates, there should be little surprise that a friendly reception is not awaiting the prodigal

[14] See *Bulletin,* January 16, 1965.

[15] *Catholic Worker* (Melbourne), January 1964. In the same issue, also see the observations of H. White.

DLP—quite apart from genuine differences of view on the substance of policy.

It would be difficult to assert that Australia is a central concern for China, or even that China has anything like an explicit "Australian policy." There are, of course, numerous evidences of Chinese interest in Australia and Australian affairs. The Chinese have cultivated two-way trade with Australia on the best terms available to them. They have fostered the movement of people in both directions. They have encouraged the operations of the ACS, China's principal lobby in Australia. They encouraged the split among Australian Communists and extend special favors to the Hill branch of the party. They have apparently taken a dislike to Radio Australia broadcasts and have responded by jamming them. They would, of course, like to bring about Australia's detachment from the anti-Communist alliance and from America in particular. But they would hope to accomplish this with many countries, of which Australia is only one, and to such pressures Australia is highly resistant. Australia is a stable, established, prosperous, and European country, quite unlike her neighbors in Asia. Neither is she geographically susceptible to a quick thrust of Chinese armies nor are her political or socioeconomic systems especially vulnerable to threat, blandishment, or revolutionary incitement. Chinese foreign policy therefore concentrates on resisting the principal antagonist, the United States, and on neutralizing, weakening, or overthrowing Asian nations which are accessible and/or vulnerable. In this sense, Australia is relegated to being a secondary, not a primary target of China.

But for *Australia,* the China issue has become central, and far more than the concern of policy makers alone. It has generated warm debate and the establishment of assorted and often competitive groups. It has affected political life considerably. Indirectly at least, elections have been influenced by it, and therefore the determination of those who were to be in or out of office. It has contributed to the persistence of the cleavage in political labor, and thereby served to produce exaggerated, often unreal fulminations on all sides. Through it all, however, emerges the fact that Australia's China policy has, at minimum diplomatic and material expense, served her national interests well.

# BIBLIOGRAPHY

## OFFICIAL MATERIALS

*Australia*

*Parliamentary Debates,* House of Representatives and Senate; *Commonwealth Acts; Statutory Rules; Parliamentary Papers*—"First Report from the Joint Committee on Foreign Affairs Relating to the Peking Peace Conference," 1952, "Reports of the Australian Government, Employers' and Workers Delegates to the Fortieth Session of the International Labour Conference, Geneva, 1957," 1957; and various Tariff Board Reports; Dept. of External Affairs, *Current Notes on International Affairs;* Dept. of External Affairs, *Select Documents on International Affairs, Korea* (Canberra: Government Printer, 1950–54), 3 parts in 2 volumes; Bureau of Census and Statistics, *Commonwealth Yearbook(s),* various years; Bureau of Census and Statistics, *Balance of Payments* and other related trade figures materials.

*New Zealand*

*Parliamentary Debates,* House of Reprsentatives; Dept. of External Affairs, *External Affairs Review.*

*Canada*

*Parliamentary Debates,* House of Commons; Dept. of External Affairs, *External Affairs.*

*United Kingdom*

*Parliamentary Debates,* House of Commons and House of Lords; *Board of Trade Journal.*

*United States*

*Department of State Bulletin;* Senate, Committee on the Judiciary, *Hearings on the Institute of Pacific Relations,* 82nd Congress, 1st Session, 1951, part 5; Senate, Committee on Foreign Relations, Hearings, *Mutual Defense Treaty with Korea,* 83rd Congress, 2nd Session, 1954; House of Representatives, Committee on Foreign Affairs, *Report of the Special Study Mission to the Far East, South Asia, and the Middle East.* House Report no. 1946. 87th Congress, 2nd Session, 1962.

*International Organizations*

United Nations, *Official Records* of the General Assembly,

Security Council, and Trusteeship Council; *Yearbook of National Accounts Statistics 1963* (New York: United Nations, 1964); International Labour Conference, *Record of Proceedings* (Geneva: International Labour Office, various years).

## NEWSPAPERS

*Australia*

The *Sydney Morning Herald, Sydney Sunday-Herald,* and *Sydney Sun-Herald* were systematically reviewed for news and commentary. Extensive use was also made of the Melbourne *Age,* Sydney *Daily Telegraph,* and *Canberra Times.* All major Australian papers were covered for editorial opinion.

*New Zealand*

*New Zealand Herald* (Auckland) and *Dominion* (Wellington).

*Canada*

Toronto *Globe and Mail* and Montreal *Gazette.*

*United Kingdom*

*The Times* (London).

*United States*

*New York Times.*

*Japan*

Japan *Times* (Tokyo).

*Indonesia*

Djakarta *Daily Mail.*

*Burma*

*Nation* (Rangoon).

*Malaysia*

*Straits Times* (Singapore).

## GENERAL AUSTRALIAN PERIODICALS

*Bulletin* (Sydney); *Nation* (Sydney); *Observer* (Sydney); *Australian Financial Review* (Sydney). Selections from these periodicals have been omitted from the compilation of articles listed below.

## PARTY AND SPECIALIZED PUBLICATIONS

*Fact* (Melbourne), ALP; *Labor* (Melbourne), ALP; *A.C.T.U. Bulletin* (Melbourne); *News Weekly* (Melbourne), National Civic Council; *Facts* (Melbourne), National Civic

Council; New South Wales *Countryman* (Sydney), Country Party; Victorian *Countryman* (Melbourne), Country Party; *Advocate* (Melbourne); *Catholic Weekly* (Sydney); *Canberra Letter* (Canberra), Associated Chambers of Manufacturers of Australia; *Australia China News* (Melbourne), ACS; *Australia-China Society Bulletin* (Melbourne), ACS; *Australia-China Society Bulletin* (Sydney), ACS; *China News* (Canberra), Chinese Embassy in Australia. The above items were consulted on a systematic basis or for particular periods. Various other publications of this nature were consulted from time to time.

BOOKS

Alexander, Fred. *Canadians and Foreign Policy* (Melbourne, London, and Wellington: F. W. Cheshire, 1960).

Anonymous. *China Yearbook (s)* (Taipei: China Publishing Co., various years).

——. *Important Documents of the Peace Conference of the Asian and Pacific Regions* (Peking: Secretariat of the Peace Conference of the Asian and Pacific Regions, 1952?).

Appleton, Sheldon. *The Eternal Triangle?* (East Lansing: Michigan State Univ. Press, 1961).

Australian Institute of Internationl Affairs. *Australia and the Pacific* (Princeton: Princeton Univ. Press and the AIIA, 1944).

——. *Living with Asia* (Sydney: AIIA, 1963).

Australian Institute of Political Science. *New Guinea and Australia* (Sydney, London, Melbourne, and Wellington: Angus and Robertson, 1958).

Burchett, Wilfred G. *China's Feet Unbound* (Melbourne: World Unity Publications, 1952).

Burton, John. *The Alternative* (Sydney: Morgans Publications, 1954).

Calvocoressi, Peter, ed. *Survey of International Affairs 1949–1950* (London, New York, and Toronto: Oxford Univ. Press for the Royal Institute of International Affairs, 1953).

Calwell, Arthur A. *Labor's Role in Modern Society* (Melbourne: Lansdowne Press, 1963).

Casey, R. G. *Friends and Neighbours* (Melbourne: F. W. Cheshire, 1954).

Clune, Frank. *Ashes of Hiroshima* (Sydney and London: Angus and Robertson, 1950).

Council on Foreign Relations. *Japan Between East and West* (New York: Harper and Bros. for the Council, 1957).
Crisp, L. F. *Ben Chifley* (London: Longmans, 1960).
Cusack, Dymphna. *Chinese Women Speak* (Sydney, London, Melbourne, and Wellington: Angus and Robertson, 1958).
Eden, Anthony. *The Memoirs of the Rt. Hon. Sir Anthony Eden* (London: Cassell, 1960). Vol. 2, "Full Circle."
Eggleston, F. W. *Reflections on Australian Foreign Policy* (Melbourne: F. W. Cheshire for the AIIA, 1957).
Epstein, Leon D. *Britain—Uneasy Ally* (Chicago: Univ. of Chicago Press, 1954).
Farley, Miriam S. *United States Relations with Southeast Asia* (New York: Institute of Pacific Relations, 1955).
Fitzgerald, C. P. *Flood Tide in China* (London: Cresset Press, 1958).
——. *Revolution in China* (London: Cresset Press, 1952).
Gilmore, Robert J. and Denis Warner, eds. *Near North* (Sydney and London: Angus and Robertson, 1948).
Goddard, W. G. *Formosa* (Taipei: P.O. Box 337, 1958).
——. *The Story of Chang Lao* (Melbourne: Australian League of Rights, 1962).
——. *The Story of Formosa* (Taipei: P.O. Box 337, 1960).
Goodwin, Geoffrey L. *Britain and the United Nations* (New York: Manhattan, for the RIIA, 1957).
Grattan, C. Hartley. *The United States and the Southwest Pacific* (Melbourne: Oxford Univ. Press, 1961).
Greenwood, Gordon and Norman Harper, eds., *Australia in World Affairs 1950–55* (Melbourne: F. W. Cheshire for the AIIA, 1957).
——. *Australia in World Affairs 1956–1960* (Melbourne, Canberra, and Sydney: F. W. Cheshire for the AIIA, 1963).
Harper, Norman, ed. *Problems of Contemporary Australia* (New York: IPR, 1949).
Harper, Norman and David Sissons. *Australia and the United Nations* (New York: Manhattan, for the AIIA, 1959).
Harrison, W. E. C. *Canada in World Affairs 1949 to 1950* (Toronto: Oxford Univ. Press for the Canadian Institute of International Affairs, 1957).
Haylen, Leslie. *Chinese Journey* (Sydney, London, Melbourne, and Wellington: Angus and Robertson, 1959).
Kirkpatrick, Evron, ed. *Year of Crisis* (New York: Macmillan, 1957).

Legge, J. D. *Australian Colonial Policy* (Sydney, London, Melbourne and Wellington: Angus and Robertson for the AIIA, 1956).

Leng, Shao-chuan. *Japan and Communist China* (Kyoto: Doshisha Univ. Press, 1958).

Levi, Werner. *Australia's Outlook on Asia* (Sydney, London, Melbourne, and Wellington: Angus and Robertson, 1958).

Lindsay, Michael. *China and the Cold War* (Melbourne: Melbourne Univ. Press, 1955).

London Institute of World Affairs, *Year Book of World Affairs* (London: Stevens and Sons for the Institute, 1956).

Luard, Evan. *Britain and China* (London: Chatto and Windus, 1962).

Modelski, George, ed. *SEATO. Six Studies* (Melbourne, Canberra, and Sydney: F. W. Cheshire for the Australian National University, 1962).

Pao, Chun-jien, ed. *A Century of Sino-Australian Relations* (Sydney: 1938).

Passin, Herbert. *China's Cultural Diplomacy* (New York: Praeger, 1962).

Rosecrance, Richard N. *Australian Diplomacy and Japan, 1945–1951* (Melbourne: Melbourne Univ. Press for the ANU, 1962).

Shepperd, Jack. *Australia's Interests and Policies in the Far East* (New York: IPR, 1939).

Truman, Tom. *Catholic Action and Politics* (Melbourne: Georgian House, 1959).

Tsao, W. Y. *Two Pacific Democracies: China and Australia* (Melbourne: F. W. Cheshire, 1941).

Vassilieff, Elizabeth. *Peking-Moscow Letters* (Melbourne: Australasian Book Society, 1953).

Warner, Denis. *Hurricane from China* (New York: Macmillan, 1961).

Webb, Leicester. *Communism and Democracy in Australia* (Melbourne: F. W. Cheshire for the ANU, 1954).

Whiting, Allen S. *China Crosses the Yalu* (New York: Macmillan, 1960).

Whitington, Don. *Ring the Bells* (Melbourne: Georgian House, 1956).

Wilkes, John, ed. *Asia and Australia* (Sydney, London, Melbourne, and Wellington: Angus and Robertson for the AIPS, 1961).

——. *Australia's Defence and Foreign Policy* (Sydney, London, and Melbourne: Angus and Robertson for the AIPS, 1964).

Woodbridge, George, ed. *UNRRA* (New York: Columbia Univ. Press, 1950), 3 vols.

ARTICLES

Albinski, Henry S. "Australia and the China Problem Under the Labor Government," *Australian Journal of Politics and History* (*AJPH*), Vol. 10 (August 1964), pp. 149–172.

——. "Australia and the Dutch New Guinea Dispute," *International Journal,* Vol. 16 (Autumn 1961), pp. 358–382.

——. "Australia Faces China," *Asian Survey,* Vol. 2 (April 1962), p. 16–28.

——. "Australia's Defense Enigma," *Orbis,* Vol. 4 (Winter 1961), pp. 452–466.

Alexander, Fred. "Australia in World Affairs," *Australian Outlook* (*AO*), Vol. 10 (March 1956), pp. 5–19.

Anonymous. "Australia Prepares Big Export Drive," *Far East Trade* (*FET*), Vol. 16 (December 1961), pp. 1478–1479.

——. (Various authors) "The Base," *Dissent,* Vol. 3 (Winter 1963), pp. 6–11.

——. "Be Less Chinese," *Far Eastern Economic Review* (*FEER*), Vol. 36 (April 19, 1962), pp. 126–127.

——. "Between Moscow and Peking—The C.P. of Australia," *Current Affairs Bulletin,* Vol 34 (June 22, 1964), 14 pp.

——. "China-Canada Trade," *FEER,* Vol. 26 (June 4, 1959), p. 774.

——. "China Trade," *FEER,* Vol. 22 (June 27, 1957), pp. 823–824.

——. "China Trade Lures Japan—I," *FET,* Vol. 16 (May 1961), pp. 575–577.

——. "China Trade Lures Japan—II," *FET,* Vol. 16 (June 1961), pp. 693–694.

——. "China's Policy Towards Far Eastern Countries," *FEER,* Vol. 25 (August 14, 1958), pp. 193–196.

——. "Chuo [*sic*] -Ishibashi Communique," *Oriental Economist* (*OE*), Vol. 27 (October 1959), p. 565.

——. "Communist China and Japanese Socialists," *OE,* Vol. 27 (April 1959), pp. 170–171.

——. "Cost and Returns in Primary Industry," *Bank of New South Wales Review,* no. 48 (March 1962), pp. 3–7.

——. "Decade of Sino-German Trade," *FEER*, Vol. 35 (February 1, 1962), pp. 203ff.

——. "Easier Trade with China," *OE*, Vol. 25 (August 1957), p. 391

——. "From Moscow to the Flag," *FEER*, Vol. 28 (April 14, 1960), p. 789.

——. "How the Department of Trade Aids Australian Businessmen," *Australian Grocer*, Vol. 52 (February 1963), pp. 94–99.

——. "Japan-U.S. Trade Problems," *OE*, Vol. 31 (May 1963), pp. 265–267.

——. "A Look at the China-Britain Trade Situation," *FET*, Vol. 12 (December 1957), pp. 1404–1405.

——. "More Australian Trade with China," *FET*, Vol. 14 (April 1959), p. 498.

——. "The New Wheat Stabilisation Scheme," *Trends* (Rural Bank of NSW), Vol. 6 (December 1963), pp. 6–9.

——. "Our Mission to Britain," *FET*, Vol. 13 (January 1958), pp. 54–55.

——. "Outlook for China Trade," *FET*, Vol. 12 (July 1957), p. 735.

——. "Peking's Boycott of Trade Accord," *OE*, Vol. 26 (May 1958), pp. 234–235.

——. "Pressure to Ease China Embargo," *FET*, Vol. 12 (April 1957), p. 392.

——. "Promise of Communist China Trade," *OE*, Vol. 29 (March 1961), pp. 133–137.

——. "Prospects for Trade with China. Part 1," *FEER*, Vol. 19 (September 29, 1955), pp. 395–399.

——. "Prospects for Trade with China. Part 2," *FEER*, Vol. 19 (October 6, 1955), pp. 425–427.

——. "Relaxed Restrictions on China Trade," *OE*, Vol. 25 (September 1957), p. 478.

——. "Re-Start of Sino-Japanese Trade Seen," *OE*, Vol. 28 (November 1960), p. 625.

——. "Sino-Japanese Economic Severance," *OE*, Vol. 26 (June 1958), p. 291.

——. Special Supplement on Japan, *FEER*, Vol. 26 (April 23, 1959), esp. pp. 571–572.

——. "Stalling on Seats," *FEER*, Vol. 30 (October 6, 1960), p. 3.

——. "Tokyo-Peking Trade Accord," *OE*, Vol. 26 (April 1958), p. 175.

——. "Tokyo-Peking Trade Agreement," *OE,* Vol. 30 (December 1962), pp. 682–683.

——. "Trade Triangle," *FET,* Vol. 18 (September 1963), pp. 938ff.

——. "Trade with Australia," *FEER,* Vol. 36 (April 12, 1962), p. 54.

——. "U.S.-Japan Relations," *OE,* Vol. 32 (March 1964), pp. 136–140.

Attlee, Clement R. "Britain and America: Common Aims, Different Opinions," *Foreign Affairs,* Vol. 32 (January 1954), pp. 190–202.

J. H. W. B. [Burton, John W.] "Australia and the Asiatic Area," *Anglican Review,* no. 7 (August 1949), pp. 8–12.

——. "Australia and Communist China," *Anglican Review,* no. 8 (November 1949), pp. 18–21.

——. "Korea," *Anglican Review,* no. 13 (February 1951), pp. 26–32.

Ball, W. Macmahon. "Observations on Britain's Attitude to Asia," *Australia's Neighbours* (*AN*), 3rd Series, no. 60 (February 1956), pp. 1–2.

——. "The Pacific Defense Pact," *Nation* (U.S.A.), Vol. 175 (November 29, 1952), pp. 488–490.

——. "A Political Re-Examination of SEATO," *International Organization,* Vol. 12 (Winter 1958), pp. 17–25.

Barcan, Alan. "Australia and Malaya," *Eastern World,* Vol. 9 (September 1955), pp. 19–20.

——. "Australian Labour Party and China," *Eastern World,* Vol. 8 (May 1954), pp. 15–16.

Beddie, B. D. "Australia and the Recognition of China," *AO,* Vol. 13 (June 1959), pp. 129–135.

Bell, Coral. "Australia and the American Alliance," *The World Today,* Vol. 19 (July 1963), pp. 302–310.

Biehl, Max. "The West and Trade with China," *FEER,* Vol. 22 (February 14, 1957), pp. 208–211.

Boyce, Peter. "Canberra's Malaysia Policy," *AO,* Vol. 17 (August 1963), pp. 149–161.

Burns, A. L. "Australia, Britain, and the Common Market," *The World Today,* Vol. 18 (April 1962), pp. 152–163.

——. "Overseas Bases and Alliances: The Australian Case," *AN,* 4th Series, nos. 3–4 (March–April 1963), pp. 5–8.

——. "A Regional Problem: The American Signalling Station in Western Australia," *Disarmament and Arms Control,* Vol. 2, no. 1 (1964), pp. 23–33.

Casey, R. G. "New Plan to Defend Southeast Asia," *U.S. News and World Report* (July 16, 1954), pp. 50ff.

Clubb, O. Edmund. "Chinese Communist Strategy in Foreign Relations," *Annals,* Vol. 277 (September 1951), pp. 156–166.

Cox, Harry. "The Chinese in Australia," *Pix* (January 23, 1960), pp. 16–23; (January 30, 1960), pp. 16–21; (February 6, 1960), pp. 18–23.

——. "The Ear of the World," *People,* Vol. 14 (October 23, 1963), pp. 19–21.

Crawford, D. L. "Direct Shipping Opens up Taiwan Market," *Overseas Trading,* Vol. 12 (August 19, 1960), pp. 364–367.

——. "Prospects in Taiwan for Australian Exports," *Overseas Trading,* Vol. 11 (May 6, 1959), pp. 174–175.

Crawford, Sir John. "The Jolt of the Common Market," *Saturday Review* (January 12, 1963), pp. 31ff.

——. "The Significance of Recent Developments in Asia for the Economic Future of Australia," *Economic Record,* Vol. 37 (September 1961), pp. 273–293.

Dickinson, George. "Manus: Land of Beginning Again," *Walkabout,* Vol. 18 (October 1, 1952), pp. 30–33.

Dixon, J. P. F. "U.N. Embargo on China," *AN,* 3rd Series, no. 11 (July 1, 1951), pp. 2–4.

Donath, E. J. "Australia's Wheat Sales to China," *FEER,* Vol. 37 (August 30, 1962), pp. 387–389.

——. "Australia's Wheat Sales to Communist China," *AN,* 3rd Series, nos. 126–127 (April–May 1962), pp. 7–8.

——. "Changes in the Direction and Composition of Australia's Trade in Wheat," *Australian Accounting Student,* Part 1-Vol 15, pt. 3 (1962), pp. 87–91; Part 2-Vol. 15, pt. 4 (1962), pp. 111–113; Part 3-Vol. 16, pt. 1 (1963), pp. 20–22.

——. "China: Australian Dilemma over Wheat Sales," *FEER,* Vol. 39 (January 31, 1963), pp. 197ff.

——. "China—Australia's Fourth Best Customer," *Australian Institute of Export. Monthly Bulletin,* no. 24 (December 1963), pp. 42–46.

Dulles, J. F. "Security in the Pacific," *Foreign Affairs,* Vol. 30 (January 1952), pp. 175–187.

Fitzgerald, C. P. "Australia, Japan and Formosa," *Spectator,* no. 6455 (March 14, 1952), pp. 318–319.

Fletcher, Arthur. "China and the U.N.," *FEER,* Vol. 38 (October 4, 1962), pp. 21–22.

Garratt, Colin. "How to Pay for the Grain," *FEER,* Vol. 33 (September 14, 1961), pp. 644–646.

Gelder, Stuart. "Britain *Can* do More Trade with Us, Say China's Leaders," *FET,* Vol. 16 (January 1961), p. 55.

Goddard, W. G. "Behind the Bamboo Curtain," *Australia and East Asia* (October 1952), 16 pp.

Grantham, Sir Alexander. "What Great Britain Has Gained Through Recognizing Red China," *Vital Speeches,* Vol. 21 (December 1, 1954), pp. 875–879.

Greenwood, Gordon. "Australian Attitudes Towards Pacific Problems," *Pacific Affairs,* Vol. 23 (June 1950), pp. 153–168.

Griffin, S. "China Trade Issue," *Eastern World,* Vol. 17 (August 1963), pp. 14–15.

Harper, Norman. "Australia and Regional Pacts 1950–57," *AO,* Vol. 12 (March 1958), pp. 3–22.

Hudson, G. F. "British Relations with China," *Current History,* Vol. 33 (December 1957), pp. 327–331.

Jain, J. P. "Chinese Reaction to British Recognition of the People's Republic of China," *International Studies,* Vol. 4 (July 1962), pp. 24–45.

Johnston, W. S. "Australia's Floating Shop Window," *Etruscan,* Vol. 8 (March 1959), pp. 24–27.

Lawrence, M. J. "Wool in Mainland China," *Quarterly Review of Agricultural Economics,* Vol. 15 (October 1962), pp. 188–198.

Leach, P. B. "The Wheat Industry Today. A Grower Reports," *Commonwealth Agriculturalist,* Vol. 33 (December 1963), pp. 7–10.

Leng, Shao-chuang. "Japanese Attitudes Toward Communist China," *Far Eastern Survey,* Vol. 27 (June 1958), pp. 81–89.

Lerche, Charles O., Jr. "The United States, Great Britain, and SEATO: A Case Study in the Fait Accompli," *Journal of Politics,* Vol. 18 (August 1956), pp. 459–478.

Lindsay, Michael. "Australia, the United States and Asia," *AJPH,* Vol. 3 (November 1957), pp. 33–45.

MacDougall, Colina. "Agreement of 'Intent,' " *FEER,* Vol. 32 (May 18, 1961), pp. 317–318.

——. "Australian Aid?" *FEER,* Vol. 36 (June 14, 1962), p. 551.

——. "China. A Grain Purchaser," *FEER,* Vol. 43 (January 30, 1964), p. 255.

'eople's Anti-Communist League, Melbourne, Australia." )elivered November 7, 1959. Mimeo

ociated Chambers of Commerce of Australia. "Export 'romotion," Forum Addresses Delivered at the 58th An- ual Conference of the Associated Chambers. Held at Ho- art, 2–5 April, 1962.

stralia-China Society (NSW Branch). "The Facts of the 3andung Conference" (Sydney: 1955).

stralia-China Society (Victorian Branch). "Aims and Ob- ects" (Melbourne: 1961), mimeo.

—. "Why We Should Recognise China Now" (Melbourne: ACS, 1962).

stralia-Free China Association (NSW Branch). "China. Free or Red?" (Sydney: 1963).

stralia-Free China Association (Victorian Branch). "Ob- ects" (Melbourne: n.d.).

stralian Association for the United Nations (Victorian Di- ision). "The Case For and Against Recognition of Com- nunist China" (Melbourne: AAUN, January 6, 1955), nimeo.

—. "Statement Prepared by British UNA and Circulated or Discussion-January 1951-China and World Peace," nimeo.

stralian Council of Trade Unions. Federal Congress and Executive *Reports,* various years.

stralian Country Party. "The Red Twins. Communism. ocialism" (Sydney: 1949).

—. "You Won't Vote Labour When You've Read *This* Story!" (Sydney: 1949).

stralian Cultural Delegation. "Report on China" (Sydney: ACS, NSW Branch, 1956).

stralian Democratic Labor Party. *Policy Decisions,* Com- nonwealth Conferences, various years.

—. "A New Concept in Australian Politics" (Melbourne: 961).

—. "Our Platform" (Sydney: 1963).

stralian Democratic Labor Party, Victoria. "Speakers' Notes-Part 2, 1961" (Melbourne: 1961), mimeo.

stralian Exporters' Federation. "Australian Trade Mission 958" (Sydney: The Federation, 1959).

stralian Industries Development Association. Committee on he European Economic Community. *Report on the Impli- ations of the United Kingdom Becoming a Member of the*







——. "The Wheat Deals," *FEER,* Vol. 32 (June 29, 1961), pp. 653ff.

McEwen, John. "Australia and the U.S. Wheat Surpluses," *Industry Today,* Vol. 2 (June 1959), pp. 135ff.

McHenry, Dean E. and Richard N. Rosecrance. "The 'Exclusion' of the United Kingdom from the ANZUS Pact," *International Organization,* Vol. 12 (Summer 1958), pp. 320–329.

McManus, Frank. "DLP Deal Terms," *Dissent,* Vol. 4 (Autumn 1964), pp. 10–12.

Meeking, Charles. "Long-Range Dilemma," *Eastern World,* Vol. 16 (June 1962), pp. 19ff.

——. "Red Trade—Welcome Gift or Baited Trap," *Eastern World,* Vol. 15 (April 1961), p. 26.

——. "Thoughts on Irian," *Eastern World,* Vol. 13 (February 1959), pp. 24–25.

——. "Trade with China Expanding," *Eastern World,* Vol. 16 (August 1962), pp. 19–20.

Miskoe, W. I. "Red China Trade 'A Matter of Time,'" *Australian Factory,* Vol. 13 (August 1, 1958), pp. 75–76.

Modelski, J. (George) A. "Communist China's Challenge in Technology," *Australian Quarterly,* Vol. 30 (June 1958), pp. 57–68.

Moroney, J. V. "The Wheat Industry Today. The Marketing Outlook," *Commonwealth Agriculturalist,* Vol. 33 (December 1963), pp. 4–6.

Neale, R. G. "Problems of Australian Foreign Policy January–June 1963," *AJPH,* Vol. 9 (November 1963), pp. 135–149.

Nossal, Frederick. "Wheat Diplomacy," *FEER,* Vol. 41 (July 18, 1963), p. 151.

Padelford, Norman J. "Collective Security in the Pacific. Nine Years of the ANZUS Pact," *U.S. Naval Institute Proceedings,* Vol. 86 (September 1960), pp. 38–47.

Palmier, Leslie H. "Recognition of the Chinese Governments," *AO,* Vol. 12 (December 1958), pp. 36–42.

Paltridge, Angus. "Australia's Trade with the United Kingdom and Western Europe," *Australian Accountant,* Vol. 32 (November 1962), pp. 575–582.

Partridge, P. H. "Opportunities for Close Relations," *Voice,* Vol. 5 (July–August 1956), pp. 11–12.

Paul, Robert. "China and Japan—The Mutual Attraction," *FEER,* Vol. 37 (September 27, 1962), pp. 582–584.

Pillai, K. S. C. "What Prospects for Australia's Trade with China?" *FEER,* Vol. 38 (October 4, 1962), pp. 23ff.

Poynter, J. R. "ANZUS and the Crisis," *AN,* 3rd Series, no. 45 (August 1954), pp. 2–4.

——. "Britain and ANZUS," *AN,* 3rd Series, no. 27 (January 1953), pp. 1–3.

——. "Treaty Commitments," *AN,* 4th Series, nos. 3–4 (March–April 1963), pp. 1–3.

Pyke, N. O. P. "Australia's UNRRA Contribution," *AO,* Vol. 3 (March 1949), pp. 70–81.

Quigley, Harold S. "Trade with Communist China," *Current History,* Vol. 35 (December 1958), pp. 353–357.

Rose, A. J. "Strategic Geography and the Northern Approaches," *AO,* Vol. 13 (December 1959), pp. 304–312.

Samuel, Peter. "Australian Economic Aid," *AN,* 4th Series, nos. 15–16 (May–June 1964), pp. 6–8.

Santamaria, B. A. "The Federal Election, 1963, and the American Alliance," *Twentieth Century,* Vol. 18 (Autumn 1964), pp. 247–251.

——. "A Pacific Confederation," *Quadrant,* Vol. 6 no. 1 (1962), pp. 25–35.

Sawer, Geoffrey. "Problems of Australian Foreign Policy, June 1956–June 1957," *AJPH,* Vol. 3 (November 1957), pp. 1–17.

Stone, Julius. "Problems of Australian Foreign Policy, January–June 1955," *AJPH,* Vol. 1 (November 1955), pp. 1–26.

Stove, Vincent W. "Australia Probes Asian Markets," *FET,* Vol. 14 (July 1959), pp. 935–936.

Sung, Kayser. "The China Trade Riddle," *FEER,* Vol. 29 (September 1, 1960), pp. 504ff.

Takita, Kazuo. "Seeing the Red Light," *FEER,* Vol. 42 (October 10, 1963), p. 55.

——. "Tough Trade," *FEER,* Vol. 33 (September 14, 1961), p. 650.

Tapp, E. J. "New Zealand: The Seventh State of Australia?" *Australian Quarterly,* Vol. 34 (December 1962), pp. 74–81

Tay, S. I. "Sukarno's Chinese Minority," *FEER,* Vol. 43 (March 20, 1964), pp. 617ff.

Tehan, J. "Trade with Communist Countries," *Pastoral Review,* Vol. 72 (February 1962), pp. 117ff; (March 1962), pp. 230–231; (April 1962), pp. 350–351; (May 1962), pp. 461–463.





Vinacke, Harold M. "United States Policy An Appraisal," *Far Eastern Survey,* Vol. pp. 65–69.

Walker, Richard L. "Australians in Wonde Vol. 4 (Autumn 1960), pp. 3–11.

Wilczynski, J. "Dilemmas in Australia's Tra munist Bloc," *Australian Quarterly,* Vol. pp. 9–19.

Wolf, Elizabeth. "No-Hopers in Never-Ne *land,* no. 18 (Winter–Spring 1960), pp.

Wolfstone, Daniel. "The Envious Oregoni 42 (October 17, 1963), pp. 143–144.

Wolpert, V. "Minister Lu in London," *FE* 9, 1963), pp. 313ff.

Wu, T. F. "Overseas Chinese in Australia (September 11, 1958), pp. 328–329.

Younger, Kenneth. "An Analysis of Britis in the Far East," *Eastern World,* Vol. 7 10–12.

Yu, Frederick. "Prospects for Australian 30 (December 8, 1960), pp. 551–552.

OTHER MATERIALS

Aitkin, Donald A. *The Organisation of t try Party (N.S.W.), 1946 to 1962.* Ph.D National University, 1964.

Albinski, Henry S. *Australia and the Ch the Korean War Period* (Canberra: D Relations, ANU, 1964).

——. *Australia's Search for Regional S Asia.* Ph.D. Thesis, University of Mi

Anonymous. "Formosa. Danger Spot for Victorian Peace Council, 1953).

——. "The Future of Australia," Social 1951 (Carnegie, Victoria: Renown P

——. "Students in China." Report of th National Union of the Australian Uni People's Republic of China (Melbo 1957).

Asian People's Anti-Communist League Chang-kang, Chairman of the Counci Communist League, and President of

*European Economic Community* (Melbourne and Sydney: AIDA, February 1962).
Australian Labor Party. "The Australian Labor Party. Speakers' Notes" (Brisbane: ALP Federal Secretariat, 1958).
——. *Federal Platform Constitution and Rules,* 1961.
——. *Official Reports,* Federal Executive and Commonwealth Conferences, various years.
Australian Labor Party, Victoria. Central Executive and Conference *Reports,* various years.
Australian Liberal Party. "The Case Against Socialist Labour." Background Notes for Candidates, Speakers and Canvassers (Sydney: Liberal Party Federal Secretariat, 1949).
——. " 'Dangerous and Frustrating'—A.L.P. Decisions on Defence and Foreign Relations" (Canberra: Liberal Party Federal Secretariat, 1963).
——. "Liberal Facts. Federal Election Campaign, 1963" (Canberra: Liberal Party Federal Secretariat, 1963).
——. "Peace Through Security" (Canberra: Liberal Party Federal Secretariat, 1963).
Australian Wheat Board. *Annual Report. Season 1962–63* (Melbourne: 1964).
Barwick, Sir Garfield. "Australian Foreign Policy 1962." Roy Milne Memorial Lecture, Perth, July 31, 1962 (Melbourne: AIIA, 1962).
Brand, Allan D. "I Preached Peace in U.S.S.R. and China" (Sydney: NSW Peace Council, 1953).
Burchett, Wilfred G. "News from China" (Banksia Park, Victoria: World Unity Publications, 1951).
Bureau of Agricultural Economics. *Wool in Communist Countries.* Wool Economic Research Report no. 1, June 1960 (Canberra: 1960).
Burton, John W. "The Light Grows Brighter" (Sydney: Morgans Publications, 1956?).
——. "The Nature and Significance of Labor." Chifley Memorial Lecture, Melbourne, September 11, 1958 (Melbourne: 1958).
——, *et al.* "We Talked Peace with Asia" (Sydney: 1952?).
Caine, Gerald. "Towards the Pacific Community" (Ballarat: Cripac Press, 1963).
Calwell, Arthur A. "Labor's Policy." ALP 1963 policy speech, November 6, 1963 (Melbourne: 1963).
Chapman, B. Burgoyne. "China Revisited" (Sydney: ACS, NSW Branch, 1957), mimeo.

Cole, George R. "Joint DLP-QLP Policy Speech." Delivered November 8, 1961. Mimeo.

Donath, E. J. "1961–62 Was Another Memorable Wheat Year," *Economic and Financial Survey of Australia 1961–62,* no. 15 (Sydney: Birt and Co., 1962).

Ellis, Ulrich. "The Case for New States" (Canberra: 1950).

——. "New England. The Seventh State" (Armidale, NSW: New State Movement, 1957).

Evatt, H. V. "Policy Speech of the Australian Labor Party." Delivered October 15, 1958 (Brisbane: ALP Federal Secretariat, 1958).

Export Payments Insurance Corporation. *7th Annual Report and Financial Statements, 1963* (Sydney: 1963).

External Affairs, Dept. of. "Sir Garfield Barwick's Statements on Possible Applicability of ANZUS and Australian Forces in Malaysian Borneo" (Canberra: Dept. of External Affairs, 1964), mimeo.

Fitzgerald, C. P. "China and the United Nations." Delivered September 16, 1961 (Melbourne: ACS, Victorian Branch, 1961), mimeo.

Fitzgerald, C. P. and P. H. Partridge. "Report to the Council of the Australian National University on the Visit to China of the Australian Cultural Delegation" (Canberra: ANU, 1956), mimeo.

Goddard, W. G. "Peaceful Co-Existence?" (Melbourne: Victorian Chinese National Salvation Association, 1955).

——. "Report on Formosa" (Brisbane: R. G. Gillies and Co., 1954).

Gott, K. D. "Australian Trade with China." Reprinted from *South Australian Farmer,* July 23, 1954.

Greenwood, Gordon, ed. *Australian Policies Toward Asia.* Australian Papers, IPR Conference, 1954 (Melbourne: AIIA, 1954).

Healey, G. "The Truth Behind the 'Nuclear-Free Zone' Campaign" (Melbourne: Australian Catholic Publications, 1963).

Hughes, William Morris. "U.N.O., Dr. Evatt and World Peace" (Sydney: 1949).

Institute of Social Order. *A Pacific Confederation?* (Melbourne: The Institute, 1963).

International Wheat Council. "Review of the World Wheat Situation 1962/63" (London: The Council, 1963).

Joshua, R. "Address to Third Commonwealth [DLP] Conference." Delivered August 8, 1959. Mimeo.
——. "[Anti-Communist Labor Party] Policy Speech." Delivered November 10, 1955. Mimeo.
Kent-Hughes, Sir Wilfrid. "Appreciation of the S. E. Asian Situation January-February 1964." Private paper. Mimeo.
Liu, William J. L. "Chinese-Australian Trading Relationship" (Sydney: 1932).
Lockwood, Rupert. "China Our Neighbour" (Sydney: Current Book Distributors, 1951).
Martin, A. D. P. "The Role of Export Credit Insurance in Australia's Export Drive." Economic Monograph no. 252, June 1963 (Sydney: Economic Society of Australia and New Zealand, NSW Branch, 1963).
Maynes, J. P. "Conquest by Stealth. Communist Plans in the Unions Exposed" (Melbourne: 1961?).
——, compiler. "Report of the First Delegation of Australian Trade Union Officials to Visit South-East Asia." Issued 1957. Mimeo.
Menzies, Sir Robert. "Federal Election, 1963." Policy Speech, November 12, 1963 (Canberra: Liberal Party Federal Secretariat, 1963).
Millar, T. B. "China's Asian Policy" (Sydney: AIPS, 1964), monograph no. 4.
National Civic Council. "Conflict. A Nation Faces the Challenge" (Melbourne: NCC, 1961?).
Oakley, M. W. "Australia's Trade with Asia." Section P, Australian and New Zealand Association for the Advancement of Science (Canberra: 1954).
Palmer, Helen G. "Australian Teacher in China" (Sydney: Teachers' Sponsoring Committee, 1953?).
Playford, J. D. *Doctrinal and Strategic Problems of the Communist Party of Australia, 1945–1962*. Ph.D. Thesis, ANU, 1962.
Ray, J. Franklin, Jr. "UNRRA in China." Secretariat Paper no. 6, IRP Conference, 1947 (New York: IRP, 1947).
Returned Sailors', Soldiers' and Airmen's Imperial League of Australia. *48th Annual Report 1963* (Canberra: RSL National Executive, 1964).
Santamaria, B. A. "New Guinea. The Price of Weakness" (Fitzroy, Victoria: Australian Catholic Publications, 1959).

——. "Peace or War? The Global Strategy of World Communism" (Fitzroy, Victoria: NCC, 1958).

Thomas, Pete. "As We Saw it . . . China's Great Leap" (Sydney: Current Book Distributors, 1958).

Turner, Ian. "Nuclear Bases in Australia?" In "The Questions for Labor—Foreign Policy and Defence," an *Outlook* publication, March 6, 1963.

United States Information Service. "The China of Mao Tse-tung" (Sydney: 1954?). Mimeo.

Victorian League of Rights. "Dr. Evatt and Communism" (Melbourne: The League, 1955?).

Victorian Sponsoring Committee for Delegates to the Asian and Pacific Regions Peace Conference in Peking, China, September 1952. "Proposals" and "Draft Resolutions" (Melbourne: 1952).

Watt, Sir Alan. *Australian Defence Policy 1951–1963* (Canberra: Dept. of International Relations, ANU, 1964).

Whitlam, E. G. "Australian Foreign Policy 1963." Roy Milne Memorial Lecture, Armidale, July 9, 1963 (Melbourne: AIIA, 1963).

Wilczynski, Josef. *Australia's Trade with the Communist Bloc.* M.Ec. Thesis ANU, 1963.

Wright, Tom. "Australians Visit People's China" (Sydney: Federal Council, Sheet Metal Working, Agricultural Implement and Stovemaking Industrial Union of Australia, 1952).

# INDEX